THE LAST RESORTS

CLEVELAND AMORY

HARPER & BROTHERS, PUBLISHERS, NEW YORK

M-B

For permission to reprint the following selections, grateful acknowledgment is made to:

Appleton-Century-Crofts, Inc., for a selection from *Manners for the Metropolis* by Frank Crowninshield.

Doubleday & Company, Inc., for a selection from *Such Was Saratoga* by Hugh Bradley, copyright, 1940, by Doubleday & Company, Inc., and for "If Once You Have Slept on an Island" from *Taxis and Toadstools* by Rachel Field, copyright, 1926, by Doubleday & Company, Inc.

Harms, Inc., for "Florida, The Moon and You," copyright, 1926, by Harms, Inc.

Library of Congress catalog card number: 52-8456

To the memory of my uncle, the late Cleveland Cobb

Contents

The Last Resorts

I

The Grand Tour— From Berkshire Wit to Southampton Charm

IN THE year 1908, the late Frank Crowninshield—who was called by his friend Clare Boothe Luce, "the last and probably the greatest of a species known as the gentleman" —was persuaded to rate, for the express benefit of "millionaires from the West whose wives are bent upon breaking into Society," this country's great Eastern resorts. Crowninshield's ratings, which took the form of a tip sheet for a social steeplechase, advised that "the safest graded order of jumps" was as follows:

1. PALM BEACH.	Not exclusive, but merry, sumptuous, and expensive. Chance to meet many men in the gambling rooms.
2. HOT SPRINGS, VA.	Depressing, but many "classy" invalids.
3. NARRAGANSETT PIER.	Geographically speaking, this is nearly Newport, but the social tone, though "nobby," can hardly be called A-1.
4. THE BERKSHIRES.	Dull and dowdy, but full of genteel old families in reduced circumstances who are willing to unbend—if properly propitiated.
5. TUXEDO.	Excellent opportunities here, particularly in the Tuxedo jiggers (i.e., cabs) and at the club on rainy days, when a fourth is needed at bridge.
6. LONG ISLAND.	This is the Tattenham Corner of the social Derby—(many bad falls here—due to riding too hard)—the last great turn before the finish. (Try Hempstead, Westbury, and Roslyn—in order.)

7. NEWPORT. Having finally reached Newport, be very careful about the pace. Begin cautiously with Bellevue Avenue and the casino. Gradually, however, you may hit up the pace and try the golf club, Bailey's Beach, and, finally, you may dash past the judge's stand and weigh in at Ochre Point.

As a list of what to Westerners were once America's far-away places with the social-sounding names, Crowninshield's roll call is a convenient jumping-off place; certainly the year 1908 was at least close to the heyday of the great Eastern resorts. Nonetheless, there are some possible changes. Bar Harbor, for example, would seem Crowninshield's most notable omission; it was here that the elder J. P. Morgan, indefatigable man-about-resorts, made perhaps his sternest social observation. "You can do business with anyone," he said, "but you can only sail a boat with a gentleman." Baedeker's *United States*, published in 1909, the year after Crowninshield made his listing, rated Bar Harbor the only resort at the time "vying in importance" with Newport; certainly in the salad days of resorts, it was, after Newport, the recognized second stop on the socially popular Grand Tour of resorts—one which also included the Berkshires in the early fall, Hot Springs or White Sulphur in the late fall, and perhaps spring also, and Palm Beach in the winter.

Saratoga would also seem deserving of a place on the Crowninshield roll call, if not for home Society and the *haut monde*, then at least for hotel Society and the *beau monde*. Newport, with its ocean and its palaces, was the Queen of the Watering Places, but Saratoga, with its springs and its horses, was the King of Spas. As far back as 1865

Godey's Lady's Book, properly offended by the fact that the ladies of Newport and Saratoga were using mascara, coupled the two resorts together as "the Sodom and Gomorrah of our Union," and Newporter Henry Clews, whose *Fifty Years of Wall Street* was published the same year Crowninshield made his roll call, unhesitatingly nominated Saratoga as a recognized West-to-East gateway into New York Society:

> The ladies of the West of course have heard of Saratoga, the far-famed spa of America, and as the fortunes of their husbands mount higher and higher into the millions, they become more and more anxious to see this great summer resort of wealth and fashion. Their influence prevails, and at the height of the gay season they may be seen at the United States or the Grand Union. They are in practically a new world. There is the rustle and perfume, the glitter and show, the pomp and circumstance of the more advanced civilization of the East, and the ladies, with innate keenness, are quick to perceive a marked difference between this gorgeous panorama and the more prosaic surroundings to which they have been accustomed.

Even giving the Crowninshield roll call the addition of Bar Harbor and Saratoga, adding White Sulphur to Hot Springs, and giving Long Island the benefit of Southampton, the story of what has happened to these once hallowed addresses is an extraordinary tale of how have the mighty fallen. The Westerner of today, following the tips on his Crowninshield form sheet of less than half a century ago, would find that what once represented the recognized millionaires' meccas now stood, if for anything at all, for a succession of social ghost towns. While this switch—of the Westerner finding ghost towns in the East—is not without its irony, it is also not without its final justice. For generations the Pittsburgh Steeler, the big butter-and-egg man, the mining man and the oil man have beat their collective heads, and particularly the heads of their various wives, against these social walls, and for generations they have been taken to task for their *lèse-majesté*. Mrs. Edith Wharton, of Newport and Lenox, the country's most literary social resorter, could not resist anti-Western *nouveau riche* stories; her private favorite was the one in which her own husband, the late Edward Wharton, took the measure of a Newporter who had newly arrived from the wide-open spaces. Late for a luncheon engagement, Mr. Wharton had one day on the spur of the moment successfully thumbed a ride up Bellevue Avenue in a passing butcher's cart. Sometime later, the Westerner, meeting him, took him to task. "Wharton," he said, "I hear you rode up the Avenue in a butcher's cart. I wouldn't do that if I were you." Mr. Wharton was unmoved. "No," he said, "if I were you, I wouldn't do that either."

Whether or not that particular Westerner was a meat packer, the meaning of the story is clear from the point of view of the age-old social double standard which existed for the East-ins and the West-outs. Today, however, the shoe is on the other foot. Riding high, wide and handsome on oil wells and expense accounts—two forms of wealth which because of current tax structures are really the last remaining "money" in the old sense of the word—the West's great resorts, Palm Springs and Sun Valley, Reno and Las Vegas, Tucson and Phoenix, Prescott and Santa Fe, Colorado Springs and Aspen, are, in contrast to the East's ghost towns, all social boom towns. Furthermore, the anti-Western story of today has deteriorated. Not long ago Mrs. William Ladd, of Southampton and Palm Beach, discussing a favorite theory of old-time Eastern resorters that yachts have of late years come into the wrong hands, commented on a disturbing yachting experience with newcomers to the Florida resort. "They were people from Detroit or somewhere," she declared, "and the entire time we were on board their boat they ran the generator or the vibrator or something. Why, the boat shook so you could hardly hold a cocktail!"

Somewhere along the line, the ring of authority which marked the Wharton story has disappeared. More than this, the Westerner of today sees small reason to bow to Eastern condescension, and, if necessary, even answers back. When Mrs. Claude K. Boettcher, who had been voted one of the ten best-dressed ladies of Denver, arrived in Palm Beach, she was challenged by an elderly Eastern *grande dame* who spotted her one morning wearing diamonds. "Oh, no, my dear," said the Eastern lady patronizingly, "you mustn't. One simply doesn't wear diamonds in the daytime." Mrs. Boettcher smiled. "I thought not, too," she said pleasantly, "until I had them."

The story of the decline and fall of the great Eastern resorts, however, is more than a West-East engagement. The late resort sport Alexander Phillips, a man who died in 1950 after a lifetime career of bacheloring Newport, Bar Harbor and Palm Beach, once declared that while he felt Old Guard Society could be better distinguished at the old-line resorts than it could in the confused milieu of the big cities, he nonetheless felt that all over the country Society as he had known it was a thing of the past. "The '400,' " he said, "has been marked down to $3.98." Furthermore, the story of what has happened to these resorts is not only a story of what has happened to Old Guard Society but also to Old Guard Business—which was, of course, the foundation of that Society. Railroader Robert R. Young, premier businessman resorter of today—he summers at Newport, winters at Palm Beach, and springs and falls at White Sulphur—finds himself almost alone in his social pilgrimages; even he feels it necessary to define his position. "I find I can work more effectively in these resorts," he explains. "When I'm in New York I spend 80 per cent of my time doing someone else's work. When I'm in Newport or Palm Beach I can escape."

In the old days no such explanation was necessary; the Big Businessman who did not attend at least one resort in season was socially suspect. As recently as August, 1930, Newport was the birthplace of the famous list of the late Ambassador James W. Gerard of the so-called "Sixty-Four Men Who Run America." Not only was Gerard visiting the late General Cornelius Vanderbilt at Newport at the time he made out his list, but also, of the fifty-nine men originally named—Gerard later expanded it to sixty-four—no less than fifty were recognized men-about-resorts. "They themselves," said Gerard with some irony, "are too busy to hold political office but they determine who shall hold such offices." Further back, in the same year that Crowninshield made his roll call, gaping tourists were regularly taken by boat to glimpse the simple brown clubhouse of Bar Harbor's famous Pot and Kettle Club; they were invariably assured by the captain of their sight-seeing tour that the membership of this club—one which never, in those days, exceeded fifty men—represented 85 per cent of the wealth of the United States.

If the story is a large one, it is also, at least to the thin red line of social heroes at these resorts, an extremely sad one. Outsiders like New York's Elsa Maxwell may be unmoved—"I always think of Newport," she says, "as the city of the living dead"—but to insiders their ghostdom is a stern matter indeed. "There's no use talking about it," says Miss Edith

Wetmore of Newport's "Chateau Sur Mer," "we're the end of an era, if you please." Miss Wetmore, whose grandfather, George Peabody Wetmore, built Newport's first large mansion just a hundred years ago, has in her will left "Chateau Sur Mer" to the Society of New England Antiquities; she feels that, socially speaking, Newport is within eight of being a complete ghost town. "I mean to say," she says, "if you know what I mean, there are just eight families left. Fortunately, I like very few people." At Bar Harbor, Tuxedo and Southampton the story is the same; down at White Sulphur Springs Mrs. Quintard Taylor, speaking for both that resort and Hot Springs, declares: "We used to be two lovely old places. It was sort of like Harvard and Yale—but in the South. We were rivals but we really loved each other and we all knew everybody and everybody knew who we were. Now we're just nothing and nobody knows who we are and we're just like anywhere." And finally at Palm Beach Mme. Jacques Balsan, the former Consuelo Vanderbilt and ex-Duchess of Marlborough, who lives ten miles outside the resort, declares that the place is actually so dreadful that she won't go near it. "The only time I go to Palm Beach now," she says, "is to get my hair washed and to get some money out of the bank."

The Berkshires are perhaps the sharpest example of the change. Here the stranded gentry are in a high state of social bereavement. "We are burying the Sedgwicks one by one," says Stockbridge's Tom Carey, who describes himself as the last liveryman east of the Hudson River, "and there is no one to take their place." At "Chesterwood" Mrs. William Penn Cresson, talented daughter of sculptor Daniel Chester French, has a standing reply to people who ask to see the social sights. "Come on down," she says, "and view the remains." At "Laurel-Mere" Mrs. George Otis Rockwood, great-great-great-granddaughter of Harvard Professor John Webster who murdered Dr. George Parkman in Boston's most distinguished Society killing, feels that, as of a century later, the younger generation does not care anything about background or social tradition. "They don't even talk family anymore," she says. "The whole thing's gone fluey. We're all gobbled up."

Lenox, social capital of the Berkshires, was once a social household word. In the same year that Crowninshield made his roll call the Lenox Library voted to give up renting out its Assembly Room for balls, because, stated the minutes of the Library meeting, "every palace now created has its own ballroom." In the same year also Grover Cleveland died, and the *Berkshire Evening Eagle* found it hard to believe the President had escaped Lenox. The headline of the paper read, PRESIDENT DEAD; underneath there was a subhead, "May Have Fished Here." Today, in contrast, Lenox is known only for its Tanglewood Music Festival, one which, remarkably enough, Newport turned down. "Elm Court," grand castle of the last of the Lenox *grandes dames*, Mrs. Emily Vanderbilt Sloane White, was, after Mrs. White's death in 1946, converted into a hotel; for five dollars the tourist can sleep where the Vanderbilts slept and for twenty-five he can sleep in Mrs. White's own bed. Here, fortunately, some protocol is still observed. "Of course," says George Wilde, owner of the hotel, "if we have the kind of tourist who wants to rent the room because it was Mrs. White's, we don't rent it." At "The Gables" Mrs. Alexandre Hoppin ticks off on her fingers the names of the old-time Lenoxers who are left. "There's Granny Schenck and there's my sister and there's me," she says, "and there's the Bristeds and the Fields and the Danas. And there you are." In the old days, in the opinion of Mrs. Hoppin, Lenox was always on the go. "We were a very sporty community," she says. "We had the Berkshire Hunt and Tub Parades and Gymkhanas and tetherball tournaments and we even had a ladies' baseball team. We slid the bases, too—in long skirts and picture hats. Today if you want to show the younger generation a horse you have to take them to the zoo."

To the historian of the future, looking back on the great American resort extravaganza, it is quite possible that its most outstanding single feature may be the use of the simple word "cottage." Through the years this word has been used, with remarkable aplomb, to denote the million-dollar mansions, marble palaces and château castles which today, in various stages of destitution and distress, still adorn such streets as Newport's Bellevue Avenue, Bar Harbor's West Street and Palm Beach's Ocean Drive. Always thought-provoking—the Henry Sage cottage on Long Island was, for example, called "the peaks and turrets of outrageous fortune"—it is a curious fact that originally, in the early days of resorts, the word "cottage" was used humbly. It was then used in the dictionary definition of "a modest country dwelling" to denote the small buildings which were built around the large hotels to care for the overflow of guests. Soon, because of the extra space and privacy these cottages provided, they became more socially desirable than rooms in the hotel; their patrons became known as the "cottagers" or the "cottage colony," in any case, the social leaders of the resorts. Then, when these patrons broke away from the hotels entirely and built their own resort homes, they were loath to lose their social eminence and so kept the word, if not the spirit, when they built their mansions, palaces and castles.

Today, of course, the word has come back to haunt the resorts; the million-dollar cottages, many of them unoccupied, sold to institutions, or cut-up and subdivided, are now the haunted houses of the resorts.

Curiously enough, even the names of these cottages seem of some significance. The most prominent of them not only evoke a sort of picture of the life they once represented but also seem to symbolize the individual differences of the resorts. "The Breakers" and "Marble House," "Vinland" and "Beaulieu" somehow conjure up a picture of the pomp and circumstance of the life in the almost side-by-side castles along Newport's Bellevue Avenue and Ochre Point, while Bar Harbor's "Chatwold" and "Baymeath," "Pointe d'Acadie" and "Reverie Cove" call to mind a more sequestered life by the ocean and mountains of Maine, and Lenox's "Shadowbrook" and "Bellefontaine," "Wheatleagh" and "Clipston Grange," bring at least a glimpse of upper-strata pastoral life amid the autumn foliage of the Berkshires; in the same way "El Mirasol" and "Playa Reinte," "Mar-a-Lago," and "Casa Bendita" seem to picture the man-made qualities of tropical Palm Beach.

Unfortunately, such stateliness was not to last. As a self-conscious era of wealth set in, Newport descended to such names as "Chateau Nooga," "The Rocks' Kiss," and "Little Clifton Berley," while Bar Harbor, which in its great days went so far as to have private signals regularly run up on cottage flagpoles to salute incoming ships, was reduced to "Mainstay," "Camp o' the Woods" and "Bishop's Gate Within." Southampton traveled from such names as "Chestertown House" and "Hampton Court," "Old Trees" and "Appletrees" into a new era of "El Nido" and "Peep o' Day," "Cherubian" and "Laffalot," "Duke Box" and " '21' Cottage," and, as might be expected, Palm Beach went all the way with names like "Peewita" and "Casa Veeva," "Kathwill" and "Gumbo Limbo," "Villa Aujourd'hui" and "Villa Toi-et-Moi." Today it is possible to find, in the best of resorts, names which range from pig Latin to pidgin Indian, from "Ediewantsit" to "Pnegokihlasis II" and self-conscious names are the rule—names like "Careaway" for a Carey family, "Baker's Acres" for a Baker family, and, inevitably, for a Whitney family, "Whitsend." All over the East for every "Fairholm" and "Brightholme," "Sundansea" and "Wyndansea," "Mon Repos" and "Sans Souci," there is certain to be, as a sign of the times, a "Dearuin" and a "Hardscrabble," a "Broome Hall" and a "Witch Cliffe" and even "Gruesome Gables" and "The Wrecktory." Finally, at Aiken, South Carolina, the late Thomas Hastings named his cottage, which was unique in that it included cottage and stable all in one, "Horse Haven." As the designer of the New York Public Library, Hastings was obviously the man for the job. During the controversy about the money for the library, a politician asked Hastings why he had spent the extra required to put the lions outside. Replied Hastings patiently, "So that everyone who goes into the library, takes out a book and walks down the stairway, can, if they desire, read between the lions." Hastings had other competitors in the field. Ring Lardner named his cottage "The Mange" and the late Philip Barry, who lived at East Hampton beside a cottage in which a man had hanged himself, used the name "Chez Noose." But it remained for the late Arthur Samuels, editor of *House Beautiful*, to satirize the era most delicately. Painted in small letters on the outside of the door of Samuels' small apartment at 277 Park Avenue were the words, "The Breakers."

The real "Breakers" at Newport, the most famous resort cottage ever built in this country, was built in 1895. In 1948 it was leased by its owner, Countess László Széchényi, the former Gladys Vanderbilt, to the Newport Preservation Society for the sum of one dollar and opened to the public. Today, for the sum of one dollar and fifty cents, a visitor can see a cottage which cost five million dollars in the days when a million dollars was a million dollars and could not now be duplicated for twenty million dollars. Designed by Richard Morris Hunt, who made a specialty of turning foreign palaces into American cottages, and vice versa, "The Breakers" boasts an ornamental wrought-iron fence outside which currently costs over five thousand dollars a year just to keep painted. The front doors—there are two sets of double doors even after you get by the outside gate—are no come-ons either; one set weighs seventy tons. In the entire cottage, in order to insure a completely fireproof building, not a single stick of timber was used; the chandeliers are both wired for electricity and piped for gas, and the bathrooms are fitted with outlets for both hot and cold salt, as well as fresh, water. Four floors and a total of seventy rooms (thirty-three of them for servants) center around a monumental hall which rises over 45 feet through two floors to what is undoubtedly the most breath-taking interior of any house—let alone cottage—ever built in this country. The dining room, which is covered by a distant ceiling painting of Aurora at Dawn, has been called more ornate than any single room in any palace abroad, and even the Billiard Room, in which the walls are faced from floor to ceiling with matched slates of pale gray-green Cippolino marble, is by no means to be confused with a rumpus room.

Tourists often overlooked this cottage's motto; this is engraved in French over the library fireplace. Translated, it reads: "Little do I care for riches, and do not miss them, since only cleverness prevails in the end." In this library, in the confusion of one of the first public tours of "The Breakers," a lady guide noticed a rather lost-looking young man who, all of seven years of age, appeared not to be a member of any of the several touring parties in various parts of the cottage. "Young man," she commanded sternly, "you are not allowed to wander around by yourself. Come over here and join my group." The young man obediently joined up, and as the tour progressed, the lady guide was distressed to note he seemed to have a vast disinterest in the whole affair. Finally, determined to bring him into line, she stopped her prepared spiel in the middle. "Young man," she said, "how would *you* like to live in a house like this?" The young man looked up at her for the first time. "I do," he said.

The young man's grandmother, Countess Széchényi, long Newport's most charming First Lady, also has her memories. She recalls, as a child hardly older than her grandson, sitting inside "The Breakers" and hearing cab drivers take sightseers up to the outside of the wrought-iron gates. "Those drivers used to say," she recalls, " 'It takes four footmen to open the door and they have ice cream there every day.' Today footmen have disappeared and everybody has ice cream every day. But are people any happier? Today your child wants to be like your chauffeur's child more than your chauffeur's child wants to be like your child. But is that any better?"

"Shadowbrook" at Lenox is second only to "The Breakers" among the country's resort cottages; it too is haunted by ghost stories. Built by the late Anson Phelps Stokes, a huge 100-room turreted granite castle occupying half a mountain, it has always dwarfed all other Berkshire cottages. Today

Canon Anson Phelps Stokes, son of the original owner of "Shadowbrook," lives in what was once the dairy of the main cottage; a distinguished church historian, he works in what was once the ice house. In happier days when he was attending Yale in the class of 1896 he once wired his mother in "Shadowbrook," ARRIVING THIS EVENING WITH CROWD OF NINETY-SIX MEN—only to receive from his mother the return wire, MANY GUESTS ALREADY HERE. HAVE ONLY ROOM FOR FIFTY. In 1916 "Shadowbrook" was purchased by Andrew Carnegie, and, following his death there in 1919, the house was, in 1922, like so many other resort cottages since, sold by Mrs. Carnegie to the Roman Catholic Church—in this case for a Jesuit Novitiate. Some years ago Mrs. Stokes, meeting the Director of the "Shadowbrook" Jesuits for the first time and knowing at first hand the shortcomings of what is generally regarded as the country's all-time cottage monstrosity, was extremely puzzled over the Director's obvious enthusiasm for the cottage's qualifications for a school. First she guessed politely that the Director must be pleased with the outside anyway, even if he couldn't be with the inside, and admitted that "Shadowbrook" had a fine view of the surrounding countryside. The Director smiled and shook his head; he declared that no, it wasn't the view. Mrs. Stokes tried again, this time guessing that what he probably liked was the huge size of the rooms; she knew that the proportions of the ballroom had proved right for a chapel and hazarded that the other rooms had proved equally serviceable. Again the Director smiled and shook his head; no, it wasn't the size. Mrs. Stokes tried still a third time; she supposed the terraces must be a beautiful place for reciting. Once more the Director shook his head, and this time Mrs. Stokes gave up. "Well, you tell me, Father," she said, "what *do* you like about it?"

"Madam," said the Director, "before our boys even come to us, they have been tested as rigorously as it is possible to test them in three different ways. They have been tested physically, they have been tested mentally and they have been tested spiritually. 'Shadowbrook,' Madam, tests our boys still a fourth way. 'Shadowbrook' tests them *socially*."

Curiously enough, a brief history of the ups-and-downs of fashionable resorts reveals that what is today a complete resort ghost town—the little village of Stafford Springs, Connecticut—has the honor of being the first recognized Society resort in this country. Though it still boasts an ancient mineral spring beside its library and a sulphur spring in its park, Stafford Springs wears its honors lightly and has not even a Chamber of Commerce. Nonetheless, this spa was frequented, as far back as the seventeenth century, by fashionable Pilgrims. These Pilgrims had heard of its charms from a tribe of Indians known as the Nipmucks, who, whether fashionable or not, at least looked down on the neighboring Podunks and had for many years been vigorously promoting their springs for summer gatherings for Indian tribes from all over New England.

In second and third position for resort age honors were two Pennsylvania Springs, the Yellow Springs in Bucks County and the Bath Springs at Bristol. Both claim discovery from the year 1722, and though they never attained high social standing, they were soon followed by a veritable procession of Virginia Springs which did. These Virginia Springs, dating from about 1750, were, in order, the Old Warm (later

Bath and then Berkeley), the old Little Warm (later the Hot), the old Sweet and the old White; there were also, however, the Red Sulphur, the Salt Sulphur, the Blue Sulphur, the Gray Sulphur and the Yellow Sulphur, as well as the Montgomery White Sulphur, the Fauquier White Sulphur and the Jordan White Sulphur and also the Rockbridge Chalybeate and many others. Second only to the Virginia Springs came New York's Saratoga Springs, closely followed by Maine's Poland Springs and New York's Richfield Springs; Saratoga, antedated by a few years by nearby Ballston Spa, could in fact claim by 1783 that George Washington had slept there—a boast that Virginia's Old Warm could take with the old salt, the Father of his Country having first visited that resort as a young surveyor, at the age of eighteen, in 1750.

At all of these early-day resorts, health was the primary attraction. "One twinge of the gout in *pater familias'* toe," says Harrison Rhodes, "sufficed to start a whole caravan to the Springs." Second only to health, however, was attention to religion. Even Saratoga, in its early days far from the den of iniquity it was later to become, saw this country's first Temperance Society organized as far back as 1808. In the same year, the Englishman Edward Kendall, visiting Stafford Springs, declared that "prayers, hymns and chapters of the Bible were quoted before breakfast" and that "evenings at the Springs were generally spent by the young women in singing hymns." It is hardly surprising that America's first resort had also the honor of being the first to be a last resort; in the words of John King, Stafford Springs was, in the year 1840, "old-fashioned" and full of "sad bores." "They drank," he said, "really without exaggeration, twenty-eight tumblers of water each day."

The nineteenth century not only saw the inland resorts begin to cast off the shackles of religion—by the 1840's Saratoga had become an acknowledged center of gambling—but this century also ushered in the great era of the social seaside resorts. Newport, first and greatest of these, had been a going resort concern since well before the Revolution; indeed Newport's late Mrs. John King Van Rensselaer always maintained that the proper date of Newport's origin as a summer resort was 1729, one which would make it not only the oldest seaside resort, but also the third oldest of all resorts. Whatever the actual date, Newport's beginning as a resort, as befitting its eminence in pre-Revolutionary days as a larger and more important city than New York, was in trade. Newport's first trade was the familiar Triangular—when molasses from Jamaica was converted into rum in Newport, rum being in turn traded in Africa for slaves and slaves being in turn exchanged in Jamaica for more molasses. Following the Revolution Newport had a second trade basis. Each June rich planters from the West Indies and Southern states would come north with their families in sailing packets on their way to get nitrates and fertilizers from Fall River; instead of returning South, they let the boats take the fertilizer home and stayed on to enjoy the cool summers on Rhode Island's most famous island. Then in September their boats came north once more bringing the plantation crops to the Fall River mill; this time the boats also took the planters and their families home.

With this well-fertilized foundation Newport was soon nationally known. During most of the nineteenth century, however, it played second fiddle to the famous New Jersey resorts of Cape May and Long Branch. "Saratoga and Newport in the North," says Jefferson Williamson, "Cape May and Long Branch on the New Jersey coast, and White Sulphur in the South were the great match-making and social-climbing center of the middle decades of the nineteenth century." In this era New Hampshire's White Mountains were also highly regarded socially. Here indeed there was actual climbing, one hotel proprietor advertising that "Pemigewasset," his local mountain, "could easily be ascended by ladies as well as gentlemen." But the seaside resorts had come to stay and by the 1870's Long Branch, summer capital of presidents from Grant to Arthur, was a rival of Newport itself. If the Rhode Island resort, having been deserted by its Southerners during the Civil War, had by this time New York's Astors and Vanderbilts, Long Branch had, if not Philadelphia's Biddles and Cadwaladers, at least Drexels and Cassatts.

As Long Branch and Cape May belonged primarily to Philadelphia, and Newport belonged first to the Southerners and then to New York, Boston was responsible for the country's fourth seaside resort. Boston Society, founded on three cardinal points of faith—the fatherhood of God, the brotherhood of man and the neighborhood of Boston—did not, of course, go far. At the southern end of what was later to become the resort area known as Boston's North Shore, the Bostonians established on a sandy spit off two high cliffs stretching out into the sea from Lynn the ancient resort known as Nahant. This name, pronounced with the Proper Bostonian accent, was virtually unintelligible to any outlander. "I think," says young Mrs. John Roosevelt, who grew up at Nahant, "that it's pronounced sort of the way I was brought up to say 'banaa-na' but nobody can ever understand that, either." If Nahant's pronunciation was difficult, so too was its Society; the resort, at which the son of the king of

Boston's merchant princes, the younger Colonel Thomas Handasyd Perkins, built the first cottage in 1817, became known for all time by the epithet given it by the Boston wit, Thomas Gold Appleton—"Cold Roast Boston."

The latter half of the nineteenth century saw the discovery of other social resort areas. The Berkshires saw the beginning of their invasion when Samuel Gray Ward, New York banker, built a "farm" in 1846. After the Civil War the real "cottage" invasion of the Berkshires began; Lenox had thirty-five cottages in 1880, and by the turn of the century seventy-five. Mount Desert, island home of such social resorts as Bar Harbor, Northeast, Southwest and Seal, was socially pioneered as far back as 1855 by Charles Tracy, father-in-law of the elder J. P. Morgan; twelve years later Bar Harbor had a dozen boardinghouses which called themselves hotels and, more important, its first separate cottage. Southampton, social dean of Long Island resorts, saw its first cottage in 1875. This cottage was built by the New York dry goods merchant, Leon Depeyre De Bost, and when, two years later, De Bost induced his family physician, Dr. T. Gaillard Thomas, to follow his patient to the resort, Southampton was on its way. In its early days, on Lake Agawam, Southamptonites had lanterns on their docks with different color combinations—white, red, green, etc.—to indicate who was who, and who was home; when the Betts family after a trip to Venice installed a gondola in the lake the resort began to be called, as it later actually became, New York's "social annex." Its first invasion was Irish Catholic when Judge Morgan O'Brien and his daughters, living in innocence and virtue at Hampton Bays—a town which had earlier been called Good Ground but had to change its name following a murder—suddenly "longed for the fleshpots," as the saying was, and moved to

Southampton; the O'Brien family was followed by the Murray and McDonnell tribes and later by a host of Pittsburghers including Mellons, Camerons, Thaws, Dilworths, Reas and Byers. Narragansett Pier, across the bay from Newport, had its first sojourn of summer boarders in 1856 and cottages a few years later. The Pier, as it was always called—with the hurricane of 1938 the actual old pier vanished from the scene altogether—had in its early days a specific character among summer resorts, long before the advent of Philadelphia's Wideners and Wanamakers and other iniquities. "The Pierian World," recalled Providence's late George Carroll, "was metropolitan society on the basis of light but graceful *negligé*."

Society's love of the horse—one which has not always been returned—found its highest expression in South Carolina's famous Aiken, another major resort development of this era. Long before Aiken was thought of as a town, nearby Kalmia was the fashionable resort for Charleston people in stagecoach days; Aiken itself may be said to have been socially "discovered" by New Orleans' Miss Celestine Elizabeth Eustis, aunt of the famous horsewoman, the late Mrs. Thomas Hitchcock of "Mon Repos," who first came to Aiken in 1872. Tuxedo Park, next in point of age and the resort which was to give its name to the tail-less dinner coat, was established single-handedly by Pierre Lorillard V, of the snuff and tobacco empire. Located 25 miles northeast of New York, in the Ramapo Hills overlooking Tuxedo Lake, it was officially opened on Memorial Day, 1886. Palm Beach, the last social resort development of the nineteenth century, was also established almost singlehandedly—in this case by the late Standard Oil man, Henry M. Flagler. Although well ahead of Miami, it was not the first Florida resort. Fernandina, just east of Jacksonville, had been advertised as "the Newport of the South" as early as 1878. Flagler's first Florida hotel was the Ponce de Leon at St. Augustine which opened in 1888. After this establishment proved successful he moved farther South to Palm Beach to build the incredible Royal Poinciana —a hostelry which opened in 1894 and lasted until it was finally razed by fire in 1932. Flagler took no chances with its early-day social promotion. The first train to cross Flagler Bridge to the Poinciana, on March 14, 1896, bore a shipment of no less than four Vanderbilts—out of a total of seventeen passengers. The train was not only a private-car affair but was also an entirely private train. "It was like a houseparty," says Countess Széchényi who, as a young girl, was the youngest of the Vanderbilt *avant garde*. "We had a sleeper for the men and a sleeper for the women, a sitting room and a dining room car and even a car for our luggage. On the way back we stopped at Aiken."

Today's resort old-timers believe firmly in a curious theory of resorts. This theory is that, generally speaking, the following groups have come to the social resorts in this order: first, artists and writers in search of good scenery and solitude; second, professors and clergymen and other so-called "solid people" with long vacations in search of the simple life; third, "nice millionaires" in search of a good place for their children to lead the simple life (as lived by the "solid people"); fourth, "naughty millionaires" who wished to associate socially with the "nice millionaires" but who built million-dollar cottages and million-dollar clubs, dressed up for dinner, gave balls and utterly destroyed the simple life; and fifth, trouble.

Actually, this theory, which amounts to a sort of Gresham's Law of Resorts—i.e., that bad millionaires drive good millionaires out of circulation—holds up remarkably well. It does not fit Newport entirely; the Southern Planter era was not preceded by artists, writers or any other intellectuals. On the other hand, in the nineteenth century, in the gap between the Southern Planters and the coming of the New York Astors and Vanderbilts, Newport had a definite intellectual period. At this time men like Bancroft and Longfellow, the Jameses, the elder Agassiz and Professor Gibbs, gave the resort a high mental reputation, and before the coming of New York's "naughty millionaires" Newport was populated by both "solid people" and "nice millionaires"—a group which included William Beach Lawrence, Prescott Hall, Henry Durand and Delancey Kane. The Boston resort of Nahant was also in its early days a stronghold of New England intellectuals. Not only were Bancroft and Longfellow here before they were at Newport, but there were also Webster, Choate, Willis, Prescott, Motley, Whittier, Holmes and many others; these gave the resort a flavor which, as late as 1904, was repeated when the Elder Lodge, speaking at the fiftieth anniversary of the incorporation of Nahant, concluded his speech with fourteen lines of Latin poetry. Even Southampton, today hardly thought of as intellectual, was originally settled because of a minister. The grandfather of the resort's first cottage builder, Leon Depeyre De Bost, was a minister in the town of Southampton.

Bar Harbor and Lenox are perhaps the two best examples of Gresham's Law of intellectual pioneers and of first good and then bad millionaires. Bar Harbor's first cottage was not built until 1867, but as early as 1844 Thomas Cole, founder of the Hudson River School of painting, came there and sketched; other artistic luminaries were in turn followed by writers, professors, doctors, bishops and other "solid people." Even Bar Harbor's first cottage-builder, the Bostonian Alpheus Hardy, a clipper trade man, ranked, among millionaires, as "nice." It was Hardy's practice to commute by sail from Bar Harbor to Boston, leaving Sunday night and, if the wind was right, arriving in time for two days' work before sailing back for another week end.

At Lenox the intellectual colony was far in advance of the millionaire cottagers. Led by Mrs. Fanny Kemble, English actress who first came to the Berkshires in 1836 and settled in her cottage "The Perch" in 1849, as well as by Catherine Sedgwick and other literary Sedgwicks of Stockbridge, the Berkshire's literary colony soon included such celebrities as Hawthorne and Melville, Holmes and Longfellow. At Lenox the famous Philadelphia resorter, Dr. Weir Mitchell, also a Newporter and Bar Harborite, called on Mrs. Kemble and, starting to go, was begged to stay. "No, do not go yet," said the aging actress. "I am old and lonely, and never again will you have these chances to talk with the woman who has sat at dinner alongside of Byron, who has heard Tom Moore sing and who calls Tennyson 'Alfred.' " Lenox's most famous literary lights were perhaps even more atmospheric. It was on "the dear, wide, sunny terrace of 'The Mount' "—as Edith Wharton called her cottage, which is today a girls' school—that Henry James told Mrs. Wharton that he thought the most beautiful combination of words in the English language was "summer afternoon"; it was here also that Mrs. Wharton recorded the age-old story of author versus author:

> I remember a painful moment, during one of his visits, when my husband imprudently blurted out an allusion to "Edith's new story—you've seen it in the last 'Scribner'?"

> My heart sank; I knew it always embarrassed James to be called on, in the author's presence, for an "appreciation." He was himself so engrossed in questions of technique and construction—and so increasingly detached from the short-story form as a medium—that very few "fictions" (as he called them) but his own were of interest to him. . . . In the present instance, as usual, he instantly replied: "Oh, yes, my dear Edward, I've read the little work—of course I've read it." A gentle pause, which I knew boded no good; then he softly continued: "Admirable, admirable; a masterly little achievement." He turned to me, full of a terrifying benevolence. "Of course so accomplished a mistress of the art would not, without deliberate intention, have given the tale so curiously conventional a treatment. Though indeed, in the given case, no treatment *but* the conventional was possible; which might conceivably, my dear lady, on further consideration, have led you to reject your subject as—er—in itself a totally unsuitable one."

But Lenox's literary "summer afternoon" was not to be permitted to go on for long. With the millionaire cottagers the resort was changed until, says Walter Prichard Eaton, "Hawthorne in his humble red house would have felt like a Fresh-Air Child at a charity picnic." Fortunately Hawthorne, who, ironically enough, had named the little stream that flowed by his red house "Shadowbrook," had fled before the invasion; his cottage, which he called "Tanglewood," later gave its name, as well as the original location, to Lenox's music festival. Another author, however, Mrs. Burton Harrison of Lenox and Bar Harbor, stayed to see the change. After speaking of "the Robert Olivers' merry tea-table where wit flew like thistledown," she gives in her *Recollections Grave and Gay* one of the best pictures extant of resort life of the 1870's:

The people who met there, summer after summer, were of the cultured and refined class of American Society, knowing each other intimately, and satisfied to exchange simple entertainments in their pretty picturesque homes. We had tea-parties followed by games of twenty questions, by charades, and dumb crambo, where fun and wit were the order of the hour. We walked to and from each other's houses, attended by maids with lanterns. Every Saturday evening there was a gathering at Sedgwick Hall, for dancing and reunions, to which the new-rich magnates of New York came as total strangers. Young men called for young women to walk to the ledge in the Woolsey woods, whither they were seen wending their way, with a cashmere shawl upon the gentleman's arm for the lady to sit upon, and with a blue-and-gold volume of some favorite poet in his hand, from which to read selected passages, under dropping nuts in an amber atmosphere. People met at the post-office after church on Sunday, when the elm-shaded street became alive with gay faces and graceful figures with attendant cavaliers. On Sunday afternoons we walked up to see Mr. Goodman's cows.

Then Mrs. Harrison's pastoral idyl is broken, and she records the change—one which was taking place not only at Lenox but at all the great social resorts the country over:

I lived there long enough to see a mighty change. The rural hillsides and pastures, bought up at fabulous prices, were made the sites of modern villas, most of them handsome and in good taste. The villas were succeeded by little palaces, some repeating the facades and gardens of royal dwellings abroad. Instead of the trim maidservants appearing in caps and aprons to open doors, one was confronted by lackeys in livery lounging in the halls. Caviar and *mousse au truffes* supplanted muffins and waffles. Worth and Callot gowns, cut low and worn with abundant jewels, took the place of dainty muslins made by a little day dressmaker. Stables were filled with costly horses, farm yards with stock bearing pedigrees sometimes longer than that of the owner; the dinner-hour moved on to eight o'clock, and lastly came house-parties, 'week-ends,' and the eternal honk and reek of the motorcar.

It was at Lenox, ironically enough, that the great library-builder Andrew Carnegie asked Frank Doubleday about the publishing business. "Frank," he said, "how much did you make last month?" Doubleday, in the time-honored manner of his profession, replied nervously that you could not figure publishing like that. "Frank," said Carnegie again, "I'd get out of it."

A few early-day Lenox cottagers felt so strongly about the change that they refused to enter the new era at all. Mrs. Goodman, who kept the cows, and Mrs. Auchmuty, aunt of Lenox horsewoman Kate Cary, both wore the same clothes of the era in which they were married until they died; both also disliked automobiles and the first time Mrs. Auchmuty ever rode in one was in her own funeral procession. Of the new "naughty millionaires," dominated as they were by New Yorkers like Sloanes, Schermerhorns and Parsons, the most puritanical was Lenox's late Grenville Winthrop. His wife having died after the birth of his second child, Winthrop brought up his two daughters so severely that they were never allowed to speak to a boy unless a chaperone was present. In September, 1924, the two girls engineered a clandestine double-elopement, marrying, respectively, an electrician and a chauffeur. The event, in the days when Lenox was the focal point of fall Society the country over, made world news; the Paris edition of the *Herald Tribune* headlined PURITAN'S DAUGHTERS ELOPE WITH OVERALLS. In sharp contrast to Winthrop was the late Cortlandt Field Bishop of "Ananda Hall." Bishop's will, still discussed at all

Berkshire tea tables, left his money to be shared in equal proportion by two women—one his wife—on the condition that they remain living under the same roof. When "Ananda Hall" was torn down, Mrs. Bishop and the other woman, who has since married, moved to another cottage, but to this day, abiding by the terms of Bishop's will, they still live together.

Other Lenoxers were more picturesque. Mrs. George Westinghouse, brought up in a dirty mining town, insisted that everything in and out of her cottage, "Erskine Park," be white. Outside she had an artificial lake, elaborate fountains and a massive bridge—all white—and even the driveway and connecting roads were white marble; inside all the rooms were white and several had both walls and ceilings made of tufted white satin and buttoned like upholstered chairs. Mrs. Westinghouse herself, the wife of a man who was at one time president of no less than thirty corporations, always dressed in white. Under a glass globe on her living room table she kept a stuffed white fox terrier. An extraordinary number of the new Lenoxers collected more lively animals. William C. Whitney stocked a whole zoo on October Mountain; he imported a herd of moose from Canada and a herd of cowboys from Arizona to conduct hunting parties. Mrs. Charles Lanier of "Allen Winden" kept a pet bull; each morning she would ride down on it from her place on the hill to get her mail, and the man at the post office, afraid of the animal, opened the window and handed her out her mail on a pitchfork. Mrs. Edwards Spencer of "Shipton Court" loved all kinds of animals, her favorite being a smartly groomed pig named Rosie which she kept as a pet in her parlor. Rosie later became so much a part of the resort's social whirl that she more than once attended desirable functions without her mistress. Old Lenoxers still recall her appearance at the finals of a tennis tournament held at Mrs. White's "Elm Court." Mrs. White, then Mrs. Sloane, at first mistook her guest for an ordinary pig and set her footmen on her, but when it was explained to the *grande dame* that it was Rosie, Mrs. Sloane immediately clapped her hands, called off her footmen, and had Rosie escorted home in style by her butler.

Today most Lenoxers date the end of the Berkshires as a social resort with the death of the late Giraud Foster in 1945. Born in 1850, Foster was so highly regarded at the resort that he was elected president of the old Lenox Club for thirty straight years, his final re-election coming at the age of ninety-four. Foster's cottage, "Bellefontaine," was as symbolic at the resort as its master or, for that matter, its mistress, who always wore black velvet eyebrows. Modeled after the Petit Trianon, this white marble showplace boasted on the exterior an enormous gilt and wrought-iron gateway, half a hundred regularly placed statues, a symmetrical garden and a long, straight driveway lined with an even row of poplars. The interior of "Bellefontaine" was even more remarkable. Built in 1898 it had furniture, hangings and rugs of such quality that not a single item was ever repaired or replaced to the day of Foster's death. Nor did Foster permit any additional furnishings; when his wife shot a moose he insisted that the stuffed moose head be placed in her own Marie Antoinette boudoir. Unfortunately, with Foster's death, the showplace of the Berkshires, like the wonderful one-hoss shay, fell into disrepair all at once. Afterward, "Bellefontaine" was bought by a man who owned a chain of mortuaries. The man's wife, however, took one look at the cottage and persuaded her husband to resell it. It was unsuitable, she felt, even for the dead.

Beloved as Foster was at the resort there was at least one

instance of unfavorable comment upon the Lenox patriarch. As at other resorts, Lenox cab drivers made a habit of taking sight-seers on tours of the great estates. Normally these drivers maintained a firm reticence about the private lives of the cottagers and merely stated the name of the owner and the name of the cottage, the source of income and the price paid for the estate. Unhappily Foster one day told his butler to forbid the cab drivers to tour the driveway of "Bellefontaine" —a privilege to which they had long been accustomed. The following day, as Foster was giving an alfresco luncheon on the sun porch of "Bellefontaine," the cab driver drove his party as close as he could. "Here," he shouted, "lives the only millionaire who made all his money in one day." As Foster and his luncheon guests stirred uncomfortably, a tourist in the cab promptly asked how that could be. And once more the driver raised his voice. "He married it!"

Today's resort old-timers blame economics for all their woes. "It's just plain a matter of money," says Bar Harbor's Mrs. William S. Moore. A daughter of the elder Joseph Pulitzer and a great-granddaughter-in-law of the man who wrote "The Night before Christmas," Mrs. Moore feels that at present she is living in a sort of Night before the Deluge. "Now," she says, "the richer you are the poorer you are." In happier days Mrs. Moore was once told that a friend had a "trade last" for her. "You never talk money," her friend said. "Why should I?" replied Mrs. Moore, with a candor she wishes she could use today. "I've never even had to think about it." Other resorters, from Bar Harbor to Palm Beach, are also suffering from taxitis. "We're the New Poor, you know," says Bar Harbor's Mrs. John DeWitt Peltz, the former Mary

Opdycke, while Palm Beach's Mrs. Frederick E. Guest, the former Amy Phipps, gazing contemplatively at her swimming pool in the center of a Grecian temple, adds, "We're left with a mere pittance." Southampton's distinguished art collector, Chester Dale, joins the chorus. "Look at your income tax schedules," he counsels sternly. "They're the timetables of resorts." The Hon. Sumner Welles, of Hulls Cove, Bar Harbor, and Via Bellaria, Palm Beach, concludes the discussion; he gives the resorts less than five years more of even a semblance of the kind of life to which they have become accustomed. "We're living on capital," he declares flatly, "and that's that."

These complaints are sad. "Heaven knows," Newport's late Miss Maude Wetmore used to sigh, "there's nothing as pathetic as the poor rich." The day is gone when, as Frederick Lewis Allen has pointed out, Andrew Carnegie could take $23,000,000 tax free in personal income in one year from his steel works at a time, 1900, when his workers were receiving for the same period $450. The day is also gone when the late Frank Gray Griswold, father of resort polo and the author of such books as *The Gourmet, Old Madeiras,* and *French Wines and Havana Cigars,* could pay for his income tax in 1914 a grand total of three cents; in a recent year Palm Beach's Hon. Joseph E. Davies paid an income tax of close to a million dollars. But taxes are by no means the whole story; indeed current tax structures, which permit the idle rich to remain both idle and rich through oil depletion allowances, capital gains deals and tax-exempt bonds are by no means entirely unfavorable to old-time wealth. Furthermore, although Bernard Baruch maintains that it is five times harder to become a millionaire today than it was in the days when he made his first million, the fact remains that families which have had wealth for half a century have also vast profits from securities. Such fortunes, 1929 crash or no 1929 crash, still present some striking instances of gain. A hundred shares of Sears Roebuck, for example, bought in 1906 for $5,700—and at that time it was one of 1906's most obvious growth stocks—would be worth, as of 1952, $350,000; a hundred shares of Eastman Kodak, bought for $10,000 in 1906, would be worth, in 1952, $300,000. Today the noted Society orchestra leader, Meyer Davis, who married a Bar Harbor girl and whose business qualifies him as a first-hand expert on Society spending, believes that there is just as much "big money," as he puts it, around today as there ever was—and also that this money is being spent. Davis specifically recalls a recent Palm Beacher's party in which he had an orchestra of 110 playing for a total of 87 guests. "I have bigger and better things booked for this summer," says Davis, "than I have ever had." Whether this spending is due to the fact that the present-day rich believe the end of all wealth is in sight and are out for one last fling, or whether it is due to shrewdly manipulated expense accounts, Davis is not prepared to state. Of one thing, however, he is sure—a matter which comes down to the same change to the self-conscious, defensive era of wealth as was evident in the names of the cottages. This is that the old-time show of wealth, at least in the social resorts, is a thing of the past. "In the old days they all loved to show it," Davis concludes, "at Newport, Bar Harbor, Palm Beach or where have you. Nowadays, no matter who's giving the party, they all keep telling me 'No publicity, no publicity.' It makes it very tough for me and the boys, too."

"No man," Newport's late Charles May Oelrichs used to say, "ever made more than a million dollars honestly." Oelrichs, father of Michael Strange and a man who was not as successful as some of his neighbors, was understandably hard on wealth. Today, at any resort, he would find support. Probably the first resorter who saw the change in times was the late Boston banker and yachtsman, Thomas W. Lawson, of Egypt, Cape Cod. Primarily known for such books as *Frenzied Finance*, in which he exposed many of his fellow Wall Street speculators, Lawson also wrote, as far back as 1913, another book entitled the *High Cost of Living*. On Cape Cod Lawson had a baronial cottage in which he endeavored to carry on the Old Way of Life. Nearby he had a little housekeeping cottage in which, under professional instruction, his four daughters were taught cottage-keeping. When each of these daughters could cook a large, formal dinner for the entire family—even including making the bread and butter—she received $100,000.

A few old-time resorters today manage to be philosophical about their descent to the ranks of the New Poor. One of these is Princess Laura Rospigliossi, who, as one of the legendary Stallo sisters of Cincinnati, was once the possessor of a large fortune. "*Somebody* must have my money," she says from her Palm Beach florist shop, "but that's the way it goes. There'll always be Leland Hayward and there'll always be me." The Princess has many confederates in *dégrandé* circumstances. A number of these bravely carry on in millinery and accessory shops, jewelry and interior decorating concerns, tearooms or boardinghouses, all of which, whether they are located in Newport, Bar Harbor or Southampton, are still socially severe. Many resort gentlemen, for their part, work in the trade they know best and may be located in resort bars or liquor businesses. At the same time, there are also a large number of old-time resorters who have taken sterner measures. Palm Beach's William Donner gave up not only Palm

Beach but America also and became a citizen of Switzerland. Southampton's William Greve chose Liechtenstein and Hot Springs' Charles Munroe selected the principality of Monaco, Monte Carlo; in extreme cases resorters have even been known to attempt to put to sea in their yachts for long periods of time and thus live nowhere. At least one resorter, Miss Eleonora Sears, of "Rock Edge," Prides Crossing, noted Boston walker, has contemplated mass action; she is currently in the process of forming a ten-million-member "Eleonora Sears Committee" to contribute one dollar apiece for the purpose of reducing Federal Income taxes to the point where, as she puts it, "we won't all be reduced to poverty."

Miss Sears, whose program includes, if necessary, the staging of a "Second Boston Tea Party," is, in the opinion of old-time resorters, off on the wrong foot in the matter of her ten-million-member committee; mere numbers, these old-time resorters point out, have never saved social resorts in the past and they will undoubtedly not save them now. As a matter of fact, numbers have proved distinctly antisocial. Coney Island, originally and at first unsuccessfully promoted by the old Commodore Vanderbilt as far back as 1840, is one illustration of this. Another is Atlantic City which came into high social favor with the decline of Cape May in the 1890's and the building of its modern fireproof hotels after the great fire of 1902. Today, fifty years later, Atlantic City has no less than 1,200 hotels which attract a total of 12,000,000 visitors a year; as a social resort, however, the Jersey mecca has hardly more standing than does Long Island's incredible triumph of resort democracy—Jones Beach. Even far-off Santa Barbara, Western outpost of Eastern resort Society, saw an illustration of the fact that numbers do not make a social resort when, in the 1920's, an overeager Chamber of Commerce distributed huge placards reading "A Bigger and Better Santa Barbara." Immediately this was answered in the Montecito area by the distribution, on the part of Santa Barbara's Roger Boutell, of little banners reading "a smaller and quieter santa barbara." At Hot Springs the story is told of a Virginia lady who became extremely irritated with the mass of tourists visiting her state; she was promptly reminded of the fact that those tourists brought more than a hundred million dollars a year to the state of Virginia, "But why," she protested, "couldn't they just *send* the money?"

At Southampton, today in season perhaps the most crowded of all old-time resorts, Mrs. Goodhue Livingston of "Old Trees" puts the matter of numbers in strong terms. "We are letting down, down, *down*," she says. "Why, I don't even use the word *nouveau riche* anymore." The last of Southampton's so-called "Dreadnaughts"—a group of ladies who received that name because they were, according to old-timers, the mistresses of the social seas—Mrs. Livingston has summered at Southampton since 1887. In 1941, for the first time, she let all her footmen go. "They had to go to war," she says, "and after it was over, my butler said not to even try to get any more. Of course there are a few of us left," she continues, "but we've opened the doors, you know. The rest are very dear and sweet and they are lovely people, but it isn't the same thing at all. It isn't just Southampton either. We're no longer, dear knows, an American country. Look at New York. Why, you can walk down the street and not hear a word of English!"

Today the ragged remnants of the great resorts' Old Guards look back from their crumbling cottages to the era of the 1920's as financially the last of the Good Old Days. Those were the days, they say, in between two-cents-a-point bridge and canasta sessions, before they had to chest their cards—the days of the private yachts and the private railroad cars, the private golf courses and the private polo fields, the private balls and private art collections. Of all the personalities of those days, the two who are best remembered for cutting the largest swath in the era were unquestionably Philadelphia's famous pair of men-about-resorts, E. T. Stotesbury and A. Atwater Kent; indeed, current resorters feel that the whole era of the 1920's was far better symbolized by this pair than by the late F. Scott Fitzgerald, a gentleman who, they feel, merely wanted to be in such rarefied Society. Mrs. Kent, who still summers at Bar Harbor and winters at Palm Beach, recalls one symbolic moment of these 1920's, when her husband called her on the carpet. "Mabel," said Kent sternly, "you aren't spending enough money."

Mrs. Stotesbury, greatest of all latter-day resort spenders, had no such difficulty. On her honeymoon at Palm Beach she wore so many jewels that she was forced to take along a detective as well as a husband; on a later occasion she did over the entire patio of "El Mirasol" from midnight to morning while Mr. Stotesbury, who knew nothing about it, peacefully slept. In Mrs. Stotesbury's heyday at Bar Harbor, she was queried on the matter of having gold bathroom fixtures—perhaps the ultimate largess of the 1920's era—and gave a characteristic answer. "They're very economical," she said. "You don't have to polish them, you know." In another era shortly before her death in 1946, Mrs. Stotesbury wrote a friend who was at the time visiting the author Booth Tarkington in Kennebunkport, Maine. Mrs. Stotesbury spoke feelingly of the difficulties of the new times and then concluded with a postscript. "Tell dear Mr. Tarkington," she wrote, "that I am reading all his old books. I can't afford to buy any new ones."

Second only to the Stotesburys and the Kents among the individual pecuniary portraits of resort 1920's was the late Colonel H. H. Rogers, who had not only one cottage in Southampton, but two—one on the water and another in the interior, the so-called "Port of Missing Men," bachelor headquarters of Southampton's gayest days. A grandson of Colonel Rogers is currently engaged in tearing down a large part of the "Port"; asked what he considers the high point of his grandfather's luxury, he recalls that the sheets and bedcovers were pressed every day and that his grandfather never spoke to the footmen but gave all his orders to the butler. To other Southamptonites, more luxurious than Colonel Rogers' $250,000 swimming pool, or even his famous beach parties, which participants describe as being "like nights in Italy," were the Colonel's means to carry out projects that other resorters have apparently always yearned to accomplish. In particular they recall one occasion when the then current Mrs. Rogers had become enamored with the poetry of the famous Indian poet Rabindranath Tagore and formed the habit of regularly reading to her husband any Tagore poem which was published in the New York *Sun*. One evening Colonel Rogers picked up the paper. "Here's another poem by that dope," he said. "I can't make head nor tail of it." His wife took the paper and proceeded to read out loud. "It's just beautiful," she said lovingly. "You just haven't any aesthetic sense at all." Colonel Rogers smiled. "Maybe not," he said quietly, "but it may interest you to know that I have had this entire page of the *Sun* printed specially for me. It is correct in every detail except for one item. Mr. Tagore's poem this evening, Mrs. Rogers, was authored by your husband."

Symbolically enough, the great men's clubs of the resorts were bolstered from the gala 1920's into the dire 1940's by long presidential tenures. In a true *après moi le deluge* spirit, Maximilian Agassiz at Newport, Giraud Foster at Lenox, Charlton Yarnall at Bar Harbor and Nicholas Murray Butler at Southampton all presided over their respective citadels for fifteen years or more and all set a tone that is still remembered, despite sinking finances, as true Old Guard club spirit. Their clubs, originally called "Reading Rooms" from the fact that the Newport Reading Room was originally a place where Newport gentlemen foregathered to read the papers, soon lost their literary tone—"They changed," says one old-timer, "from literature to liquor"—but as Newport and Saratoga have still kept their Reading Room names, so the leaders of these clubs did their best to preserve the Old Order.

Of all these men the late Dr. Butler, who was not only president of the Southampton Club but also of Columbia University as well, was undoubtedly the most memorable. Not content with his annual Labor Day oration at Southampton's Parrish Museum—one in which the oratory was of such high order that Southampton's Finley Peter Dunne, alias Mr. Dooley, claimed it was possible to waltz to it—Dr. Butler also presided each morning before beach time at the Southampton Club's famous group of so-called "Occasional Thinkers." This group included not only humorist Dunne but also such Southampton worthies as Judge O'Brien, Patrick Francis Murphy, Adrian Larkin, Morris Carnegie and Samuel Parrish; regularly they would gather round the club's famous marble-top table to discuss whatever came into their heads. Unfortunately, into Dr. Butler's head, invariably interrupting whoever had started the discussion, came such remarks as, "Well, I said to Teddy," or "I said to Calvin," or "I said to Herbert," thus introducing a personal note that to some of the less fortunate Occasional Thinkers became, in the course of fifteen years, a little tiresome. Finally Dunne decided to introduce a subject with which Dr. Butler could not possibly have had any personal connection; the next morning, as the Thinkers took their seats, Dunne started rapidly on the subject of the Franco-Prussian War of 1870. Immediately Dr. Butler interrupted. "Well," he said, "I said to Bismarck, 'Bismarck, why didn't you bring in Austria?' and Bismarck said, 'Butler, I'll tell you, it's very simple . . .' " Suddenly, for the first time in the history of the club, the rest of the Thinkers rose in rebellion. For once Dr. Butler had gone too far. They demanded an explanation of how he could possibly have spoken to Bismarck. "Well," replied Dr. Butler patiently, "I'll tell you. It's very simple. I was a student in Berlin in 1884. I was fortunate enough to secure an interview with the German chancellor. We happened to discuss the Franco-Prussian War and I said to Bismarck. 'Bismarck, why didn't you bring in Austria?' and Bismarck said, 'Butler, I'll tell you, it's very simple . . .' "

Dr. Butler was not again interrupted. The Old Order at the resorts, however, was not as fortunate. "My grandmother's world," says Eleanor Roosevelt, "never changed, and she never thought it would. She was too young for the Civil War—she barely remembered it—and when the First World War came, she was too old to be bothered much about that. She died in 1929." Mrs. Roosevelt feels that the vast changes of the present world simply took the Old Order by storm and that the Old Order's present-day representatives, as illustrated by the great social resorts, have been literally forced into their current defensive attitude. A visitor to Newport at the age of eighteen—"I still get the shivers when I think of it," she says. "Newport was no place for a country cousin"—Mrs. Roosevelt had a later experience with this inability to cope with the modern world in the person of Newport's Mrs. Frederick Vanderbilt. It happened right at Hyde Park where, besides her Newport cottage, Mrs. Vanderbilt also had another cottage which, like the Roosevelt estate, is now open to the public. Each day in her later years Mrs. Vanderbilt always went out driving alone, unattended save by her coachman; since she did everything else with a great many other people around—even her bed had a royal rail surrounding it—Mrs. Roosevelt became frankly curious about the driving and once questioned Mrs. Vanderbilt about it. "When I go driving," replied Mrs. Vanderbilt, "I do my mental exercises." Mrs. Roosevelt, also understandably curious about these, pursued the discussion further and asked politely what the exercises might be. "Well," said Mrs. Vanderbilt, "first I do the kings and queens of England, forward and backward, with their dates, then I do the Presidents of this country, forward and backward, with their dates, and sometimes," she added, "if I take a long drive, I get as far as the kings and queens of France."

Today this sort of regality is gone—apparently to the lasting detriment of its resort citadels. A Newport Vanderbilt, the granddaughter of the man who in 1887 coined the phrase "the Public be damned," attended in New York, during the winter of 1951, a Dale Carnegie course on "How to Win Friends and Influence People." Outside of the Vanderbilts, other changes have been going on. The whole tenor of old-time resort life has altered. Morning "calling," afternoon "drives" and evening "balls" all have disappeared; even the words of the times have changed—particularly the French words and phrases, which were the holdovers from the days when the resorters learned more French from their French governesses than they did English from their English "nannies." Old-line resorters do not remember the exact date when the "tripper" became the tourist, the "hired house" the apartment, the hotel "hop" the club dance and the *thé dansant* the cocktail party, but somewhere along the line it just happened, the way a girl's "limbs" became her legs, her "bosom" her breasts, her "gray matter" her I.Q., and her "come-hither" her sex-appeal; she no longer went to "prink" or "arrange her veil" but first to the "powder room" and, finally, to what to most resorters is the most irritating of all present-day phrases, "the little girls' room." The camelia gave way to the gardenia and finally they both gave way to the orchid; in the same way the Pomeranian disappeared before the Pekinese and finally both bowed to the poodle. People no longer "visited" and had "at-home" days, and words like "creature comforts" and "in the altogether" became as unknown as "to the manner born"—a phrase which is still, Shakespeare to the contrary, believed, by most cottage-bred resorters, to be only properly spelled "to the manor born." Of one thing all the old-line resorters are certain—that it all happened for the worse and Society has descended into a cheap-John *hoi polloi* who have so little *savoir faire*, let alone *cachet*, that they have never heard of a "pink tea" or a *fête champêtre*, think *tableaux vivants* stands for T.V., and couldn't tell the difference, if their lives depended on it, between *de rigueur*, *au fait*, and *comme il faut*.

As a final *bouleversement*, New York's Ritz Carlton Hotel, long the resorters' favored between-season *pied-à-terre*, has lately fallen by the wayside; resorters who for so many years were invariably well-recognized there have been reduced to rattling around in intolerable anonymity in such hostelries as the Plaza, the Pierre, the St. Regis and the new Carlton. Recently Chicago's ageless Mrs. George Alexander

McKinlock, of Palm Beach, Saratoga and the Ritz, was given a perfunctory welcome at the Plaza—"Honestly," she says, "as if they had no idea who I was." Asked how long she intended to stay, she replied sternly, "That's up to you. I'm just trying you out you know." A friend, sensing further trouble, promptly offered to register for her and started to write "Mrs. George A. McKinlock." Mrs. McKinlock took her friend's arm. "Put in 'G. Alexander McKinlock,' " she said firmly. "It sharpens it." Actually Mrs. McKinlock's point was well taken. Charles Dudley Warner, touring American resorts in 1886, declared that the "evolution from the businessman into the full-blown existence of a man of fashion" involved just such a step:

> The process is perfectly charted. Success in business, membership in a good club, tandem in the Park, introduction to a good house, marriage to a pretty girl of family and not much money, a yacht, a four-in-hand, a Newport villa. His name had undergone a like evolution. It used to be written on his business card, John B. Glow. It was entered at the club as J. Bartlett Glow. On the wedding invitations it was Mr. Bartlett Glow, and the dashing pair were always spoken of at Newport as the Bartlett-Glows.

Most of the elderly *grandes dames* at the resorts have lived from a day when they had to leave the room when the subject of divorce was mentioned to a day when a wedding invitation has only approximately a fifty-fifty chance of being issued by parents of the same name as the bride. Summing up the vast changes which have taken place, Miss Mabel Choate of "Naumkeag" in the Berkshires believes that the two most important differences between the Old Way of Life and the New are the automobile and the telephone. "But also," she says—and she feels that this latter matter is characteristic of modern peoples' lack of restraint in liking to bask in publicity —"they've taken down all those lovely old picket fences and hedges and everybody has those awful new chairs with no hind legs." Miss Rosalie Coe of "Appletrees Cottage," Southampton, feels that despite the automobile and the telephone and the modern hurry, people no longer have any sense of time. "My father always used to say," she says, " 'The wheel turns at four,' and he meant the carriage wheels actually started moving then. Today everybody's in such a hurry they're never on time for anything." Narragansett's Mrs. Post McMurtry of "Shadollan" believes that the world has passed into a kind of *servus servorum* age—one which involves, instead of a Deity, the absolute autocracy of the servant. "Why," she says, "you don't even dare open your mouth in your own house." Mrs. Herbert Pell, of "Pellbridge," mourns the passing of the tea table; she remembers, among other things, judging her daughter's beaux by whether or not they took plenty of sugar in their tea. "Gentlemen of good manners," she declares, "took two lumps. They craved sugar. The others, of course, got it from alcohol."

Aiken's Mrs. C. Oliver Iselin of "Hopelands" feels strongly on the subject of the passing of the great English tradition in American Society; in order to preserve what she can of this, she has instructed her social secretary to use all English spellings, "honour" for "honor," "cheque" for "check," and even "banque" for "bank." Mrs. Charles Mitchell, late of Tuxedo and now of Southampton, believes that most of the trouble nowadays is due to the younger generation and that most of this is due to the fact that the young girls have cross expressions. "It's because they don't wear hats," she says. "We had lovely expressions under our hats." Mrs. Henry C. Beadleston, late of "Beadlyn House," Narragansett, and now of "Ossory House," Newport, believes that the passing of hats has less to do with the difficulty than the passing of the chaperone. "The mothers themselves have abdicated," she says. "They're just *jeunes filles*—they're actually competing with their daughters. What little chaperonage is left, for mercy sakes, is left to the poor fathers!" Bar Harbor's Miss Alice Van Rensselaer believes that the whole matter comes right down, in the last analysis, to morals. "The granddaughter of the girl who wouldn't show her instep," she says, "now shows her step-ins." Finally, East Hampton's Mrs. Carman Messmore concludes the discussion. "Why even I can remember," she declares, "when it was considered fast to play net at tennis!"

Hand and glove with the disappearance of the Old Order and the Old Way of Life has gone, in the opinion of resorters, the actual disappearance of Society. "In my generally ignored opinion," says Newell Tilton, last of the resort species once known as the *arbiter elegantiarum*, "there is no such thing as real Society any more. The aristocratic family standard is at half mast and the gold standard has been furled by the income tax." Born in Newport in October—"an unfashionable time of the year," as he describes it—Tilton is today president of the Southampton Beach Club as well as a familiar figure at Tuxedo, Saratoga and Palm Beach. After thirty years of observing Society on the beaches he believes it has followed the trend of the bathing suit. "Young ladies no longer come out formally any more," he says; "they just emerge from the sea like Venus on the half shell." At the same time, Tilton maintains that, in some respects at least, Southampton has held up better than the other resorts. "There's very little incompatibility here," he declares, "if the husbands have income tax ability." Irving Terry, however, discounted even this mild optimism. The owner of the Irving Hotel, he was once asked if he was also a member of the old Southampton Club across the street. "No," said Terry, "but I am president of the Southampton Cemetery Association."

Down at Palm Beach Hugh Dillman, retiring president of the Everglades Club, is equally wary of present Society. "You have to be psychic," he says, "to know who's who nowadays." Up at Saratoga, Monty Woolley, the Beard of the Spa and the son of the Grand Union's illustrious W. Edgar Woolley, believes that even if people do matter socially they don't stay anywhere any more. "Look at Jock Whitney," he says; "he's always going somewhere else." At Aiken, which is now in the process of being overwhelmed by a huge new hydrogen bomb plant fifteen miles away, the handwriting was on the wall as long ago as 1929 when the porter on the Aiken Special brought an afternoon report to the daughter of the late Mrs. Thomas Hitchcock. "Miss Titine," he said, "I have been through the whole train. There ain't no one you would like to dine with." At Lenox, Mrs. George L. K. Morris, the former Estelle C. Frelinghuysen of "Brookhurst," all but wrote *finis* to resort Society entirely when she formally entered, in the Summer *Social Register* for the year 1936, her four-year-old Pekinese dog Rose. "There was no particular reason," she says. "I was just filling out the thing and I did it. No, Rose didn't have any pedigree."

The complaint that resort Society is not what it used to be is, of course, an ancient one; at Stafford Springs the Pilgrims were undoubtedly told by the Nipmucks that it was too bad they didn't see the place in the Old Days before the Podunks came. Nonetheless, current complaints on this score are so stern that they appear to challenge the very foundations of Old Guard Society itself. Furthermore, at least one such challenge has already come—and from no less a personage than Frank Costello, noted resort gambler. Costello recently confided to intimates that he wished to set up a research foundation to inquire into the family-founding forebears of the Astors, Vanderbilts, Whitneys, etc., his aim being to prove that such forebears were as partial to financial legerdemain and social skullduggery as he was and hence, conversely, that he should be entitled to as high a position in Society as they.

Palm Beach's great architect, the late Addison Mizner, always maintained that Old Guard Society simply bored itself to death. A faithful seasonal attendant at other resorts as well as at Palm Beach, he declared of the formal dinners of the day, "I never saw one that wouldn't bore a present-day debutante to tears." Mizner's "present-day" debutante—as of 1932—was not alone in her ennui. The Hon. Herbert Pell, who started going to Newport dinners in 1899 at the age of fifteen—"I was tall for my age," he says, "and there was a shortage of men even then"—recalls that he was almost suffocated with boredom. "The richest man present always sat at the hostess's right," he declares, "and the next richest at her left, and so on right down the table. After dinner, when the men separated, we sat around and listened to the richest man tell us how to make money." Even in the era of the 1920's formal resort Society was evidently not always as gay as it is now nostalgically pictured. Mrs. Atwater Kent recalls one particular day at Bar Harbor when she had four formal engagements in a row—a luncheon, a tea, a cocktail party and a dinner; in the midst of making the third of her four dress changes for the day, between the cocktail party and the dinner, she was compassionately addressed by her maid. "Madam," she said, "I wouldn't change places with you for a million dollars."

It is a long jump, of course, from the so-called "Smart Set" of Bar Harbor's or Newport's 1920's to the so-called "Jet Set" of Southampton's 1950's—or even, specifically, from the fabulous Cushing sisters of yesterday to the Gabor sisters of today; Southampton's Gabors have, in fact, been called by their friend Doris Lilly the "West Side Cushing girls." Nonetheless, certain aspects of the narrowness of the old-line resort Society have continued, not the least of which is the question of anti-Semitism. Although certain Jewish families, notably the Pulitzers, the Belmonts and the Goulds, have played their parts in resort Society—and Otto Kahn, Henry Seligman, Jules Bache and Frederick Lewisohn have cut sizable individual figures—the general record of resort intolerance is an extraordinary one; it reached perhaps its lowest point when Palm Beach's Bath and Tennis Club sent out a letter asking members not to bring into the club guests of Jewish extraction. Among those who received this letter was Bernard Baruch, then a member of the club and a man whose father, Dr. Simon Baruch, pioneered the Saratoga Spa. Several of Baruch's friends advised him to make an issue of the affair; instead, he quietly resigned. "No one," he says today, "has had this thing practiced against him more than I have. But I don't let it bother me. I always remember what Bob Fitzsimmons said to me—he wanted to make me a champion, you know—'You've got to learn to take it before you can give it out.' "

"I hate resorts," says Mrs. T. Markoe Robertson, one of the most popular Society sirens of today, "but I *adore* Southampton." Actually Mrs. Robertson, of "Wyndcote," the former Cordelia Drexel Biddle Duke—who feels that Newport is like "a bowl of rose leaves which have lost their smell" and that Palm Beach is dull indeed compared to what it was in the palmy heyday of her brother, A. J. "Tony" Drexel Biddle, Jr.—represents the typical present-day resort viewpoint. In the old days, before the present defensive attitude set in, the so-called Society "Sun-Followers" loved all the great resorts and took in all of them on their Grand Tour; the story is told of a Farmington Country Club debutante who, asked by her beau where she came from, sharply replied, "What season?" Today, however, with the social blackout that has descended, old-timers are agreed that resorts in general are terrible places but their particular resort —though not, of course, what it was in the days of the "old" club or the "old" hotel or the "old" something or other—is still better than any other place in the world. Even those who still go to two or more resorts feel this way. Many Southamptonites, for example, also go to Palm Beach; if they do, they choose one of these resorts, usually Southampton, as wonderful and say that the other, usually Palm Beach, is terrible. As for the servants, they too have become selective, and one leading New York employment agency now lists its domestics with their resort preference.

With all this, there is an intense personal identification. "I love my Southampton," says Miss Ethel Wickham of "Rosemore," who has been resorting there since 1883, "and I really think of it as mine. I grew up here, you know." Even resorters who have left the resorts use "my" Newport, Bar Harbor or Southampton for the resort as it was in their day and "your" Newport, Bar Harbor or Southampton for the way the resort is today. "Write whatever you want about your Newport today," says Washington's illustrious Alice Longworth, daughter of Theodore Roosevelt, "but remember my Newport was *pretty*." Moreover, Mrs. Longworth, who remembers that her father once asked the novelist Owen Wister when he was going to "smash the divorce-ridden, arrogant, preposterous Newport," feels that her father never understood her Newport—or simple Newport—which she means by the use of her word "pretty." Bar Harbor's Gretchen Finletter, talented daughter of the late Walter Damrosch and wife of the present Secretary of Air, is equally emphatic on this point. "Everyone's eyes sort of roll," she says, "when I say I'm going to Bar Harbor, but I don't think of it like that at all." Mrs. Finletter recalls as a young girl surreptitiously counting the evening dresses visiting guests brought and thinking that there wouldn't possibly be enough formal affairs to use them up. "Say something nice about it," she says earnestly. "It's such a sweet little place. I still feel, whenever the world gets too mean, that I can go back to Bar Harbor." At Southampton Mrs. Albert Jaeckel, who apologizes for having been at the resort "only twenty-seven years," advises giving up the idea of writing anything at all. "We don't want the kind of people that sort of thing attracts," she says. "Southampton is a little backwater of God."

The intense seriousness with which such views are expressed must be heard to be believed. "We're not funny, you know," warns Mrs. J. Howland Auchincloss of "Redwood," Bar Harbor. "People are not as funny in the summer as they are in the winter." Even this observation, however, finds its answer—an obvious one, according to Southampton's Mrs. T. Reed Vreeland. "People are more sympathetic," she says, "undressed." One thing is certain; old-timer resorters are convinced, also defensively of late years, that if their resort does not seem simple to outsiders, it is at least simple in comparison to Newport. Mrs. Goodhue Livingston of Southampton, for example, decries the fact that Miss Julia Berwind of Newport uses gold service. "I don't even bring my real silver," she says, "I just use plate." In the same way Mrs. Livingston is indignant that the two resorts should be lumped together merely because Mrs. Henry F. du Pont and a few other *grandes dames* still have, in the manner of Newport, footmen. "Southampton has footmen," she says, "but we've never had footmen in knee britches." All resorters feel equally strongly that their resorts have been much maligned from the point of view of family life—that actually the resorts are a perfect place for the whole family and a wonderful place to raise children. Sunday lunch at "Driftwood," Southampton rendezvous of the Henry Ford II's, is held up as a sterling example of this. "We spend all day," says Mrs. Ford's sister, "just sitting around in old shirts and wet bathing suits." Chicago's young Mrs. Marshall Field Jr. is just as adamant. "We don't even go to the Beach Club," she says. "We just sit on our own beach and play chess."

These changes are large ones and in the old days no such arguments could have been made—particularly in the matter of the resort's being a wonderful place to raise children. Canon Stokes at Lenox recalls that when his family built "Shadowbrook," though they carefully planned ninety-nine other rooms, they completely forgot a room for him; his quarters were added, as an afterthought, in the attic. The late Stuyvesant Fish, son of Newport's greatest hostess, had a room of his own all right, and not in the attic, but he never felt it was his. "Whenever I went away," he recalled, "even for just a day, I'd come back and I'd find there was a guest in it." In the same way, though Mrs. Stotesbury, at Palm

Beach, ran seventy-two servants and scores of guests on such a close schedule that it necessitated the use of a printed program delivered to each guest on arrival, she completely forgot a grandchild one Christmas vacation; the child was left at school. But even in such days, when claims of simplicity were impossible, resorters always maintained that their retreats were, if not simple, at least healthy. The genuine spas, such as Saratoga and Hot Springs, had no more devoted admirers on this score than Newport, Bar Harbor and Southampton. Today this point of pride is still challengingly echoed. "Southampton has the strongest air in the world," says Mrs. Livingston. "It's the suction, you know. You feel it the minute you leave Westhampton."

If resorters are stern on the subjects of simplicity and health, they are even sterner on the subject of their resort's history. They are certain that their resort is the only one with a history which is "really interesting," as they put it, and they identify themselves, through their various Historical Societies and Village Improvement Societies, back to the very dawn of American history itself. Although in certain cases this identification has been difficult to prove—Newport's claim that its Old Stone Mill was built by the Vikings is the outstanding example—the claims continue nevertheless. Mrs. Henry G. Trevor of "The Snuggery," as her room in her Southampton cottage was called, went so far as to write the history of every piece of furniture in her cottage. Writing on a more general subject, in her typewritten scrapbook entitled *Memories of a Southampton Child*, she declared: "We owe a debt of gratitude to the first cottage colonists at Southampton. . . . No trolley or bus or Merry-go-Round or any form of commercialism was sanctioned by them. Imagine if our roads (First Neck Lane, Job's Lane,

Captain's Neck Lane, Ox Pasture Road, Toylsome Lane, Gin Lane, Meeting House Lane, etc.) had been rechristened Sea View Avenue or Ocean Boulevard!" Finally, if all else fails, resorters will invariably discuss the age of their golf course; at each resort the course is, if not the oldest in the world—St. Andrews in Scotland is generously accorded that honor—then the oldest in this country. Failing that, each resort's golf course is always the second oldest, and, failing that, then at least the second oldest continuously operating eighteen holes in the same territory with no women allowed on Sunday. Near the Greenbrier at White Sulphur Springs resorters make no claims for any one course; in the *area* near one of their courses, however, they claim the game was first played. The Homestead at Virginia Hot Springs, in turn, claims the country's oldest continuously operating *tee*. Saratoga, which claims only the country's third oldest continuously operating golf course, makes up for this by claiming the country's oldest continuously operating race track—continuously operating except, of course, in World War II.

Actually golf was derived from the Dutch word *kolf*, meaning "club" or "stick." It was first imported from Holland and played in the New Netherlands so ferociously that authorities forbade it "within thickly settled areas." Dying out in that warlike form, the game was later revived along the more peaceful Scotch lines with Charleston, South Carolina, taking the honors for having the first recorded golf club and clubhouse, on Harleston's Green, as far back as 1795. The first American golf club in the modern sense was the St. Andrews Club of Yonkers, New York, which was established in 1888, the name Yonkers being conveniently forgotten by resorters who think only in terms of the Scottish St. Andrews. Mrs. Trevor's memory book, on the subject of golf at Southampton, is typical of the scene which in the early 1890's was being enacted at virtually all the major social resorts:

> The climax in Southampton's growth and the reason for its change from a simple country place to a fashionable resort was the discovery that the Shinnecock Hills was a naturally ideal golf links. Edward Spencer Meade, returning from a winter spent in Pau, described a game called Golf, which he said should be pronounced "Goff." He was founder and first president of the club. Stanford White designed the clubhouse. The members all had scarlet coats and the insignia of the club on the brass buttons. The small Shinnecock Indian boys were trained as caddies and a Scotch professional was imported to teach the members. Saturday afternoon all Southampton would gaze admiringly at each contestant as they "drove off" from the first tee. Woe betide them if they foozled the ball. Once Mr. Walker Breese was playing and the professional told him he must keep his eye on the ball, and as he had one glass eye he took it out and placed it on top of the ball.

Another severe point of pride which all resorters share in common is their claim to like their particular resort best, not during the regular season but only during the off season when, apparently, only the "real Newporters" or the "real Bar Harborites," are present. This leads, of course, to a corollary to this point of pride—the love of the native. In the old days, while a few distinguished natives were cherished—such as Old Foley, Bar Harbor taxi driver, Old Pyrrhus, Southampton's Lake Agawam paddler, Old Eddie at the Lenox Club or Old Brooks at the Tuxedo Club—the natives in general were regarded as pretty terrible people who were always out, as the expression was, to "do" the resorters. In recent times, with the changing world outside and the new defensive attitude, resorters have come around to loving their natives dearly and have even attempted to provide a substitute for a word which they feel is too undemocratic. "I'm sorry," a Bar Harbor debutante recently told a prospective native beau, "but I never go out with winter boys." Unhappily neither "winter boys" nor "year-round residents" nor several other expressions which have been tried have yet proved satisfactory; nonetheless the current affection is as remarkable as the old-time animosity. Even Palm Beach's famous fishing guide "murderer," a man who has dispatched his wife's boyfriend and two of his most irritating in-laws, has been regularly defended by the resort lawyer, Charles Francis Coe, and is now regarded as a grand fellow and as nice a one as anyone would care to meet. In some cases, notably at Southampton and Tuxedo, sons of distinguished old members are actually working in the resort clubs, side by side with the natives, in a paid capacity, and although these club staffs are not what they were in the Good Old Days—Southampton's Meadow Club, which once had a lady's maid for each lady visitor, is now down to one housekeeper—the camaraderie between native and resorter has never been higher. On their side the natives have endeavored to do their part to promote this era of good feeling, an era which reached its peak following World War II when Bar Harbor's Shirley Liscomb summoned his caddies at the Kebo Valley Club and delivered a short speech. "It has been years," he said, in an address which warmed the hearts of all resorters, "since anyone looked aggressively for a golf ball."

Old-time resorters are particularly proud of the fact that their natives, far better than other people in these trying times, can tell the "right" people from the "wrong" people. A typical present-day resort story is the one told of Mrs. Jackson Boyd of Hot Springs who returned to Palm Beach after long absence and saw a man she recognized—the colored operator of a Palm Beach "afromobile." This vehicle, which is one of the prides of Palm Beach, is a combination of a two-seated chair in front and the business end of a Negro-pedaled bicycle behind. Mrs. Boyd had not seen the man, who was at that moment engaged in pedaling a newcomer to Palm Beach, for many years. "Hello, Uncle," she said. When the colored man acknowledged the greeting, the newcomer in the wheelchair turned around to address the pedaler. "Your niece?" she inquired. The pedaler, according to the story, smiled at Mrs. Boyd and then solemnly addressed the newcomer. "No, ma'am," he said, "when an old-time lady meets a colored man whose name she does not remember she calls him 'Uncle' as a term of respect." Not all native stories have as happy an ending from the point of view of resorters. Some years ago at Southampton the favored native taxi driver, who was also widely reputed to know all the "right" people from all the "wrong" people, was delegated to take home from a gay Angier Biddle Duke party a particularly paralyzed gentleman. The driver, in keeping with his trusted position, not only took the gentleman safely home but also went to the trouble of escorting him into his cottage, upstairs to his room and even putting him to bed beside his wife—a lady who, having taken sleeping pills, was slumbering heavily. All went well except for one matter which, unhappily enough, was not discovered until the next morning. Unknown apparently to the taxi driver, who knew everyone, was the fact that Southampton that season had two families of exactly the same name; the next morning it was discovered that the driver had delivered one of the "right" people all right—but to the wrong wife.

One curious fact about the new defensiveness in present-day resort life is that even the youngest resort patrons long for the old days. "I used to know everybody," says Southampton's young Thomas E. Murray, Jr., "now I don't know anybody." Murray, whose immediate family alone is so large that Newell Tilton has called the resort "Murray Bay," might understandably have difficulty in knowing outsiders as well. However, he is joined in his complaint by other resort stalwarts, such as Mrs. Alfred Gwynne Vanderbilt, of Southampton and Saratoga, a lady still in her twenties. "These places," she declares firmly, "are nothing like they were in the old days."

This sort of nostalgia has its charm in that it perpetuates, against the new defensiveness, the same sort of stories that have been told at each resort apparently ever since the resort was started. The favorite of all is probably the story of the resort's leading hostess who is invariably presented by a newcomer with the same problem. "I've had thirty-six"—or twenty-four or twelve, the story is told differently—"of the top drawer people to dine," the newcomer is said to report, "and I've had thirty-six"—or twenty-four or twelve—"of the second drawer. Now who shall I have?" The answer, whether the story is told of Countess Széchényi at Newport, Mrs. Livingston at Southampton or Madame Balsan at Palm Beach, is always the same. "My dear," she replies, "why don't you just have your friends?"

A second type of story concerns the old-time resorter's belief that no newcomer is ever able to handle servants. The favorite in this category is told of the George Goulds, who in 1896 built their cottage "Georgian Court" in Lakewood, New Jersey, a cottage which included, among other things, a forty-bedroom casino and a race track equal in size to that of Madison Square Garden. As the story is usually told, the Goulds had hired their battery of servants directly from England and, when the servants had arrived, en masse, all members of the Gould family promptly retreated upstairs. Even after the servants had dressed and, headed by the butler, were waiting patiently in formation downstairs, the family, huddling upstairs, still refused to go down and face them. Finally Tuxedo's late Bruce Price, architect of the cottage and a guest at that time, took over, boldly marched downstairs and apparently handled the situation satisfactorily. In the opinion of old-time resorters he was the perfect man for the job. "Why," they say, "he was not only the spit and image of a duke himself—he was the father of Emily Post!"

A specific matter of deterioration which all old-timers have noticed at the resorts is the matter of the emergence of what they call, in the old manner, the *demi-monde*. In the early days, with the exception of Saratoga, which always had its share of the *demi-monde* mixed with its *haut monde* at the United States Hotel and its *beau monde* at the Grand Union, the social resorts were notably free from this element; in fact, in 1894, the French traveler Paul Bourget noted that at Newport, in sharp comparison to the European watering places, there was a total absence of adventurers and adventuresses. "It is easy," he declared, "to deceive a composite society but not a society of businessmen." Bourget spoke too soon. The very next year, in 1895, Newport's Consuelo Vanderbilt married His Grace the Ninth Duke of Marlborough and, following Miss Vanderbilt's nuptials, a veritable tidal wave of titled foreigners swept over American heiresses. Not only have they been sweeping, with notable aplomb, over these heiresses ever since, but they have been followed by a constantly growing army of café royalty. Coupled with this latter-day foreign element—most of whom speak English fluently when they first arrive at the resorts and worse and worse as the years go by—has come wave after wave of a native element, a group which used to be known as the "little brothers of the rich" but might be more clearly identified as resort sports. Old-time resorters believe this latter group to be a throwback to the old days of the beach gigolo—a species of resort life which sprang from the ocean around Long Branch in the 1890's. According to a Long Branch guidebook, the beach gigolo superseded the old bathing machines of the early part of the nineteenth century and were, in the latter part of the century, a vital part of swimming etiquette:

> "To bathe" a lady rather than to dance with her was the first function of many attractive young men who hired themselves out by the hour, the day or even the entire season. Although the practice was confined to fashionable Society, it was unmistakeably a gaucherie for a lady to appear on the beach without an escort no matter how completely swathed she might be in skirts, pantalettes and long stockings.

Unfortunately, the resort sports did not confine their activities to the bathing; undoubtedly many of them saw the possibilities contained in the opinion of the late Frank Crowninshield that, in resort Society, "Married men make very poor husbands." In any case, of late years, starting slowly, properly "sponsored" or being "taken up," as it is still called, by a recognized Society matron, the young sport visits first his sponsor and then whomever else he can. Invariably in demand because of the perennial shortage of resort men, he must indicate only a willingness to play cards for high stakes—in many cases he is actually staked to these stakes—as well as to attend cocktail parties, dress for dinner and dance. Since he is moving into a now decadent Society primarily dominated by widows who, among other things, are always on the lookout for the possibility of making a joint return on their income tax, he has excellent opportunities of marrying for money. Beyond this, if he proves sufficiently incompatible, he has equally excellent prospects of divorcing for money. The story is told that an ex-grocery boy received, according to Palm Beachers, the sum of $350,000 for his Palm Beach divorce alone, not including what he was able to save during his tour of actual marriage. In some cases, the resort sport has even more intriguing avenues open to him—and age is no problem. In one of Newport's most celebrated attachments of recent years eighty-year-old Mrs. Hamilton Fish Webster legally adopted as her son a fifty-seven-year-old retired Brigadier General.

"Nowadays an awful lot of unscrupulous fellows come to these resorts," says Schuyler Livingston Parsons of Newport and Palm Beach, "primarily to make deals." Parsons, though he is now a resort bachelor himself, is far from the type of resort sport he discusses. So, too, is Philadelphia's William Levino of Bar Harbor and Palm Beach, an equally popular bachelor of recent years. Nonetheless even such distinguished resorters as these are, humorously at least, aware of their position. Once, during a Palm Beach dinner, Levino, who has no regular occupation, met several gentlemen, all of whom, resort fashion, were being introduced by their businesses. "This is Mr. So-and-so," the introduction ran, "steel; Mr. So-and-so, oil; Mr. So-and-so," railroads," etc. Asked what business he was in, Levino smiled. "Monkey," he said. Unhappily the situation is not as humorous for the most faithful of present-day resort bachelors, Arthur Bradley Campbell, of Newport, Bar Harbor, Tuxedo, Hot Springs and Palm Beach. A rotund gentleman who speaks with a pronounced English accent—his mother's third husband was the Eleventh Marquis of Huntly—Campbell feels that no resort is what it was. "Nowadays you do nothing but hear about people nobody ever heard of before," he says, "and they're all from nowhere." Asked why, in view of this, he continues to make the Grand Tour, Campbell is resigned. "Where else can you go?" he asks. "Why in New York there's no use even going to the theater any more. The audience isn't worth seeing."

Second only to the question of the appearance of the *demi-monde* as evidence of resort Society deterioration is, in the opinion of old-timers, the question of the disappearance of wit. Indeed most resorters nowadays would settle for conversation, let alone wit; at most of the major resorts card-playing has actually taken the place of conversation. Mrs. Ralph Robertson, of Hot Springs and Palm Beach, is a particularly indefatigable card-player. Formerly married to two bankers, James Clews and George Blumenthal, Mrs. Robertson is currently married to a Major-General. "We spend so much time with the same people," she says, "that card-playing saves our lives." Nor is the lack of conversation at the resorts by any means confined to the ladies. Mrs. Arthur White of Middleburgh, Virginia, recently evolved a conversational gambit which she recommends as extremely efficacious in all dinner-table conversations involving difficult gentlemen. "When I get between two duds—" she says, "I mean complete duds—I always turn to one of them and say, 'May I ask you something personal?' They all love that, you know, and then I say, 'Where do you get your clothes made?' Then they just beam. They turn their cuffs inside out, roll their trousers up to their knees, and off we go. Tailors and valets, tweeds and flannels, England and Scotland—it opens up all avenues of textile conversation."

This sort of persiflage is indeed a far cry from the great days—of Nahant's Thomas Gold Appleton who coined the phrase, "Good Americans when they die go to Paris," or, more recently, of Palm Beach's late Addison Mizner who originated "God gives us our relatives, thank God we can choose our friends." Actually only a handful of resorters still remember the gentleman who was in his day—he died in 1887—regarded as the greatest of all the old-time resort wits; his name was William R. Travers. Newporter and Saratogian, lawyer and *bon vivant*, Travers had two town houses, three resort cottages and belonged to twenty-seven clubs; he was the founder of the Racquet Court Club, predecessor of today's Racquet & Tennis Club, and the Travers Stakes at Saratoga, oldest horse race in the country, was named for him. A genial man with a port wine complexion, "Old Billy," as he was affectionately called, had a wit which was heightened by the fact that he stammered. Once accused by a friend of stammering worse in New York than he had in his native Baltimore, Travers replied, "This is a d-d-damned sight b-b-bigger city."

Back in Baltimore, Travers' first home was furnished in the early Victorian manner with a sign in worsted work hanging on the dining room wall; the sign read, of course, "God Bless Our Home." One day, after a prolonged period of servant trouble in the home, Mrs. Travers, who was nearsighted, noted a new sign which, painstakingly made to parallel the old, had been placed on the opposite wall. Adjusting her glasses, she read, "God Damn Our Cook." One night Travers arrived home late and tiptoed upstairs. "Is that you, Bill?" his wife called out. "Y-y-yes," called back Travers. "Wh-wh-whom did y-y-you expect?" After the Travers family had bought a small farm in New Jersey, a large landowner from upstate New York became engaged to Travers' daughter and, on visiting the Travers farm, was surprised to find only a row of box stables, some gamecock walks and a few paddocks. "What do you raise here?" he asked Travers sharply. Travers sighed. "H-h-hell," he said.

Travers' most famous resort observation was undoubtedly the one which he made at Newport after being shown a vista of beautiful yachts, almost all of which, upon inquiry, he discovered belonged to Wall Street brokers. "Wh-wh-where," he asked, "are the c-c-customers' yachts?"

In New York one day, passing the Union Club, Travers was asked if all of the men who could be seen in their chairs from the street outside were actually habitués of the club. "N-n-no," said Travers, "s-s-some are s-s-sons of h-h-habitués." A Democrat in politics at a time when such feeling in resort circles was as akin to heresy as it is today, Travers particularly enjoyed taking the measure of a rising group of Republican millionaires. On one occasion A. T. Stewart, owner of Saratoga's Grand Union Hotel, took over a meeting, pulled a gold pencil case from his pocket and rapped for order. Cried Travers sharply, "C-c-cash." On another occasion seeing Newporter Henry Clews, who always boasted of being a self-made man, pompously enter a room, Travers stopped him. "I say, Cl-cl-clews," he said, "s-s-since you are a s-s-self-made man, why the d-d-devil didn't you put more h-h-hair on your h-h-head?"

Unlike most wits, Travers was haunted by the fear of

repeating himself; with his wife and children he worked out a special arrangement of signals. If he began on a story which they knew the company present had heard him tell before, they would discreetly hold up one finger if he had told it once before, two fingers if twice before, and so forth. Unlike most wits also, Travers was funny to the end. He spent his last winter, at the age of sixty-eight, in Bermuda, in the hope that the climate might affect his diabetes. Unfortunately it did not. On his deathbed a friend called on him and mentioned what a nice resort Bermuda was for rest and change. "Y-y-yes," replied Travers wearily, "the w-w-waiters get the ch-ch-change and the h-h-hotel the r-r-rest."

More celebrated as a resort wit even than the great "Old Billy" Travers was the late Hon. Joseph Hodges Choate of the Berkshires. Born in Salem, Massachusetts, in 1832, the son of a doctor who received seventy-five cents a visit and five dollars for delivering a baby, but who nonetheless had four sons all in college at the same time, Choate soon established himself as one of New York's greatest lawyers. Settling in Lenox in 1874 and three years later moving to Stockbridge—he built his famous cottage "Naumkeag" in 1885—he lived in the Berkshires until his death in 1917 at the age of eighty-five, a death that coincided, curiously enough, almost exactly with the beginning of the end of the resort era. A tall handsome man with alert boyish eyes set in a stern thin-lipped 1890 face—Sargent once said he despaired of painting him because of his constantly changing expression—Choate actually symbolized this era. Although he played no games, looked down upon tennis and golf and did not belong to the fashionable Lenox Club, he was practically personally responsible, in 1895, for enabling the resort way of life to last another twenty years when he successfully fought, before the Supreme Court, the constitutionality of the graduated income tax.

In his best-remembered case today, Choate successfully undertook the defense of a distinguished yachtsman and resort sport by the name of Joseph Florimond duc de Loubat who, on the evening of November 28, 1881, was asked by one Henry Turnbull, in the inner sanctum of the Union Club, why he did not marry a rich widow and, according to Turnbull, slandered the lady's daughter. Although Count Loubat always denied the slander—and in this outspoken age the affair seems a tempest in a teapot—the Count was expelled from the Club and the case created the greatest furore in its time. When Count Loubat sued for reinstatement, Choate's victory, which proved that club members have a vested interest in their clubs, was of such importance that all clubs to this day take heed of it; as a member of the Board of Governors of New York's Harvard Club puts it, "Ever since the Loubat case we never expel members, we just suspend them."

If Choate's oratory was effective, his wit was even more so. His *bons mots* alone would have made him a man of national eminence. As he grew in stature as a humorist he found himself in the position of having all manner of witticisms attributed to him which were not authorized; he was once asked by his daughter if he was disturbed by this position. Choate shook his head. "I acknowledge them," he said, "only if they're good enough."

Much of Choate's wit had for its locale his beloved Berkshires. Only barely dissuaded from naming his cottage, because of a slope and an oak, "Slopoke," Choate was anything but slow when it came to commenting on his fellow resorters. It was he who named the famous Sedgwick Graveyard—one which fans out all around in ever-increasing circles from the two central headstones of the family's original progenitors—the "Sedgwick Pie." It was he also who declared that the Sedgwicks had thought up the arrangement so that the entire family, arising on Judgment Day, would see nothing but Sedgwicks. When Choate himself, who later bought a lot in the same graveyard, was asked to subscribe to a fund to build a fence around the cemetery, he refused to do so. "No one who is in wants to get out," he said, "and no one who is out wants to get in." Choate's Berkshire neighbor and partner in law, the late Charles F. Southmayd, was an almost perfect foil for his wit—a lifelong bachelor of such conservative habits that when he was asked by the minister of the Stockbridge church to be a warden, said that he would do so only "if I don't have to pass that damned plate." The minister appealed to Choate, but the latter declared the case was hopeless. "Other men," he said, "have five senses, but Southmayd has a sixth—a sense of property."

In his own way Choate, too, was a man of severe routine. Disliking games, he nonetheless rode horseback before breakfast every day in his life until his last illness, even when he was in New York. Commuting to work he invariably made for the end seat in the elevated and there buried himself in the paper. One day a fellow passenger, whose curiosity at this routine was aroused, went over, sat down beside him, and asked the lawyer why he always chose the end seat. "So," replied Choate, without looking up from his paper, "I can be bored from only one side at a time." One day a pompous young man came into his office and, though the lawyer was busy, demanded to see him immediately. "Take a chair," said Choate quietly, still working. "But I am Bishop So-and-so's son," declared the young man. "All right," patiently replied Choate, still continuing his work, "take two chairs." One prominent clergyman, who had engaged the lawyer in the settlement of a large and involved estate, was upset by receiving the bill. "I always understood, Mr. Choate," he protested, "that you gentlemen of the bar were not in the habit of charging clergymen for your services." Choate was unmoved. "You are much in error," he said. "You clergymen look for your reward in the next world, but we lawyers have to get ours in this."

In court Choate's repartee was proverbial. On one occasion he asked a witness how he was able to remember so well events which had happened so long ago—only to receive the reply, "Oh, Mr. Choate, I am older than you think I am." Choate stopped. "Indeed?" he countered. "Now just you tell me how old you think that I think you are." On another occasion an opponent, engaged in a long fruitless cross-examination, swung around at Choate, who was chuckling out loud, and demanded to know what he was laughing at. "Oh," replied Choate, "I was not laughing at you at all. I was laughing at something that happened at the Union League Club last night when one of the speakers had gone on so long that he had to be reminded by the president that there was danger of the discussion becoming tedious." After such a sally in another case, the judge took sides against him, blocked him at every turn, and finally gave him an actual calling down. When Choate turned his back for a moment, the judge became infuriated. "Mr. Choate," he asked, "are you trying to show contempt for this court?" "No, your Honor," replied Choate quickly, "I am trying to conceal it." Probably Choate's most memorable court repartee occurred in an exchange with the opposing lawyer John Parsons, who had not only a cottage in Lenox but also a home in Westchester County. In his final address Parsons warned the jury against being swayed by what he called Choate's "Chesterfieldian urbanity." Choate, rising in rebuttal, promptly counterwarned the jury—against Parsons' "Westchesterfieldian suburbanity."

As Ambassador to England Choate saw his fame as a wit become international. Since American ambassadors did not then, and still do not, wear the trappings of other visiting diplomats, they have often suffered the indignity of being mistaken for butlers and footmen. Choate was no exception. A particularly homely English duke mistook him at the door for a servant. "Call me a cab," he said abruptly. "You're a cab," replied Choate quickly. "I wish I could call you a hansom cab." Dining with a Lady who complained that her King had decided a question in favor of the House of Commons and against the House of Lords, Choate consoled her. "Do not worry, my Lady," he said. "King George does not reign—he only sprinkles." At another time breakfasting formally at a country-house another Lady seated beside him suddenly turned to him and exclaimed, "Oh, Mr. Ambassador, what shall I do? I have just dropped an egg in my lap!" Choate checked the situation briefly, then said gravely, "Why, cackle, Madam, cackle."

Probably the most popular resorter of his era among the ladies, Choate took no stock in the opinion of the bachelor Berkshirite Southmayd that "your womenfolk will be the death of you yet." Nonetheless he had many theories about women, his favorite being that they always showed their character in one way at least—by their hats. Wittily cynical about morals, he was once asked at Newport to help a young bachelor millionaire who was being pursued by a married woman. "Tell the lady," he advised, " 'Madam, I have no time for a liaison, but I am willing to oblige you, if you promise that our adultery is not to be of a serious nature.' " On the other hand, Choate's toasts in favor of the fair sex were almost as famous as his *bons mots*. Once, in a speech lauding the Pilgrims, he suddenly switched his tack in the middle and concluded that the Pilgrim Mothers were the most devoted martyrs of all the country's early settlers. "The Pilgrim Mothers," he said, "not only had to bear with all the hardships—they also had to bear with the Pilgrim Fathers."

Often challenged by other wits of the day, Choate's most remarkable engagement was probably the one with the late Simeon Ford, proprietor of New York's old Grand Union Hotel. Ford was an extremely clever man himself; it was he who, when told indignantly by a fellow Union League Clubber that he had been offered five hundred dollars to resign from the club, promptly replied, "Don't take it, man; wait 'til you get a better offer." Ford had, however, one Achilles heel, the then extremely shady reputation of his hotel. The occasion of his run-in with Choate was a banquet at which he had the honor of introducing the lawyer, and, determined to make the most of it, he made a long and witty speech in which he noted that the man he was to introduce had the same first name as the Biblical Joseph who had so much trouble with Potiphar's wife. "I suppose, Mr. Choate," he concluded, "you too have such distinction." The audience roared with laughter as Choate stood up. "I am sorry," he said, "but I do not. However, if I did I should certainly know, Mr. Ford, to which hotel to take the young lady."

If Choate was among the most famous resorters of his day he was also among the most modest; his intimates cherish most a story which occurred at a simple dinner party with a few Berkshire friends. Even here he was bearded. A friend suddenly turned to him and asked who, of anybody, he would prefer to be if he could not be himself. The table fell silent, awaiting his answer. Choate smiled. "Why," he replied quietly, "I should like to be Mrs. Choate's second husband."

Along with the great wits of the great days of resorts, at least two events of the Gay Nineties are still recalled by all true resort old-timers. The first of these was the remarkable case, in the Berkshires, in the summer of 1893, of the "Gentleman Burglar." A tall dark and handsome man who wore a finely hemstitched handkerchief over the lower part of his face and who carried a beautifully carved revolver which he never pointed directly at anybody, the burglar worked nightly except Sundays with no accomplices and with a high feeling for the romance of his profession. He made extremely orderly entrances into all the best cottages, usually by means of a straightforward outside-the-door argument that he wished to avoid breakage, and, using as a getaway car a well-upholstered carriage drawn by two smart horses, extremely orderly exits. His actual methods of burglary were equally exemplary; in fact, even the Berkshires' most cantankerous spinsters, amid much fluttering of old maidenly breasts, spoke so highly of his bedside manner that they were of little help to the police in running him down.

A Miss Stetson, a resort visitor at the home of Stockbridge's Miss Grace Parker, was responsible for the burglar's title. After having been held at bay in a cottage which he had burgled for the better part of an hour, Miss Stetson reported that not only was her blind date "to the manner born" and "every inch a gentleman" but also that his voice was "low, musical, soothing and even mesmeric in its effect" and that she for one "should dislike to know he was taken up."

Furthermore, as the man proceeded with his work—he disdained money and took only jewelry and silver—all agreed that success did not go to his head and that, while he must have been cognizant of the fact that not to be visited by him was something of a social snub at the resort, he nonetheless never took advantage of this, or, as the saying was, "forgot his station." When it came Mrs. John Bulter Swann's turn to be burgled, she reported happily to the police that the man had seemed in no hurry to leave her cottage at all; she also admitted that toward the conclusion of his tour of her bedroom she had cautiously peeked out from under the bedclothes and asked to see what he was taking. With a smart, "Yes, madam," the burglar had obliged; in fact, at Mrs. Swann's suggestion he had put down a costly diamond ring which she had told him was a memento of her mother and had substituted another far less valuable. Mrs. Swann next reported that having been encouraged by his attitude she had sat up in bed and gently scolded him. "Do you not think," she had asked, "that you might choose some other form of employment?" But this, she reported, had been unsuccessful. She had been met only by "an icy stare from his delicately arched eyebrows" and then the burglar had at once disappeared—"as if hurt."

By this time the cottagers, as baffled as the police, began entertaining the theory that the "Gentleman Burglar" was a butler. At the very next cottage he visited, however, before settling down to the serious burgling of the evening, he decided to open a champagne bottle; unfortunately it made a loud "pop." The theory was, of course, instantly exploded—all cottagers reasoning that any resort butler would at least know how to open a champagne bottle without making such a vulgar sound.

Mrs. David Dudley Field, next on the burglar's schedule, took sterner measures. Jumping at the man as he leaned over her bed, she threw her arms around his neck and attempted, as she told the police, to hold him prisoner. Stiffening up, the burglar bristled. "I must warn you," he said, "if you do not let go, I shall have to shoot you." But this time the shoe was on the other foot; Mrs. Field hung on and, in fact, was still around the burglar's neck as he left the bedroom and made for the stairs. Crying out for help as she passed the back of the house, Mrs. Field roused the valet. The latter, according to the report of the Berkshire *News*, was a true resort valet:

> But what appealed to the valet more than the necessity of securing the burglar, dead or alive, was the necessity of dressing according to the hour and the company. He begged to be excused while he put on his dressing gown, and disappeared without waiting for the consent of Mrs. Field or the burglar. . . . A few minutes later, attired in gown and trousers, and armed with a Civil War pistol, he rushed downstairs and in his rush to get out after the burglar he blew the lock off the front door with a blast from his pistol. But he was too late.

Finally only three socially front-running Stockbridge cottages remained to be burgled—the Sedgwicks', the Choates' and the Southmayds'. Southmayd, Choate's penurious partner, acted in character. He engaged a night watchman with a dinner bell, double-bolted his front door and ordered no one in his cottage to open it after dark under any circumstances. The very next night there was a knock on the front door. "Mr. Southmayd," a voice called out, "your house is on fire." Southmayd himself rushed down the stairs, opened the door and, of course, personally admitted the "Gentleman Burglar." Later the entire resort rejoiced when they learned that the burglar, descending to such stern measures for the first time in his career, had taken not only money as well as jewelry and silver, but also Mr. Southmayd's trousers.

Only when the burglar broke from the cottage field and began taking on all comers, did he meet with disaster. Entering the Rectory in Lenox he was chided by the Rector; ashamed and protesting he was a good churchman himself, the burglar agreed to take only a box of cigars and immediately left. Unfortunately, these cigars proved his undoing. They were a special brand smoked only by the Rector, and when cigar papers of this brand were found in the bottom of a buggy which was later proved to have been stolen from Stockbridge's William Pitt Palmer, the "Gentleman Burglar," to the distress of many, was apprehended. His identity proved to be Thomas Kinsella, a man whose previous field of social activity in the Berkshires had ranged from serving as a stonecutter on Joseph Choate's cottage in 1885 to shooting his mother-in-law in 1887.

The second Gay Nineties' event which lives on in the minds of all true resort old-timers was Southampton's famous Charm Contest of 1899. Originated by the prince of resort sports, the late Peter Marié, a lifelong bachelor yet a perennial proposer to all the debutantes of Newport, Bar Harbor, Lenox and Southampton, the Charm Contest was announced early in the summer by large posters put up in conspicuous places at the various Southampton Clubs:

A PRIZE

will be awarded to the person who will give the best written answer to the question

WHAT IS CHARM?

The answers must be original and written, not oral, but may be in prose or verse, and should not exceed one hundred words—and should be a definition of Personal Charm.

Answers to be sent in over noms de plume accompanied by a sealed envelope bearing real name by Monday, July 24, 1899, addressed Charm, Meadow Club, Southampton.

Also 5 honorable mentions.

Committee

Mrs. Thomas H. Barber — Mrs. Duncan Cryder
Mrs. James L. Breese — Hon. Horace Russell
Mr. James C. Parrish

Everyone knew, of course, that Marié was behind the contest and that gentleman himself, who even in those days felt that charm was disappearing from the resorts, was entirely serious about his project. Having failed in New York to revive, by means of dinners, what he called "the art of intellectual conversation," he was in no mood to abandon charm at the resorts; his contest recalled, he felt, "the open competition of the medieval Troubadours." In any case, the entries poured in and on the afternoon of July 25, 1899, at four o'clock, by invitation of Samuel L. Parrish, an "informal tea" was given at the Parrish Art Museum where two hundred guests assembled to hear the reading of the papers of the successful contenders. For the first time the sealed envelopes, containing the names of the authors, unknown up to that time to the Committee, were opened and the prizes awarded. Charm, as it turned out, had been defined by the competitors in almost every conceivable way—from "the essence of good breeding and refinement" to "the open sesame to love." The prize itself, a pin in the form of an enameled laurel leaf bearing on its face, in brilliants, the word "Charm," was awarded to Mrs. J. Metcalfe Thomas, née Louisa Carroll Jackson. Mrs. Thomas' poem was written under the pseudonym "A Dune Dweller":

WHAT IS CHARM?

Charm is the measure of attraction's power
To chain the fleeting fancy of an hour
And rival all the spell of Beauty's flower.

A subtle grace of heart and mind that flows
With tactful sympathy; the sweetest rose,
If not the fairest, that the garden knows.

A quick responsiveness in word and deed,
A dignity and stateliness at need,
The will to follow or the art to lead.

She to whom this most gracious gift is known
Has Life's great potent factor for her own
And rules alike the cottage and the throne.

Following the reading of the prize poem, the Committee reported that a certain prose piece signed "The Philosopher" had given the most accurate definition of charm, but since it exceeded the prescribed limit of 100 words—it did so by 108 words—it could not be given the prize and was therefore given a special consolation prize. The prose piece was written by Dr. H. Holbrook Curtis:

CHARM

Charm may be approximately defined as the faculty of inducing an agreeable emotion without conscious effort, through the medium of an inherent intensity of those attributes of mind and body to which we give the names imagination, suggestion and grace.

The person who possesses Charm is sensitive, sympathetic, politic, and combines repose of manner with incisiveness of thought and speech.

True Charm must react on all classes and pervade all conditions; consequently, keenness of intuition is an indispensable component of Charm.

Charm is more subtle than so-called magnetism, for it suggests a more delicate texture and greater refinements of those qualities which make a man or woman magnetic. Though perhaps not ethically conceded, physical perfection is an augmentative factor of Charm, for Charm must always be associated with a certain relationship of individual to individual, as well as of mind to mind.

Charm, however, subordinates the objective to the subjective, the physical to the psychical.

Charm deals in suggestion; it is a telepathic influence exerted upon the mental environment. It is synonymous with no other term; it cannot be analyzed. It is as complex and indefinable as love. It cannot be taught. It is an accidental constituent and must be acquired unconsciously, hence its delightful and seductive fascination.

Among the honorable mentions, and, judging by the applause of the Art Museum Tea, by all odds the popular favorite of the entire contest was a short poem contributed by Mrs. Henry May; it was signed "Anna Conda":

Charm is a power,
Charm is a spell,
Charm is enchantment
And sometimes—
Hell!

II

Tuxedo and the Social Islands —Fishers, Hobe and Jekyll

You don't know what life really is
Till you've been to Tuxedo Park!
—Chorus of song from *Tuxedo*,
by Henry J. Sayers, 1891.

IN VIEW of the importance of clubs in the resort way of life, it is not surprising that more than once resorts have been founded which have been all club; the greatest of these, all club and some five thousand yards wide, was Tuxedo Park or, as it became more familiarly called, Tuxedo. Located forty miles northwest of New York City in the rugged but picturesque Ramapo Hills overlooking Tuxedo Lake, Tuxedo was incorporated in 1886, originally as a hunting and fishing resort—in the words of its founder, a "short season place between New York and Newport." Gradually Tuxedo, which was between New York and Newport seasonally but not geographically, became not a resort at all; old-time resorters deserted it because they found it too hot in the summer and too cold in the winter and, in between times, neither one thing nor the other. Nowadays, though still clubbable, it is nothing more or less than a year-round community outside of New York which, like the ancient resort of Nahant outside of Boston, still clings to its age-old reputation but which, in the final analysis, is really one more on the list of social ghost towns.

To call Tuxedo one more of anything, however, is an injustice. No other community in this country ever started off on a grander social scale, and therefore no other may be said to have fallen so hard. Today, with several cottages in the hands of tax-free institutions, with some so-called "Young Marrieds" living in Stable Row (or converted stables of the great estates), and with a sizeable group of residents apparently happily not belonging to its club (to which in its great days all belonged) Tuxedo has been called, with some justice, the Graveyard of the Aristocracy. Nonetheless, no other community of its size—roughly two hundred families—still attracts so much curiosity. Chambers of Commerce throughout the country invariably write to Tuxedo to find out how it operates—actually the Tuxedo Park Association runs all major matters of heat, light, water, sewage, policing, etc., for a 2 per cent annual property assessment—and to this day no one who has ever lived in Tuxedo for any length of time has ever been allowed to forget it. Governor Thomas E. Dewey, a resident of Tuxedo many years ago, recalls that the most definite bit of advice he ever received concerning his proposed active entry into politics was to get out of Tuxedo. "No one," he was told, "could be elected to anything from such a social place." The Hon. Katharine D. P. Collier St. George, Republican Congresswoman from the area, has disproved this prediction by her ability, charm and personal popularity; nonetheless, even Mrs. St. George can be leery of the subject. "I always say I'm from Tuxedo," she says. "I never say Tuxedo *Park*." More severe is the story of Clermont L. Barnwell who, born June 7, 1888, was the first baby ever born in the Park and has been known ever since as the Tuxedo Baby. Although he deserted the community as far back as 1923, Barnwell is still plagued every time he is forced to make reference, public or private, to his birthplace. "All my life," he declares, "it's been almost as much of a cross to bear as a bar sinister."

The late Price Collier, who made his home in Tuxedo

from 1898 until his death in 1915 once said, "The best society of Europe is success enjoying an idle hour or so; the best society here is idleness enjoying its success. . . . Society, to be permanently interesting, must be made up of idle professionals, not of professional idlers." Today Mrs. Price Collier, who ranks as Tuxedo's First Lady, believes that in its great days Tuxedo Park came at least close to her husband's European ideal but that it is now far from it indeed. Now ninety-two years old, she has in her lifetime traveled all over the world ever since she first went to China with her father, Warren Delano, at the age of two. "Tuxedo," she says, "has changed more than any place I know of. My father used to say, 'This place is perfection' and I remember the wife of the Old Squire telling me, 'If you live in Tuxedo one year, you will meet everybody you've ever heard of.' I don't mean to sound crotchety, but, oh dear me, what a change."

Mrs. Collier, who now spends her winters in two rooms in the Tuxedo Club's bachelor quarters, has of course seen this change at first hand. So, too, has Miss Dorothy Kane, daughter of Grenville Kane, whose family homestead did not even have electricity until 1941. "My father and mother were putter offers," she says, "but finally one summer when they went to Newport I had it put in." Although both Mr. and Mrs. Kane died within two years of the installation, Miss Kane feels that the present-day situation at Tuxedo has been exaggerated and points to families like the Seton Porters and the Frederick Frothinghams, the George Amorys and the George Bartletts, the Casimir de Rhams and the William M. V. Hoffmans, as well as Mrs. Stanley Mortimer, Mrs. Ernest Adee and Mrs. Pendleton Rogers, all of whom still cottage in the Park in the old sense. Another Tuxedo old-timer discusses this group. "The ones who had three places now may have only two, and the ones who had eight servants now may have only four," she says, "but they're all still ladies—to use an absolutely extinct word."

Tuxedo's younger contingent are also vocal, if even less optimistic. "I like it here," says Mrs. Eric Archdeacon, a relative newcomer to the Park, "but mentally Tuxedo has always been slow-moving. I always think of this place as a beautiful cemetery." Jay Rutherfurd, scion of a distinguished Tuxedo family and a young man who in 1927, at the age of nine, was editor and publisher of the only newspaper the Park has ever had, is more philosophical. But today he sees vast changes from the Golden Days of the Tuxedo *News* which, though it lasted only six months, maintained, right to the end, a circulation of an even four hundred.

"It's the most beautiful place in the world," he says, "but it's full of midgets. The midgets are trying to hold down the tent—and the kings are all gone."

The story of Tuxedo Park goes back to the first Pierre Lorillard, original prince of the snuff and tobacco empire who, in 1814, foreclosed a mortgage upon part of the Tuxedo territory. This Pierre I was a true empire-builder of the Old School. On his death in 1843 one newspaper coined the word "millionaire"—which had never before been used—and another newspaper was moved to remark, "He led people by the nose for the better part of a century and made his enormous fortune by giving them to chew that which they could not swallow." According to Fairfax Downey, Lorillard historian, the Lorillards had a straightforward four-point program for business success:

1) Find out what the public wants, then produce the best of its kind.
2) Advertise the product so that everybody will know it's available.
3) Distribute it everywhere so that everybody can get it.
4) Keep making the product better so that more people will like it.

A member of a family which has usually been numbered rather than named, Pierre Lorillard V came into the possession of 600,000 acres around the present Tuxedo partly by inheritance, partly by buying out others and partly by defeating his own relatives at poker. The owner of Iroquois, the only American-bred horse ever to win the English Derby, he too had an equally clear program for his dream community. Stated in four roughly parallel points this program might be put as follows:

1) Find out who the leaders of Society are and produce the best place for them to live in.
2) Tell nobody else about it so that nobody else will know it's available.
3) Keep it a private club so that other people, even if they do hear about it, can't get in.
4) Keep the place exactly as it was in the beginning so that other people, even if they do hear about it and somehow do manage to get in, won't ever like it anyway.

Taking over in September, 1885, with Bruce Price as his architect and Ernest Bowditch as his engineer, Pierre Lorillard V proceeded rapidly. It was in the days before strict immigration and labor laws, and Lorillard imported 1,800 workmen directly from Italy. On the almost deserted property, which was then known as the Erie Railroad's "Wood Pile," the first thing these workers had to do was build a small city of shanties for themselves—like an army in barracks. Lorillard himself, though a severe man socially, was a remarkable general of this army. "He talked rapidly," his architect Bruce Price once said, "and thought twice as fast as he talked and wished his orders carried out at a speed that equaled the sum of both." Once, as Lorillard was leaving Price's office he called back. "By the way, make it four cottages instead of two. Show me the plans tomorrow and break ground for them next Monday." Incredibly enough, since the workmen had only the simplest equipment and the winter was a severe one, eight months to the day from the September 30th start, Lorillard had a seven-thousand-acre, eight-foot barbed-wire fenced park, thirty miles of graded dirt and macadam road, a complete sewage and water system, a park gatehouse described by its architect as looking "like a frontispiece to an English novel," a broad-verandaed clubhouse staffed with English servants, twenty-two casement-dormered English-turreted cottages, each surrounded by a square of new green lawn, two blocks of stores, a score of stables, four lawn tennis courts, a bowling alley, a swimming tank, a boathouse, an icehouse, a dam, a trout pond and a hatchery. The total cost was $1,500,000. On Memorial Day, 1886, three special trains from New York brought seven hundred guests and Tuxedo Park was opened for inspection.

Nothing had been left to chance. Even the streets of the workers' shanties had been named circumspectly; one was "Fifth Avenue," another "Broadway." The mess hall was "Delmonico's." During the construction of the Park the grounds were carefully guarded and, warned the New York *Herald*, "Woe to the unlucky stranger who strays across the posted boundaries." As far back as October Lorillard had completed the membership list of his club. Described at the time as "a guide to Who is especially Who in the Four Hundred," it consisted of William Waldorf Astor, T. Burnett Baldwin, George S. Bowdoin, Lloyd S. Bryce, William P. Douglas, Robert Goelet, John G. Heckscher, Henry H. Hollister, C. Oliver Iselin, Grenville Kane, William Kent, Lawrence Kip, Herman R. LeRoy, Pierre Lorillard, Pierre Lorillard, Jr., Ogden Mills, Herbert C. Pell, Allen T. Rice, F. Augustus Schermerhorn and William R. Travers. Among other things these members also sported the club badge which, designed to be worn as a pin, was an oakleaf of solid gold; club governors had acorns attached to their oakleafs and later all Tuxedoites were to wear ties, hatbands, socks, etc., in the club colors of green and gold. At first Lorillard had intended to own all the cottages himself and rent them out to his friends, but gradually he was persuaded to parcel them out for purchase. While this was done on a sort of social first-come first-served basis, no one who was not a member of the club was allowed to buy property; the first outsider to be admitted was Sir Roderick Cameron, the British Consul in New York.

From miles around the country folk gathered to witness the coming of the New York trains. Even the engineers felt the fever; despite the complaints of the passengers in the rickety coaches, the ride from the Jersey City terminal, supposed to take an hour and a half, was made in forty minutes flat. On their arrival at the Tuxedo station, the seven hundred guests were directed to newly painted coaches and Brewster wagonettes which, sporting the Tuxedo colors with their leaf-green bodies and bright yellow-gold wheels, waited to take the visitors on tour. Architecturally the original idea of Tuxedo had been to blend everything into the surrounding woods; the shingled cottages were stained russets and grays, and the gatehouse, as well as the post office, drugstore and market, all were patched with lichen and moss and were supposed to look at least a hundred years old. As the coaches and wagonettes drove around the Park, beds of flowers lined the roads, while private Tuxedo policemen, chosen for their height and good looks, pointed the way. Tirolean-hatted gamekeepers, also in club uniform, darted in and out of the forest on a regular in-and-out schedule. Out on the lake crews in blue and white sailor suits manned eight-oared sight-seeing barges. From one hilltop a red flag flew; Lorillard's idea of this flag, said *Harper's Weekly*, was that it would serve as "a warning to hesitating lovers that the beauty of the place will turn their thoughts to love."

The high point of the visit, which included a luncheon reception, an afternoon of sports and an evening dance before the special trains returned, was the trip to the New Club, or the Old Club as it is called today. Up until the time of Tuxedo the few country clubs which existed were relatively simple, small-roomed farmhouse affairs. Tuxedo's Club was something else. Although it would seem primitive by today's standards—there were one hundred bedrooms and only one private bath—it was the marvel of its time. A square wooden building, surrounded by porches, it boasted a large paneled living room, long leather sofas and wide open fireplaces burning five-foot logs; everywhere the appointments were the last word in smartness. Hallmen, footmen and waiters were in full Tuxedo Club livery, green with gold-striped waistcoats, the service was excellent and the food generally regarded as the best this side of Paris.

Of all the features of what to Tuxedoites will always remain their beloved Old Club the most remarkable was its large circular ballroom, eighty feet in diameter, which was actually a separate building from the main club and was connected to it by a long corridor. This ballroom had not only a parquet floor which was reputed the best dance floor of its time but also a handsome domed ceiling supported on a set of Corinthian columns. Behind these columns were the built-in divans, or high-chair seats, which were reserved for the Tuxedo dowagers who, complete with lorgnettes, spent the dance evenings happily strafing their offspring. Finally, opposite the entrance of the ballroom, was a stage fully equipped with footlights, drop curtains and all the trimmings. There was some irony in connection with this stage since when James Brown Potter proposed the English actor Kyrle Bellew for membership in the club, there was such consternation that a special *ad hoc* committee was called of the Tuxedo Governors. Immediately they passed a rule that no actor should ever be permitted to become a member of the club—a rule which has never been erased from the books. Actually, it was on this stage, as amateurs, that two of Society's best known actresses, Mrs. James Brown Potter and Miss Elsie de Wolfe, later Lady Mendl, both got their start. Today Tuxedoites recall in particular Mrs. Potter's moving recital of George R. Sims' poem "'Ostler Joe," the story of a poor but honest hostler who had the misfortune to be deserted by his beautiful but willful wife in favor of a more glamorous life. Following her Tuxedo success, Mrs. Potter embarked on a full-time professional career and in 1900 divorced her husband. As for the late Lady Mendl, later a leading figure in international Society, she too never forgot Tuxedo Park. "It was at Tuxedo," she said, "that I had my first glimpse of the ends to which women, and men too, will go in order to get into Society."

Today old Tuxedoites become misty-eyed at the mere thought of the Old Ballroom and firmly believe that the famous cotillions at the old Autumn Balls had a dignity and charm unequaled in any other resort Society. These balls were led by one of the well-known beaux of the day, such as Elisha Dyer or Stowe Phelps. These leaders took no partners themselves but their word was law in directing the various figure formations such as the Windmill, the Grand Chain and the Mirror. The Mirror figure was perhaps the most memorable. In this a chair was placed in the center of the ballroom, and the leader, with some ceremony, escorted a girl to sit in it; he also presented her with a looking glass. Then he led up from behind a potential partner who presented his face, over the girl's shoulder, to the mirror. If the girl was dissatisfied with the choice, she shook her head and another potential partner was led up. Finally, when an acceptable reflection appeared, the girl nodded and then arose and danced, after which another girl took the throne. Tuxedo belles recall this Mirror figure with extreme affection, Tuxedo beaux, understandably enough, with considerably less. At the same time, all agree that the Tuxedo Autumn Balls were never the same after the fox trot and the bunny hug, let alone the rhumba and the samba, appeared on the scene. "It became," says Tuxedoite J. Earle Stevens severely, "a free-for-all."

Free-for-all or not, the annual Autumn Ball is the only feature of Tuxedo Society which has continued more or less intact to the present day. Though held in considerably reduced splendor—"Somebody's gardener," says Mrs. Clarence Bartow, "just sticks a few branches around"—the Balls are still the opening gun of each New York debutante season, and a debutante who receives an invitation feels confident that she is a member of New York's inner circle. This Ball has a justly famous place in the history of American Society, for it was at the first Autumn Ball in October, 1886, that young Griswold Lorillard, son of Pierre V, wore the tailless dress coat to which the resort gave its name. Today all Tuxedoites agree that, once having seen the coat, "everyone wanted one like Grizzy's," but how the coat came to be worn in the first place, or even whether it was first worn at Tuxedo, can still start an argument in any resort Society. Some resorters trace the origin of the coat to James Brown Potter's visit to the Prince of Wales, who wore a somewhat similar smoking jacket, some to the late E. Berry Wall, King of the Dudes, who was put off the dance floor of the Grand Union Hotel in Saratoga for wearing such a coat, and some to an anonymous leader of Irish Society who sported the coat at a dance at one of the Bowery's Chowder and Marching clubs. Perhaps the simplest explanation is that given by Newport's young Louis Lorillard, great-great-grandson of Pierre V. "I've always heard," he says, "they just got tired of sitting around on their tails, so they cut them off." Two things are certain. One is that the coat which Griswold Lorillard wore was designed by his father and was a scarlet satin-lapeled affair which was tailored, if not tailed, along the lines of the pink coats worn by hunters riding to hounds. The other is that the coat was not an instant success. The Society journal *Town Topics* claimed that Griswold Lorillard looked "for all the world like a royal footman" and that he and his friends who wore the coats "ought to have been put in strait jackets long ago." Even today it is an ironical fact that in Society the word "tuxedo" is itself considered taboo, the use of "dinner jacket" in its stead being as mandatory as the Society patois which insists on "to-mah-to" for "to-may-to" and "my-onnaise" for "may-onnaise."

The immediate success of Tuxedo Park, entirely apart

from its coat, was a phenomenon of the great resort era. In social prestige Tuxedo quickly outranked other New York resorts such as Richfield Springs and Sharon Springs, Lake Placid and Lake George, and even challenged Saratoga; soon Tuxedo was a rival of Newport itself. Any Tuxedoite, merely by showing his gold oakleaf pin, could have any Erie train, even those which did not stop except at the largest stations, stopped at Tuxedo, and Mrs. William Pierson Hamilton, daughter of the elder J. P. Morgan, even had her own railroad station; the last before Tuxedo, it was called "Sterlington" and dutifully the Erie trains stopped there as they did at "Arden," the station beyond Tuxedo belonging to the railroad king, E. H. Harriman. Among other distinctions Tuxedo was the first community in the country to have telephones installed in all its cottages; today Tuxedo still has its own private telephone exchange and battery of operators who work inside the Park. Also in those early days the Park soon received a new name for its taxicabs, which were nondescript single traps with a canopied top, a rear entrance and seats on the side. When these vehicles were brought up to the club for inspection, Lorillard's daughter, Mrs. William Kent, was standing beside him. "Surely," she said, "you don't expect anyone to drive around the Park in those nasty little jiggers!" Lorillard, having already made up his mind to use the cabs, did indeed expect that; from that time on all Tuxedo taxicabs have been "jiggers."

By the 1890's the fame of Tuxedo had spread to Broadway. On the evening of October 5, 1891, George Thatcher's Minstrels allied with Rich and Harris' Comedy Company under the management of Henry J. Sayers to present at the New Park Theatre *Tuxedo*. This production, though regarded at the time as the first attempt to combine minstrelsy with farce comedy, was unfortunately never published; not even the Library of Congress boasts a copy, and the playbill reveals merely that it was advertised as "refined even as it must be to secure popular patronage." Old-time Tuxedoites recall that it was divided into two parts. The first part, entitled "On the Lawn at Tuxedo for Sweet Charity's Sake," took place outside a Tuxedo cottage where an entertainment for charity is planned and the title song is sung:

You don't know what life really is
Till you've been to Tuxedo Park!

The second part of *Tuxedo* took place outside the Tuxedo clubhouse and concerned the entertainment itself; in this, since the amateurs fail in their play-within-a-play scene, George Thatcher's minstrels, including the famous Henry Dougherty, are substituted and take over the show from there. Apparently the author of the farce, Ed Marble, who later admitted he had never been to Tuxedo, had little confidence in his work. To the title of the playbill he appended the line, "For the individual who can discover the plot there is a barrel of red apples at the box-office." The next morning the reviewers to a man supported Marble's lack of confidence; the critic of the New York *World* began his review with a story:

> There was one very funny thing during the evening. It was just at the close of the second part. A little girl who had been sitting down in a very picturesque pose arose and started to walk across the stage; her foot was asleep. The manner in which she walked set the whole audience to shrieking. A fat woman went into hysterics, and there was no end of fun.

If *Tuxedo* was not a critical success, there was at least one memorable thing about the show. This was the fact that it popularized the famous song "Ta-ra-ra Boom-der-é"—later changed, for the benefit of the American public, to "Ta-ra-ra Boom-de-ay." Henry J. Sayers, the adapter if not the author of the song, first heard the refrain in a Negro resort run by "Babe" Connors in St. Louis. Later it was popularized in England by Lottie Collins. As used in *Tuxedo* the Sayers' verses, still lovingly recalled by old-time Tuxedoites and sung with French endings on the "Boom," ran as follows:

A sweet Tuxedo girl you see,
Queen of swell society.
Fond of fun as fond can be
When it's on the strict Q.T.!
Ta-ra-ra Boom-der-é [Four times repeated]

Not too young and not too old,
Not too timid, not too bold,
But just the very thing, I'm told,
That in your arms you'd like to hold.
Ta-ra-ra Boom-der-é [etc.]

With the singing of "Ta-ra-ra Boom-der-é," Tuxedo reached the crest of its wave. Gradually there had begun to be intimations that all was not well with Society's Utopia. The first chink to appear in the Tuxedo armor occurred in 1892 when Julia Ward Howe, author of "The Battle Hymn of the Republic," journeyed up from Newport and made a visit to the Park. On her return she was asked by her daughter, Newport's beloved Maud Howe Elliott, what she thought of the place. Replied Mrs. Elliott briefly, "White of an egg." This opinion, coming from one of the social oracles of the age, was widely repeated at the time, and although no one was quite sure what it meant, the consensus was that the opinion was by no means favorable. At about the same time the Park also suffered a severe blow from within. This occurred with the report handed in to the executive committee of the Tuxedo Park Association from another committee which was headed by William Waldorf Astor and which was entitled "The Committee Appointed to Examine into the Original Historical Names of the Tuxedo Region." This sort of search for the historic is, of course, a familiar defense in which all the great resorts have indulged in order to take the edge off the purely social; in Tuxedo's case, the report, which still reposes in the Tuxedo Club safe, was supposed to prove that the name Tuxedo meant "beautiful view"—an opinion widely held by Tuxedoites:

> The name as found in 1754 is undoubtedly the corruption of one or more Indian words. The language of the Algonquins, who occupied this region, was examined. It is found that the letter X, being unknown in their dialect, is represented in the fragments that remain by KS. It is also found that "to" or "tough" means "a place." The best authorities upon the language of the Algonquins have found that the name Tuxedo, no matter how spelled, contains no elements that mean pond, lake, or water; nor can the word or any of its variants be made to mean anything like "beautiful view," as has been stated.
>
> It was suggested that a frequent habit of the Indians was to name a place after the chief whose tribe occupied it, and this view being taken up, mention was discovered of a sachem named P'tauk-Seet, "the bear," who, in the seventeenth century, ruled over a tract of country including Tuxedo. Uniting his name with "tough," the Algonquin for "place," we should infer the original spelling to have been P'tauk-Seet-tough, and its meaning "The Home of the Bear."

If not "beautiful view," neither was "The Home of the Bear" by any means a perfect habitat for sport. Article I of

Tuxedo's Constitution had clearly stated that the resort was established "for the protection, increase and capture of all kinds of game and fish," and a gallant effort subsidized by Lorillard's money was made to carry this out. Fishing, expected to be Tuxedo's main sport, was the first to suffer. Originally Tuxedo Lake had a reasonable supply of black bass; unfortunately German carp were soon added under the mistaken idea that they would breed and that the carp fry would furnish good bass food. Instead the grown-up carp, hungry in the meantime, ate the bass fry. Tuxedo had even more trouble with game. Though no expense was spared and ring-necked pheasant from New Jersey, quail from North Carolina and wild turkey from Texas were imported with abandon, all either found Tuxedo's eight-foot fence no bar to their desire for less social areas or else became so tame that not even elder resort sports, who had been prevented by state law in 1894 from such cruelties as live pigeon shooting, had the heart to molest them. Tuxedo's white-tailed deer, also an imported item from New Jersey, were particularly pacific. In the early days a favorite story of the Park was the occasion when a group of eager sportsmen, out from New York to Tuxedo for the first time, suddenly thrilled by the sight of a doe springing through the woods. Up went their guns, only to come down again when, sighting closer, the sportsmen observed that the animal wore, handsomely bowed around her neck, a large red ribbon.

Still Tuxedo refused to give up. Failing in its fish and gaming, the Park turned to other endeavors. In short order the Park built not only a mile-long, electrically lit toboggan slide—one which was the subject of a famous Tuxedo short story entitled *A Kiss in the Toboggan*—but also a race track complete with a grandstand for horse shows and dog shows.

On the lake the Park went in heavily for canoeing and sailboating in the summer, and in the winter for both curling and ice skating; old-timers recall with relish the "black ice" days when the lake froze over. These days were not many—"No matter what year you were there," says Herbert Pell, "somebody was always complaining that the lake wasn't freezing properly"—but on the occasions when the lake did freeze properly, Tuxedoites skated as romantically as they tobogganed, often in the evenings by lantern light, later coming in, two by two, to the club's hot spiced punch and sugared doughnuts. In common with other resorts Tuxedoites claim that their first golf course, established in 1889, was the second oldest course in the country. On their second course, in 1894, they also claim that the country's first inter-club match was played. Four teams competed—Yonkers' St. Andrews, Boston's Brookline Country Club, Southampton's Shinnecock Club and Tuxedo—with St. Andrews winning. This match was the major social sporting event of its time and not until after it, Tuxedoites say, did the country's golf craze begin in earnest. Today, ironically enough, a new turnpike threatens to destroy some fourteen holes of Tuxedo's present course.

One sport has to this day been kept almost entirely safe from democracy; and Tuxedo played, characteristically, a stalwart role in its promotion. Known as court tennis, not to be confused with lawn tennis or squash tennis, squash or squash rackets, or even just plain rackets, the sport has, according to Gamesman Allison Danzig, "the most complicated rules of any game played by man" and is so aristocratic a sport that with the exception of a handful of racket clubs and private courts it has never been played anywhere in this country except at Tuxedo, Newport, Aiken and Harvard. If to outsiders it appears like an involved family joke, to insiders like Mr. Danzig it is not only several centuries older than lawn tennis or tennis, but it is also the granddaddy of all ball and bat games:

> It is the game of youth and the game of age, but he who would be king in this game of kings must have both the coursing blood of vigorous manhood in his veins and the ripened experience of years spent in the courts. Its highest honors are not for the schoolboy of shining morning face, nor for the soldier bearded like the pard seeking the bubble of reputation in the cannon's mouth, but for the student and the campaigner, the man of brains and the man of action, who has won many a battle and lost even more, and who has profited by both.

Even the spectators to this remarkable sport do not watch in ordinary manner; they sit in an opening in the wall at the back of one end of the court which is known as the "dedans"—from the French "within"—protected by a net. As these spectators view a court and see the many curious buttresses, grilles, roofs, netted window, "tambours" and penthouses around them, they often feel they are in the back side of an ancient monastery—and, indeed, they may well be; the English *Saturday Review* of 1884 declared that the court was the result of an accident of ground and "is, in fact, a copy of a monastery courtyard turned by the monks to the purpose of an improvised game." The ball, however, which looks like an ordinary tennis ball but is heavier and appears to bounce about as well as a badly baked biscuit, is far from monastic in origin; all true court tennis adherents subscribe to the theory that these balls are still the same as they were in the days when they were made from the hems of the petticoats of the ladies-in-waiting who watched the French and English princelings play *jeu de paume*, as the game was once called. The rackets are also unique; unlike either tennis or squash bats, with their large faces and bulging sides they look rather like old snowshoes and in the hands of a player of less than several generations' experience seem to be about equally effective—even though, with court tennis' so-called "chases," the game is the only racket game in which, under certain conditions, the ball is permitted to bounce twice.

From the first the Tuxedo fathers of court tennis appeared to realize that they had in their hands the last sport of the last resorts—in other words, a gentleman's sport, as lawn tennis and golf once were, and one which so few people could understand, let alone have any facilities for practice, that it was almost possible to announce yourself as champion without playing at all. Even if you did have to play, the chances were good that your opponent would not know the rules, and if he did know the rules, the chances were even better that he would not know how to keep score; no game can be played without a "marker" or umpire, and even then the scoring is so complicated that many players have played for years without understanding it. At first serene in their club championship, in which good Tuxedoites like T. Suffern Tailer, William B. Dinsmore, Clarence C. Pell, C. Suydam Cutting, Stanley Mortimer and Pierre Lorillard VI happily took turns in sharing the honors, Tuxedo gingerly started in 1903 their famous Gold Racquet Championship. For the first year and for two years following, this was won, satisfactorily enough, by the neighboring Hudson Valley socialite Charles E. Sands, a young man who kept the game even more in the family by playing both under his own name and the alias "E. Edwards." When the outlander Jay Gould, however, came over from Lakewood in 1906 and won, not only that year but also for the next two years, the tournament was promptly abandoned, and although it was revived in 1926 following the retirement of Gould—some idea of the sport may be gained from the fact that Gould was amateur champion for twenty straight years—Tuxedo took no chances. The tournament was revived only on condition that no one who had won the national championship could also play for the Gold Racquet.

Today perhaps the last example of the old-time gentleman champion at court tennis, or in fact at any other sport, is Ogden Phipps of Long Island, Palm Beach, Saratoga, Tuxedo and other points social. Phipps first won the national court tennis championship in 1938—he retired undefeated in 1949—and is also in the championship class of a variety of other sports including squash, squash rackets, tennis, golf, shooting, etc. Some years ago he made a wager that no athlete anywhere in the country, amateur or professional, at any three sports of his own (*i.e.*, the challenger's) choosing would be able to defeat him (*i.e.*, Phipps) in more than one of the three. To date there have been no takers.

In the boom 1920's, as in the case of the other old-time resorts, Tuxedo, believing that the Old Order would continue *ad infinitum*, dug in. A new clubhouse with long stone lines, contrasting sharply with the old square wooden building, was designed by John Russell Pope, a new swimming pool replaced the old swimming tank, and the resort ushered in a new generation of millionaires—the "bad" millionaires in the view of the old "good" millionaires. By this time also Tuxedo led all other resorts in the beginning of a new difficulty, the servant problem. Because of the Park gatehouse rigamarole—by which any visitor to Tuxedo still cannot get by the gate policeman until his purpose has been checked by telephone with his destination—servants found it extremely difficult to entertain their boyfriends; their boyfriends in turn usually persuaded them to leave for more accessible areas. Still remembered at Tuxedo today is Newell Tilton's *bon mot* on a subject which became far from funny at all resorts with the passing years. "We have ten servants," said Tilton, "five coming and five going."

The era of the 1920's was ushered in by at least one specific tempest in the Tuxedo teapot. The year was 1921 and the resort was in a turmoil. Word was passed around that one of the Park's most charming ladies was writing a book. Furthermore, the dark story went, she was putting all her friends in it. Fortunately the fears were unfounded. The book, published in 1922, was *Etiquette*; the author Mrs. Price Post, better known as Emily. For many years the literary adviser of Funk and Wagnalls had tried unsuccessfully to persuade Mrs. Post, who was the daughter of the architect of Tuxedo and author of several novels contrasting European with American standards, to undertake such a book; Mrs. Post had steadfastly refused. One day the Funk and Wagnalls man surreptitiously left another book on the subject, published by Doubleday, in Mrs. Post's Tuxedo cottage. Picking it up one night, Mrs. Post was horrified with its gaucheries. "Doubleday!" she says today, recalling the event, "Doubleday! And I knew they were ladies and gentlemen, too!"

Mrs. Post was never one to brook gaucheries. Among other distinctions, she had been named, at the age of eighteen, by Ward McAllister, as one of the ten ladies in New York who could gracefully cross a ballroom floor alone; furthermore she had learned the art, wearing a sandbag on her head, at Miss Graham's Finishing School for Young Ladies—a school which also taught, in the same manner, the art of curtsying. The next day Mrs. Post sat down and began her book, and today *Etiquette*, born in Tuxedo Park, is currently in its seventy-seventh edition. Mrs. Post herself, who no longer lives in the Park, still ranks as Tuxedo's most distinguished ex-hostess. "I go to Edgartown in the summer now," she says. "Edgartown is distinguished, but it is not fashionable. It is just a lovely return to the day before yesterday."

Tuxedo, in Mrs. Post's opinion of October, 1911, as expressed in the *Century* magazine, was evidently a return to the day before that. Admitting Tuxedo was indifferent to change, Mrs. Post refused to concede that the Park was actually inhospitable:

> It does not matter nowadays whether John Smith and his family, taking a cottage for the summer or for the winter, know anyone in the "A" group of people or not. If they do not know anyone in the "C" group, they surely will know, and like, some of the "D's" or "B's."

Today—"nowadays" of forty years later—Mrs. Post still looks back on Tuxedo less as snobbish than as formal. As an example of this formality, Mrs. Post recalls at the age of fifteen going out to dine alone with a young lady whose husband was away; she was received by her hostess standing in the door of her drawing room with her gloves on. Only once, apparently, did Tuxedo break down and attempt to enjoy what the world outside the Park was later to call the Gay Nineties. This occurred with the promotion on the part of James L. Breese, Tuxedo's leading resort sport of the day, of a craze which turned out to be, for a brief period at least, the Park's favorite indoor activity—tobogganing down the Club stairs on trays. Young ladies in voluminous party dresses, beaux in tail coats (more often than tuxedos), each mounted a tin tray at the top of the stairs—on one special occasion silver tea trays were used—and slid down with a bang only to be caught at the landing by faithful extra beaux with pillows. For several weeks Tuxedo enjoyed its iniquity; then one evening when Miss Grace Carley, later Mrs. Oliver Harriman, and other belles were engaged in the sport and their dresses were opening up like umbrellas, one of the young beaux at the landing sounded the death knell of the sport with a remark widely quoted at the time as the height of boldness. "Did you see," he asked a friend in goggle-eyed excitement, "all the lovely laces?" Immediately a storm gathered around all participants of the sport; under severe stigma James L. Breese left for Southampton, and Mrs. Post recalls that, following his departure, the Park reverted to its accustomed formality.

"Tuxedo was the most formal place in the world," Mrs. Post concludes today, summing up the resort. "Nobody ever waved or hello-ed or hi-ed at Tuxedo. You bowed when you shook hands and the manners at the balls were something wonderful. You never slopped. You sat up perfectly straight. And first names were considered very bad form. You might be Johnny in private, but you were Mr. Jones in public. There were only five men in Tuxedo who called me Emily—and never in formal Society."

One gentleman whose formality is legendary at the resort is Philadelphia's Rodman Wanamaker; even his wife never called him by his first name. For one birthday ball Wanamaker imported from New York a famous colored quartet. At the height of the proceedings the bandleader stopped the music, held up his hands, ordered a roll of the drum, and then led his orchestra into "When you wore a tulip, a bright yellow tulip, and I wore a big red rose." The quartet, to this tune, then proceeded to render their special song—one which, unknown to Wanamaker, had been composed for the occasion:

We all call him Rodman
Our glorious Rodman—

The quartet had intended to sing as their third line "The Prince of Tuxedo Park." Unfortunately two "Rodmans" had been too much. Drowned by the roars of laughter from the audience the quartet stopped singing. Once more they started. This time they got no farther than the first "Rodman." Finally the quartet gave up entirely and not until the end of the evening did they receive an explanation of how they had committed Tuxedo's most glaring *faux pas*.

Mrs. Post is not the only eminent ex-Tuxedoite who remembers the Park as formal. Mrs. Tuckerman Draper, better known as Dorothy, is another. Tuxedo's gift to the field of decorating, Mrs. Draper recalls that her mother, Tuxedo's Mrs. Paul Tuckerman, was the first lady to wear a divided skirt riding horseback. "All her friends were terribly shocked," says Mrs. Draper today. "It was a *cause célèbre*." Mrs. Draper's resort decorating has been characterized by its modernity and informality—"Change something," she says, "and something delightful usually happens"—and in this spirit she has redone such resort hotels as the Greenbrier at White Sulphur, the Gideon Putnam at Saratoga and the Arrowhead Hotel, at Arrowhead Springs, California. Mrs. Draper herself represents a Tuxedo rebellion. "As a resorter," she says, "I go back to the eighteenth century. My great-great-great-grandfather George Gibbs had seventy-five ships in the harbor of Newport at one time. But I couldn't stand Tuxedo. I can't stand any place with a fence around it. Tuxedo had holes in its fence and I escaped through one of them and married George Draper. But I still don't like the idea of that fence."

From the beginning, fence or no fence, Tuxedo was for its size the most attractive of all resorts to royalty; even today a spare Hapsburg or a miscellaneous Hohenzollern may be flushed, along with the tame quail, from almost any given spot in the Tuxedo woods. In the memory of Tuxedo old-timers, however, one regal visit of the winter of 1927 still stands out. The visit began quietly enough when Mrs. Charles E. Mitchell, wife of the National City banker, innocently playing a double concerto on the piano in her New York home, was summoned to the telephone to receive a long-distance call from Louisville, Kentucky; the call was from a former acquaintance, a man she knew so slightly that she hardly recalled his name. The man informed Mrs. Mitchell that he was on tour with Queen Marie of Rumania and that Her Majesty was coming to New York and would like very much to visit Mrs. Mitchell in Tuxedo rather than stay in a New York hotel. When Mrs. Mitchell asked how many people there were in the Queen's party, the man informed her that there were sixteen—including nine servants.

At first Mrs. Mitchell, relatively new to the ways of visiting royalty at resorts, was sure the whole thing was a hoax. Her Tuxedo cottage was closed for the winter and neither she nor her husband had ever met the Queen of Rumania. As Tuxedo's leading hostess of the era she had already been subject to many practical jokes and in the case of this one, she refused to bite. She merely said politely she should be delighted, hung up the telephone and returned to her double concerto. But at dinner she received a telegram from the same man who had telephoned her. The telegram was to the point:

HER MAJESTY WISHES ME TO EXPRESS HER DEEP APPRECIATION FOR THE HOSPITALITY WHICH YOU AND MR. MITCHELL HAVE SO KINDLY OFFERED WHICH SHE ACCEPTS WITH PLEASURE.

To this day Mrs. Mitchell does not know how she did it. The telegram arrived Thursday night; the Queen and her army were to arrive in Tuxedo Saturday afternoon. Mrs. Mitchell's Tuxedo cottage had no linen or silver in it, the water and electric lights were turned off and winter shutters boarded all the windows. She does recall, however, her very first step—which was to wire the go-between and ask if Her Majesty preferred seclusion or if she wished to be entertained. Promptly she received an answer in the form of her second wire of the evening—one which contained a list of friends Her Majesty would be happy to see. "It was," says Mrs. Mitchell, recalling the incident, "an abbreviated little yellow edition of the *Social Register*."

Since the Mitchells' cottage was not large enough to include both the Queen's servants and the Mitchells' servants, the latter were farmed out to neighboring cottages, the Mitchells being traded, in return, extra butlers and footmen in day and night shifts. Meanwhile, the Mitchell children were dispatched to the Tuxedo Club. For the first dinner not only was there a guest list prepared to the Queen's taste but also Ruth Draper was pressed into service to give monologues and Ernest Schelling to play Chopin. By Saturday afternoon the Mitchells were ready on their doorstep—royalty at resorts must always be greeted from outside, rather than inside, one's cottage—when the Queen and party, accompanied by the sirens of police escorts, screamed up the Tuxedo hills. During the entire visit only two mishaps occurred. At the first dinner a novice butler spilled a melon of ice cream down the back of Princess Ileana—who, since the Queen's luggage did not arrive until the next day, was wearing Mrs. Mitchell's black velvet Chanel dress—and midway in the visit Master Craig Mitchell's American cocker spaniel, high-hatted by the Queen's cocker spaniel, bit Her Majesty's dog in the behind. There was also one error in protocol. This occurred at the first dinner when the Queen found herself seated at Mr. Mitchell's right; actually, of course, she should have been on his left—or, in other words, Mr. Mitchell should have been at *her* right. Evidently such discrepancies did not trouble the Queen at all, for she promised the Mitchells before leaving that when she got home her first act would be to summon the Grand Keeper of the Scrolls and instruct him to strike off, for the Mitchells, one of the most prized Rumanian medals. Furthermore, to one Tuxedo old-timer, the Queen confided, with what that gentleman described as her "infectious wink," that she had completely forgotten the matter of the dinner protocol. "Mr. Mitchell has been so royal," she said, "that I felt common."

In many ways the recent story of Tuxedo Park can be summed up in the story of the last of its great estates. Known as "Duckhollow House," a beautiful white Georgian building, directly across the lake from the club, it consists, among other things, of twenty-five air-conditioned rooms, an all-mirrored master bathroom, a movie theater, a swimming pool, a life-size granite Buddha, a boathouse, an electric motorboat and thirty thousand dollars' worth of shrubbery; the total cost was staggering even for 1937. Designed by Architect T. Markoe Robertson, this charming cottage was presented to Mr. and Mrs. Angier Biddle Duke as a wedding present by their parents, the Duke and St. George families. Following the divorce of this couple, "Duckhollow House" was sold to Mr.

and Mrs. John Astor Drayton, also of Tuxedo. When Mr. and Mrs. Drayton reached the end of their marriage too, "Duckhollow House" was again resold, but on this occasion for the first time the cottage came into ownership which, by Tuxedo standards, involved an outsider. The new owner, Nathan Berkman, a wealthy New York tax consultant, was charmed with "Duckhollow House." When, however, he went down to his boathouse and put out to sea at a fast ten knots in his forty-battery electric motorboat—since the lake is the source of the Park's drinking water all boats have to be electric—he was promptly informed by letter from the Tuxedo Park Association that since he did not belong to the Tuxedo Club, and the Tuxedo Club claimed exclusive use of the lake for its members, he could not use it.

Berkman was promptly disenchanted. He was, however, as a tax consultant, a man who knew his way around in law books; when the club threatened with an injunction, he decided to fight back. He not only traced deeds to the lake far beyond those the Tuxedo Park Association had ever heard of—one being a manuscript map made for George Washington—but he also declared that if the club sued him he was prepared to maintain that if the lake was indeed a private reservoir then it should have an eight-foot fence around it—the same height of fence, ironically enough, which surrounds Tuxedo Park and even more ironically perhaps, surrounds "Duckhollow House." Finally both the Park Association and Berkman dropped both suits and threats of suits and Berkman was once more permitted to put out to sea. "I found," he says today, above the puttering of his forty batteries, "that I had no less and no more privileges to the lake than the club itself."

Today at Tuxedo, if the situation in the lake is fraught

with peril, the situation in the club itself is even more so. In the early days so great was the prestige of being a member of the club's fifteen-man Board of Governors that these Governors cheerfully paid the deficit, which often ran as high as fifty thousand dollars a year, out of their own pockets; no statement was ever even rendered to ordinary members. But with the depression, as well as the fact that the new club was vastly more expensive than the old, this situation could no longer exist. Today's clubhouse, which is in reality Tuxedo's third—the second was partially destroyed by fire during World War II—is now supported by all manner of desperate measures, including renting out the premises to the employees of Time, Inc., for a so-called "Time Out." While such heterogeneous outsiders enjoy using the tradition-hallowed facilities, insiders have not taken kindly to the change, and even the trusted old employees of the club, men like "Chris," "Scott" and "Carter," all of whom have served more than forty years, view the present with distaste and the future with alarm. Actually "Brooks," the predecessor of these men, also viewed the past with alarm. One afternoon when the late James Henry "Silent" Smith was preparing for one of his famous parties in his large cottage up on the hill, his friend T. Suffern Tailer telephoned down to Brooks for an extra man. Brooks carefully scrutinized the Tuxedo gentlemen who were sitting reading their papers, then, in his loud English-accented voice, gave his report. "There are several people here, sir," he said, "but there is nobody you would want."

Coupled with the club's current money-raising programs has come another modernism which to elderly Tuxedoites is equally dangerous—a sort of social inflation in the electing of members. Recently Tuxedoite Charles Coulter of "Wee-Wah" cottage, following the election of a new member of whom he did not approve, announced that he would never cross the threshold of the club again, and while the club pondered this blow Coulter's motion was promptly seconded by action on the part of Mrs. E. John Heidsieck of "To the Point." Following the election of a member of whom she did not approve, Mrs. Heidsieck, daughter of the late railroad man James J. Hill, ordered the portrait of Pierre Lorillard VI removed from the club's ballroom. In her opinion Tuxedo's beloved Squire, who was her second husband and of whom she was the second wife, should not have to view, even from the wall, the sort of modern goings-on in the club he loved so well. For a while the space was blank. Then quietly one day in the place of Squire Lorillard a new portrait was hung, and all good Tuxedoites breathed a sigh of relief when it turned out to be the familiar, chop-whiskered visage of the greatest of all the Gods of the club, the Titan of Tuxedo himself, the late George F. Baker. In the opinion of old Tuxedoites no man in his life ever personified better than the great banker the virtues of the era which had passed; in their opinion, also, no man after death was so eminently fitted to warn the moderns, by the stern, disapproving look from the wall, of the wages of their sins.

It is doubtful if Tuxedo could have made a better choice. Certainly the career of Banker Baker, who lived from 1840 to 1931, was the antithesis of the modern, high-pressure, publicity-charged success story of today. Whether or not he was, as Tuxedoites claim, the "third or fourth richest man in the history of the country," he was in any case the only man in the country's history who ever made fifty million dollars in his ninetieth year; even John D. Rockefeller, Sr., Baker's latter-day golfing companion, had long since retired from money-making before reaching that age. As for the elder J. P. Morgan, the man Baker succeeded as the country's greatest money captain, Morgan met Baker at Tuxedo shortly before sailing abroad following the panic of 1907. "If anything happens to me," he said in the time-honored Morgan manner, "I want you to know that my association with you has been one of the most satisfactory parts of my life."

The feeling was mutual; in one transaction alone, involving the sale of the Jersey Central Railroad in 1901, Morgan had given Baker a check for twenty-three million dollars—up to that time the largest single check ever drawn. But even the great leaders of Baker's own day, Morgan, Rockefeller, Ford, etc., led lives which were, compared to his, an open book. Variously called the Father, the Dean, the Grand Old Man and the Sphinx of Wall Street, Baker had for his lifetime motto, "Silence Is Golden," and in the entire course of his ninety-one years he granted just one newspaper interview and made just two speeches which might even be considered public. One of these was a speech of just six words at a testimonial dinner given in his honor by the Bond Club of New York and the other, an equally brief thank-you, at the Tuxedo Club following his donation of funds for a new golf house. Although late in life he was finally prevailed upon to have his life written up, and Albert Bigelow Paine, biographer and friend of Mark Twain, was commissioned to undertake the job, at Baker's own wish just six copies of the book were ever printed—all six to this day owned and privately held by members of the Baker family.

In view of this secrecy, it is not surprising that Baker is Society's least known Horatio Alger hero; even old-time Tuxedoites know only the outlines of the Farmer-to-Four-

Hundred rise of the man who, from 1901 to his death in 1931, was Tuxedo's First Citizen and who remains today the resort's most unforgettable character. Born in Troy, New York, March 27, 1840, the son of a father who was uninterested in business and of a mother who died when he was young, Baker was sent as a child of eight to live with his grandparents on a farm in Dedham, Massachusetts. One day, hoeing corn with his Uncle Fisher, Baker observed another uncle, his Uncle John, sitting comfortably on the veranda rocking. "Uncle Fisher," the boy asked between hoes, "what does Uncle John do?" His Uncle Fisher stopped and mopped his brow. "Do, child, why nothing now. He don't have to. He lives on interest money." For a while young Baker went back to his hoeing, then suddenly he brightened. "Uncle Fisher," he said, "when I grow up I'm going to be like Uncle John and live on interest money."

Actually young Baker did not wait to grow up; the first money he ever earned was selling, for seven dollars, a load of cranberries which another boy had picked and decided were worthless. Early also Baker exhibited his passion for anonymity. At the age of eleven in a letter to his Uncle Fisher from school, he wrote: "I would write more confidentially but there is a saucy fellow looking over my shoulder and reads every word I write. The fellow hollered out you lie I have not read a word you've written, so he exposed himself nicely."

Completing his schooling at sixteen, Baker clerked for seven years in the State Banking Department at Albany, New York. With the first one hundred dollars, which he saved out of his salary of five hundred dollars a year, he bought one share of American Express stock. He also made other speculations. In between speculations he was the most earnest of clerks. Once, set to signing bank bills with no one to help him handling the sheets and taking time off only to run out to a hydrant to cool his cramped wrists, he numbered and signed 4,080 bills in four hours and twenty minutes. When the First National Bank of New York was organized July 1, 1863, he became, as paying teller, its first employee. He also bought thirty shares of stock; a few years later, liking his work, he bought the bank.

During the Civil War Baker, still under twenty-five, was often called to Washington for banking conferences with Secretary Chase. At the reception following Lincoln's second inaugural, the banker was standing close by the President who was wearily and methodically shaking hands with his well-wishers, when a pretty red-haired girl stepped up. "Mr. Lincoln," she said, "I wish you would say something to me that I will always remember." Lincoln leaned over and kissed her on top of the head. "I think," he said, "you are the prettiest girl I have seen this evening." All his life, Baker declared, he wished he could have found out what became of that girl; he never did, however. In 1869, at a time when he reckoned his fortune at an even $100,000, he married another Baker. The young lady, Florence Tucker Baker from Louisville, Kentucky, was no relation of his but a friend of his sister; her father was connected with the Treasury Department. Traveling to Europe on his honeymoon, Baker was most impressed by his first sight, in Paris, of an apartment; to Baker it represented the perfect home and he expressed the wish that New York might someday have something like it. Back in New York, during a three-week period when his wife was visiting her parents, Baker himself bought and furnished their future home at 427 Lexington Avenue.

As a resorter, Baker started slowly. He loved horses and drove a lively pair; one day he drove out to a race track. One of the bank's largest customers spotted him. "Have good luck today, cashier?" he asked. Baker never went to a race track again. In those days few people had summer homes, and summer vacations for everybody were still unheard of. A fortnight at Saratoga or Long Branch was the extent of resorting for the gay blades, and while a few extremely wealthy indulged themselves in cottages at Newport, Baker did not believe he was ready for this. The era of spas also passed him by. Once, during a week end at Lake Mahopac, some ladies approached him. "My dear Mr. Baker," said one, "how well Mrs. Baker looks. Where have you been with her?" Replied Baker: "At 427 Lexington Avenue."

In 1880 Baker bought his first and only yacht; once rather timorously he ventured in her to Bar Harbor. Inland the couple made several trips to the Berkshires. Finally, in 1884, Baker built his first resort cottage at Monmouth Beach, north of Long Branch; at the time it was the first really substantial cottage there. Baker's son George, Jr., loved the place and soon found a rowboat for sale for fifty dollars. Asking his father for the money he was promptly refused. "George," said his father, "if you can buy that boat for forty dollars, you can have it." The son, failing to make the deal, never had the rowboat; later in life he was to own a magnificent yacht and Baker, who by that time had no yacht at all, was asked to explain the situation. "My son can afford it," he said. "He has a rich father." In New Jersey, Baker also bought a farm, five miles from his cottage on Monmouth Beach because, he declared at the time, he wished his children to get some idea of farm life. Unfortunately, "Wolf Hill," as the farm was called, was well named; Baker, who said that even twenty-five dollars a year profit would have satisfied him, could not make it pay—and promptly sold it. "The man who redeemed the Jersey Central," says Albert Bigelow Paine, "could not redeem a Jersey farm."

On his trips abroad Baker became, like other Society figures of his day, interested in art. Although his collection included such items as Regnault's "Salomé" and Rodin's "The Kiss," he bought not for artistic value or personal appeal but only for intrinsic worth. "Of all my investments," he once said—and by 1900 he was officially connected with thirty-one corporations—"my art collection has shown me the largest proportionate increase of value." This was no mean statement. Some idea of the extent of the financier's wealth may be gathered from the fact that after the birth of his son, George, Jr., in 1878, it occurred to Baker that he should start an account, for the benefit of his son, of his directors' fees alone; in those days the fees were just ten dollars. In 1916, by which time Baker was a director of forty-three corporations, the fees so deposited, with the interest compounded, amounted to a piggy bank of $700,000. In 1899, when his son graduated from Harvard at the age of twenty-one, Baker gave him a separate $100,000. "I could have put the sum in a bag," he said, "and dropped it from the ferryboat and ceased to think of it by the time I got to New York. There would have been nothing problematical about that. But this was a different matter." One morning following the gift Baker was walking down Wall Street with his son. "Son," he said, "when are you going to work?" The son took one look at his father, then without a word stopped in at a cigar store and left his cane and started that very morning as a runner in the bank.

In 1901, having sold his Monmouth Beach cottage, Baker bought "Imlagh," the original Lorillard cottage at Tuxedo Park. Mrs. Baker, a woman of far more charm than her husband, fitted immediately into the resort's social pattern. Although she died in 1913, eighteen years before her husband, she was a part of Tuxedo's recognized Old Guard of the day—a group which has undoubtedly its final counterpart in today's group of Mrs. Paul Tuckerman, Mrs. Frederic Carey, Mrs. Louis Ogden, Mrs. F. Kingsbury Curtis, Mrs. Theodore Frelinghuysen and Mrs. Pierre Lorillard Barbey. For all his eminence, Baker never fitted into the pattern; following his wife's death he spent most of his evenings alone, many of them merely sitting on his cottage's wide terrace looking out over the moonlit water of the lake and listening to his stable clock with its famous Big Ben chimes. Tuxedoites across the lake enjoyed the chimes less; they reverberated over the water every quarter hour like thunder. Gruff as Baker was and often entirely derelict in the social graces, Tuxedo knew him as an almost impenetrable conversationalist—one who never talked of his business affairs to anyone save his actual business associates, and of his private affairs, never to anyone. On all sides were stories of his economy. Down at the bank, Baker ordered two different sized memo pads, and woe betide a bank officer who, using a small pad for a large note, wasted an extra page. During the panic of 1907, Baker's own son-in-law, Newport's William Goadby Loew, was forced to borrow $100,000, and inquired gently of Baker if there would be any interest involved. "There will," replied Baker. "Twenty per cent." Loew took the money, then looked at his father-in-law. "There's a hell of a lot of nepotism in this bank," he said, "isn't there?" On one occasion late in his life Baker attended a large dinner party accompanied by a young man in his office. The young man had never experienced anything like the dinner and afterward asked Baker frankly if he had made any social errors. Baker said only one—when the butler had passed the cigars the young man had said, "No thank you, I have one." "It was not only questionable manners," said Baker, "it was poor economics."

In Baker's will his charitable bequests were conspicuously modest. In his lifetime, however, the man who had never been to college gave Harvard $5,000,000, Cornell $2,000,000, Dartmouth $1,000,000 and Columbia $700,000. Although two of these bequests—Dartmouth's Baker Library and Columbia's Baker Field—later bore his name, he liked such charities to be announced when he himself was a full day out to sea on a trip to Europe. When in 1926 he gave in such a manner a bonus of a year's pay to the 148 officers and clerks of his bank—a total of $300,000—he returned to find that the clerks had written him a thank-you note. "Your wonderful career," the note read, "a record so admirably wrought that to consider is to marvel." Once as he entered the Union League Club, a member from a black leather chair suddenly, and for no apparent reason, jumped up and proposed three cheers for Mr. Baker. "I was too moved to make any reply," Baker said. "I could only bow and sit down and I left at the first opportunity. I could not get home soon enough to tell Mrs. Baker about it." At one of the two recorded speeches of his career, at the Bond Club, the full text of his remarks was, "Thank you and God bless you." At the Tuxedo Club following his gift of the golf house the text was, "God bless you and thank you." On both occasions, as indeed on several others where he was made the center of attention, he actually wept with emotion. In 1927, as the largest stockholder of the Erie Railroad, Baker was visited at his Tuxedo cottage by the fabulous young Van Sweringen brothers of Cleveland, who were interested in acquiring the road. The bankers entered his living room. "Do you work hard?" asked Baker without any preliminaries. The brothers, who never took a vacation, nodded. "Do you sleep well?" Again the brothers, who, until the crash of their empire at least, were among Wall Street's soundest sleepers, were able to answer yes. "Very well, then," said Baker, concluding the interview, "you may have the stock."

Only once in his life did Baker ever make a public appearance—and this he was forced to do. The occasion was his appearance at the famous Pujo Committee "Money Trust" Hearings in Washington in the winter of 1912-13. At these hearings, in which the Government was attempting to prove that Big Business was dangerously overconcentrated in the hands of a few men, it was the elder Morgan, who was to die within the year, who was the central figure. But it was Baker, with his mutton-chop beard, his square-cut stiff hat and his umbrella, who best symbolized the era which, with Morgan's death, he was to lead until his own death. It was also Baker who provided the reply for which the government lawyer Samuel Untermyer had sought in vain from Morgan. Untermyer, pressing Baker to admit the potential danger involved in the concentration of wealth, finally asked the banker point-blank if he thought the country was in "a comfortable situation." For once Baker's reply was more than one word. "Not entirely," he said. "The spectators," said the New York *Tribune*, "sat back with a sigh."

In 1910 Baker, who was a lifelong Unitarian, took up for the first time smoking, drinking cocktails and golf. Stories of his latter-day links efforts are still part of Tuxedo conversations; among other things if Baker wished a round before dinner, the train stopped right at the first tee of the golf course. Once playing in the pouring rain with Edward E.

Loomis, president of the Lehigh Valley Railroad and a man thirty years younger than he, Baker insisted on continuing a tied match. "Mr. Baker," gasped Mr. Loomis, "you are a wonder for a man of your age." Baker teed up his ball. "The difference between you and me," he said, "is that I never began to dissipate until I was seventy." But even at golf the banker could not forget himself entirely. On losing a ball he would become so distressed that he would hunt for it with his caddy as long as there was even a remote hope of finding it. Nor were tees items to be taken lightly. One of the banker's golfing companions, a Tuxedo "little brother of the rich," made a practice of surreptitiously placing broken tees where Baker would find them; the disappointment on Baker's face on picking up one of these tees was, according to this "little brother," something to see. To players following Baker around the course, the Titan's game, a severe point of which was to let no one else through, was little pleasure indeed. One Saturday afternoon when the course was crowded and Baker, at eighty-five, was being slowly pushed up a hill by the strong arm of his caddy, a fellow Tuxedoite cupped his hand in desperation. "Mr. Baker," he called out, "I've got to catch a train." Then, dropping his hand, he added, "Monday morning."

The various attempts to interview Baker during his long career are a story in themselves. Baker's secretary, at the office of the First National Bank, made it a regular practice to tell whoever wished to interview the banker the number of years since 1863, a year in which, as assistant military secretary to the Governor of New York, Baker had been forced to give a brief public announcement to a reporter on the subject of the Civil War. Each year following, the secretary would take note of the new year and add sternly, "This is the passing of one more year since Mr. Baker has spoken." Not even one word would the Sphinx speak, although every sort of dodge was attempted. One reporter, seizing an opportunity, asked him what time it was. "Mr. Baker," he reported, "suspecting a trick, merely stared at me."

In August, 1923, a young lady from the New York *World*, Georgette Carneal, attempted a new approach. Journeying out to Tuxedo Park, she attempted to beard the lion in his den. Stopped by the guard at the Tuxedo Gate, who warned her that her mission was hopeless, she nonetheless called Baker's cottage. The housekeeper promptly informed her that an employee had once been discharged because he admitted a reporter; she added that Mr. Baker was very fond of a very fierce police dog who also disliked reporters. Miss Carneal still persisted. Finally the housekeeper brought the banker himself to the telephone. "I haven't been interviewed for sixty years," said Baker, "and I'd rather support you for life than talk to you for a minute." Miss Carneal hesitated, then said if Baker would only talk to her that she could support herself; the managing editor of the *World* had promised her a permanent job if she procured the interview. It was Baker's turn to hesitate. "Come into the bank tomorrow," he said.

The next day Miss Carneal entered the First National Bank at 2 Wall Street. Up one flight of stairs she walked—past a guard who wore no military trappings, past tellers' cages which dated to Civil War days, and past the other officers of the bank, all of whom worked behind quaint roll-topped desks amid surroundings which were older than any one of them. Once admitted to Baker's private sanctum, Miss Carneal described the whole effect of his office as one of "dignified quietude"; Baker himself, on first impression, reminded her of her mental picture of George Eliot's Silas Marner. "I don't talk, you know," he told her, opening the interview, "because silence is the secret of success. Silence spells financial happiness."

"Is financial happiness real happiness?"

"Yes, of course," replied Baker. Then in one brief paragraph he gave, for the first and only time in his life, his own story of his life:

> I did nothing unusual when I began. My first job that I choose to call a job was in a small bank at Albany. I was a very quiet worker and that served to distinguish me. It was there I made and invested my first thousand dollars. It was with this money that I bought the First National Bank. But I don't remember anything about that. You see, I have a very poor memory.

Miss Carneal also procured one other brief statement:

> Everything is all right. The country is on the road to prosperity, perhaps the greatest prosperity that any country ever attained. But I shouldn't be talking about it. Business men of America should reduce their talk at least two-thirds. Everyone should reduce his talk. There is rarely ever a good reason for anybody to talk. Silence—it uses up much less energy.
>
> There—you have it. Those are the first words I've spoken to a newspaper since 1865. There! I've broken my record! Tell the others they needn't come in. And get out!

During the boom 1920's Tuxedo joined with the entire country in each day trying to figure the result of the bull market on Baker's personal fortune. When, for example, the First National Bank stock, of which it was common knowledge in the Park that Baker owned some 25,000 shares, touched $8,500 a share, they quickly multiplied it out and found Baker worth \$212,500,000 in that stock alone; they knew that besides he was also the largest single stockholder in such companies as American Telephone and U.S. Steel. Few of Baker's friends at Tuxedo actually banked with him. The story was that it took \$100,000 to open an account and even today, since the bank is primarily a banker's bank—one for other banks and corporations—the average individual bank balance is something over \$300,000. On the golf course or in the train, no one could get an individual market tip from Baker; at the same time his general market slogans were common currency. One, apparently for a rising market and also credited to J. P. Morgan, was, "Never sell America short"; another, for a falling market, "When the house is on fire, the good girls have to get out as well as the bad ones." Although in 1929 97 per cent of Baker's total fortune was in common stocks, he had but one complaint when the market broke. Sick in bed, he begged to be allowed to go downtown. "This is my ninth panic," he protested. "I have made money in every one of them." The following year, true to his word, Baker made, by the estimate of *Fortune* magazine, fifty million dollars at a time when he was ninety years old.

In the last two years of his life, though suffering from diabetes, Baker attended no less than 150 directors' meetings, his favorites being those of companies on the so-called "tontine" system. At these meetings the directors present divide the fees of directors absent; Baker, characteristically, especially enjoyed such meetings in inclement weather. Unfortunately they proved the death of him. In the last week of his life he attended four directors' meetings. At the final one, the Consolidated Gas Company, which was held on a bad day, he caught the cold which led to the pneumonia from which two days later, on May 2, 1931, he died.

The banker's funeral was typical of his life. The most important in the history of Tuxedo Park, it was limited to three hundred guests and held in the reception room of his cottage. The immediate family remained apart in a small parlor opening in one side of the reception room, while the congregation itself was chiefly made up of special funeral delegations from the First National Bank, J. P. Morgan and Company, Harvard, Columbia and Cornell. The services were conducted by the pastor of New York's All Souls Unitarian Church, of which Baker had been for fifty years a trustee and to which he had recently given $100,000. In New York, flags on all the financial institutions flew at half-mast. Two special trains operated between Jersey City and Tuxedo and a third special train carried the flowers. To this third train, the Erie Railroad attached as its special tribute Observation Car 901, the famous Tuxedo Club Car; a wreath marked Seat Number 7, which had long been permanently reserved for Baker. At Baker's own wish there was no music in the service and only during the prayer was the banker mentioned at all. He was, said the pastor, "an example of courage and a memorial of virtue not only to the young men but to the whole nation." After the services all the guests were invited to a luncheon at the Tuxedo Club.

If Gresham's Law of Resorts is that bad millionaires drive good millionaires out of circulation, Newton's Law is that for every fashionable resort, there is, close by, another less fashionable which has grown up as a reaction. Thus for every Bar Harbor there is a Northeast Harbor, for every White Sulphur a Hot Springs, for every Lenox a Stockbridge and for every Southampton an East Hampton. In general, these latter resorts have been for generations defensively recommended by their adherents by such a line as, "Oh, you don't want to go *there*"meaning Bar Harbor (or White Sulphur, Lenox or Southampton)—"you want to come *here*"—meaning Northeast Harbor (or Hot Springs, Stockbridge or East Hampton). The recommendee, who generally does want to go where he said he did, is then in for a lengthy discussion of his initial choice being too fashionable and too formal, full of awful people and a terrible place for children, the lesser resort, of course, being invariably upheld as, in comparison, a paragon of all the resort virtues—completely unspoiled and informal, full of lovely people, a family place perfect for all ages, etc.

In these latter years when the major resorts have suffered far worse than the minor as a result of having become overextended in the boom 1920's the tail has come in many instances to wag the dog; the social distinction, however, remains almost as sharp as it was in the old days. Even Stockbridge's Joseph Choate, who originally settled in so-called "wicked" Lenox and then moved to "virtuous" Stockbridge, was not immune to the struggle. "In Lenox," he said, "people are estimated. In Stockbridge they are esteemed." In the time-honored war between "wicked" Bar Harbor and "virtuous" Northeast Harbor, there is even the added question of a third resort, Seal Harbor, right in the middle. Since this resort has Rockefellers and Fords as well as simple virtues, it is difficult to classify in the struggle, particularly so because the Seal Harbor Club has curious social distinctions of its own; nurses, for example, may swim in Seal's swimming pool, governesses may not. "You might say," says Bar Harbor's Gretchen Finletter helpfully, "that Seal Harbor is, like Switzerland, neutral."

The case of East Hampton vs. Southampton is a particularly interesting battle. This too is complicated by the presence of a third resort—Westhampton. As far back as 1868 East Hampton is mentioned by at least one guidebook as "a place where the blasé tourist won't find all the parvenus." Today Pan American's Juan Trippe and other financial luminaries of East Hampton have given rise to a saying that Southampton is for the sporting rich, Westhampton the nearly rich and East Hampton the really rich. Nonetheless, East Hamptonites, who pride themselves on getting along with just one club, the Maidstone, and on their traditional simplicity, still vehemently scorn their more fashionable neighbors; Southamptonites, on their part, return this scorn with interest. Southampton, they say, is for presidents, East Hampton for mere vice-presidents. "Why, do you know," says Mrs. George Pynchon, "in East Hampton they actually *eat* at seven?"

To the Bostonians, characteristically, goes first credit for pioneering the search for simplicity in resorts; they were particularly vigilant in maintaining this simplicity at such Maine resorts as Dark Harbor, York Harbor, Prout's Neck and North Haven. Dark Harbor, or Islesboro, was not only the final resort to give in to the automobile but it was also the last to go formal; there is a saying at the resort, which has been credited to Bostonian Dudley Howe, that "Dark Harbor never dressed for dinner until the Dillons came." At North Haven, as a bulwark against the formidable Lamonts and Morrows on the island, Boston Cabots even set up their own resort-within-a-resort. Here, in "Cabotville," as it is affectionately called, four Cabot families of various generations all crowd themselves into Spartan-simple cottages and all use one telephone in a farmhouse more than a mile away. Finally, in Naushon, an island off Wood's Hole, on the south end of Cape Cod, Boston has one resort which is famous for being not only all Bostonian but all Forbeses; just one Boston family, the Forbes, with its many branches, vacations there. Among other distinctions, the Forbes' retreat of Naushon is especially remarkable as being the outstanding example of Old Guard Society's habit of being careful with electricity. This habit goes back to the social saying that it is possible to tell how long a person has had money by how quickly, on leaving a deserted room, he turns out the lights behind him. If he has had money in his family since the days of gas, or at least since the days when electricity was expensive, he will turn out the lights immediately; if his money is brand new, he will not turn them out at all. At Naushon, though the Forbes' servants have electric lights in the back part of the island's "Mansion House," the front part of the house, by order of Forbes' patriarch, Cameron Forbes, has candles only.

The fact that Dark Harbor, North Haven and Naushon all are islands is not without significance. Although large islands like Newport, Mount Desert and Palm Beach have been for generations the centers of resort fashion, small islands, particularly those difficult to reach, have always played a large role in the fulfillment of Newton's Law of Resort Reaction or the search for social simplicity. Indeed, from the Thousand Islands up in the St. Lawrence River on the Canadian border—actually there are 1,700 of these—to the hundreds of Shangri-las off Nassau, the entire history of resorts could be written in the desire for resorters to own their own island. Failing outright ownership, resorters have established a distinct trend to make their jointly owned islands at least as private as possible. In many ways the two sturdiest examples of this trend are Fishers Island, off New London, and Jupiter Island, or Hobe Sound, twenty-five miles north of Palm Beach.

In resort history Fishers belongs in the Newport reaction category, while Hobe Sound is a reaction against Palm Beach; nonetheless, both of these islands, separated as they are geographically, are today populated by so many of the same people that they can almost be considered together. At Fishers, for example, the Island Country Club is staffed with the same ménage that operates the Jupiter Island Club at Hobe Sound. Furthermore, at either of these resorts, when the resorters themselves are visible it is immediately apparent that, despite small cottages, dirt roads and other misleading externals, the majority of these resorters are so extremely well off that nobody tries to impress anybody with money; instead they impress each other with their homey qualities. This keeping down to the Joneses, in such select social areas where there are no Joneses to keep down to, is no easy task, but both islands do their level best. Men rarely dress for dinner and women go in heavily for the dirndl and the peasant motif. For more formal attire all ladies of Fishers and Hobe wear what amounts to a uniform—a well-cut shantung or linen dress which is topped off by a cashmere cardigan sweater. The latter, quietly but healthily jeweled, is always worn casually over one's shoulders; a lady putting her arms actually in her cardigan is socially suspect. At both these islands the resort set of Greenwich, Connecticut, many of whom winter at Hobe and summer at Fishers, may be said to set the standards of activity. "We do everything we do in Greenwich," explains Mrs. Robert Noble of the Life Saver fortune, "but faster." If the standards of activity of these islands are local, the social significance of Hobe and Fishers, in the opinion of their adherents, is national in scope. Mrs.

"Bud" Adams, wife of a popular realtor who operates at both islands, expresses this significance with some finality.

"Everyone knows," she says, "that Fishers Island is the last stand in the North, and Hobe Sound is the last stand in the South."

One reason, despite Mrs. Adams, that everyone does not know about Fishers Island and Hobe Sound is that these islands do not wish to be known; in fact, their anonymity has been largely responsible for making them perhaps the most formidable social resorts still in existence. At Fishers, a seven-mile hook-shaped island which belongs to New York state but which is only a forty-minute ferry-boat ride from New London, Connecticut, simplicity is carried to the extreme. For one thing no outsider ever knows when the ferries run or exactly where in New London they run from; for another, Fishers is spelled without even an apostrophe. More important, though the island has a few small stores and one small movie theater, it has often gone long periods without a single doctor on the island and still today does not even boast a drug store. Even the movie theater is no concession to modern night life; it was formerly the property of Fishers' army post, and there is always a question each summer of whether or not it will be running. Fishers' financial anonymity is carried even further. "We don't have what you might call the wrong element of the rich," says Henry L. Ferguson, whose family once owned the entire island. "We have people with twenty million dollars but you wouldn't know it."

Fishers' First Citizen, who fits this definition with some to spare, is the modest, public-spirited, ex-Newporter John Nicholas Brown. As far back as May, 1900, at a time when he was three months old, Brown held the title of the world's richest baby. At that time his father, who had no other children, and his uncle, who was childless, had both died within a few months of each other and had left him sole heir to two multimillion dollar fortunes. At "Harbour Court," Newport, Brown got his first taste of resort life in a dark, Victorian feudal castle. He was literally tied to his governess—bound, from her wrist to his, by a blue silk cord—and, surrounded by guards, was permitted only one regular playmate, a friend named "Akerbodie" whom he had made up. As a reaction from this, Brown and his wife, the former Anne Kinsolving, of one of Fishers' most prominent families, lead a very different kind of life on their island. Their cottage, designed by the California architect Richard Neutra, is Fishers' showplace—an almost entirely glass house which perches conspicuously on the crest of the island. Kleig-lighted and equipped with photoelectric cells, the cottage has much of its furniture built in to the floor, has several rooms which may be transformed from indoor to outdoor merely by pressing buttons, has a soda fountain in the rumpus room, twin bathtubs in the master bathroom and has all twenty-four rooms, including the servants' rooms, piped for Bach and Brahms. The name of the cottage is "Windshield," and when, during the 1938 hurricane, the entire top story of the cottage blew away, Mrs. Brown was forced to take refuge on the second floor under the butler's bed. More recently, after rebuilding their cottage, the Browns, in a typical Fishers Island economy wave, refused to protect their view by buying a neighboring hill and promptly saw a new cottage, owned by the Lammot du Ponts, built practically on top of them. Fisherites call this cottage "Windshield Wiper." In the summer of 1952 the Browns gave up their cottage altogether and rented it to Palm Beach's

Consuelo Vanderbilt Balsan; they themselves rented one of Fishers' beloved Hay Harbor cottages. Nonetheless, in the true spirit of resort reaction, the Browns remain steadfastly pro-Fishers and anti-Newport. "John just goes to Newport now," says Mrs. Brown, "in the off season."

Equally pro-Fishers are two newcomers to the resort, the much-traveled John Hay, or "Jock," Whitneys, who recently built the island's second most honored showplace. Described by Fishers' natives as looking, from the roadside, like a Coca-Cola factory, the cottage was designed by Erard Matthiessen and is, from the shore side, one of the few modern houses which manage to blend in with the landscape. Fishers' simplicity notwithstanding, the Whitneys have a seaplane ramp at their back door and all manner of modern luxuries throughout the cottage proper. At the same time, Mrs. Whitney, the former Mrs. James Roosevelt and Betsy Cushing, yields to no one in her love of the island. "It's just heavenly," she says. "Take tonight for example. The children are all going out with blankets to lie on the road and look at the stars."

In Fishers' early 1900's the island's most noted cottage was built by the late Garrett Linderman, coal-mine operator and banker of Bethlehem, Pennsylvania. Linderman's idea was to build the indestructible resort cottage, and the foundations of his island fortress alone would have served a forty-story skyscraper. Almost entirely built of solid mahogany, the cottage boasted half a hundred rooms and picture windows which were made of glass bent in Belgium. Outside there was an artificially tiled garden with a drainage system which would have done credit to a small town. Neither the first nor the last resorter to get in deeper and deeper in the matter of cottage building, Linderman went on spending and spending. Finally, just when his cottage was completed and he was ready to move in, he was found guilty of embezzling $53,000 from the estate of his cousin. In August, 1908, instead of moving in style into his indestructible million-dollar island fortress at Fishers, Linderman moved, without style, to jail; for his first few days he shared a cell with a common pickpocket. In the World War I era Linderman's cottage was bought by New York's esteemed Madame Alma Gluck. Madame Gluck particularly desired to fit into the resort's early-day search for simplicity and ordered a horse brought over from the mainland; she also ordered a tailor-made harness and a smart lemon-yellow patent leather trap. Unfortunately Fishers was ill-equipped to handle the last of the horse-and-buggy era, and the horse's fodder, like the horse, had to be imported from the mainland. When the horse arrived, she proved to be an enormous Percheron named "Lizzie." "Lizzie's feet," recalls Mrs. Gluck's daughter Marcia Davenport, "were the size of dinner plates and when you got behind her in the trap you couldn't see anything. But Mother said it didn't matter. Lizzie only cost thirty-five dollars. And we had only two choices. Either to drive in a Cadillac with a chauffeur or drive Lizzie. Mother always drove Lizzie. Even in those days Fishers was full of the kind of people who were so rich that nobody ever heard of them. They weren't even chic."

In the old days also Fishers boasted such large hotels as the Munnatawket, the Mononotto and the Mansion House. Following World War II, however, cottage-owning Fisherites gleefully applauded the tearing down of the last of these, the Mansion House, and today there is no resort hotel on the entire island; unless an outsider is fortunate enough to be put up at the Fishers Island Country Club, he is obliged to take the night ferry back to New London. Although Pittsburghers, Wilmingtonians and Baltimoreans have been known to invade the island with some success—at one time there was even a saying that no one could get on at Fishers unless he could "buck Baltimore"—today getting on at Fishers is a question of bucking Manhattan, Long Island and Greenwich. And a newcomer can have hard sledding indeed. Some years ago a family of means from Bedford, New York, rented a cottage on the island for the summer and each afternoon around six o'clock, hopefully ran up a flag with a cocktail glass on it; nobody, however, came. At the end of the summer the newcomers folded up the flag and left—never to return.

Even more remarkable was the arrival off Fishers, during the summer of 1946, of Baron Hans de Meiss-Teuffen of Zurich, Switzerland; the Baron, who had sailed all alone from Casablanca in a thirty-two-foot yawl, had just completed the fastest East-West solo sailing passage ever made—a trip of fifty-eight days. Since he could not see water on the other side of Fishers and since his chart did not show Fishers at all, the Baron thought he had hit New London. Anchoring his boat, he quickly paddled ashore in an inflatable rubber dinghy, still dressed in his sailing uniform—a one-piece Annette Kellerman bathing suit with a Swiss emblem on it. Unfortunately he had not only hit Fishers Island instead of New London, he had also hit the island at its most forbidding spot, the Club Beach, and at its most forbidding possible time—the fashionable bathing hour of high noon. There was no hero's welcome for the strange-looking man in his strange-looking bathing suit; in fact there was no welcome at all. No one spoke to him. Finally, after what seemed to the Baron almost as long a time as he had been at sea, a Swiss governess, moving over to guard her children from the intruder, recognized the emblem on the bathing suit. Engaging him in conversation she confirmed the fact that he was in reality a Baron and promptly spread the good word. Immediately Fisherites crowded around and led by Greenwich's Mrs. J. William Moore Robbins, gave the Baron a royal welcome. "She said," says the Baron today with a wry smile, "that glad she was that I had that day come because it happened she was an extra man short for lunch."

If Fishers is careful with outsiders, it nonetheless promotes a way of resort life which is entirely satisfactory to its insiders. "We're very independent here," says Mrs. E. C. Houghton of "Money Pond," whose land mercifully encloses one of Captain Kidd's buried treasures. "It's my inflation hedge," she says. "All I need now is a dredge." Mrs. Francis K. Kernan is impressed with the life of Fishers' children. "At what other resort," she asks, "could you see a mixed foursome of nine-year-olds on a golf course on a Saturday? You'd certainly never see that at that 'Shinnycook'—or whatever they call it—at Southampton." Mrs. John Gaston, of the island's prominent Talbot family, is proud of Fishers in another way. "They have very little scandal here," she says. "People are out-of-doors so much."

This is no idle boast. Even the island's so-called "dirndl set," which consists of such attractive divorcees as Mrs. Cushing Emmet and Mrs. E. Bliss Parkinson and regularly entertains such perennially eligible bachelors as Washington's Joseph Alsop, never causes the kind of gossip which is standard dinner-table conversation at other resorts, and Fishers' so-called "red hats," a clubby group of ladies who meet together at regular intervals all winter, are primarily suburban rather than resorty in tone. Fishers' Du Ponts, of whom there are families of Reynolds and Pierre III, as well as two families of Lammot, are probably the resort's best example of simplicity. At first the Du Ponts all rented small cottages at Hay Harbor. Then, even after they had branched out and bought large cottages of their own, they still went back, on several occasions, to their Hay Harbor rentals, meanwhile subletting their own cottages. Only once have these distinguished Wilmingtonians, who ask no indulgence save that their name be accented on the large "Pont" rather than the small "du," stepped out of line. This occurred two years ago when the Reynolds du Ponts of "Grey Gulls" gave a so-called "Fireworks and Whisky" party on the Fourth of July. Although invitations had been issued, Fishers Island style, on penny postcards, and most of the display was quiet enough to suit Fishers simplicity, the final burst proved too elaborate for the taste of at least one conservative. "My God," she exclaimed, in the rockets' red glare, "there goes next month's dividend!" The next year the Du Ponts, severely chastened, gave a "bottle party"—all guests being invited to bring their own refreshments.

At Fishers' most elaborate post-World War II party not only the Du Ponts but all islanders learned perhaps their most severe lesson. This party, which occurred during the summer of 1948, was a fancy-dress circus ball, and for once Fisherites went all out. There was a portable dance floor out on the lawn, the Du Ponts came as elephants and Pittsburgh's James Hillman came as a seal-trainer; the three attractive Hillman daughters, dressed in tight black satin, rolled around on the dance floor as trained seals. Unfortunately, during a lull in the festivities when Mrs. Erard Matthiessen, wife of the architect of many of Fishers' cottages, was in the bar, she noted the loss of a valuable diamond and emerald bracelet. Promptly she went out and notified the orchestra leader of her predicament. The predicament was worse than Mrs. Matthiessen thought. In the time she had been off the floor, a lady had found the bracelet and had given it to the orchestra leader; meanwhile, unknown to Mrs. Matthiessen, the orchestra leader had stopped the music and announced the finding of the bracelet—only to have the bracelet promptly claimed by someone else. To this day Fisherites have never been able to find out who claimed Mrs. Matthiessen's bracelet, nor has the island ever had another fancy dress affair. The hostess of the ill-fated ball puts the matter severely. "We learned our lesson," she said. "Those masked balls were all very well in the days when everybody knew everybody, but they're very dangerous nowadays."

Today, when Fisherites pay up to two hundred dollars for one month's supply of electricity, stories of the old days have unusual charm. Even in the boom 1920's, all the lights on the north end of the island began blinking at quarter of twelve. The lights went out completely at midnight and Fisherites were thus given just fifteen minutes to get to bed; if out of their own cottages, just fifteen minutes both to get home and get to bed. In this era, also, Fishers was actually a tight little island. During prohibition in one winter season the island experienced no less than three rum-running wrecks in a row. Before the close-following revenue agents arrived, Fishers' natives stowed away hundreds of cases of Vat 69, Haig and Haig, etc., in such hideaways as asparagus beds; what they couldn't stow they attempted to imbibe. Ever since that time Fishers' natives have been known beyond all resort natives for their liquor capacity, perhaps the best example of this being the stock answer of Will Sinclair, Fishers' hunting-dog expert, as to whether or not he would like a drink. "The only time I ever said 'no' to that," says Sinclair, "was once when I misunderstood the question."

During the summer, of course, in the time-honored manner of resorters, Fisherites take stern care of native morality —if not in the specific matter of drinking, at least in the matter of reading. The little island library, which is run by a Library Board of both summer and year-round residents, has perhaps as strict a code as exists anywhere in the country. The general policy of this library is to try out a book of uncertain morality on a member of the Library Committee; then, judging by that opinion, the Library decides whether or not to make the book available to its general readers. "We have *Forever Amber*," says the librarian quietly, "but no one knows that we have." The case of *How Green Was My Valley* presented a particularly knotty problem, all but four pages of the book being judged suitable for both summer and winter readers. Finally a compromise was effected. Back on the Fishers' shelves went *How Green*—without, however, the offending four pages; they were simply torn out.

Like other resorts, Fishers has seen great changes. The most recent of these was the sale of the Fishers Island Country Club to the Remington Rand Company, which now operates it as a training school for its employes in the winter and then turns it back to the members for a club in the summer. This is the sort of change, however, which Fishers, chary of becoming as financially overextended as the other great resorts, has been able to take in stride. Only on the matter of the island's becoming too popular do Fisherites take a firm stand. "We don't mind it getting crowded," says Mrs. Leslie Allen, a longtime Fishers resorter, "if only it's all our crowd." Even failing this, Fisherites are likely to give a sturdy account of themselves—as witness the story of Baltimore's late Rev. Arthur B. Kinsolving. The father of New York's rector of St. James and Fishers' present summer rector, Rev. Kinsolving, like his son, was a staunch Episcopalian; despite this, he lived to see his daughter marry a man of Jewish faith and his own wife embrace Catholicism. Asked in his last years if he minded the arrangement, Kinsolving replied he did not. "I feel," he said, "that I am the only link between Abraham and the Pope."

In the final analysis, the quality of Fishers as a resort comes down to the fact, in the minds of its devotees, that it is an island. Old-time Fisherites point out that even the Indians once used the island as a summer resort and though no one knows the standards of Society they maintained, Fisherites are convinced they must have been high. Mrs. Kernan is a lady who describes herself as a refugee from both Watch Hill and Southampton. "Being on an island is everything," she says. "It's that little jump over the water that makes all the difference." Greenwich's Mrs. Grant G. Simmons, of the bed and mattress fortune, is perhaps the resort's most devoted island worshiper. "Here," she says, "I feel I am growing a piece of soul." Mrs. Simmons' cottage-castle "Whitecaps"—one which is built medieval style completely surrounding a lawn in the middle—stands on the east end of Fishers and is not only the island's largest residence but has the most remarkable view. "On a clear day I could see the people on Block Island drinking martinis," she says, "if they drink martinis on Block Island. They used to, you know. Block Island used to be very fashionable." In keeping with her position as Fishers' leading island-worshiper, Mrs. Simmons has, in contrast to lesser resorters, not only named her cottage but also poemed it. Cast in bronze on the gatepost of "Whitecaps" are four lines:

Where the Isle to the Eastward points sharper
And her green floor glitters with fire
The Sea has the Sun for a Harper
And the Sun has the Sea for a lyre.

This poem was written by Mrs. Simmons' husband, but inside "Whitecaps," hung on the wall at the foot of a circular staircase, Mrs. Simmons has another poem, which was written in 1929 by the late Rachel Field, author of *All This and Heaven Too.* Originally composed in honor of Sutton's Island near Northeast Harbor in Maine, the Simmonses feel that it expresses better than any other poem the feeling of all good resort islanders:

If once you have slept on an island
You'll never be quite the same;
You may look as you looked the day before
And go by the same old name.
You may hustle about in street and shop,
You may sit at home and sew,
But you'll see blue water and wheeling gulls
Wherever your feet may go.

You may chat with the neighbors of this and that
And close to the fire keep,
But you'll hear ship whistle and lighthouse bell
And tides beat through your sleep.
And you won't know why and you can't say how
Such change upon you came,
But once you have slept on an island
You'll never be quite the same!

Whether or not Fishers Island is specifically a reaction against Newport, its southern counterpart, Hobe Sound, or Jupiter Island, is specifically a reaction against Palm Beach and is only a forty-five-minute drive from it. A banana-shaped island, thirteen miles long, varying in width from a mile to twenty-five feet, between the Atlantic Ocean and Florida's Inland Waterway, Hobe has had a varied history. In early days the island was owned by a Britisher who tried to raise pineapples on it. In more recent times Hobe passed through a Florida boom period in which it was promoted by such come-on names as "Olympia Beach" and "Picture City." But when in 1933 the Hobe Sound Company, its present owners, acquired the property, all promotion ceased and Hobe became not only a social island but also the most publicity shy of all resorts. When *Life* magazine recently expressed interest in Hobe Sounders giving a party for the magazine to go to, the offer was summarily rejected. "The vote," says the manageress of the Jupiter Island Club, emphasizing her words, "was *u*nanimous." Even more recently, Hobe Sounders petitioned Florida officials to get Route 1-A off Jupiter Island entirely. Privately, of course, Hobe Sounders cherish stories of their public modesty—in particular one which occurred several years ago when a Jupiter Island Club *grande dame,* about to disembark from the train at what is still the flagstop of Hobe Sound, saw a fellow passenger turn to the porter. "What is this Hobe Sound?" the man asked. "I've never even heard of it." The porter, replete with the luggage of the *grande dame,* drew himself up. "Mister," he said, "it's a small stop, but it sure is snappy!"

"Snappy" is not the word the average sight-seer would use for Hobe Sound. At first impression it is, like Fishers, extremely unprepossessing. The vegetation is slightly greener than it is in the territory around Palm Beach and there are more trees; nonetheless, in sharp contrast to Palm Beach, Hobe Sound's large cottages seem almost purposely hidden, there are no visible private swimming pools—actually there are only a handful at the whole resort—and what passes for the "town" has, in the same manner as Fishers, not even a drug store. There is the Jupiter Island Club where people stay and the Beach Club where people swim but there is no hotel and there are no natives. There is a Yacht Club but no dock, a Hunt Club but no horses, a Skeet Club but no pigeons and a Golf Club but no place to get a drink. The whole area has a temporary and even a lost look—a little like the Hobe Sounders themselves who look perhaps most typical gingerly picking their way home from late dinner parties, with flashlight beams to guide their steps between the rattlesnakes.

The first impression, however, is extremely inaccurate. Hobe Sound is simple in outward appearance only because it wants to be. It is the northernmost point of Florida's so-called "Gold Coast" and as this Gold Coast begins with Miami and moves north it becomes progressively less garish until, after the burst at Palm Beach, it reaches the height of resort reaction at Hobe. Here, hidden in the wilds as carefully as the rattlesnakes, are a hundred-odd havens of the harried rich—all living in million-dollar simplicity in an area which is not only all club but also the only club in the country which refuses to exchange membership cards with any other.

In season, January to April, Hobe Sound is a community of some two hundred, including just four types of resort citizens—those who own their own cottages, those who rent club cottages, those who, as members, stay at the club, and those who stay at the club as guests; not even a man who owns his own cottage, however, can sell this cottage until the buyer has been accepted by the Jupiter Island Club. There are big frogs from big puddles and big frogs from little puddles but there are no little frogs from any kind of puddles. There are Pryors from Greenwich, Whitneys from Long Island, Fords from Detroit, Armours from Chicago, Strawbridges from Philadelphia, Ayers from Cleveland and Bullocks from Cincinnati—there are the Worthington Scrantons from Scranton, Pa., two families of Bassetts from Bassett, Va., and the Thomas B. Stanleys from Stanleytown, Va.—but there are no Smiths and no Joneses. Industrialists like Mt. Kisco's Carll Tucker, Wilmington's Walter S. Carpenter and Pittsburgh's Ernest T. Weir mingle with eminent politicos like Long Island's Robert Lovett and Averell Harriman, who in turn are at least on a bowing basis with *grandes dames* like New York's Mrs. William S. Barstow and grandees like His Eminence Samuel Cardinal Stritch from Mundelein, Illinois. Even in the matter of royalty Hobe Sound refuses to bow to any other resort. If, for example, Palm Beach has the Duke of Windsor and the Duchess, the former Mrs. Warfield Simpson, Hobe has the Marquis of Milford-Haven and the Marchioness, the former Mrs. William Simpson. Not the least remarkable part of Hobe Sound are the cottages themselves. Despite lanai porches, coquina-paved patios, manicured lawns and, for those who live on the water, incredibly expensive sea walls, these cottages not only contain what is undoubtedly the most curious collection of the hidden rich to be found anywhere in the country today but they also bear the most curious collection of last resort names—"Guestproof," "Ditty Box," "Tackle Box," "Moon and Sixpence," "South Moon Under," "Pieces of Eight," "At Long Last," "Lirala," and, inevitably, a "Folie du Bois" owned by Philadelphia's Henry C. du Bois.

As at Fishers, there is one movie theater at Hobe—the Tangerine Theatre—but that is the extent of night life.

There is the so-called Island School which has teachers but no regular classes; lessons are merely sent down from whatever northern school—up to the seventh grade—the child is attending and the child is kept up on a sort of correspondence school basis. The search for simplicity at the resort is particularly evident in the matter of bicycling. All Hobers do a certain amount of this and some ride bicycles everywhere. Simplicity also extends to yachting. There are yachts anchored off the island which would compare favorably, in social if not financial displacement, with any to be found at Palm Beach, but visitors are much more likely to be shown the island's beloved fleet of sixteen-foot sailboats—the so-called "Wood Pussies."

Above all, Hobe Sound prides itself on informality; there are no Garden Clubs, lectures or indignation meetings of any sort and a Club dinner dance Thursday night is the only formal entertainment. At this, according to Detroit's Mrs. Ernest Kanzler, a sister of Edsel Ford, "You dress for dinner but you do not put on a diamond tiara." Any other night in the week a Hobe Sounder who dresses may have to face West Orange's George W. Merck of the Merck Chemical Company; Merck has a standing promise that if he sees a stiff shirt on anyone, he will tear it off. It was Merck also who pioneered the recent Hobe movement to have a special Beach Club hamburger stand, at which, in contrast to the main lunch area, bathing suits might be worn. Furthermore, if Hobe Sounders are publicity-shy, they are also extremely immune to being name-impressed. Some years ago Gary Cooper arrived at the Beach Club at the cocktail hour before lunch; all the seats were taken and Cooper drank his martini sitting on the steps. "I remember it lividly," says Chicago's Mrs. Valentine Bartlett, the resort's favorite Mrs. Malaprop, while Mrs. Averell Harriman, who named a long-haired dachshund after the actor, told a friend, "Cooper loved it. Nobody paid any attention to him at all." Unfortunately Hobe realtors do not share the resort's passion for anonymity. When a friend sent a postcard to the dachshund as a joke, addressed "Mr. Gary Cooper, % The Harrimans," the arrival of the card was immediately followed by the arrival of a realtor. He wished to see Mr. Cooper. "He must be around somewhere," said the maid. "Here, Gary! Here, Gary!"

Only on one matter do Hobe Sounders take a united stand; this is on the question of Palm Beach. Palm Beachers regard Hobe as a quaint little suburban dictatorship with "so little behind it," as the saying goes, that even its beach is rapidly disappearing. In turn, Hobe Sounders regard Palm Beach as a *nouveau riche* nightmare and fling back the challenge of their beach disappearing with the statement that Palm Beach would be far better off if their beloved Lake Worth would disappear; in the opinion of Hobers, it is nothing more or less than one big septic tank. "Palm Beach is so *busy* now," says Mrs. Kay Denckla, while Mrs. Charles Shipman Payson, an ex-Palm Beacher herself, ends the matter on the same note. "We just go to Palm Beach," she says, "to shop."

Although Hobe Sound was discovered, in the geographical sense, by Ponce de León in the season of 1513, Hobers are inclined to credit Mrs. Robert Lovett, wife of the present Secretary of Defense, with the discovery of the resort, in the social sense, in the season of 1931. One day Mrs. Lovett picked up a map of Florida and determined to pick out a location which she felt would be similar in general sand-and-sea formation to Palm Beach but which would never be allowed to become, as she put it, "Palm Beachy." An expert gardener, Mrs. Lovett chose Hobe—one of Florida's few unspoiled garden spots, which had already been pioneered by such individualists as the actor Joseph Jefferson and the engineer John Jessup, both of whom were ex-Palm Beachers, as well as by such "solid" people as Chicago's Dawes family and Rochester's Gordons. The actual responsibility of building up the resort, however, fell to Greenwich's Joseph Verner Reed, who bought the Inn and cottages then existent during the depth of the depression. A possessor of a large mining fortune and a former theatrical angel, Reed not only produced the present Hobe Sound but also cast it. Among his new theatrical acquaintances he moved, understandably enough, with the utmost social caution; finally, however, he selected just one of them, the late Philip Barry. The socialite playwright, a perennial East Hamptonite, was just the type of anti-major resort man that Reed was looking for. "I'd like to have a cottage at Newport," he once said, "but it's such a bad address." Hobe Sound, which in those days had literally no address at all, appealed. Furthermore, as Reed had rounded up Barry, Barry in turn cast about among the stars he knew and finally rounded up Katharine Hepburn. Today the picture of the socialite star, together with her younger sister Peggy, in a Hobe Sound cottage with no running water, hanging their clothes out to dry on a broomstick, is still regarded as the typical view of Hobe in its unspoiled days.

Unfortunately Hobe Sound, moving into the current era, refused to remain unspoiled. "Fishers," says Mrs. John Hay Whitney, who no longer goes to Hobe, "is the way Hobe used to be. Hobe isn't." Ex-boxer Gene Tunney, another ex-Hober, is even more heretical. "If you don't want to go to a cocktail party," he says, "you have to pretend you're sick and go to bed—or at least pull your shades down. Otherwise everybody can just look in and know that you just didn't want to go. Today Hobe Sound out-Palm-Beaches Palm Beach." Finally the Hobe Sound story of John P. Marquand is perhaps the saddest of all. One fall, so the story is told, Ferry Marquand, the author's eight-year-old daughter, who was at the time attending the little Woodbridge School in Newbury, Massachusetts, came home to ask her father a question. "Daddy," she said, "are you the richest man in Newbury?" Marquand, taken aback, wanted to know why she thought so. "Everybody at school," said Ferry firmly, "says so." That winter the Marquands went to Hobe Sound; their cottage, oldest on the beach, was between the president of Du Pont on one side and the president of Morton Salt on the other. Ferry, installed in the Island School, once again came home to ask her father a question. "Daddy," she asked, "are you the poorest man in Hobe Sound?"

Today friends of the Marquands admit that it is characteristic of the resort that the author, one of the most successful writers in the world, was invariably treated by the majority of his fellow resorters as delightfully Bohemian. Hobe Sounders used to say, "Let's go over to the Marquands' " in the same spirit that Park Avenue once said, "Let's go down to Greenwich Village," and they were even too polite to criticize what they regarded as the author's misspelling of his name for his cottage—"Nervana." Mrs. Marquand was called "gallant" for trying to cope with a writing husband and at the same time, as the saying was, "keep up her standards"; she won particular commendation for the way she made a so-called "go" of her chowder dinners. At the most successful of these affairs Henry Ford II volunteered to "handle things" in the kitchen, and the next day, legend has it, Hobe friends sent around, in Thanksgiving baskets, avocados, grapefruits and goodies. Finally the Marquands had enough. The author, always sensitive on the subject of his Hobe Sound poverty as reported by his daughter, moved to Nassau. Not as polite as Marquand's guests was Frederick Pope, the seventy-five-year-old Boston-born corporation official to whom the Marquands sold "Nervana." "The draperies in the house," Pope said, "were fit only for polishing my Cadillac."

Besides playing host to many theatrical and literary lights, Hobe Sound has also been known, in the relatively brief course of its social history, for the presence of many political bigwigs—so many, in fact, that it has been said in Washington that a man who has not spent at least one week end at Hobe Sound during the winter is socially, if not politically, on the outs. Caliph of the Hobe Sound cabal is Greenwich's Samuel Pryor who, like so many politically minded resorters, has made almost a full career out of his opposition to the late Franklin D. Roosevelt; the causes with which he has been closely identified have ranged from that of the Pan-American Airways to the Republican Defenders of the Constitution of Old Greenwich. Nonetheless, in contrast to most other resorts, Hobe Sound has also included large political representation from both sides of the fence. Not only do Lovett and Harriman regularly vacation there but Hobe has regularly played host to such a variety of Washington headliners as Paul Hoffman, Stuart Symington, Donald Nelson, Louis Johnson and the late Edward R. Stettinius, as well as representatives of high Army and Navy brass like General Somervell and Admiral Halsey. "You see everything here," said one veteran Hober early in 1952, "from Averell Harriman calling up Truman in between croquet shots to Joe Martin fishing in high button shoes."

In view of this political atmosphere it is not surprising that, also in the resort's brief history, its virulent anti-Semitism has had severe repercussions. Some years ago a Jewish New York book publisher whose daughter was ill rented a cottage owned by the then president of the Hobe Sound Company. When the publisher wished to return the next year, he was told by the president that though everybody liked him, the resort was being turned into an all-club affair and would henceforth be restricted. The publisher wrote back that though he would not mind being refused if someone did not like him, he did indeed object to being turned down because of a policy such as that; he even brought up the possible effect of the new policy on another Hobe Sound visitor, a distinguished Jewish playwright whom the president of the Hobe Sound Company had often been quoted as saying was his best friend. "Whose best friend," replied the Hobe Sound president, "isn't Jewish?" Several more letters were exchanged and finally, after a lapse of several years, the issue involved none other than the late Wendell Willkie himself. Willkie, visiting at Hobe Sound following his defeat in 1940, heard both sides of the case and said that if Hobe Sound authorities did not rescind their blanket policy he would leave the resort. Following this blow, the resort reversed itself. Even sterner, perhaps, was the rebuke delivered by Hobe Sounder Robert Lovett who, representing the resort's more forward-looking contingent, recently announced that he would bring anyone he wished to Hobe. "What is this, anyway?" he asked. "Germany?"

Of late years the admitted queen of Hobe Sound and the official manageress of the Jupiter Island Club is the wife of the man who built up the resort, Mrs. Joseph Verner Reed. The former Permelia Pryor, a sister of Greenwich's Samuel Pryor, she is a small dynamic woman who is not only the archetype of the resort clubwoman but also one who holds a position which, in spite of the eminence of her subjects, comes perhaps the closest to absolute power as that existing in any resort, either major or minor, today. In Mrs. Reed's opinion the American hotel, in contrast with the European, has been allowed to run down and no longer has any idea of what constitutes real service. "What we really do here," she says briskly, "is provide a good hotel." Mrs. Reed's idea of a good hotel—or Hobe Sound—is one which involves, before entering, a proposer, a seconder and two other letters of recommendation; her first question to any stranger who inquires about the resort is, "Who do you know?"—the "who" meaning, of course, not who of just anybody but who of regular Hobe Sounders or, preferably, of Hobe Sound Governors. Mrs. Reed believes in no public advertising at all. "Word-of-mouth," she says, "is not only the strongest advertising there is, but it is the only kind that doesn't get you involved." Through the years, Mrs. Reed has also developed several other methods of not becoming involved. One is to play with all newcomers what is known in Hobe Sound as "Musical Chairs." This game means that all newcomers are constantly moved around from room to room. Not only does this allow veteran Hobers, as they arrive, to use the rooms they have always had, but it also permits a severe testing of the newcomer's devotion to the resort. If the newcomers fail to measure up to Hobe Sound standards they receive what is jocularly referred to at the resort as their "numerals"—in other words, they are placed on probation. If they fail to get off probation by the time of the Easter week end they receive what is known as Mrs. Reed's "sweater"—in other words, they are told that there are no rooms available for them the next year.

The fact that few newcomers complain is a tribute not only to Hobe Sound but also to Mrs. Reed herself, whom resorters cherish not only as an excellent tennis partner but a lady who is particularly kind to her subjects in time of personal distress; among both newcomers and old-timers alike, she is regarded not as a tyrant but as a benevolent despot. Furthermore, if Mrs. Reed is autocratic socially, she prides herself on being democratic geographically. "Why," she says, "this very year we have a charming couple from Oklahoma City!"

Two years ago Mrs. Reed also took for the first time at Hobe Sound a young couple from a city in the social wilds. Although the couple were, in the Hobe Sound sense, "well-connected"—the wife was a sister of the husband of the sister of Jock Whitney—their first season at Hobe was a difficult one, primarily because their so-called "sponsors," or the Hobe Sound regulars who had recommended them, were not at the resort that season. For the first three days, no one spoke to them at all; on the fourth day someone nodded to them and on the fifth, to their great excitement, someone addressed to them a casual remark on the state of the weather. Shortly after this, early in February, they were invited to the so-called "Governors Tea." This affair, a "must" on any Hobe newcomer's calendar, is not only attended by all the Governors of the resort and their wives, but also by the minister of Hobe Sound's church, who is, characteristically enough, no ordinary minister, but a Bishop. Since the tea is the only regular occasion during the resort season when everybody has a chance to get to know everybody else, the young couple, who were not entirely satisfied with their progress up to this time, were determined to make the most of it. The young wife dressed in her best bib-and-tucker, including a pre-Easter hat and long white gloves, and the husband donned a new blue suit and a pre-Easter necktie. Arriving they suddenly had a feeling, in view of Hobe's informal reputation, that they might be overdressed and took the precaution of tiptoeing up to a side window and peeking in on the tea. When they saw that the other ladies were hatless and gloveless and the men were in sport shirts, they stole back to their car and deposited their formal items of apparel. Then once more they approached, this time boldly up to the front door —which to their surprise was wide open. Entering they attempted to join various groups but unfortunately met with no success. Again and again they tried but finally, having stayed more than a full half hour, they went home. "During the entire time we were there," says the young wife today, "the only person who spoke to us was the Bishop and the only thing I can remember him saying was that he always tried to speak to everybody."

Mrs. Reed, who herself makes it a point to call on all newcomers—she always wears long white gloves when she does so—would be the first to be disappointed at such a story. Nonetheless, she feels that, when all is said and done, the rigors of Plebe Year at the Sound make for better Hobers in the end. Among other things she points to the fact that Hobe Sound, like Fishers, is apparently scandal-proof. "We have never had a scandal here," she says, "of any sort." Asked if people ever find Hobe a little too quiet, she smiles. "They can always move on, you know. Take people who are always the life of the party. I keep them just two years. That's enough."

So far the only Life-of-the-Partyers who have been coming longer than two years are Chicago's Henry Rowland and Wilkes-Barre's John C. Haddock. Henry Rowland, or

"Hank" as he is affectionately called, leads the Chicago contingent and is especially in demand during the Easter vacation for his rendition of the song, "I Want to Go Chair-Chair." John C. Haddock, or "Uncle Jack" as he is called, publishes a weekly news bulletin at the resort and has a high reputation for both humor and community spirit. Some years ago he sent out under the heading of the Hobe Sound Improvement Society a letter asking all resorters to report in a prescribed area, on the morning of April 1, to save Hobe's prized *ficus Benjaminum,* a species of rubber tree which he claimed was suffering from a blight. Some idea of the spirit of the resort was given when a large proportion of all able-bodied Hobers, dressed in overalls, working gloves and sun-hats, and carrying trowels and shovels, obediently turned up —only to be greeted by "Uncle Jack's" loud war cry, "April Fool!"

Only once each season does Hobe Sound burst at its seams. This occurs during the Easter vacation when the resort is treated to the en masse arrival of the collegiate and boarding-school contingent of Hobe Sound families. Curiously enough, this contingent is welcomed by Mrs. Reed with open arms. Although the young people are put up in what is jokingly called the club's "Slave Quarters," for the two weeks they are in residence the queen all but abdicates in their favor and they rule the roost. Regulations are relaxed, the Beach Club is opened up at night and all manner of youthful iniquities ensue. This seeming inconsistency in Mrs. Reed's otherwise Spartan regime is, however, duly explained, and by none other than the queen herself. "I want the young people," she says firmly, "to have a good time. We take no seasonal reservations here—our limit is two months. Otherwise we'd get all old people. It's much more trouble but we are resolved never to let our age level get too high. We *love* young people."

Just why Hobe Sound should welcome a youth movement so warmly still seems inconsistent. But suddenly Mrs. Reed becomes, in conclusion, extremely adamant even for a queen.

"We learned our lesson," she says, measuring her words, "from Jekyll Island."

On this score Mrs. Reed might well be stern. Certainly the lesson of the late Jekyll, a twelve by two mile area off the coast of Brunswick, Georgia, was a sharp one. Once called the resort of the "100 Millionaires"—its club was limited to just a hundred members—Jekyll was not only the greatest of the country's social islands, but one so legendary in prestige that in its heyday the claim was made that its clientele controlled one-sixth of the world's wealth. While this claim was undoubtedly even more exaggerated than the claims made for Newport or Bar Harbor, the fact remains that Jekyll was unquestionably the island epitome of this country's Big Business Society. Furthermore, whether Jekyll fell solely because of its high age limit or whether also because it ran the matter of privacy into the ground and in the end, like Old Guard Society, simply bored itself to death, the fact also remains that its fall was the largest in the history of old-line resorts. Even the closing of the Adirondacks' famous Tawahus Club, solid center of the millionaire "camp set" could not match, in the opinion of old-line resorters, the significance of the end of Jekyll. "When Jekyll went," says Greenwich's Henry J. Fisher, who with the late J. P. Morgan the Younger closed the resort for the last time in 1941, "it was not only the end of an era. It was the end of a way of life."

In keeping with such heroic stature, Jekyll's fall, unlike the fall of any other old-line resort, was complete. In its salad days the resort was even spelled differently—as just plain Jekyl. "When the world went to hell," says one old-timer poetically, "then Jekyll doubled its 'l.' " In June, 1947, the state of Georgia started condemnation proceedings against the island and in October of that year took Jekyll over, lock, stock and barrel, for the sum of $675,000, for a State Beach Park. But even at the end with two "l's," Jekyll was still a name to conjure with. A candidate for the governorship of Georgia, knowing that only 3 miles of his state's 149 miles of beaches were open to the public, made large campaign issues out of Jekyll's ultra-private 12 miles. As one of his chief platforms he announced that it was his purpose not only to acquire Jekyll for everybody but also to have every man in the state sleep in the bed J. P. Morgan slept in.

Today, as Georgia has marched through Jekyll, this curious ideal is at least approachable, or at least will be as soon as Georgia's proposed new causeway from Brunswick over to Jekyll via bridge is completed. Already Morgan's bedroom in Jekyll's once extremely private "apartment house," the so-called "Sans Souci," has been prepared for tourist accommodation at the Park. So too is his beloved "Mistletoe Cottage," once the scene of Jekyll's famous lawn parties. In the great days these lawn parties featured, among other things, the Jekyll Island Club specialties, "Jekyll Oysters" and "Jekyll Terrapin," both of which were accurately named since the island boasted both its own oyster bed and terrapin pen. The Jekyll Island Clubhouse itself, together with the Club Annex, is now a hotel. Elsewhere on the island, in various stages of weed and vine-grown disrepair, the once vaunted cottage hideaways of Rockefellers and Bakers, Goodyears and Fergusons, Goulds and Pulitzers are now open to all; those on the north end will shortly be used, ironically enough in view of Jekyll's stern clubbiness, to house Georgia 4-H clubbers. All over the island ghost stories still cling like the Spanish moss. On the golf course the visitor can see the place where the elder John D. Rockefeller is supposed to have lost, one early morning, a golf ball. All day, it is said, he hunted and late in the afternoon, disgusted, finally gave up—and gave his caddy a dime. On Jekyll's beach the visitor can see a place where the elder Mrs. J. P. Morgan got stuck in the sand in her "red bug"—one of Jekyll's beloved little electric cars. She was pushed to safety, the story goes, by a Rockefeller and a Harkness. Another Morgan story concerns Jekyll's game, for originally, like Tuxedo, Jekyll was primarily a hunting and fishing resort. Soon added to the deer, turkey, duck and quail was a herd of wild boar which King Humbert of Italy had presented to the elder Morgan. The latter had difficulty keeping them in "Camp Uncas," his Adirondacks camp, and shipped them to Jekyll; today their snooty descendants may still be found on the island.

The story of Jekyll goes back to the great era of resort building of the 1880's. At this time a group of simplicity-minded New York businessmen, led by the elder Morgan, Cyrus McCormick, James J. Hill, William Rockefeller, William K. Vanderbilt and George F. Baker, reacting resort-wise against Newport and Bar Harbor, etc., determined to search for a rock-ribbed winter refuge where they would be free from reporters, salesmen, social climbers, extortioners and people who would make them dress for dinner. Perhaps fortunately for them, there was no Palm Beach in 1883, the year the plan took shape, and in fact the whole idea of a winter resort was itself a novel one. Nonetheless, money was no object and the group turned their problem of a search over to two doctors from Johns Hopkins. Dutifully the doctors scouted not only America but also Europe and the Near East. They reported that the French Riviera was too rowdy and public, Italy too unpredictable and public, Egypt too hot and public, etc; in fact, the good doctors found only one spot to meet the exacting requirements of privacy—St. Simons Island, home of the present Sea Island, a winter resort off the coast of Georgia. Unfortunately St. Simons was not for sale, but sometime later one of the original group of businessmen, the Brooklyn dry goods merchant John Claflin, was invited to a wild turkey and duck shoot on Jekyll Island, neighboring St. Simons; he returned to announce that Jekyll's owner, John Eugene du Bignon, was at least open to an offer. On Claflin's report the New York group paid Du Bignon $125,000 and on February 1, 1888, the Jekyll Island Club came into being. Immediately work began on the clubhouse and cottages and natives were hired to guard the island year-round. "For sixty years," says J. Bryan III, "no unwanted foot ever walked Jekyll soil."

Almost at once club members fell in love with Jekyll. Besides twelve miles of beaches as hard as a shell road the island soon boasted thirty miles of roads made of crushed oyster shells as well as intriguing bridle paths and bicycle trails. Soon side by side with the Old Shell Road, Jessamine Road and Old Plantation Road there was Morgan Road and Rockefeller Path and Baker Trail. Long-leaf pines coming down to the water's edge and a variety of other trees, including Bayonet palmettos, holly, oaks, magnolias and wild oranges, made the island a scenic paradise. Flowers bloomed all winter long and climbing vines were everywhere—the Cherokee rose, the wisteria and the trumpet creeper. From the trees mockingbirds sang. In later years Buffalo's John J. Albright, wholesale coal baron, became so taken with these birds that he planted a row of redwood trees for them to sit and sing on; he announced that in his next incarnation he wished to come back and join them.

The Jekyll season was always from January to March; few stayed into April and the swimming was a cold proposition even at that time. While the beach was fine for bicycling or for driving "red bugs," it was so shallow that a Jekyllite could wade as far as two miles out to sea before getting in over his head. In time a swimming pool fed with warm sulphur springs was installed, but this pool, along with a new eighteen-hole golf course and two indoor tennis courts, were Jekyll's only latter-day concessions to high life. Otherwise, simplicity prevailed. The Edwin Gould cottage was the island's most elaborate but even this was a minor matter compared to Newport's castles; other Jekyll cottages were Spartan in the extreme. The rambling old brick clubhouse, painted yellow, never pretended to magnificence. To the end it had only an ancient creeping elevator; the Sans Souci apartment house had none at all. Although the club *décor*, at least in the women's drawing room, was primarily chintz with wicker chairs, the men's smoking room, with its elephant sized table, a five-hundred-pound sofa and heavy black leather chairs, was somber in extreme. In the library in the manner of New York's Union Club was a large sign which read in capital letters, "SILENCE." Nowhere in the club was there a bar to which everyone stood up; there was merely a den in which drinks were served. Inside the front door of the club was probably the most typical feature of all—a hundred hooks marked with each Jekyll clubber's name.

"At Jekyll," says Henry Fisher, " 'Jack' Morgan was strictly

John Jones. That was the idea of the place." At the Golf Club Karl Keffer, the famous island professional, treated everyone alike. Jekyllite Langdon P. Marvin recalls one day when he went down and apologized to Keffer for not having had time to play golf that particular visit—and being promptly answered by what the lawyer feels should be his epitaph. "Mr. Marvin," said Keffer sternly, "you do too many things." In the general camaraderie, only Jekyll's help seem to have kept their heads. During the bank holiday of 1933 Morgans and Rockefellers, Vanderbilts and Whitneys, Harknesses and Sloans all were caught short of cash; "Henry," the head bellboy at Jekyll, saved the situation with loans for everybody. Not the least of Jekyll's legends concern the caddies which were recruited from a colored orphan asylum. On one occasion Railroader Edward E. Loomis, was so loath to leave Jekyll at the end of the season that he played golf up to the last minute before his ferry left. Coming off the last green he hurriedly gave the caddy house boy four dollars, telling him that he wished him to take two of the four dollars up to the clubhouse boy. The next year Loomis, returning, asked the clubhouse boy if he had received his two dollars. The clubhouse boy shook his head. Loomis explained that he had asked the caddy house boy to deliver it. Once more the clubhouse boy shook his head. "Mistah Loomis," he said solemnly, "you might jus' as well of sent a lettuce-leaf by a rabbit."

Like other resorters Jekyllites became fascinated with their island's history. Digging back from Du Bignon, the original owner, they found that Jekyll's only previous owner had the island directly from King George III. Known to the Indians as Ospo, the island was later called Jekyll by Georgia's first governor, General Oglethorpe, in honor of Sir Joseph Jekyll, who made a generous contribution to the Georgia colony. These historians, led by Standard Oil's Walter Jennings, also found that the first syllable of Jekyll should be pronounced to rhyme with "cheek"—but this, like the two "l" spelling, was never accepted by old-timers who continued to rhyme their pronunciation with "check." Farther back, Jekyllites discovered that the first historical report of the island was delivered by none other than Sir Francis Drake. Jekyll's ever pro-English Society, however, had difficulty swallowing the findings which seemed to be at sharp variance with the way they had learned English history. The report related how Sir Francis and his men, attacking the island in force, first "hung and burned" the Spanish captain and seventeen other Spaniards, then:

> Having in mind the merciful disposition of your Gracious Majesty, we did not kill the women and children, but having destroyed upon the island all their provisions and property, and taken away all their weapons, we left them to starve.

Some of Jekyll's history was closer at hand. Near the island church still stands today a huge kettle—a memorial to the fact that the greatest of social islands was also the scene of the arrival of the last cargo of slaves ever landed in the country:

> This kettle from Slave Yacht Wanderer,
> Captain Corry
> Used for feeding the slaves landed
> on Jekyl Island, November 28, 1858,
> Yacht owned by Charles A. L. Lamar, of
> Savannah, Georgia

Soon Jekyll's "100," most of whom were leading figures in the so-called "Invisible Government" of the period, were making history themselves. After the Panic of 1907 and its attendant bank failures, the country demanded revision of national and state banking laws, and Congress appointed Rhode Island's Senator Nelson W. Aldrich to head a commission to study the matter. The Aldrich Commission made its study, then one day in the autumn of 1910 Aldrich himself telephoned to four men and told them to pack their bags and meet him at a little-used platform of the Jersey City terminal. The four did as they were told—a group which included Frank A. Vanderlip, president of the National Bank, Henry P. Davison, right-hand man to the elder Morgan, Paul M. Warburg, of Kuhn, Loeb & Company and Abram Piatt Andrew, Assistant Secretary of the Treasury. At the Jersey platform Aldrich ostentatiously talked of a sporting trip but privately swore the men to silence and told them to address each other by first name only. He then herded his group into a private car where great care was taken so that not even the train crew would recognize them. The men left the car at a siding in Georgia and they were then marched down to a deserted pier and rowed to Jekyll Island. Here, for the next ten days, with only one day off for shooting, Wall Street's "First Name Club"—as the group later came to be known—drew up the report which, later made to President Taft's Congress, laid the foundation for the establishment in President Wilson's administration in 1914, of the Federal Reserve System.

If Jekyll could secretly found the Federal Reserve System, the island could also, in another off season, provide a rather different kind of social history. Some years before the arrival of the first-namers, a Jekyll clubber came to the island, one late autumn, on his honeymoon. His bride, later one of Newport's greatest belles, was at that time only sixteen years old;

foreign-born and exotic looking, with long jet-black hair, a well-curved figure, huge black eyes and a tiny retroussé nose, she was generally regarded as the most beautiful girl ever to set foot on the island. Unfortunately the occasion was not a happy one. The young lady had married, in the manner of the worst features of the Society of the day, someone rich enough to pay off her father's debts; at the time, as she later admitted, the only thing she knew about marriage, before entering into it, was that it involved leaving one's own family in favor of another. Her bridegroom, all-time black sheep of men-about-resorts, was the worst possible she might have chosen. An eccentric, sadistic roué, not only was he close to three times her age but he had just two interests in life—the breeding of horses and the seduction of women. He especially enjoyed combining his two interests and taking young girls to his farm in Kentucky where, if they proved difficult, he would tie them up without their clothes and force them to witness, at close range, the breeding of his horses. Before her wedding, the girl knew nothing of this. During her courtship the man had behaved in approved carriage-ride and candy tradition. Following their wedding night at the Waldorf-Astoria, however, one which involved most of the hotel staff before it was over, the sinister bridegroom had determined to take his recalcitrant bride to his club at Jekyll; here, in the autumn season, he expected to find no one except caretakers to interfere with the various entertainments he planned for her.

The entry of the couple into the dining room that first night was an unforgettable sight. In her arms the bride clutched a sickly mongrel dog she had found on a station platform and had since shielded, as a companion in misery, against her now-thoroughly-hated husband. To the latter's horror, on entering the Jekyll dining room, there were four other men eating their dinner. At one table sat Henry B. Hyde, insurance magnate, with one of his associates; at another, Joseph Pulitzer, the famous publisher, with one of his editors. These men, on an off-season vacation at the island, knew and despised their fellow clubman and, despite the latter's fulsome efforts to make them think he was enjoying a happy honeymoon, immediately made plans to foil him. Following dinner, they not only saw to it that the bride was given a room by herself but even protected her dog. Then for the next week, since Hyde played the principal role of protector, the island witnessed a most remarkable real-life Jekyll and Hyde drama. Not only did Hyde and his associates never leave the bride alone with her husband, but also they sat with her at all meals and rode, walked or bicycled with her in between times. Always in the background was Pulitzer ready to aid, if need be, with the power of his press; in later years the bride used to say she never forgot the comforting presence of the voice of the sick, blind publisher who, unable to sleep, dictated to his secretary far into each night. Finally, with the arrival of other Jekyllites, the drama came to an end. The bride left the island without her husband and her marriage ultimately ended in divorce; the bridegroom, who never came back to Jekyll again, was later expelled from the club.

No women were ever allowed as regular members at the Jekyll Island Club; wives and daughters came in under family memberships, and others came only as guests. For Jekyll house parties, however, the island always had its share of the fair sex. Old-timers recall, in particular, New York's late James Alexander Scrymser, submarine cable king, who used to invite down to the island bevies of young girls from the Farmington School and, despite the presence of his meek little wife, would exact each night from each of the girls a good-night kiss. Nor did all the old Jekyllites submit meekly to the nightly division of male and female after dinner. On one occasion the late James Rowland Angell, president of Yale, stayed right with the ladies and refused to join the gentlemen. "I wish," he said, "to know what my boys are up against."

Despite Dr. Angell, the real core of life at Jekyll Island, in its great days, was to be found in the men's after dinner talks. "For hours," New York's late Dr. Walter B. James, who presided at many such discussions, once declared, "the men would sit and talk and the talk was always of great things, of visions and developing. If they did not have a map of the United States or the world before them, they had a map of industrial or financial empire in their minds." Dr. James succeeded Singer Sewing Machine's "Commodore" Frederick Bourne as president of Jekyll and was, in turn, on his own death, succeeded by Standard Oil's Walter Jennings who also served until his death in 1933, at which time he was succeeded by J. P. Morgan the Younger. But with the death of the elder Morgan as far back as 1913—Pulitzer had died at Jekyll two years before—the position of patriarch of the island had fallen to none other than the archetype of latter-day Big Business Society himself—George F. Baker. Always legendary on the island, Baker had a custom-built car with a built-in toilet and carried an ancient canvas bag in which he used to carry one-dollar gold pieces for tips. In his last days, when the Titan of Tuxedo was unable to come down to the club for dinner, regular Jekyllites usually carried the after-dinner discussions on up to his cottage. The naïveté of the banker in his off-guard moments charmed his listeners. On one occasion Baker told how "that young man at the telephone company"—a man who can be identified today as Walter S. Gifford, ex-president of the American Telephone Company and current Ambassador to England—had run a private line into Baker's room. "Wasn't that an awfully nice thing to do?" he asked. Since his listeners knew that at that time Baker owned 63,443 shares of American Telephone stock and could easily have reorganized the entire management if he had wished, they merely smiled their agreement.

On another occasion Baker was upset by the question of honorary degrees. "A lot of these colleges want to give me these things," he said disarmingly. "What do you fellows think?" His listeners told him frankly that they believed that the colleges to which he had already given money wished to show their appreciation, while other colleges, to which he had not yet given, undoubtedly hoped to get something in the future. "Oh," replied Baker slowly. "Well, I've taken Harvard and Yale. I think that's enough."

Only one Jekyllite, Boston's great fund-raising Bishop William Lawrence, was bold enough to go to Baker for money—and this was done circumspectly. Coming to Jekyll in the winter of 1923, the good Bishop began dropping all manner of hints about the wonderful idea Harvard had to build a Business School. In glowing terms, at every possible chance, he pictured to Baker what the school could mean to businessmen of the future; the Bishop's idea was to raise a million of the proposed five million project from Baker alone. Unfortunately, Baker, whose conversation on matters which involved his pocketbook was limited to a slight raising of his full eyebrows, refused to bite. Finally Bishop Lawrence, irritated with the failure of his masterful hinting, which had always proved so successful in other money-raising projects, came right out with his plan. "Mr. Baker," he said, "how would you like to give a million dollars?" Without a moment's hesitation Baker replied, "I would not," he said. "I would not like to give a million dollars, and I would not like to give even half a million dollars." Then, while Bishop Lawrence stirred uncomfortably in his chair, Baker gave him the same treatment he had been receiving. In the same way the Bishop had talked of the Business School, Baker talked of his own pet project—a bridge between the Palisades and New York, where the present George Washington Bridge now stands. The banker pictured in glowing terms what such a bridge could mean to motorists of the future. "I like the idea of my children and grandchildren driving over the George F. Baker Bridge," he said. "It may not be the right kind of pride but it appeals to me. I should rather like," he concluded, "to drive over it myself." By this time Boston's Bishop was extremely uncomfortable. Suddenly Baker looked at him. "Bishop," he asked, "if I give up my bridge, do you think that Harvard will let me give five million dollars and have the privilege of building the whole Business School?"

The sort of resort idyl of Big Business which Jekyll represented could not continue with the changing times. In the early days not even the women dressed for dinner and no Jekyll man ever took a dinner jacket to the island. In those days being invited to a Jekyll dinner party consisted merely of moving from one table in the club to another; all good Jekyllites retired promptly at ten-thirty or eleven at the latest. Four, or at the most six, people for dinner was considered the dinner-party limit and all true Jekyllites shuddered when Mrs. Hyram Edward Manville, Sr., of Johns Manville, moved two tables together and started giving formal dinners for twelve. When Vincent Astor came down to the island with his yacht *Nourmahal* they were sure the end had come.

"In the early days," says Greenwich's Mrs. Roger S. Baldwin, whose late husband was an island leader, "everyone let their hair down *en vacance* at Jekyll. Not even Mr. Baker was forbidding. Then all the fluffy people started coming down and the whole thing lost its purpose."

Before the fluffy people came, one letter from a Jekyll visitor, a guest of James Alexander Scrymser, is still prized in the last official club book as the most nostalgic picture of the great days of the resort in existence:

> I thank you for my two weeks at Jekyl Island. They were most enjoyable and how could they be otherwise, surrounded as I was with charming, well-bred people, with an interesting golf course, and men to play with whose keen interest in the game and the spirit of fun made eighteen holes a real treat.
>
> Then along a drive through those woodland groves, along that wonderful beach, and, after a good dinner, an evening before the wood fire in the smoking room, listening to men who have seen and done things, men with war experiences and stories of hunting and yachting and traveling, here and in other lands, interspersed with wit and humor, and, think of it, no gossip. I, for once, did not miss the band and music and the dancing which are found in so many of our Southern watering places. Those beautiful moonlight nights and the days when the air was filled with a perfume of flowers and the mocking birds were singing in the trees, were much more to my taste, and when it came to Sunday, the services in the little Chapel, where eminent bishops and divines discoursed upon things which every thoughtful man is thinking about, suited me.
>
> It is certainly a unique place. I know of no resort of the kind in this country or any other country. And when you see the tired men and women, who come there, restored to health and strength, you feel that there must be some combination of circumstances that makes the place so attractive

> and restoring. The real spirit of comradeship, which makes all young and old feel that they belong to the family, stimulates one to give of their best for the pleasure of others.

Today several old Jekyllites are among the 150 members of the resort club of Yeamans Hall, an old Southern plantation, one thousand acres in size, located on a salt swamp twelve miles outside of Charleston, South Carolina—a development which can be considered a social island since it is almost entirely surrounded by Goose Creek. Established in 1924 and designed by Gamble Rogers, Yeamans promotes the same sort of search for simplicity which Jekyll represented in its day; the Hall even boasts one of Jekyll's latter-day bartenders. Here, New Yorkers such as John W. Davis, Henry R. Luce and John D. Rockefeller III join with a few non-New Yorkers such as Wilmington's Mrs. du Pont Clark, Connecticut's Judge Thomas W. Swan and Charleston's Benjamin R. Kittredge in golfing, fishing, eating and drinking—there is virtually no riding—as well as card-playing for low stakes and once a week moving their chairs around in the club library and watching a movie. There is no dressing for dinner and no drinks are allowed to be served at the table while eating. The annual event of the season, which also parallels the old Jekyll season, is the birthday party of New York lawyer Harris Colt, a gentleman in his nineties; at this function, champagne is permitted. "You might say," says one old Haller, "that this is the last refuge of both gentility and gentilety—but it's a very sleepy sort of life. If anyone gets here after nine-thirty in the evening he'll find everybody in bed—and in their own beds too."

The success of this kind of resort in these modern times remains, of course, to be proved, but even in the old days there were dissenters. To at least one couple visiting Jekyll

Island the picture painted in the letter to Scrymser was an over-idyllic one. Banker Charles Mitchell and his wife, late of Tuxedo, recall going down to Jekyll for a three-day vacation in the boom 1920's; neither had ever seen the island before, and, as they admit today, great were their expectations. Arriving Friday night the Mitchells smiled their greetings to one and all and Mr. Mitchell immediately ordered his golf clubs to be sent down to the golf house. He wished, he said, rubbing his hands cheerfully and gazing around him, to tee off first thing in the morning. Promptly he was informed that he would not tee off first thing Saturday or anytime Saturday or, indeed, anytime Sunday; the golf course was reserved the entire weekend for a golf tournament for members over sixty-five. While Mr. Mitchell pondered this blow, Mrs. Mitchell went on a tour of the premises to see what was in store for their evening's entertainment. She returned crestfallen to report to her husband that the choice appeared to lie between a game of croquet out on the lawn and a showing of Mr. Morgan's color photographs in the teahouse.

Somehow the Mitchells got through their first evening. The next morning, however, there occurred an event which neither one of them will ever forget. At the time, as they recall, they were, Jekyll Island style, separated—Mr. Mitchell in the men's smoking room watching a game of backgammon and Mrs. Mitchell in the ladies' drawing room watching a game of mah-jongg. Suddenly a woman's piercing shriek resounded through the club. Such unseemly noise in the well-mannered quiet was unbelievable. Out of the ladies' drawing room rushed the ladies; out of the men's smoking room ran the gentlemen. In the hall they found the cause. Boston's Mrs. William Vaughan, chairman of the Jekyll Island Library

Committee, had just opened the club's incoming mail. In her hand she held a large envelope. Turning excitedly to the Jekyllites crowding toward her, she waved the envelope over her head.

"Look," she shouted again, unable to contain herself, "look what's happened! The *Atlantic Monthly* has come a day early!"

III

Newport—
Of Cottages and Queens

Now, don't go gettin' cross about th' rich, Hinnissy. Put up that dinnymite. Don't excite ye'ersilf about us folks in Newport. It's always been th' same way, Father Kelly tells me. Says he: "If a man is wise, he gets rich an' if he gets rich, he gets foolish, or his wife does. That's what keeps the money movin' around. What comes in at th' ticker goes out at the wine agent. F'river an' iver people have been growin' rich, goin' down to some kind iv a Newport, makin' monkeys iv thimsilves an' goin' back to the jungle. 'Tis a steady procission. Aisy come, lazy go. In ivry little hamlet in this broad land, there's some man with a broad jaw an' th' encouragement iv a good woman, makin' ready to shove some other man off his steam yacht. At this very minyit whin I speak, me frind Jawn Grates has his eye on Hankerbilk's house. He wud swing a hammock in th' woodshed this year, but nex' he may have his feet up on th' bannister iv th' front stoop. Whin a captain iv industhry stops dhrinkin' at th' bar, he's near his finish. If he ain't caught in his own person, th' constable will get to his fam'ly. Ye read about th' union iv two gr-reat fortunes. A dollar meets another dollar, they are conganial, have sim'lar tastes, an' many mutual frinds. They are marrid an' bring up a fam'ly iv pennies, dimes, thirty-cintses an' countherfeits. An' afther awhile, th' fam'ly passes out iv circylation. That's th' histhry iv it," says Father Kelly. "An'," says he, "I'm glad there is a Newport," he says. "It's th' exhaust pipe," he says. "Without it we might blow up," he says. "It's th' hole in th' top iv th' kettle," he says. "I wish it was bigger."

—*Observations by Mr. Dooley*, F. P. Dunne, 1902

EXACTLY fifty years have passed since the late F. P. Dunne, alias Mr. Dooley, gave the Queen of Resorts perhaps her most philosophical blessing. In those fifty years, in the opinion of Emil Jemail, editor of the Newport *Daily News*, the time for philosophy has passed. "To be objective about Newport—and that's a very easy thing to be," he says, "there's been a revolution here."

Jemail, who has been editing his paper since 1920, has seen the greatest of the resort revolutions at first hand. In 1925 both he and Washington's late Edson Bradley, liquor manufacturer and ex-Tuxedoite, built houses. Jemail built one which had four bedrooms and two bathrooms and cost fifteen thousand dollars. Bradley built one which had forty bedrooms and twenty bathrooms and cost two million dollars; the largest ever built in Newport, it was French Renaissance in design and among other features had a chapel which seated 150 people. In 1949 Bradley's house, which was called a cottage and named "Seaview Terrace," sold for eight thousand dollars. Jemail's house, which had never been called a cottage and has never had a name, has never been for sale. "I wouldn't take twenty-five thousand dollars for it," he says, "today."

This sort of revolution must be seen to be believed, and it is not an easy thing to see. Newport, which is located in Rhode Island, is an island itself, and it has always been physically, let alone socially, an extremely difficult place to get into—or, once into, out of. All Newporters pride themselves on the fact that there are few murders there. The methods of exit afforded the prospective murderer are but three and all involve either a bridge or a ferryboat. As for the methods of entrance, the usual one from New York, since the passing of the old Fall River Boat Line, is either by train or plane to Providence and a taxi or taxi-plane from there, or else by automobile over the Mount Hope Bridge and the Jamestown Ferry. Both are expensive. At the Mount Hope

Bridge, which was at one time entirely controlled by the Vanderbilts, Steven Smith, the tollkeeper, has a standing reply to sight-seers who, knowing that a dollar-fifty ferry trip also lies ahead, often complain of his ninety-cent charge. "It may interest you to know," Smith answers with a wry smile, "that the bonds of this bridge are owned entirely by widows and orphans."

If there are three entrances and exits to Newport, there are also three separate Newports to view. The first Newport, or Navy Newport, becomes visible in the ride over by the Jamestown Ferry. Entering Newport Harbor, between old Fort Adams on one side and the U.S. Naval Training Station and War College on the other, the ferry moves between warships whose ancestors have been riding Newport waters since the days of John Paul Jones. During the Civil War the Naval Academy at Annapolis was, as a precautionary measure, evacuated to Newport and today, three and a half wars later, Newport still ranks, along with Norfolk, as one of the two main fleet bases on the Atlantic. Newport's chief industries include the making of electrical instruments, household appliances and prophylactics; the latter are, perhaps fortunately, extraordinarily often confused, in the minds of Old Guard resorters, with toothbrushes. Newport's water system, on the other hand, is rarely confused. Outsiders often become actually ill before they get used to the water, and ever since the hurricane of 1938 there has been a legend that one Newport reservoir alone contains the still undiscovered bodies of "three cows, a padre and a woman in a red dress."

The second Newport, or Historic Newport, is the sight which becomes visible when the ferry docks alongside Newport's ancient Long Wharf. This sight is not of Newport at all but of "Oldport," as Thomas Wentworth Higginson spoke of it in the nineteenth century, of a Newport which was old even then—a fascinating Colonial town whose narrow cobbled streets open on vistas which come to an end, said Henry James, "like the quick short steps of little old ladies." Thames Street, Newport's waterfront thoroughfare, is a curious Old World version of Main Street. Resorters pronounce it "Tems," natives usually use the "h" as well as the "a"; here, during the British occupation in the Revolution, Hessians shot down Newporters for target practice. In and around Thames' quaint side streets, where hollyhocks and petunias still hang on the fences, there are enough historic buildings to delight the most severe antiquarian. There is the Wanton-Lyman-Hazard House built in 1675, Richard Munday's Trinity Church built in 1726, Dean Berkeley's Whitehall built in 1729, Peter Harrison's Redwood Library built in 1749 and the Touro Synagogue built in 1763. The Redwood Library antedates all such institutions in New York and Boston and the Touro Synagogue was not only the first synagogue in this country but it was for many years the only one. Of all these museum pieces, only the so-called "Old Stone Mill" in Touro Park, a peculiar round stone tower built on open arches supported by pillars, has no date; all true Newporters believe, periodical reports by archeologists to the contrary, that this tower was built by the Vikings.

The third Newport, or Social Newport, begins at the top of the hill with Bellevue Avenue. Here, moving out past Ochre Point toward Bailey's Beach and the famous "Ten Mile" or Ocean Drive, on an avenue which was once called Jews Street, the visitor sees for the first time a sight which is unduplicated anywhere else in the country—the sight of the castles which once represented the height of the great American resort extravaganza. Here, side by side, in extraordinary proportions, in an extraordinarily small area—less than half of the castles are actually on the water—are represented every kind of architectural crossbreeding from a weird Queen Anne gingerbread sired by an errant Florentine *palazzo* to a medieval marble blockbuster out of Versailles by the Grand Central Station. Although some of these castles date to the nineteenth century and some to the twentieth, all have at least two things in common; all were originally committed in the sacred name of the word "cottage," and all bear actual names which, if they mean anything at all, are roughly translatable in reverse. Thus "Chateau Sur Mer" is not on the ocean, "Champ Soleil" is in the shade, "Land Fall" is the home of an Admiral, "Quatrel" means the home of four "l's," or Lorillards, and such a name as "Bel'Napoli" was never apparently meant to mean anything except that it was once owned by a family named Belknap. "The white elephants," Henry James called these cottages as long ago as 1907, "all cry and no wool." Concluding "The Sense of Newport" in his *American Scene,* James found that the resort made little:

> What an idea, originally, to have seen this miniature spot of earth, where the sea-nymphs on the curved sands, at the worst, might have chanted back to the shepherds, as a mere breeding-ground for white elephants! They look queer and conscious and lumpish—some of them, as with an air of the brandished proboscis, really grotesque—while their averted owners, roused from a witless dream, wonder what in the world is to be done with them. The answer to which, I think, can only be that there is absolutely nothing to be done; nothing but to let them stand there always, vast and blank, for reminder to those concerned of the prohibited degrees of witlessness, and of the peculiarly awkward vengeances of affronted proportion and discretion.

Half a century later, after such a vast reshuffling of the social deck as even James might have doubted possible, James has his wish. The castles of Newport still stand, as mute testimony to the Newport revolution. The figures of this revolution are far from mute. The ten largest cottages were in 1925 assessed for $2,773,000; in 1950 they were assessed for $823,150. In 1950 also, only four of the ten cottages were still in private hands and tax-producing, and one of these, "The Breakers," has since been producing as a paying museum. In 1900 Newport's summer estates accounted for 50 per cent of all Newport taxes; in 1950 they accounted for less than 20 per cent. And, if tax records and per cents seem a mundane way of expressing what has happened at Newport, Newporters themselves are happy to supply more colorful expressions. "Isn't it terrible?" asks Mrs. Cornelius Vanderbilt. "And you know," she adds, "*our* heads were the first to fall." Schuyler Livingston Parsons, dean of Newport "extra men," is still in a daze. "It all stopped at once," he says. "I can't remember when I had a white tie on last." Even Mrs. "Kitty Mouse" Norman Cook, one of the most popular social figures on the island, and a lady whose cottage is only half in Newport—the other half is in the neighboring town of Portsmouth—has not escaped. "It's not so bad for us," she says. "It's awful for the servants."

In their great days Newporters themselves were by no means averse to using figures. "A man who has a million dollars," old John Jacob Astor once told Julia Ward Howe, "is as well off as if he were rich." Other Newporters also talked in equally round numbers—Newport's "newspaper dollars," they were called. "We are not rich," Mrs. Stuyvesant Fish used to say. "We have only a few million." Maude Parker recalls that one Newport hostess barred from her dinner table people who had less than *five* million dollars; another hostess barred people whose cottage, furnished, cost less than a million. Mrs. O. H. P. Belmont was, of course, on safe ground. Her "Marble House" cost $2,000,000 to build and $9,000,000 to furnish. The Pembroke Joneses used to say that they set aside $300,000 at the beginning of each Newport season for "extra entertainment." In a similar manner, Mrs. Henry Clews, grandniece of Dolly Madison and reputed to be Newport's best-dressed lady of her era, declared that each summer she set aside $10,000 for "mistakes in her clothes." Richard Lounsbery recalls that a single Newport ball cost $200,000—in the days, of course, when not only dollars were dollars but also when balls were balls.

Dinners were dinners, too. Both Mrs. Ogden Mills and Mrs. Elbridge Gerry used to boast that they could give a dinner for a hundred without calling in extra help. There were hand-painted individual place cards at every place and between every two guests there was an elaborate French menu in front and a powdered-haired, knee-breeched, liveried English footman behind. Ten-course meals were eaten off solid gold services. At one dinner a stream flowed down the middle of the table in which "vivid fish swam pleasantly"; at another there was a cage in the center of the table filled with parrots of "singular hues and utterances." At still another the center of the table was covered with sand; at each place was a small sterling silver pail and a matching shovel. At a given signal half a hundred guests dug frantically into the sand in front of them for their favors—thousands of dollars' worth of rubies, sapphires, emeralds and diamonds. Ordinarily, however, the pace was leisurely. The late Mrs. Maud Howe Elliott recalls a dinner at the cottage of George Wales. "We were at the table," she said, "three mortal hours."

When such dinners palled, Newporters took strong measures. At the most memorable dinner in the resort's history Newport Society was introduced to Prince del Drago from Corsica. The Prince was ersatz—a monkey attired in full evening dress. Second only to this famous "Monkey Dinner" was the so-called "Dogs' Dinner." In this, a regular Newport dinner table was taken off its foundations and placed on a veranda—on trestles about a foot high. A hundred dogs participated, most of them in fancy dress; the menu was stewed liver and rice, fricassee of bones and shredded dog biscuit.

At human fancy dress affairs Newport costumes were the height of invention. At one costume ball Philadelphia's Henry Carter and his wife arrived and explained their costume to the announcing footman at the entrance of the ballroom. Carter, a small man, was dressed as Henry IV; his wife, a large woman, represented a Norman peasant. "Henry the Fourth," shouted the footman, "and an enormous pheasant."

Grand Duke Boris, brother-in-law of Czar Nicholas II, compared pre-income tax Newport and pre-revolution Russia. "I have never dreamed of such luxury as I have seen at Newport," he said. "We have nothing to equal it in Russia." Costume balls and ten-course dinners were not the only way Newport had of showing this luxury. Philadelphia's Fairman Rogers, author of the authoritative manual of coaching, was particularly grand; he personally landscaped his estate by throwing down a magnificent Persian rug on his lawn and ordering his army of gardeners to follow its colors and patterns in exact detail. At "Bois Doré" Harrisburg's William Fahnestock hung from his trees artificial fruits which were made, like the faucets in his bathroom, of fourteen-carat gold.

On the Arthur Curtiss James place in Sunrise Valley there was a complete Swiss village. There were half a hundred beautifully kept-up farm buildings and a complete roster of animals, each eulogized by a pictorial signboard in verse. In the James piggery each pig had his own individual yard and sty.

Newport built few swimming pools because its lush era antedated them; nonetheless, the resort posted many achievements in sports. Pierre Lorillard achieved what construction men at the time believed was impossible when he built a pier over the reefs in front of "The Breakers" and was thus enabled to bring his enormous yacht *Rhoda* right up to his front door. On the other hand, Philadelphia's Mrs. Richard Cadwalader could not bring her 408-foot *Savarona* even into Newport's harbor, or indeed into any port in this country. Mrs. Cadwalader refused to pay the duty involved, and her yacht, largest in the world, was reduced to ports abroad. It was fitted with antique rugs and tapestries, gold-plated bathroom fixtures, and a full-sized pipe organ. T. Suffern Tailer built the country's most elaborate private golf course. His "Ocean Links," as it was called, reproduced the most famous individual holes of all the world's most famous courses. Newport's horse-and-buggy days were unequaled anywhere. Several Newporters had as many as twenty different kinds of carriages in their stables and in the old Alfred Gwynne Vanderbilt stables the horses' names were inscribed on gold name plates. O. H. P. Belmont could not bear to have his horses under another roof; the ground floor of "Belcourt" was an all stable affair. Here, in stalls designed by Richard Hunt, with a tasteful barracks for a battery of grooms alongside, the Belmont horses had a change of equipment morning, afternoon and evening. For the night they were bedded down on pure white linen sheets with the Belmont crest embroidered on them. Above the stables, in the salon of "Belcourt," Belmont kept two stuffed horses, old favorites of his, which were mounted by stuffed riders in chain armor.

What any other social resort had, Newport had also and more besides. If Lenox's Mrs. Edwards Spencer kept a pig as a pet in her parlor, Newport's Mrs. John King Van Rensselaer recalls seeing a Newport dowager drive down Bellevue Avenue with a pig seated in her victoria beside her and a monkey on each shoulder. If at Saratoga a President of the United States, Martin Van Buren, was snubbed by Mrs. DeWitt Clinton, at Newport President Chester A. Arthur was snubbed not only by resorters but also by footmen; on the steps of the Newport Casino he was reduced to calling for his own carriage. If Bar Harbor's Joseph Pulitzer imported the entire New York Symphony Orchestra to play for himself and his guests, Newport's Mrs. Cornelius Vanderbilt, Jr., thought nothing, in 1902, of closing for two days a New York hit show of that era, *The Wild Rose*, and having the entire company transported for a private performance at "Beaulieu." Even as late as the depression era the resort was in a class by itself. The late Atwater Kent was perhaps the country's greatest latter-day party-giver. His affairs cut a swath through the societies of Bar Harbor, Palm Beach, Southampton and, finally, in his last days, Hollywood itself. But even at his best party weight—which consisted of three orchestras and some three thousand guests—Kent was not up to Newport. Bar Harbor's Mrs. John DeWitt Peltz recalls that after watching Kent for several seasons at the Maine resort she had the pleasure of going down to Newport and attending several functions there. Returning to Bar Harbor, she was asked to describe them. "Why," she said, "they made At Kent look like pot luck!"

In Newport's Golden Age Newporters even went to church in a memorable manner. The box pews of old Trinity were upholstered in the same colors as the liveries of the worshipers, with the Hon. Edwin Morgan's pew taking first honors. In the rear of this, which was known as the Morgan Parlor Car and was sumptuously swathed in crimson damask, were two large armchairs. These were for Mr. and Mrs. Morgan. In front were a trio of tastefully tapestried and well-oiled swivel chairs—these, of course, for the Morgan children who, when affected by the tedium of worship, could twist and turn to their hearts' content.

It is not surprising that from such pews Newporters faced the hereafter, with its uncertain standard of living, with some alarm. Old John Jacob Astor was particularly concerned about his future life. One day, to his faithful coachman, William, he put the fateful question. "William," he said, "where do you expect to go when you die?" The answer was hardly calculated to settle John Jacob's mind.

"Why, sir," replied William, "I have always expected to go where the other people go."

Newport's great social tradition was pioneered as far back as the eighteenth century by the redoubtable Godfrey Malbone. Newport's first merchant prince and king of its slave-traders, Malbone was born in Virginia but in 1744 he built Newport's first showplace. The estate cost $100,000—an enormous sum in those days—and it included not only ten acres of terraced gardens but also an underground passage to the beach, by which Malbone was apparently able to land his cargoes without the knowledge of customs officers. Malbone's parties were princely affairs. In 1756 he entertained George Washington, on the latter's twenty-fourth birthday. In the Library of Congress, in Washington's own handwriting, is a record of Washington's having paid for the affair: "By cash to Mr. Malbones servants, four pounds. To a Bowle broke, four pounds." Breakage was considerably higher at the parties for Malbone's returning ship captains. If their voyage had been a successful one they were permitted, at the conclusion of the dinner, to break every dish and glass on the table. Finally, in 1766, Malbone gave the most elaborate dinner in Newport's early-day history. As his slaves were serving the first course, a fire broke out. When guests and slaves failed to extinguish it, neighbors also arrived to help. Mrs. Malbone, however, barred the door. The neighbors' feet were dirty, she noted, and she did not wish them to soil her "immaculately clean floors." When it became apparent that the house was going to be lost, Malbone joined Mrs. Malbone at the door. "By God," he said, "if I have to lose my house, I shall not lose my dinner." Whereupon he ordered his slaves to set the table out under the trees and there, by the light of the now blazing house, Malbone, Mrs. Malbone and their guests finished their banquet. Late in his career Malbone became convinced that money was everything. "What," he asked, "will not money buy?" The next day, on Newport's Town Hall, an anonymous poem was posted:

> All the money in the place
> Won't buy old Malbone a handsome face.

Before the Revolution Newport was, as a port and city, at the peak of its prosperity. It was led in commerce only by

Philadelphia and Boston—although in 1770 a visitor to New York wrote back to the Newport *Mercury* that "at its present rate of progress New York will soon be as large as Newport." The Revolution put an abrupt end to this commercial supremacy; the town not only suffered greatly under British occupation but also, in the years following, grass grew in the principal streets. As early as the summer of 1784, however, the sailing packet *Governor Gerard* brought a sizable contingent of Charleston planters to Newport. By the early part of the nineteenth century the resort boasted Rhetts, Middletons, Rutledges, Alstons and Gists from South Carolina, as well as Randolphs, Myers and Lathams from Virginia. In the early days these Southerners either stayed in boardinghouses or rented farmhouses, and the social life was simple. A characteristic feature of the life was the so-called "joggle-board." This board, a kind of social seesaw, had chair seats and backs affixed to each end, and each farmhouse boasted one—out under the trees. Ladies of the day, who found that superintending their servants failed to give them enough exercise, invited a friend over and daintily pushed up and down for a half hour or so.

Newport's first summer hotels, which date from the 1830's, were the Bellevue and Whitfield's, Whitfield's being later renamed the Touro House. Although the Aquidneck House, the Perry, the Freemont, the Fillmore and the United States followed in rapid succession, only one Newport hotel became nationally famous. A "huge, yellow pagoda factory," as George William Curtis called it, it was named Ocean House and its opening in 1845, according to Henry Tuckerman, "reduced Saratoga to being a hotel while Newport was a realm."

Along with this all but forgotten hotel period, between

the Southern planters and the coming of the New York cottagers, the resort also had a distinguished intellectual period. In later days Edith Wharton, whom old Newporters recall as "Pussy" Jones of "Pencraig," and who wrote her first book at Newport—a study of interior decoration written in collaboration with Newporter Ogden Codman—was never happy there. "I did not care," she wrote, "for watering-place mundanities." But in an earlier era, in the days following the Civil War, when Colonel Higginson settled at the resort, he declared that there were more authors living in Newport than anywhere else in America. This author group, which ranged from Boston's Edgar Allan Poe to California's Bret Harte, also included Dr. Oliver Wendell Holmes, Henry Wadsworth Longfellow, Henry James, George Bancroft and Julia Ward Howe; to it was added such Boston wits as Helen Choate Bell and Thomas Gold Appleton. Newport's Professor Wolcott Gibbs loved nature. "Who loves his fellow man," he said, "plants trees." Mrs. Bell disagreed. "Go kick a tree," she said, "for me." Appleton, who divided his time between Nahant and Newport, was at both resorts the prince of intellectual dilettantes. "A good mixer," the late Maud Howe Elliott described him, "of salads and of guests."

Appleton's favorite occupation at Newport—an indication of the simple life at the resort in those days—was painting oil landscapes on rocks which he picked up at Newport Beach. Already Newport had developed a high artistic reputation. Among its luminaries had been portrait painter Gilbert Stuart and miniature painter Edward Malbone, a distant relative of the merchant prince, Godfrey Malbone. These were followed by still another portrait painter, John Singer Sargent, as well as by such pioneer American artists as William Hunt and John LaFarge. Hunt's brother, the architect

Richard Hunt, was also a Newporter of this period. Born in Paris, he was acclaimed the first American architect to study his profession at the Beaux Arts; later, after he had designed "The Breakers" and "Marble House" and many other Newport cottages, it was said of him that he found Newport a town of wood and left it a town of marble.

Gresham's Law of first "nice" and then "naughty" millionaires following artists and "solid people" never held too accurately at Newport; in fact, back in its "solid people" era, the resort had at least one millionaire, William Beach Lawrence, who caused the most trouble among the natives of any resorter in Newport's history. Having married the daughter of the wealthy New York merchant, Archibald Gracie, Lawrence purchased, in 1844, almost the whole of Ochre Point for fourteen thousand dollars; many years later he sold for the same sum one acre of this property to a friend of his named Pendleton.

No sooner had the sale been made than the Governor regretted it and proceeded to build a stone wall between the properties. This wall, which extended to the water's edge, cut off the famous Cliff Walk, which even in those days had long been a favorite of native Newporters, and rising in rebellion, they pulled the wall down. Lawrence promptly rebuilt it, this time facing it with broken glass; he also bought a fierce bull which he pastured in the property. Despite the glass and the bull, Newporters once more pulled the wall down and this time they threw it into the sea. Lawrence promptly took to the courts. The case hinged on the discovery of an old right which gave the fishermen public access to the shore for fishing and collecting seaweed. Carried to the Supreme Court after years of litigation, the case was finally settled in favor of the natives and against Lawrence only after the staging of a test shipwreck. The case established a firm precedent. To this day the right of Newport natives to walk between beach and lawn around the great estates, beginning at Forty Steps and traveling around Ochre Point, Rough Point and finally to Bailey's Beach itself, is inviolate. As for Newport resorters they have had to grin and bear the intrusion—although, characteristically, they have made the Cliff Walk as difficult as possible. In some cases the walk has been pushed out on the rocks on bridges, in others it has been depressed below lawn level, and in one case at least, opposite "Marble House," the walk is a complete tunnel.

Each of Newport's great early-day hostesses, Mrs. Sydney Brooks, Mrs. Paran Stevens and Mrs. Nicholas Beach, was responsible for inaugurating at least one new form of entertainment at the resort. Mrs. Brooks introduced Newport to salons, Mrs. Stevens to musicales and Mrs. Beach to dancing receptions. With the coming of Mrs. August Belmont, however, the resort had its first real taste of New York high life. The niece of the Commodore Perry of Lake Erie fame, the wife of the Rothschild banker and the mother of Newport's noted brothers, O. H. P. and Perry Belmont, Mrs. Belmont had elegant French manners, beautiful jewels and was a pioneer resorter. When she deserted her beautiful country seat at the once fashionable Staten Island and built "Bythesea" at Newport, the event marked the beginning of a new era. All old-time Newporters today still recall stories of the sensation created by Mrs. Belmont's famous *demi-daumont*. A Paris importation, the carriage was drawn by four horses with no driver but with the two near horses ridden by postilions in short jackets, tight breeches and smart jockey caps.

But all Newport did not cherish ten-course dinners and liveried footmen and other changes which were inaugurated by the coming of the Belmonts. Mrs. John Francis felt these changes most sharply. In her one-servant cottage she had the misfortune one summer to engage a maid who had the summer before worked for the Belmonts. In the time-honored manner of her craft, the maid began unfavorably contrasting everything about her new position with her old. "Mr. Belmont," she said one day, "keeps ten servants," another day, "Mr. Belmont keeps twenty horses." Finally in the middle of still another "Mr. Belmont keeps," Mrs. Francis could stand it no longer. "Mr. Belmont," she snapped, "keeps everything but the Ten Commandments."

Even the Belmonts were nothing to what was coming. The real New York task force descended on Newport with the Kips and the Kernochans, the Lorillards and the Livingstons, the Stuyvesants and the Schermerhorns, the Tiffanys, the Rhinelanders and the Van Rensselaers—and finally the Astors and the Vanderbilts. Newport had already had its distinguished resort individuals—William R. Travers, George Gray Griswold, Bradley Martin and James Gordon Bennett, Jr.—but by far its greatest, from the point of view of the future of the resort, was the one and only Ward McAllister. "Mister Make-a-Lister," as old-time Newporters recall him, McAllister made his most famous list shortly after the momentous occasion on March 24, 1888, when he put in the American vocabulary the phrase "The Four Hundred." "There are only," he told Charles H. Crandell of the New York *Tribune*, "about four hundred people in fashionable New York Society. If you go outside that number you strike people who are either not at ease in a ballroom or else make other people not at ease."

Born in Savannah, Georgia, in 1827, the son of a Southern lawyer, McAllister as a child came north to Newport almost every summer. "A Southern colony," he later described the resort of his childhood days. "Well do I remember," he said, "with my Uncle Sam Ward and Dr. Francis of New York and my father, building bonfires on Paradise Rocks on the Fourth of July and flying kites from Purgatory." As a grown man, with a small fortune made as a lawyer in San Francisco during Gold Rush days, McAllister returned to Newport and bought "Bayside Farm." To this farm he did not hesitate to invite, as he put it, "the *crème de la crème*." Here also he would hire for his parties, for half a day, a flock of Southdown sheep, as well as cattle and cows to give his place, as he called it, "an animated look." One day one of New York's amateur farmers turned to another guest. "Well, it is astonishing," he said. "McAllister has but fifty acres and here he is, keeping a splendid flock of Southdowns, two yoke of cattle, to say nothing of his cows." McAllister smiled. "My friend," he said, "I am not a fancy farmer like yourself. I farm for profit."

McAllister meant what he said. Soon his farm began to pay large social dividends. McAllister himself grew increasingly severe. "He added to the sins of his Southern dialect," said Bar Harbor's late Arthur Train, "a Frenchman's imperial and an Englishman's morning manner." On Newport, McAllister's dictum was firm. "It was the place above all others," he said, "to take social root in." And he advised people not to be afraid of "sitting on the stool of probation" for at least four seasons. Asked by the parents of a girl wishing to enter her into Society how she should pass her summers, McAllister advised that she should have her first season at Bar Harbor. "Here," he said, "she could learn to flirt to her heart's content and vie with the other girls." For the young lady's second summer McAllister suggested Newport, where, he said, "she should have a pair of ponies, a pretty trap, with a well-gotten-up groom, and Worth to dress her." As for McAllister's own picnics, or *fêtes champêtres* as he called them, they soon outranked Mrs. Belmont's dinners and became the most recherché functions at the resort. McAllister himself describes their demand:

> Riding on the Avenue on a lovely summer's day, I would be stopped by a beautiful woman, in gorgeous array, looking so fascinating that if she were to ask you to attempt the impossible, you would at least make the effort. She would open on me as follows: "My dear friend, we are all dying for a picnic. Can't you get one up for us?"
>
> "Why, my dear lady," I would answer, "you have dinners every day, and charming dinners too; what more do you want?"
>
> "Oh, they're not picnics. Any one can give dinners," she would reply; "what we want is one of your picnics. Now, my dear friend, do get one up."
>
> This was enough to fire me, and set me going. So I reply: "I will do your bidding. Fix on the day at once, and tell me what is the best dish your cook makes."
>
> Out comes my memorandum book, and I write: "Monday, 1 P.M., meet at Narragansett Avenue, bring *filet de boeuf piqué,*" and with a bow am off in my little wagon, and dash on, to waylay the next cottager, stop every carriage known to contain friends, and ask them, one and all, to join our country party, and assign to each of them the providing of a certain dish and a bottle of champagne. Meeting young men, I charge them to take a bottle of champagne, and a pound of grapes, or order from the confectioner's a quart of ice cream to be sent to me. My pony is put on its mettle; I keep going the entire day getting recruits; I engage my music and servants, and a carpenter to put down a dancing platform, and the florist to adorn it, and that evening I go over in detail the whole affair, map it out as a general would a battle, omitting nothing, not even a salt spoon; see to it that I have men on the road to direct my party to the

farm, and bid the farmer put himself and family, and the whole farm, in holiday attire.

Old-time Newporters today hardly recall any Mrs. McAllister at all; McAllister's daughter served as hostess for his parties. In short order, however, McAllister attached himself to Mrs. William Backhouse Astor. The former Caroline Schermerhorn and the so-called "Queen of the Four Hundred," Mrs. Astor had joined the New York invasion of Newport and, in keeping with her position, had bought "Beechwood." This cottage, with its high-ceilinged piazzas on three sides, had been a Newport showplace for years; to it Mrs. Astor added Newport's largest ballroom. Nonetheless, she had hard sledding in her early days at the resort. There were two Mrs. William Astors at Newport, Mrs. William Waldorf as well as Mrs. William Backhouse, and living side by side on Bellevue Avenue both insisted on having their mail addressed simply: "Mrs. Astor, Newport." Both were equally formidable. If Mrs. William Backhouse Astor at "Beechwood" called native Newporters her "dear villagers," Mrs. William Waldorf Astor at "Beaulieu" built a brick wall between her cottage and Cliff Walk and kept them away entirely. Finally, with McAllister's help, Mrs. William Backhouse outran the challenging Mrs. William Waldorf, and the latter gave up Newport entirely and took up cottage-keeping in England.

From that time until after the turn of the century, *the* Mrs. Astor reigned supreme. Over her black pompadour, which was later succeeded by a jet-black wig, she wore a diamond tiara and even for her *intime* evenings—for just a hundred or so guests—she took little stock in Andrew Carnegie's dictum that jewel-wearing was a relic of barbarism. She wore a three-strand diamond necklace, a dazzling diamond stomacher and several chains of diamonds in lesser spots. Dignified, reserved, and aloof, she rose above everything and everybody. If her husband gave a particularly gay party on board his yacht and a gossiping lady-in-waiting at her "Beechwood" court would relay the news to her, Mrs. Astor would reply that the sea air was so good for her husband and that it was a shame that she was such a poor sailor or she would accompany him. "I have never even set foot on his yacht," she said. "Dreadful confession for a wife, is it not?"

Outwardly at least, Mrs. Astor saw no evil, heard no evil and spoke no evil. McAllister himself described her qualifications for Newport queenship. "She had," said her court chamberlain, who always spoke of her as his "Mystic Rose," "a just appreciation of the rights of others, and, coming herself from an old Colonial family, a good appreciation of the value of ancestry; always keeping it near her, and bringing it in, in all social matters, but also understanding the importance and power of the new element; recognizing it, and fairly and generously awarding it a prominent place." On young people attending her balls Mrs. Astor's dictum was stern. "I like to have them come," she said, "but they must look after themselves." On people "in trade," as she called it, she wavered; at carpet manufacturers she drew the line. "I buy my carpets from them," she said, "but is that any reason why I should invite them to walk on them?" When the early twentieth-century version of Café Society began to rear its head, Mrs. Astor showed her respect for the new development and made plans for her first Bohemian party. Surprised, the late Lady Mendl asked her whom she was having. "Why, J. P. Morgan," she replied, "and Edith Wharton."

Such majesty was made to order for McAllister, a man who said that one thing he disliked most about America was the custom of shaking hands. When the Navy, largely through the influence of Admiral Luce, established a war college and torpedo station at Newport in 1880, McAllister took full credit for it. It was necessary, he felt, to solve Newport's perennial shortage of men on week nights. "So many of them," McAllister said, "are boat men, don't you know, down Friday night and back again Sunday." With equal pleasure he watched the rapid evacuation of the New England intellectual from the resort. "Fashionable people cultivate and refine themselves," he said. "The talent of and for Society develops itself just as does the talent for art." Finally McAllister applauded Newport's biggest change of all—the end of the hotels. Although the old Ocean House lasted on until it finally burned down in 1898, McAllister had by this time founded a resort civilization so secure that it was not dependent upon mere hotels. Even today Newport remains staunchly anti-hotel. It has its modern Viking Hotel for commercial travelers, but only the Muenchinger King Hotel and the La Forge Cottages are approved social residences.

McAllister died in 1895. As if he had not done enough to establish Newport tradition for all time, his good work at the resort was soon seconded by still another protégé of Mrs. Astor, the remarkable Harry Lehr. If McAllister was the "Autocrat of the Drawing Rooms," Lehr was the so-called "King of the Gilded Age." Born in Baltimore in 1869, the son of a prosperous snuff and tobacco importer, Lehr saw his family reduced to poverty at an early age and never forgot it. "Clod-like people," he wrote in his diary, could stand "the cold grayness of everyday life" but he could not. "Other men have to sweat in offices," he said. "I made up my mind I never would." His answer was a simple one. "I saw that most human beings are fools, and that the best way to live harmoniously with them and make them like you is to pander to their stupidity. They want to be entertained and be made to laugh. They will overlook most anything so long as you amuse them. I did not mind cutting capers for them if I could gain what I wanted through it."

Lehr was admirably suited for his part. In contrast to the sternly-mustached and continental-mannered McAllister, he was blond and boyish-looking with bright blue eyes and a high-pitched voice; his outstanding feature was a humorous-looking nose which he had a remarkable ability to wiggle from side to side. Musically inclined, he had few equals as a party pianist. His first social success was scored in his female impersonation at Baltimore's Paint and Powder Club theatrical, his second on the occasion when, returning from a Baltimore party, he danced in the fountain at Mt. Vernon Place with the famous belle, Miss Louise Gebhard. Since Miss Gebhard held her evening dress up above her knees and a night watchman and several other people witnessed the spectacle, by the next day all Baltimore talked of it. Among other things, it started the Society craze of fountain-wading —one which continued into the F. Scott Fitzgerald era.

Lehr himself was soon searching for deeper waters in which to wade. Invited to "Fairlawn," the Newport cottage of Baltimore's Mrs. I. Townsend Burden, Lehr moved on to Mrs. Elisha Dyer's "Wayside" and there met Mrs. Astor herself. Their first meeting, at a large ball, was a memorable one. Mrs. Astor passed by him resplendent in diamonds and a white dress. Lehr seized a bunch of red roses out of a bowl. "Here," he said, "you look like a walking chandelier. Put these on. You need color." Late in the evening Mrs. Astor, wearing the roses, again passed close to him. This time Lehr was standing in front of a parrot's cage. He looked at Mrs. Astor, then put his finger up to his lips. "Don't interrupt," he said. No one in Mrs. Astor's life had ever spoken to her like that; the "Mystic Rose" was charmed. On the spot she invited Lehr, in preference to Elisha Dyer, to lead her next cotillion. Dyer, furious at being superseded, at once quarreled with his house guest, but Lehr refused to quarrel back. "There are three ways of taking an insult," he said. "You can resent it and walk out of the room, in which case you have committed yourself to a quarrel you may later regret; you can pretend not to hear, or you can laugh and turn it into a joke. I always choose the last, for I find it the most disarming. No one can quarrel with a man who laughs like an idiot." Certainly Newport could not. Newport's *Morning Telegraph* promptly reported Lehr's laugh the "new bona fide sensation" of the resort:

> Haven't you heard "Harry" Lehr's laugh? That shows that you have not been within a hundred miles of Newport this season. Everybody within rifle range of Newport has "Harry's" laugh down by heart. Not that it is stentorian, clangorous or of the ten-ton gun variety. Not at all. But its vibrations, once started, have an initial velocity of a mile a second, and by the end of the third peal, the very earth is undulating in unison, the church steeples begin to wag in perfect time, and the jaded souls of Newport's "h'inner suckles" seem acted upon by some new and potent stimulant.
>
> Mr. Lehr is a Baltimorean. He has money—a little, as Newport riches go; good looks—more, as Newport beauty goes; but it was the laugh that made him king. As Newport's court jester "Harry" is a wonder. He simply laughed himself into the bosom of the ultra exclusives. He has held up the town with his irresistible chuckle, and robbed it of

invitations to dinners, musicales, yacht cruises, barn dances, and heavens knows what not, at his piratical pleasure.

As a resort sport, Lehr was unequaled in Society history. Because he attracted Society's best wherever he went, everything for him was free. In Newport he visited; in New York the Waldorf, Delmonico's and Sherry's all competed for the honor of seeing that he had free board and lodging during the off season. Wetzel made his clothes free, Black, Starr and Frost lent him an endless supply of jewels, Mrs. Stuyvesant Fish and the wives of other railroad men arranged passage on all railroads, and George Kessler, the French champagne agent, paid him six thousand dollars a year for pocket money. The only expense he might have had was postage stamps. Instead of letters, he sent cables and wires—all of which, arranged through Mrs. Clarence Mackay and the wives of other cable magnates, were also free. In return, Lehr aimed to please; his insults to his hostesses and benefactors were cherished. Their diamonds he called "demimondes," their tiaras "ti-rah-rahs." All Newport delighted in his pet names. Mrs. Vanderbilt was his "Alice of 'The Breakers.' " anyone from Boston his "bean," anyone from Texas his "steer." One day he paused before the stained glass windows of "Belcourt" on which O. H. P. Belmont, in the Newport tradition of appropriating coats of arms, had emblazoned the arms of Dunois, the Bastard of Orleans. "My dear Oliver," said Lehr, "why proclaim yourself illegitimate?" On another occasion the Stuyvesant Fishes got up to leave a party. "Sit down, Fishes," said Lehr sharply. "You're not rich enough to leave first." Occasionally Newport's husbands rebelled. More often, they decided that Lehr was, at worst, the most harmless between-week-end diversion that their wives could find. Lehr himself was aware that this was the secret of his success.

"Love affairs," he once said, "are fatal to ambition. I have seen the shore strewn with the wrecks of people who have given away to their passions."

In time Lehr married, his choice falling on Mrs. John Dahlgren, the former Elizabeth Drexel of Philadelphia and later Lady Decies. Mrs. Lehr herself has written the story of her bridegroom entering her room on their wedding night. "In public," he said, "I will be to you everything that a most devoted husband should be to his wife. I will give you courtesy, respect and, apparently, devotion. But you must expect nothing more from me. The less we see of one another except in the presence of others the better." When Mrs. Lehr recovered from the shock enough to ask why he had married her, Lehr explained that it was for her money and that actually she was fortunate, because, as his wife, all doors would be open to her and she would have, as he put it, "a wonderful position" in Society. "How many among our own friends," he asked her, "have entered their wives' rooms on their wedding night with exactly my state of mind? But they prefer hypocrisy to the truth. If I am never your lover when we are alone, at least I will not neglect and humiliate you in public." For twenty-eight years, on this basis, Mr. and Mrs. Lehr carried on.

If Lehr was not serious about marriage he was actually humorous on the subject of Newport Society: "There is only one way to be sure it is safe to associate with people. Wait until you have seen them four or five times at the best cottages. Then you can make no mistake in taking them up yourself." Toward his predecessor, McAllister, he was charitable. "Wardie," he said, "was the voice crying in the wilderness who prepared the way for me." Where "Wardie" had advised that Newport was the place "to take social root in," however, Lehr called it "the Holy of Holies," and advised people to avoid it completely—"like the plague," he put it—unless they were certain they would be acceptable. Otherwise, he felt, it would be their Waterloo and he advised as much. Above all he advised people against taking a cottage and trying to give parties. "Try to get invited for a week or two on someone's yacht," he said, "as an experiment to see whether you are a success or not. In that way you will leave your retreat open to you and you can always pretend that the climate does not suit you and go back to New York without anyone having witnessed your defeat." McAllister said Newport took four seasons for assured social success; Lehr felt it was necessary to be careful even after that. His two "Golden Don'ts," as he called them, for aspiring Newport ladies, were first, Don't try to outdress, outjewel or outentertain the reigning Queens of the resort, and second, Don't try to take any other woman's man. The latter, with characteristic irony in view of his own position, he later defined as "husband, lover or well-wisher."

McAllister and Lehr were not the only luminaries of Newport's Golden Age. Mrs. Henry Barton Jacobs, who regarded even cotillions as undignified, gave dinners of such stateliness that they rivaled those of Mrs. Astor herself. Mrs. Jacobs' previous husband, Robert Garrett, former president of the Baltimore and Ohio Railroad, had for many years before his death suffered from the delusion that he was the Prince of Wales. Many thousands of dollars were spent administering to this delusion. Actors were hired on a permanent basis to impersonate Court officials and a London Court expert was imported to insure the correctness of all Court detail. Garrett himself had the uniform of the principal regiments of every country and daily received bogus ambassadors. His court favorite was Harry Lehr; in turn Lehr's favorite impersonation was the Crown Prince of Germany.

Almost equally formidable was Newport's most elegant widower, the late James J. Van Alen of "Wakehurst." Van Alen, son-in-law of Mrs. Astor, had contributed fifty thousand dollars to the 1892 Democratic campaign and wished to be appointed ambassador to Italy by President Cleveland. Unfortunately for these plans, Bar Harbor's indefatigable Joseph Pulitzer, who knew Van Alen, sent a *World* staff man to report on the potential diplomat. After the *World's* profile, several excerpts of which follow, Van Alen did not become ambassador:

> He wears a single eyeglass with a heavy string attached. He speaks with a weird bastard cockney, which fills Englishmen with wonder. It is the sort of English accent that a man with no talent for imitation might get from hansom-cab drivers and Strand barmaids.
>
> A prize-fighting gentleman of the Bowery was brought to Newport to train the fat off Van Alen. The fighting gentleman, called One-eyed Connelly, said he had never met a man who seemed less fit to be on earth than Van Alen.
>
> Van Alen has all the vanities that an American Ambassador could do without.
>
> He informs whoever will listen that he keeps English mustard in a mustard pot of English silver and French mustard in a French mustard pot.
>
> He entertains few convictions except those which refer to clothes, horses, and Scotch whiskey.
>
> He owns twenty pairs of breeches for hunting, this despite the fact that a Shetland pony could buck him off with a gentle shrug. . . .
>
> If Abraham Lincoln could meet Van Alen his inclination would be to lift Van Alen up by the coat collar and duck him in a muddy pond as a graceful compliment to the Stars and Stripes. If Mr. Cleveland knew Van Alen his inclination would be the same.

From 1890 to 1914 Newport was in its glory. Its southerners, its intellectuals, and its hotels were gone or going, and the Astors and the Vanderbilts, the Belmonts and the Van Alens, the Goelets and the Oelrichs were firmly in the saddle. Price Collier, coming down from Tuxedo, described Newport as "New York Society's best dish, garnished with a little cold Boston celery and a fringe of Philadelphia and Baltimore parsley." But if Newport was New York in the center, and Boston, Philadelphia and Baltimore on the edges, the welcome mat was also out for the Pembroke Joneses from the rice fields of North Carolina, the E. J. Berwinds from the coal fields of Pennsylvania, the tinplate Leedses from Indiana and the coke-operating Paul J. Raineys from Ohio. Out in Newport Harbor, riding at anchor, were such magnificent yachts as Morgan's *Corsair*, Astor's *Nourmahal*, and Bennett's *Lysistrata*—soon to be followed by Drexel's *Sultana*, Higgins' *Varuna*, Leeds' *Noma* and P. A. B. Widener's *Josephine*. And, says one yachting historian, recalling the scene: "Mr. Thomas Dolan's houseboat also worked her way along the shore to be with the anointed." Newporters felt strongly about the names for their yachts; the favored names were those which were Oriental and regal in origin. *Nourmahal* meant "Light of the Harem," *Sultana*, "Wife (or Mistress) of the Sultan," and *Varuna*, "The Supreme Cosmic Deity." *Noma* was the first two letters of each of Mrs. Leeds' first two names, "Nonnie May." "It's a good name to send through a megaphone," Leeds used to tell Newport dinner parties. To prove it he would cup his hands and bellow, "Noma! Noma!"

But the best place to see the splendor of Newport in the Gay Nineties was in the coaching parade. Bellevue Avenue was, every afternoon in the week, from three o'clock on, a spectacle never equaled at any other resort. Vanderbilt coachmen wore maroon coats, Astor blue. As the rubber wheels of the coaches whirred silently around behind the rhythmic clop-clopping of the horses' hooves, all Newport paused to stare. There were all kinds of turnouts—*grand daumonts de visites, demi-daumonts,* road coaches, barouches, landaus, victorias, four-in-hands, tandems, spike teams—three horses, a pair together in back and a single in front—as well as pony phaetons, governess carts, dogcarts and T-carts.

Everything was spick and span. The horses were groomed and currycombed within an inch of their lives, and the men on the box sat as stiff as statues. Richmond Barrett recalls the black dazzle of boots and the bright white of breeches being matched only by the shiny gold buttons of uniforms and the long white gloves of the ladies sitting behind. To him the coaches looked as if they had emerged not from stables at all, but from ladies' boudoirs. "The imaginative onlooker," he says of the drives, "could almost picture the maid, after she had laid out the mistress's costume for the afternoon, taking the lid off the big white box that contained the carriage, the coachmen and the horses themselves, whisking away yards and yards of tissue paper from around them and lifting them out in a cloud of fragrant sachet." When young Harry Jones, dressed in a frock coat, a tall hat and pearl-gray trousers, helped his girl into a T-cart—the girl dressed in a white silk dress with a black satin stripe, a hat wreathed with red roses and draped in a green veil—his young sister Edith, later Mrs. Wharton, thought of gods and goddesses. "What wonder," she wrote, "that an eager-eyed little girl watching the stately comings and goings from the verandah of 'Pencraig,' still thought that old Mr. Bedlow's Olympian gods and goddesses must have looked like her brother Harry and his lovely companion when they started off for a turn along some supernal Ocean Drive."

The manners on these drives were as extraordinary as the drives themselves. The wind blew the door of one lady's coach shut before she had entered; her coachman, stiff as a ramrod on the box, heard the accustomed signal, cracked his whip and took the entire drive without her. In the days before the opening of the Ocean Drive, it was often necessary for the coaches, traveling back and forth, to pass and repass each other. "The first time you met a friend," recalled Maud Howe Elliott, "you made a ceremonious bow, the second time you smiled, the third you looked away." The *faux pas* of *faux pas* was overtaking another coach of superior, or senior, social gravity. One young lady, whose new coachman did not recognize her mother's carriage, committed *lèse majesté*. The next morning the young lady hustled over to her mother's house to apologize. She explained that her coachman had no idea of his offense. "You might have told him," replied her mother.

Manners at the dinners were equally courtly. New York lawyer Lispenard Stewart, perennial bachelor, was considered the prize catch of the resort's beaux. One day, as he was escorting the young belle, Mrs. Henry O. Havemeyer, Jr., into a dinner at Mrs. Belmont's "Marble House," Mrs. Havemeyer suddenly tired of Stewart's pompous manner and, without a word of explanation, fled from him, crossed the room and drew up a chair with friends at another table. "I was faced with two alternatives," Stewart recalled. "Should I remember my birth and breeding and offer her my arm as we left the dining room, or should I obey my natural impulse and leave her to walk out alone." All the long dinner Stewart pondered his problem, and all the long dinner Mrs. Belmont and her other guests anxiously awaited the outcome. "In the end," said Stewart, "my breeding won. When we rose from the table, I bowed stiffly to her, held out my arm and escorted her back to the drawing room. But I never addressed a single word to her, and I never will again."

In its great days Newport was the center of the sporting world, and particularly the center of the new world of tennis —or lawn tennis, as it was called to distinguish it from the older court tennis. Invented in 1873 by the Englishman, Major Walter Clopton Wingfield, who first patented the game under the remarkable name "Sphairistike," lawn tennis saw its first American court at the Staten Island Cricket and Base Ball Club. When the Newport Casino opened in 1880, Newport was granted the national championship. This championship was won for eight straight years by the peerless Richard Dudley Sears, a Boston resorter of such racket eminence that in 1943 his obituary stated that his "death represented the end of an era of ruffles and parasols, roped-off lawns and sunny afternoons, lopsided tennis bats and the genteel pat of ball against languid strings." At about the same time the late Tom Pettit, Casino professional, was watching a group of modern tournament players. "If I'd known how much money there was in being an amateur," he said, "I'd never have turned pro."

But the Newport Casino, in the Gay Nineties at least, was more than the scene of Newport tennis. In fact, by 1885 the massive building on Bellevue Avenue, built by James Gordon Bennett, Jr., and designed by Stanford White, was the center of Newport life. The clubhouse, a curious combination of Victorian grandeur and Chinese detail, still stands today almost unchanged from those days; hordes of sparrows still camp on its many-gabled roof and along its vine-covered sides. Entering off Bellevue Avenue one still passes first the branch shops of the smart New York stores and then enters under a tunnel passageway into the inner circle of gardened courts and lawns. On the Horse Shoe Piazza in the old days Mullaly's String Orchestra played every morning. Here, on the high stools up on the second floor, the resorters sat and gossiped and looked down on the townspeople below, and each morning just as regularly the townspeople gathered on the Bellevue Avenue sidewalk to gossip and look up. The "rubber plants," the resorters called the starers below; nonetheless, for one dollar apiece, they were admitted to watch Casino balls and cheer for their favorite belles. These belles were almost invariably described as "willowy"—a favorite word of the day. The slim Mrs. John Jacob Astor, the former Ava Willing and the later Lady Ribblesdale, was perhaps the most famous. "I remember the extraordinary lovely lines of her instep and foot," said Michael Strange, who, as Blanche Oelrichs, was herself a Newport belle. "Sculped and isolated in a lit-up cabinet, it might have passed for an extreme sample of breeding." The resort's noted Whelan twins, Mrs. Robert Goelet and Mrs. Craig Biddle, were also in the approved Newport belle tradition. Tall and dark, with long flowing lines and only an occasional gentle curve, they were Newport's idea of perfect grace in a ballroom. "How beautifully they stood and moved!" exclaimed Miss Strange, "with their evening dresses caught up under their breasts, wearing fresh gardenias in their hair, their slim throats encircled by necklaces of emeralds and sapphires. . . ."

To many Newporters the most fascinating of all the belles was Mrs. Philip Lydig, the ex-Mrs. W. E. D. Stokes and the former Rita de Acosta. Mrs. Lydig was born in Spain, had dark velvety skin, waist-long lustrous black hair and such deep black eyes that they were unforgettable. She had delicate health and was always in intriguing difficulties, either financial or male in nature. Nonetheless, she invariably found enough admirers to extract her from these difficulties—as well as to plunge her into new ones—and whether she was at "death's door" or dancing in the most décolleté gown ever seen at Newport, she was always the center of the stage. She could be extraordinarily calm. On discovering that her husband in Paris was apparently keeping as his mistress a ballerina who dressed in shockingly bad taste, Mrs. Lydig promptly had the lady go to her own dressmaker. "I can't have you going around with a creature who looks like that," she told her husband directly. At other times her temper was equally extraordinary. One week end she drove out in her electric car to meet an ex-beau who was arriving on the ferry. On the way back he told her that he had come all the way back from Egypt to see her; he had decided that unless she would have an affair with him life was not worth living. "Very well," said Mrs. Lydig, "we'll die together." Without another word she ran her car at full speed into a telegraph pole. The car was ruined and the beau had to be taken to a hospital. Mrs. Lydig walked home unhurt.

Actually, no picture of Newport at the turn of the century would be complete without the appearance of that symbol of the new age—the automobile. More than one historian of the industry has, in fact, credited Newport with being primarily responsible for the promotion of "bubbles," as cars were then called. Newporters themselves had no idea of their service—"Nobody dreamed," Stuyvesant Fish recently recalled, "that automobiles would come into general use"—but all Newport activities were thoroughly reported and people all over the country wanted automobiles, if for no other reason, to follow the Four Hundred.

The Newport craze began in 1897 when O. H. P. Belmont imported a French machine. Harry Payne Whitney promptly replied with a whole stableful of "bubbles" and when William K. Vanderbilt and John Jacob Astor also began replacing their horses with the "White Ghost" and the "Red Devil," as they were called, the race was on. Newport's first real automobile race occurred early in 1899 when the "bubblers," attired in dusters, veils and goggles, long-gauntleted gloves and long-visored caps, vied for honors at ten miles an hour.

More memorable than this beach-racing was the first great obstacle race of September 7, 1899. For this event the grounds of Belmont's "Belcourt" were transformed into an obstacle park. The race was a kind of automobile *slalom*, the course being marked out not only by flags but also by all manner of stuffed dummy figures. These figures represented horses, dogs, nurses, children, maids, policemen and other obstacles. The idea of the race was to drive by the figures, on a time basis, without knocking them down. Belmont himself drove first with Mrs. Stuyvesant Fish as his co-pilot. Their car was decorated with an arbor of cat-o'-nine-tails with a stuffed eagle on top; in front, extending a full ten feet ahead of the car, was a long pole also decorated with flowers. Behind Belmont came Ambassador James W. Gerard and Mrs. Belmont. Their car was buried in blue hydrangeas, Newport's favorite flower, and Mrs. Belmont carried a whip made of hydrangeas and daisies. In the third car Harry Lehr drove and Mrs. Astor, complete with hydrangea-collared lapdog, rode shotgun. All three of these contestants, as well as some fifteen others, fared badly, knocking over the obstacles like tenpins, but Colonel Jack Astor, partnered by Mrs. Ladenburg, emerged victorious. "He steered," says one reporter present, "with the same cool-headed dash that distinguished him while serving under fire at Santiago."

With all this outward splendor there was, even in the utterly unself-conscious era of Newport's Golden Age, the rumblings of an inner discontent. Mrs. Lydig herself, whose own life was no small tragedy, expresses this feeling in her *Tragic Mansions*. During Tennis Week, in the resort's heyday, she took a distinguished French author on a tour:

> I took him driving, one afternoon, to show him the sights, and whenever we passed a conspicuously luxurious home, he would ask eagerly: "What is really going on inside there? Are they happy? What do they make of life?" He asked it as one might ask what sort of social relations existed in an Eskimo igloo, and in trying to give him a truthful answer, I found myself, to my surprise, invariably relating the most shocking histories of grief and scandal.
>
> He became as excited as a street gamin in the chamber of horrors of a musée of wax-works. "What misery!" he would cry. "What drama! What a plot for Dostoievsky! Do they write these tales, your American authors? How I wish I knew this American scene! We have nothing so colorful in France."

Mrs. Lydig admitted that the French author's point of view was new to her but suddenly, she admitted, she saw the mansions as he saw them—"as dramatic as the two hours of concentrated incidents that make a stage play." She first looked around her in astonishment, then began to ask herself, "Where is there a happy home among us? Is it possible that there is *none*?" Finally she wrote her conclusions—as of 1927:

> All over America, to-day, people are imitating the conduct and ideals of our fashionable rich society, the so-called

> "smart set" of the East; and I am convinced that those ideals are false ideals, tragic ideals, and that it is suicidal for America to imitate them. They are not truly American. They are largely an importation from abroad, and they are much more pernicious here than they are in the social systems that originated them.

"Many women will rise up to fill my place," said Mrs. Astor, "but I hope my influence will be felt in one thing, and that is, in discountenancing the undignified methods employed by certain women to attract a following."

There was no doubt, at least as far as Newport was concerned, whom Mrs. Astor meant. She meant the three successors to her throne, Newport's Great Triumvirate, Mrs. Hermann Oelrichs, Mrs. O. H. P. Belmont and Mrs. Stuyvesant Fish. These three had actively challenged the "Mystic Rose" long before her death in 1908; by the turn of the century they had all but seized the scepter. In her last years Mrs. Astor's mind failed. Her final summers at "Beechwood" were spent in solitary splendor. "Still erect," says Lloyd Morris, "still bravely gowned and jeweled, she stood quite alone, greeting imaginary guests long dead, exchanging pleasantries with ghosts of the utmost social distinction."

Far from ghosts were Mrs. Astor's successors. If Newport called them its Great Triumvirate, they themselves preferred the title of Newport's Social Strategy Board. The Board was jury-rigged; actually they feuded with each other as often as they did with outside challengers, and, if they had any one thing in common, it was that they were all extreme individualists. The least known was Mrs. Oelrichs of "Rosecliff." Daughter of the gaudy Irish Comstock Loder and wife of the dapper North German Lloyder, Theresa, or Tessie as she was called, had been a handsome raven-haired belle in her younger days and she refused to allow any of her later misfortunes to interfere with her career as a dowager dynamo. Troubled by increasing deafness, she simply substituted, for conversation of other people, a steady stream of her own small talk. Coupled with Mrs. Oelrichs' deafness went a remarkable tendency to put on weight. When all her masseurs and masseuses failed, she substituted such a severe corset that it required the services of a strong male servant to fit. Music, literature and art were to Mrs. Oelrichs only names but no Newporter had a higher reputation as a housewife. She ran "Rosecliff" like a first sergeant. In contrast to other Newport hostesses, she had no personal maid and up at eight each morning—after doing her own hair—she made a personal tour of inspection of every room in her cottage. Then in her electric runabout she would tour her garage and stables. Above all she had a passion for cleanliness. Every bed in "Rosecliff" was made up fresh every day and when she spent a night in a hotel she took her own bedding with her. At the Ritz in Paris she even had her own bed—a privilege for which, since the hotel staff had to set the bed up the day before she arrived and take it down the day after she left, she was always charged for two extra days. At "Rosecliff" if a marble floor was not scrubbed to her satisfaction she would take soap and mop and scrub it herself. "When I die," she used to say, "bury me with a cake of Sapolio in one hand and a scrubbing-brush in the other. They are my symbols."

Unfortunately Mrs. Oelrichs' attention to detail brought on still another misfortune. Out supervising some repairs on the cottage and shouting orders to carpenters above her, she was hit in the eye by a falling tack. She was instantly blinded in one eye. But even this she took in stride. Her vision in the other eye was unimpaired, and with one eye she was still a match for any rival hostess. Her most memorable party was her "White Ball"; for this the ballroom of "Rosecliff" was completely decorated in white and all guests came in white. The white marble balustrade of "Rosecliff" overlooked the sea—but not over Newport Harbor. Mrs. Oelrichs promptly remedied this defect by ordering a dozen full-sized skeleton ships with white hulls. She had these anchored out in the water in front of the balustrade; brilliantly illuminated at night, they gave the illusion of a full white fleet at anchor.

In spite of such luxury, and unknown to many even in the Newport swirl about her, Mrs. Oelrichs led a private life which was as difficult as her own physical ills. Although always in love with her husband, he was not with her and they had lived apart for many years, Mr. Oelrichs quietly in San Francisco, Mrs. Oelrichs noisily in New York and Newport. Finally Mrs. Oelrichs received word that he had been in the San Francisco earthquake and was returning to New York by a certain train. She fitted out her New York house with flowers, redid her husband's room and personally went down to Brooks Brothers to pick out all kinds of new clothes for him. For once she planned, instead of her usual elaborate dinners, a simple supper *à deux*; it was as if she were trying to begin a new and different kind of life—for him alone. At last everything was ready and she sat down to wait. Shortly after her husband was due to arrive the door opened. She jumped up expectantly. It was Herbert, the Oelrichs' butler. He had come to tell her that he had seen Mr. Oelrichs walking up Fifth Avenue. Mr. Oelrichs, he reported, had gone directly to his club.

Like Mrs. Astor and an extraordinary number of other Newport ladies, Mrs. Oelrichs lost her mind in the end.

"During those last years," her niece Michael Strange recalled, "when none of us ever saw her, she would wander, a fragile and still incredibly beautiful person, her raven hair with its deep wave gone snow-white, through the rooms of her immense marble copy of the Villa Trianon, reseating her guests over and over again, pressing them to take just another ice, one more glass of champagne!"

The second member of Newport's Great Triumvirate was a very different kind of lady. Her name was Alva Smith and she was born in Mobile, Alabama, in 1853, the daughter of a cotton planter. Never beautiful but rather on the plump side and with early graying hair, she had, even as a child, been driven by an impulsive kind of discontent with the world as she found it; she always preferred to read and think about the old days—particularly the days of the Medici. Traveling to France to boarding school she returned to take a trip to White Sulphur Springs in 1875. Here, at the great match-making resort of Southern belles, Alva agreed to become the wife of William K. Vanderbilt. Young Vanderbilt was a grandson of the old Commodore Vanderbilt, a man who was not only still alive but who had also, at the age of seventy-three, recently married a young Mobile belle himself. Despite this early evidence of marital proclivity, the Vanderbilts had not yet won high social recognition. As Alva, who all her life liked to remind people that her mother was "a Desha of Kentucky," then recalled, "I was the first girl of my set to marry a Vanderbilt."

With Alva, the Vanderbilts' social deficiencies were to be made up for good. Her husband, a reserved man socially, was at least wealthy. The young couple had a special train for their honeymoon and their train was given the right of way over all other trains from New York to Saratoga. Furthermore, Alva's husband soon became far more wealthy. In 1877, two years after her marriage, the old Commodore died, leaving Alva's father-in-law $100,000,000, the largest fortune in the country in those days. By the time her father-in-law also died, in 1885, this sum had become $200,000,000, and by this time Alva had seen to it that he had been persuaded to leave his fortune to his sons in equal shares—by no means always the practice in those days. Thus she, as the wife of the second son, shared equally with Mrs. Cornelius Vanderbilt, wife of the elder son. Two years before, in 1883, the young Mrs. Vanderbilt had with one blow put all Vanderbilts together on an equal footing with the Astors. This blow was struck at the $200,000 fancy dress housewarming she gave her $3,000,000 New York château. Young Miss Caroline Astor had already made plans to appear with friends in a "Star Quadrille." Hearing of these plans Mrs. Vanderbilt let it be known that since Mrs. Astor had never come to call, it would be quite impossible to ask her daughter to her château. Promptly the mountain came to Mahomet. Mrs. Astor called—and the Vanderbilts were in Society.

Moving on to Newport in the *Alva,* the world's largest yacht, Mrs. Vanderbilt built "Marble House," the world's most expensive resort cottage. An $11,000,000 undertaking, built behind fences so high that not even neighbors could see what was going on, "Marble House" was designed by Richard Hunt and was, and indeed still is, Newport's most striking cottage. With a white marble ramp for a driveway—one which sweeps in a rising arc up to the cottage from the two Bellevue Avenue gates—the cottage is itself a temple of white marble with pilasters and capitals which are modeled on, though slightly larger than, those of the Temple of the Sun at Baalbek. But Mrs. Vanderbilt, who was always, according to Harry Lehr, "knee-deep in mortar," had more building to do. She imported a corps of Chinese artisans to construct, out on the Cliff Walk in front of "Marble House," a red-and-gold lacquered teahouse. Everything about the structure was authentic and the teahouse was a truly gorgeous one. Only one detail was overlooked; there was no way to make tea in it. On discovering this, Mrs. Vanderbilt ordered the building of a miniature railroad. When this was completed her guests were treated to the spectacle of footmen in full livery, squatting in miniature cars holding silver tea trays over their heads, being whisked in and out of the hydrangeas as they wound their way from the Greek pantry to the Chinese temple.

Mrs. Vanderbilt was Newport's Queen of the Firsters. Everything she did, she pioneered. When the bicycle craze swept Newport, she was the first to cycle in bloomers. When the automobile craze began, she was the first to own a car. The first woman to be elected to the American Institute of Architects, she was also at least one of the first ladies in Society to cut off her hair at the shoulders. Finally, on March 5, 1895, she became the first widely publicized lady in American Society to get a divorce. Characteristically, she obtained this divorce right in New York where there was but one grounds—adultery. The very next week she sailed to Europe for the avowed purpose of marrying her daughter to an English title. That summer, back in Newport, on August 25, from Trinity Church Alva issued what George Leighton has called "the Vanderbilt Declaration of War."

Mrs. Vanderbilt had already issued invitations for a ball at "Marble House" three days later; by attending church services that day, with her daughter Consuelo and the young Duke of Marlborough beside her, she served public notice that she would no longer submit to the Society edict then prevailing that divorced women were beyond the pale. Actually, it was a two-part declaration of war. Mrs. Vanderbilt's daughter was also involved. The very next winter, on November 6, 1895, this daughter was forced into America's most spectacular titled match—one which was later, much to the consternation of the Protestant Episcopal Church which had married the pair, annulled by the Roman Catholic Rota. "I forced my daughter to marry the Duke," Mrs. Vanderbilt later testified. "When I issued an order nobody discussed it. I therefore did not beg, but ordered her to marry the Duke."

In 1896, at forty-three, Mrs. Vanderbilt married Oliver Hazard Perry Belmont and began a second career. Feuding with her first husband's second wife, a lady noted for her Causes, Mrs. Belmont also embarked upon Good Works and at the same time endeavored to keep up with her Triumvirate rivals, Mrs. Oelrichs and Mrs. Fish. It was a difficult task. "I know of no profession, art, or trade that women are working in today," she declared, "as taxing on mental resource as being a leader of Society." Finally the strain told—on Mr. Belmont. Five years younger than she, he died in 1908 at the age of fifty. Mrs. Belmont, however, was indefatigable. Tiring of soup kitchens, clinics for the poor, model houses, anti-drug campaigns and birth control agitation, she took on the cause of woman suffrage. The very year after her husband died, "Marble House," which had for years been boarded up, was unboarded and readied for a nation-wide conclave of suffragettes.

This "Marble House" meeting, extraordinary as it was, was Mrs. Belmont's last great Newport effort. Rarely at the resort in her last years, she lived on to die in Paris in 1933 at the age of eighty. But all Newport remembered, if nothing else, her parting shot in the suffrage movement. The shot took the form of advice delivered to a disenchanted suffragette. "Brace up, my dear," said Mrs. Belmont. "Just pray to God. *She* will help you."

Even Mrs. Belmont paled before the third member of Newport's Great Triumvirate, the irrepressible Mrs. Stuyvesant Fish of "Crossways." Mrs. Belmont was the *grande dame* of Newport's Golden Age but Mrs. Fish was its *enfant terrible.* More than any one figure of her times she is held personally responsible by old-time resorters for causing the breakdown of the classification of Society as she found it, and for causing the beginning of the end of the reign of the Four Hundred. For a lady who was by no means beautiful, who had only, as she herself put it, "a few million," and who cared little for art or theater and less for music or literature, to accomplish such a feat was remarkable enough. It was more remarkable since Mrs. Fish never went to school, could not spell even the simplest words, rarely read even a newspaper, and, if she could manage to scrawl a dash-littered letter, she could not, if her life depended on it, make such a letter legible. She had, however, two vital assets, a quick wit and a sharp tongue, and with these went a large ambition. As she once told her daughter-in-law, "It doesn't make any difference what you decide to do in life, but you must do it better than anyone else." Mrs. Fish chose to be a hostess, and today, looking back, even her enemies agree that more people had more fun on more occasions *chez* Mrs. Fish than they had anywhere else. In the bargain, it went without saying, they would be insulted. That was to be expected; it was Mrs. Fish's way. Disliking the era in which she lived, she chose to spend her life making fun of it, and a vital part of her own having fun was making fun of others. In the end, the lady who could hardly write her own name not only wrote a new chapter in American Society but also became, of the old era, perhaps its greatest satirist.

Born in New York in 1853, the daughter of the New York lawyer, William Henry Anthon, she had as her first dislike in life her own name—one which she promptly changed from Mary Ann to Marian. From the beginning her friends never called her anything but Mamie. Her father died when she was twelve years old; her family, unable to afford New York City, moved to Astoria where, alone of the three children, Mamie was able to avoid the school system entirely. If not a beautiful girl, she had striking black eyes and inherited from her French ancestry a good deal of what was then called "come hither"; characteristically she married her childhood beau from back in New York City—a young man who had been born just three blocks from her. At that time Stuyvesant Fish worked for the banking house of Morton, Bliss & Company, where his father also worked. When a check in payment of the Alabama Claims was presented to the firm, the elder Fish signed the order in behalf of the government, the younger for Morton, Bliss. A man in the office, seeing the two signatures, remarked, "I see the Father and the Son, but where is the Holy Ghost?" The younger Fish stared at him. "That, sir," he said, "is the mutual trust and confidence that makes the whole transaction possible."

Young Mrs. Fish, who made a lifelong career of running her husband, did not share his fervor for his firm. When Morton, Bliss & Company interrupted her honeymoon, she never forgave them and shortly persuaded her husband to enter the service of the Illinois Central. Of this club, the so-called "Society Railroad" of the day, Fish became president in 1887; he held the position until 1906, at which time, Mrs.

Fish having feuded with Mrs. E. H. Harriman, he was blackballed.

In between managing her husband and raising three children, Mrs. Fish also took care of Society. Moving to Newport in 1889 from "Glenclyffe," her home in Garrison, New York, she spent several summers renting cottages and then, in 1900, on the hill beyond Bailey's Beach, she built her famous "Crossways." A distinguished French nobleman once said to her, in the manner of titled foreigners angling for invitations, that he had heard she had a beautiful villa in Newport. "You have been misinformed," replied Mrs. Fish. "I have just a plain white house." Actually "Crossways," a handsome white Colonial cottage with four large Corinthian columns in front, was no castle to rival "The Breakers" or "Marble House" but it was by no means plain. And neither, Newport was shortly to learn, were the entertainments in it. Mrs. Fish had not one ballroom, but two. Despite the fact that the downstairs of "Crossways" could be transformed into what amounted to an all-ballroom floor, Mrs. Fish had an extra ballroom built on behind. Rebelling at the two- and even three-hour dinners of the times, Mrs. Fish had them served in fifty, or even forty, minutes. Her record was an eight-course dinner in thirty minutes flat. At this dinner footmen were so anxious to meet the deadline that participants recalled it was necessary to hold the plate down with one hand and eat with the other. Elisha Dyer, during the fish course, took a bone from his mouth and by the time he put it down, the meat course was in front of him. Mrs. Fish's other dining innovation was the serving of champagne, in preference to wine, from the oysters on. "You have to liven these people up," she said. "Wine just makes them sleepy."

Mrs. Fish's greetings to her guests were as unique as her

service. "Howdy-do, howdy-do," she would say impatiently, pushing the newly arrived guests at Mr. Fish with a look of keen annoyance. "Make yourselves at home," she would add. "And believe me, there is no one who wishes you were there more than I do." One guest had a special greeting. "Oh," said Mrs. Fish, surprised, "I'd quite forgotten I asked you." The conclusions of her parties were equally curious. One guest made an excuse to leave early. "I promised I would be home by . . ." he began. "Don't apologize," broke in Mrs. Fish. "No guest ever left too soon for me." Once bored with one of her own parties, she had the orchestra play "Home, Sweet Home" before the guests' carriages had even been called. An enthusiastic beau begged for one more two-step. "There are just two steps more for you," said Mrs. Fish, "one upstairs to get your coat and the other out to your carriage." A lady went out and sat down to wait for her carriage. The footman came in to report that the porte-cochere was windy and the lady was furious. "Let her stay there," said Mrs. Fish. "She'll cool off better out there than she will in here." Ladies' luncheons were her particular bêtes noires. "Here you all are," she said greeting one, "older faces and younger clothes." At another time she gave a luncheon for fifty ladies and through it all sat upstairs, refusing to come down. Finally her maid begged her at least to come down and say good-by. "But, Mrs. Fish," she said, "you invited them two weeks ago." Mrs. Fish waved her maid away. "Tell them I've changed my mind," she said.

On an individual scale Mrs. Fish's insults were even more cherished—though she never could remember names and addressed everyone as "Pet" or "Sweet pet," "Lamb" or "Sweet lamb." She was particularly acid on the favored feminine topic of babies. A lady asked her, concerning a large and constantly expanding Newport family, if she had seen Mrs.

So-and-so's last baby. "Pet," replied Mrs. Fish, "I don't expect to live that long." On another occasion Mrs. Fish was asked if she knew another lady was pregnant. "Lamb," she said, "I do. Isn't it disgusting?" When the new word "propaganda" was being widely used, a lady confided to her that she was distressed because she could not have a baby. Mrs. Fish was bored. "Perhaps," she said slowly, "you haven't got the proper gander." On the question of house guests she was particularly outspoken. Even Harry Lehr, who served her as court chamberlain as Ward McAllister had Mrs. Astor, was not above occasional reproach. One day after his marriage to Mrs. Dahlgren, a group at "Crossways" were trying to guess each other's favorite flower. "I know Mamie's," said Lehr quickly, "the climbing rose." Mrs. Fish smiled. "And I yours, pet," she replied, "the marigold." One day Lehr introduced her to the Englishman Tony Shaw Safe who had come to the resort as manager of a polo team and stayed on to marry a wealthy Newporter and hyphenate his name from Shaw Safe to Shaw-Safe. He was particularly insistent on being called by the full hyphenation. "Howdy-do, Mr. Safe," Mrs. Fish blithely greeted him. "I'm so sorry to call you Mr. Safe but I've forgotten your combination."

Other guests were even more summarily treated. One of Lehr's friends complained that there were not enough bath towels. "I had to dry myself on a bath mat," he said. "Pet," replied Mrs. Fish, "you were lucky not to be offered the doormat." Moncure Robinson had been in Europe three months. On landing in this country he came directly to "Crossways" and started in the front door. Overhead, Mrs. Fish on the balcony spotted him. "Are you in for lunch?" she called down abruptly. "Well, I really don't know," he replied. "Well," said Mrs. Fish, "I'm out." Sumner Gerard, visiting at another

Newport cottage, complained he had stayed a week and had seen his hostess only once. "I wish I could run my house as well," said Mrs. Fish. She particularly detested people who asked her the details of her menage. One lady asked her how large "Crossways" was. "I really can't tell you," said Mrs. Fish. "It swells at night." The same lady also asked her how many laundresses she employed. "I have six white ones who work all day," replied Mrs. Fish, "and six black ones who work all night. Being black, you see, you can't see them."

As a feudist Mrs. Fish was unequaled and she particularly enjoyed her altercations with other Newport hostesses. Mrs. John Drexel had a male secretary who was her inseparable companion. One day a friend of Mrs. Drexel came up to Mrs. Fish. "Mamie, have you seen Cousin Alice?" she asked. "I've looked everywhere in the house," she added anxiously. "No," replied Mrs. Fish. "Have you looked under the secretary?" With other members of Newport's Great Triumvirate Mrs. Fish feuded with equal aplomb. One day at the Newport Casino Mrs. Belmont swept up to her. "I have just heard what you said about me at Tessie Oelrichs' last night. You cannot deny it, Mamie, because Tessie told me herself. You told everybody I looked like a frog." Mrs. Fish was alarmed. "No, no," she said. "Not a frog! A toad, my pet, a *toad!*"

The privilege of being the recipient of such remarks might seem a doubtful one; Mrs. Fish made it a real one by her ability as a hostess. Mrs. Astor had tried Edith Wharton and J. P. Morgan—even, on one occasion, Isadora Duncan—but Mrs. Fish was the first hostess of the front rank to include in her invitations all kinds of celebrities. Mrs. Astor treated stage celebrities as if they were from a zoo. If they could "hold a fork," Mrs. Fish used to say, she would have them. Fighting the general social pattern of teas, card-calling and drives, she particularly disliked operas, which she often talked right through, and had a violent aversion to musicales. "I'm never sure that I have my face fixed right," she said. "Sometimes when it is just right for listening to 'The Cradle Song,' I find that I am listening to 'The Ride of the Valkyries.' " On her invitation cards she would scrawl in her illegible hand, "There will be something besides the dinner, come." There always was—and people always came. It might be Crown Prince William of Sweden or it might be a series of vaudeville acts, it might be Irene Castle or it might be John L. Sullivan, it might be the chorus of "The Merry Widow" or it might be a ballroom full of live butterflies. One thing was certain; it would be fun.

In those days celebrities were expected to give some kind of performance after dinner, and one of the difficulties was for these celebrities to make effective entrances and exits. When Marie Dressler, going upstairs to prepare for her act, found that she would have to walk down again in full view of her audience, and push her way to an improvised stage, she rebelled. Seizing an empty tray from a passing waiter, she coasted down the stairs on her stomach and slid all the way across the ballroom; then she got up, sat down at the piano and proceeded to give humorous burlesques of all the famous opera singers. Mrs. Fish was delighted. She gave Miss Dressler a handbag containing one hundred dollars. Originally Miss Dressler had not been asked to dinner—merely to come in afterward; she had called Mrs. Fish and asked to come. "I want to be able to tell my mother," she said, "I have had dinner with Mrs. Stuyvesant Fish." Mrs. Fish had been gracious. "I shall be proud to tell my children," she said, "Marie Dressler has dined with me."

Always Mrs. Fish could be counted on to provide the unexpected. When guests prepared for a really Bohemian party, she delighted to face them with a regally formal dinner. One of her most memorable was a table entirely decorated with American Beauty roses, a corsage spray of roses at each lady's place and a rose boutonniere for each gentleman. Even more spectacular was a table decorated solely with black crepe and thick white rope; the effect of this, combined with her gold service, was dazzling. Furthermore, if catholic in her choice of celebrities, Mrs. Fish brooked no general letting-down of the bars. When James Hazen Hyde appeared at a luncheon in a sports shirt, she spotted him across the room. "Who is that young man," she asked, "in a negligée?" One evening at the conclusion of a ball, when all the guests had left, Mrs. Fish found a lady's maid left over; there was no young lady left to go with her. Later the young lady, who had been out riding in a young gentleman's carriage, returned. All of Mrs. Fish's friends admired the way she handled this delicate situation. Although she cut the young lady off her list for good, she never told anyone who the young lady was. Publicity was Mrs. Fish's lifeblood, but in contrast to many present-day resort hostesses, she would not be "used," as she put it, in any way, even for causes in which she believed. Approached on having an article ghost-written under her signature about the work of a Bishop in the Philippines, she would not hear of it. "If the article was good enough to interest anybody," she said, "everybody would know I couldn't have written it. If it wasn't, I'd be mortified."

Mrs. Fish reached her strategic heights in Newport's Grand Duke war. This war began quietly enough when James De Wolfe Cutting, popular resort sport and long-time bachelor guest of Mrs. Fish, had a verbal exchange with his hostess. Mrs. Fish started it by saying, in her usual manner, that she was bored with Newport that season. "Why don't you take a moor in Scotland," suggested Cutting, "and then we could all come over and shoot?" Mrs. Fish flashed. "Why don't I?" she replied. "Because I would like to be a guest myself sometime." Cutting took offense. Promptly he transferred his guest privileges to "Ochre Court," the magnificent castle of the redoubtable widow, Mrs. Ogden Goelet. From then on he became a bone of contention. Having been a Fish protégé he was now a Goelet protégé, and Mrs. Goelet made no secret of her victory. To it she shortly added another when she secured the visit to "Ochre Court" of the Grand Duke Boris of Russia. Mrs. Fish could not let this second triumph go unanswered and she replied by inviting both Mrs. Goelet and the Grand Duke to a dinner and ball, the affair being given, of course, in honor of the Grand Duke.

Mrs. Goelet paid a call on Mrs. Fish. Mrs. Fish had forgotten, Mrs. Goelet said, to invite Mr. Cutting. "Oh, no, sweet pet," replied Mrs. Fish, "I did not forget. I have no intention of asking him. He has been to my house far too often already." Mrs. Goelet countered by saying that in that case it would be quite impossible for her to come. "Lamb," replied Mrs. Fish, "we shall miss you." Mrs. Goelet then reminded Mrs. Fish that it would also be quite impossible for any of her other house guests to come, including the Grand Duke himself. As a final blow she added that there were five gentlemen in His Royal Highness' suite, and that Mrs. Fish would not only be without her guest of honor—whose name had already appeared on her invitations— but she would also be six men short for dinner. "Sweet lamb," said Mrs. Fish, "I shall not have Mr. Cutting if I am reduced to the Naval Training Station."

Young officers from the Training Station were customarily

ordered by Newporters—by the number desired—from the Commander of the Station, who invariably supplied them, neatly uniformed and on time, for extra bridge partners or extra men for dancing. They were not, however, asked to dinner, but only after dinner. On this occasion Mrs. Fish broke precedent; she asked five of them for dinner. At the same time she was faced with a new problem. Mrs. Goelet started calling people, who had already accepted Mrs. Fish's invitation, for a rival dinner. Among those Mrs. Goelet approached in this manner were J. P. Morgan, Chauncey Depew and Lord Charles Beresford.

When the great evening came, Mrs. Fish received her guests in the hall of "Crossways" as if nothing had happened. She gave no evidence of any surprise when, with the exception of the Grand Duke, all two hundred appeared. Baffled as those asked by Mrs. Goetlet had been by the two invitations to meet one Grand Duke on the same evening, they had expressed their regrets to Mrs. Goelet; they had already accepted Mrs. Fish's previous invitation. The guests milled around, buzzing expectantly, wondering if, despite Mrs. Goelet, the Grand Duke was coming after all. Mrs. Fish, who knew the value of suspense, let them wait. "Royalty," she said enigmatically, "is better never than late." Just before eight o'clock Mrs. Fish quieted everyone. She drew herself up. "I could not get the Grand Duke Boris," she said, "but I have someone far better. Lambs and pets, His Most Gracious Imperial Majesty—the Czar of All the Russias!" At the conclusion of her introduction the door flew open—but Mrs. Fish had already swept down in a low court curtsy. All the ladies followed suit, while the gentlemen bowed deeply from the waist. Then, peering up, they saw their Emperor. He was standing utterly solemnly in a breath-taking costume of scarlet regalia, complete with a chestful of medals and a gold scepter. It was, of course, Harry Lehr. As the tension broke and everyone burst out laughing, Lehr, still solemn, played his part to the hilt. He marched down, took Mrs. Fish's arm and toured the whole circle, pausing, before each commoner, to bestow a few well-chosen words of broken English. His performance as usual was far more enjoyable than the genuine product, and the dinner was a great success.

The Grand Duke Boris dinner is often confused, in Newport annals, with the famous "Monkey Dinner." Actually, though the latter was engineered by Mrs. Fish, together with Mr. Lehr, the dinner was given, as was the "Dogs' Dinner," at "Arleigh," the cottage of Mrs. Lehr—who, curiously enough, was as much surprised by it as the other guests. In this case the "Prince," a monkey in evening dress, was led in by Washington's Joseph Leiter. Later in the evening the monkey, who had enjoyed several glasses of champagne, ascended the chandelier and pelted the guests with light bulbs. But Mrs. Fish's parties continued to be Newport's most favored functions; her annual "Harvest Moon Ball," to which all guests came in farm costumes, officially closed each Newport social season. Mrs. Fish's last large ball, on August 1, 1913, was the memorable "Mother Goose Ball," to which all guests came dressed in costumes portraying characters in nursery rhymes. At the height of the festivities Mrs. Fish stopped the orchestra and ordered the reading of a poem in honor of Mrs. Isaac Goose. Although Mrs. Fish denied writing the poem herself, she at least had a hand in its composition, and the solemn reading of the specially written verses, while Newporters stood trembling with convention, yet dressed in costumes ranging from Little Jack Horner to the Cow Who Jumped Over the Moon, represented perhaps the high water mark of her social satire:

"Crossways"
August 1st, 1913

"Here lies the body of Mary Goose, wife of
Isaac Goose, dec'd October ye 19th, 1690."
—Inscription in Granary Burying Ground,
Boston, Massachusetts

MOTHER GOOSE

In quaint old Granary she lies;
And all around her beats
The pulse life that Boston pours
Through narrow, crowded streets.

America's first woman poet;
Pause, ye blue-stockinged dame,
And you in auto, or on wheel,
And read her simple name.

That yet shall live when on your steps
Oblivion follows after;
Enduring as a mother's love,
Fresh as a baby's laughter.

And yet she was not learned or great;
No prophet of her times,
This grandam by a cradle small
Crooning her ageless rhymes.

She never tried to mold her world;
(That problem superhuman!)
She never had a higher aim
Than to be just a woman.

Yet o'er what "modern woman's" work
Such consecration lingers?
Her words are lisped by baby lips
And traced by babies' fingers.

All, all the hobbies, all the schools,
What are they worth, in one sense,
Beside her priceless gift of joy,
Her dear, delicious nonsense?

So to her name let praise be sung—
More precious than all other;
Oh, listen! down the centuries
The children call her "Mother."

As a mother herself, Mrs. Fish was a severe one. Her son Stuyvesant recently recalled a life of "children should be seen and not heard." The only meal the children had downstairs was breakfast—Mrs. Fish ate in bed. After breakfast the son remembers that the three children went through "a kind of ritual of going upstairs to say 'Good morning.' " From nine to eleven there were lessons. At eleven there was swimming. "The beach," he says, "was the only place where the children mingled with their elders."

If Mrs. Fish had guests for lunch, the children ate upstairs prior to the naps and pony cart rides which occupied the afternoon. But at tea, her son recalled, "If we were clean enough, we would be exhibited to the guests." Supper again was upstairs. "After supper, if we behaved ourselves, we were allowed to watch mother dress for dinner and leave for the party she was going to that night." If the party was to be at "Crossways," on the other hand, the children were permitted to lean over the banisters and see the guests arrive. "Sometimes," he concluded, "we stayed up long enough to raid the dinner table of the remains of the feast—after the ladies had withdrawn to the drawing room and the men to the library."

Mr. Fish was rarely in Newport more than two or three week ends a month, and even on Mrs. Fish's trips to Hot

Springs, where she went for three weeks each fall to recover from the Newport season, she was usually accompanied by a friend, Miss Lota Robinson, rather than her husband. Unlike the other members of the Great Triumvirate, however, Mrs. Fish led a private life which was an extremely happy one. In spite of the prevalence of male guests, the gossiping *Town Topics*, which haunted most Newporters, had little material at "Crossways." One night Mrs. Fish was persuaded to go on a moonlight cruise on a yacht. The night was a beautiful one, and as the couples paired off on the deck, Mrs. Fish appeared moved by it. "How lovely this is," she said to her partner in a voice which could be overheard by others on the deck. "Here, let me hold your hand." The other Newporters gasped at her action. Mrs. Fish closed her eyes. "There," she said, "now I will just imagine that you are my husband." At another time Mr. and Mrs. Fish had just returned to New York. Mrs. Fish began coughing. "Can I get you something for your throat, my dear?" Mr. Fish asked. Mrs. Fish stopped. "Yes, you can," she replied. "That diamond and pearl necklace I saw today at Tiffany's." The first time Mrs. Fish was really ill the couple were on a trip to Monte Carlo. Writing of the trip, Mr. Fish spoke of the good fortune that Mrs. Fish should be incapacitated in a "civilized place." "By the bye," he concluded, "the plumbing in this hotel is by the Jordan L. Mott Company of New York."

Mrs. Fish was as businesslike as her husband when it came to the management of "Crossways." In fact, her reputation as the most efficient of all Newport hostesses still continues. Having a far lower budget than her rivals, and only fifteen servants, she nonetheless insisted on perfect order. Even after a ball she demanded that "Crossways" be returned to normalcy by the time she appeared the next day. Her daughter-in-law recalls coming downstairs at nine o'clock the morning after a ball. "Everything," she says, "was in apple-pie order. There was no sign that a party had even taken place." She was asked if the noise of cleaning had been noticeable in the early morning. "In the early morning!" she says. "They cleaned all night long. I didn't sleep a wink. That was why I was down so early."

It is not surprising that Mrs. Fish had trouble in keeping her help. With the exception of her personal maid, Rose, a fiery-tempered Frenchwoman, who alone dared talk back to her, she rarely kept anyone in her employ over a year; even Rose, who in 1914 returned to France and went through two World Wars, declared that her later life had been a tranquil one compared to her life at "Crossways." Once a discharged butler paid Mrs. Fish a compliment. "At least I will say for you, Madam, you are a lady. You never go into the kitchen." But another discharged butler took revenge. He dismantled the entire Fish gold dinner service and left the pieces, three hundred strong, on the dining room floor. On one occasion when Mrs. Fish had managed to keep a butler just over a year Mrs. Leeds was awed by one of her dinner parties. "What wouldn't I give," she said, "to have that butler of yours." Mrs. Fish rang the bell. "Take him," she said.

Outside "Crossways" Mrs. Fish was less efficient though equally determined. Her favorite indulgence was in fortune-tellers, and she invariably believed what they told her. One reason for this was that if they told her she was to take a trip or see a long-lost friend, she would promptly take the trip or get in touch with the friend. Once, having been told she was going to take up a new sport, she was baffled. She heartily disliked yachting, as well as swimming, riding and other resort athletics. Finally, she decided to try her hand at the new sport of automobiling. She bought an electric car. The demonstrator declared that the vehicle was foolproof; there was just one lever which produced the power. The lever was pushed forward to go forward, backward to go backward and upright to stop. Mrs. Fish climbed in for her first solo drive. She pushed the lever forward and ran straight into the front door. Immediately she got out and refused to try it again. Finally she was persuaded to try just once more. This time she got by the front door safely and down the driveway to the street. Unfortunately, just after she had made the turn, a large colored man elected to cross the street. Mrs. Fish wished to slow down, but she forgot her instructions. She pushed the lever further forward. The car went into the man and knocked him down; it was a light runabout and the man was not seriously injured. By this time, however, Mrs. Fish had remembered her instructions, or thought she had, and she pulled the lever sharply back. Immediately the car went into reverse. Down went the man for the second time. Mrs. Fish was now thoroughly unnerved. She pushed the lever sharply forward again. Down went the man for the third time. This time, as he came up behind, he jumped aside and disappeared off the side of the road. Mrs. Fish, who by this time had the lever in an upright position, promptly followed suit. She stepped out of her car and walked back to her cottage. She never drove any kind of automobile again.

To the end of her life Mrs. Fish never lost her sense of satire. When Harry Lehr suffered a nervous breakdown she wrote to him that she wished him to come down to Newport immediately. "You know quite well, sweet lamb," she wrote, "that you won't need any mind to go with the people here." The hecticness of her own career—in New York, Newport and Hot Springs—continued unabated. Once, late in life, she saw a woman knitting and paused—for once reflective. "Oh," she exclaimed, "to have the time to do that!" In 1915, attempting to break in a new housekeeper and butler and at the same time plan her annual June 8 birthday party in Garrison, she suffered a stroke. She died, as she had always said she wanted to, without a day's illness. A month before she had written out several verses, which she quoted from memory from Matthew Arnold's "Requiescat," and which she wished placed on her tombstone. When it came to doing this, however, Mr. Fish looked up the verses and had them correctly inscribed. Mrs. Fish would have been annoyed; she was always irritated by her husband's attention to what she regarded as minor details. As she quoted the verses, they went as follows:

Strew on her roses, roses,
  And never a spray of rue,
For in quiet she reposes
  And I would that I could too.
The world her mirth required,
  So she bathed it in smiles of glee,
But her heart was tired, tired,
  So now they let her be.
For her life was turning, turning,
  In mazes of heat and sound,
But for peace her soul was yearning,
  And now peace laps her round.

The change in Society, from Mrs. Fish's day to the present, has been a profound one. In New York Mrs. Fish's rococo Victorian mansion at 19 Gramercy Park South is now owned by Benjamin Sonnenberg, public relations expert and one of

Manhattan's premier party-givers. But "Crossways" at Newport, owned by Mrs. Morris De Peyster, has been for many years unoccupied. In 1952 two young men in a station wagon drove up to the cottage, walked in and took out two chandeliers. Later Newport police stopped them but so weary have Newport authorities become of trying to protect the resort's long vacant cottages that the police merely took the chandeliers away from the young men and asked them please not to do it again. In the summer of 1952 the furnishings of "Crossways," including the damaged chandeliers, were sold at auction.

But Newporters would not be Newporters if they would admit the end has come—and they most certainly do not. "We're like England," explains Mrs. George Henry Warren. "We're muddling through. And," she adds, "in a funny, peculiar way this place does go on." Mrs. Warren's comparison of Newport with England is no fantasy. As president of the Newport Preservation Society, she has been for some years devoted not only to the restoration of Historic Newport after the manner of Williamsburg, Virginia, but also to the maintenance of Social Newport after the manner of England—by the opening of certain unoccupied cottage castles to the general public as paying museums. Furthermore, dazed as some Newporters are by the changes which have taken place, even relatively new Newporters refuse to admit that any other resort has fared any better. "Southampton and places like that," says Mrs. Ellen Tuck Astor, "are so *transient*." A lady who was Wife I of John Jacob Astor VI, she feels that there is real tradition at Newport. "When you sit down to dinner here," she says, "you're likely to sit down beside a nineteen-year-old on one side and a ninety-year-old on the other." Philadelphia's Mrs. Frank Griswold believes that there is not only a tradition but also a maturity to Newport Society which is sorely lacking at other resorts. "We have cosmopolitan people," she says, "people who have been out in London and Paris. When I go to dinner in Watch Hill I meet people from Detroit and Cincinnati and places like that. There's no stimulus. Why, here I am exchanging *books* with three or four people." Mrs. Warren agrees; she feels that *au fond*, as she puts it, many other resorts secretly envy Newport. She declares that on a recent trip to Edgartown she was, in common with all Newporters on their travels to lesser resorts, immediately greeted by her hostess with the line, "We lead a very simple life here, you know," and that after a meaningful silence this line was followed by the explicit one, "My husband wouldn't think of dressing for dinner." Mrs. Warren smiles. "They never did dress when they went out or when people came in," she says. "But Mr. ——— told me himself that the moment he and his wife were alone he often puts on a dinner jacket. He said it made him feel more comfortable."

The "funny, peculiar way" in which Newport goes on has never lacked further explanation. Miss Alice Brayton, distinguished Newport spinster and a member of a family which for three hundred years has been observing Newport Society from the safe distance of a farm in Portsmouth, fifteen miles away, has perhaps the easiest definition. A first cousin of the famous Lizzie Borden and in her own right credited by Newporters with originating the famous Society dictum that a lady's name should appear in the papers three times—when she is born, when she marries and when she dies—Miss Brayton believes that Newport has always been the most publicized place in the world for social climbers and that, as such, it may well go on forever. "I want to know people who don't want to know me, they want to know people who don't want to know them, and so on ad infinitum," she says. "That's Newport."

Dr. Alexander Hamilton Rice of "Miramar" brings an even wider viewpoint on the subject. Not only is he a distinguished geographer and world explorer but he is also the country's first-ranking clubman; he lists forty-three societies and twenty-six clubs in his *Who's Who* autobiography, including his membership in the Automobile Clubs of both New York and Philadelphia. "You've always had here at Newport," he says, "the er-gentleman and the er-other fellow." How successful this combination has been is emphasized by railroader Robert R. Young. An authority on Palm Beach and White Sulphur as well as Newport, Young puts Newport in a class by itself. "It is, perhaps," he says, "the last place in the whole world which is known as still standing for something."

Newport's distinguished ex-singer and collector of nineteenth-century American art, Maxim Karolik, is perhaps the most striking exhibit of Newport's world-wide appeal. "In my home town," says Karolik, who grew up in Bessarabia, Russia, "there were just three places in America I had ever heard of—Washington, New York and Newport. I didn't know much about Washington and I thought there were Indians in New York, but I did know one thing—that American millionaires spent their summers in castles in Newport." Arriving in New York, Karolik successfully avoided the Indians and sang his way down to Washington where, on February 2, 1927, he met the late Miss Martha Codman, eminent Newport heiress. Although Karolik was then in his lower twenties and Miss Codman was in her fifties, it was a case of love at first sight and after a visit to Newport that summer Miss Codman and Mr. Karolik were married on February 2, 1928, on the anniversary of their first meeting. Not all Boston

Codmans approved the marriage; Karolik recalls that an aunt-in-law asked him sternly if his wife had a sense of humor. "Of course she has," replied Karolik. "She married me." After twenty happy years of marriage during which Mr. and Mrs. Karolik built up their remarkable art collection, Mrs. Karolik died in 1948. Since that time Karolik has been living in solitary splendor in the old Ogden Codman cottage on Bellevue Avenue. "The scale here will diminish," he says, "but the style will go on. Newport consists of two kinds of people—those who know you and don't speak to you and those who don't know you and do speak to you."

As Newporters look back over their long history they are impressed by the many ups and downs the resort has witnessed. Many families, notably Philadelphia's Wideners and Drexels, have made successes at Newport before they made them in their own home towns, and conversely, other families who have made successes in their home towns have failed to duplicate these at Newport. The most curious case in Newport history concerned New York's Coogan family. Early in the 1900's the late James J. Coogan, former Manhattan Borough President and inheritor of large real estate holdings including the Polo Grounds, home of the New York Giants, decided to invade Newport. He bought on Catherine Street one of Newport's most beautiful cottages, called "Whitehall." This cottage boasted a handsome pillared portico, an enormous ballroom and music room, and solid mahogany doors with silver doorbells; Stanford White, who designed it, considered it his best Georgian work. In short order "Whitehall" became a Newport legend. This legend, as Newporters tell it, began in 1910 when, they say, the Coogans gave a housewarming to their cottage and to it invited all Newport's best. A retinue of servants readied grounds and groceries, and all manner of feasting and festivities were planned. On the night of the party the Coogans descended into their drawing room and waited. Not one guest appeared. Mrs. Fish, the legend goes, disliked the Coogans and she had sent out invitations for a party of her own on the same night; as additional insurance that no one would go to the Coogans she had announced that Paderewski would play. That very night the Coogans paid off their servants, took just one piece of luggage containing Mrs. Coogan's jewels and went back to New York. Then the Coogans took revenge. For the next thirty-five years they allowed "Whitehall" to stand just the way it was that fateful night—in its first days, with dishes and even food still on the table. As time went by, windows were smashed, the cottage broken into and everything of value stolen, including an enormous revolving statue of the son of William Tell, complete with arrow, apple and tree—a statue which took five men to lift. Outside, the once velvety lawns of the Coogans became hayfields, but each year the Coogans paid their taxes and not until 1945 did they decide that thirty-five years of revenge was enough and permit the town to tear down the dilapidated eyesore.

Actually this legend is false. The Coogans were in Newport for several seasons before the alleged housewarming took place. Mrs. Fish, who was no enemy of the Coogans, did not either have Paderewski play or indeed give any party in opposition to theirs—in fact, the Coogans that year gave no party themselves. The winter before the alleged party took place a severe fire had gutted "Whitehall" and the Coogans, believing that the cottage was totally destroyed, had not bothered to salvage what remained of their linen, clothes, silver and china; this, of course, gave rise to the legend about the dishes and food still on the table. As for the strange idea of leaving

"Whitehall" to stand as an eyesore for thirty-five years, this too is explained. Mrs. Coogan, an extremely independent woman, lived in virtual seclusion for many years in New York. She remembered liking "Whitehall" and determined that she would never tear it down; not until just two years before her death was her son able to persuade her to do so.

In spite of the lack of truth in the legend and the damage its currency did to the Coogan family, the legend is basic for an understanding of Newport Society. Far from attempting to hush the affair Coogan, Newporters enjoyed pointing out the ghost cottage on Catherine Street as a definite sight to see and a thing to know. Always sensitive to the charge that making good in Newport was primarily a matter of money, the Coogan legend was to Newport a visible example that the charge was false, and the fact that the legend too was false was to them just an unimportant technicality.

Other Newport stories on this subject—particularly in the freer and easier 1920's—have happier endings. One concerns the late John Aspegrens. The Aspegrens, who made their money in edible oils, descended on Newport by Westchester and built "Aspen Hall" on Bellevue Avenue. Although the Aspegrens owned no revolving statues they did own a pair of cockatoos named Mister Gallagher and Mister Sheehan. These, according to critical Newporters, made them suspect. When the Aspegrens issued invitations for a party, Mrs. William Burden of "Oakwood" and Newport's old guard promptly leaped into the breach and invited everyone to her cottage. But the Aspegrens had arrived primed for Newport; they let out word that they thought nothing of spending twenty thousand dollars on an ordinary evening and more, if necessary, for something special. Newporters decided that such a price warranted at least consideration and they decided to try the Aspegrens and then "go on," as the saying went, to the Burdens.

But the Aspegren party turned out to be surprisingly good. There was champagne flowing freely, tastefully lighted dancing under a marquee and all the Newport trimmings. By midnight the guests were in a quandary. They realized that it was time to move on and yet it was a close decision. Then things began to happen on the Aspegren lawn. A dozen trucks moved up like a well-trained armored division, a hundred men suddenly began fixing lights and staging, and all at once the Russian Ballet, at full New York strength, put on an unforgettable spectacle. Even after it was over, only a handful of guests went on to the Burdens. "From that moment on," declares Chicago's margarine man Frazier Jelke, "the Aspegrens had arrived socially because they knew how to play the game." In his autobiography Jelke recalls his own career at the resort:

> I played the game deliberately and for several reasons. First, it interested me and I enjoyed the companionship of well-bred, graciously mannered people. Having no family life to occupy me out of business hours, and as an unattached young man with plenty of money, many invitations came my way. Since society offered me these things, I accepted them at society's hand.
>
> Moreover, as a newcomer from Chicago to Wall Street, and without powerful family connections in the financial world, I had to establish myself, make a wide circle of friends, and build up confidence in order to win customers and have people trust my firm.
>
> I did not go to Newport deliberately as one step in the campaign to achieve this; but, having gone to Newport and having fallen under the spell of the Rhode Island shore, I would have failed my instincts as a businessman if I had not endeavored to make the most of it.

"It's wrong to think of Newport as all money," says Rear Admiral Andrews of "Land Fall." "There's something more. Waving that dollar bill won't get you all the way because for every one you can wave no matter who you are there'll be somebody else who can wave three or four." Backing up Admiral Andrews, the late Miss Maude Wetmore used to say that money was not the answer to success in Newport Society; it was a matter of *cachet*. The fact that Miss Wetmore, like most ladies of her generation, used a French word to define Newport's quality is not surprising. Many Newport ladies, brought up by French governesses, still use French idioms and the rolled French "r"; it is possible to go to a dinner party today where the conversation will be entirely French. While this makes Newport's *cachet* even more difficult for outsiders to understand, one thing is certain. Newport was able to preserve more *cachet* than any other major resort even during the dark days of the depression.

The particular bright spots were the annual Tennis Week Balls at "Miramar," the home of Dr. Alexander Hamilton Rice and his former wife, the late Eleanor Elkins Widener. These balls, which lasted all night, were still in the great Newport tradition and the behavior of Mrs. Rice, who was the donor of Harvard's Widener Library, was particularly memorable. Shortly after midnight she would disappear and take a nap. Early in the morning she would reappear and, fresh as a daisy, cheerfully breakfast with the late stayers. Equally exemplary was the fifty-fifth birthday party of Dr. Rice held at "Miramar" in 1931; at this fifty-five people were seated at two tables and the dinner had such dignity that Ambassador Gerard rose and made a short speech. "I wish a representative of the press might be with us tonight," he said, "to see for himself that Newport is not all 'Monkey

Dinners.' " Second only to the doings at "Miramar" were the balls at "Bonniecrest," the Stuart Duncan cottage. Mrs. Duncan, wife of the board chairman of Lea & Perrins, Inc., was told one night by an English guest that her cottage, which was built in the style of a Tudor manor, reminded him of "a bit of old Worcestershire." Mrs. Duncan was not surprised. "Why shouldn't it?" she said. "We made our money out of Worcestershire sauce." A more startling example of Newport's *cachet* was demonstrated by a member of the Vanderbilt family who appeared at a costume ball in 1932 clad only in a barrel. His hostess demanded an explanation. "The New York Central," he said, "took my pants." In time, of course, visitors to Newport learned something about *cachet* themselves, the favorite story on this subject being told of the violinist Fritz Kreisler who was asked by Mrs. Cornelius Vanderbilt to play at one of her parties. Kreisler said that his regular fee for such engagements was thirteen thousand dollars. To this Mrs. Vanderbilt promptly agreed, then added that she hoped he would understand but she was going to ask him not to mix with her guests afterward. "In that case," promptly replied Kreisler, "my fee is only five hundred."

Le Roy King, of "Indian Spring," a lifelong Newporter and for thirty years senior warden of Trinity Church, is a particularly formidable figure in the field of Newport's present-day *cachet*. In his long tenure at old Trinity—both his father and grandfather, as well as his uncle, were senior wardens before him—King has seen great changes at the resort, particularly in the course of his regular Sunday plate-passing. "Nowadays," he says, "they're even making change out of the plate, but I just look the other way." When it came to the matter of bringing up his two sons, however, King, at that time between wives, was faced with a problem from which he could not turn away—the matter of sex. Today, he admits, he gave his sons just one piece of advice. "Never confuse," he told them, 'I love you' with 'I want to marry you.' "

Actually, nowhere has *cachet* shown itself to better advantage than in the resort's adjustment to the confusion of marriages and divorces. For generations Newporters have married Newporters, divorced Newporters and married still other Newporters—all with a kind of show-must-go-on feeling that puts to shame the stark immorality of Palm Beach or Palm Springs. Although Bellevue Avenue is today a street composed primarily of widows and widowers—the widows living by apparent tradition on the west side of the Avenue and the widowers on the east side—Newporters have made remarkable efforts to keep their resort family together. The marriage of Louis Bruguière and Mrs. James Laurens Van Alen, both parties in their seventies, was one example of this *esprit de corps*. Even more remarkable was the late Perry Belmont, who died in 1947 at the age of ninety-seven. A widower for several generations, Belmont in his nineties still felt spry enough to tell a Newport dinner party that he wished to marry and sire an heir. "I have so many portraits," he said, "and no one to leave them to."

In the matter of divorce Newport *cachet* has also been notable, the outstanding performer being the late Illinois-born automobile man, Milton J. Budlong, who was sued by his first wife a total of twenty-one times. Denied the use of his cottage, "The Reef," by a cordon of servants who sided against him in his marital discord, Budlong would appear each morning, go through an elaborate ritual of penitence and then raise his arms. Following this, the ex-Mrs. Budlong, who always watched from one of the upper windows, would signal a heartfelt "Bravo," raise the sash and gallantly throw him one clean shirt. In keeping with such tradition, Newport weddings can be even more memorable spectacles. At one, an ex-husband gave away the bride. At another, the guests were treated to a ceremony which included not only a bride and a groom but a daughter of the bride and the bride's ex-husband, two children of the groom and the groom's ex-wife, as well as the groom's ex-wife's present husband. The only conspicuous absentee was the groom's ex-wife's present husband's ex-wife. She summers in Newport, but no offense was intended; she was ill on the day of the wedding and just couldn't make it.

In World War II Newport *cachet* was perhaps most effectively demonstrated by Miss Julia Berwind of "The Elms." One day early in the war Miss Berwind placed a large grocery order. The grocer, surprised that she could have so many points, asked her to produce her ration books. Miss Berwind was even more surprised. "Oh," she said, "I thought those were just for ordinary people." When her gasoline was also rationed, Miss Berwind, in her eighties, took to an "adult tricycle"—the first machine of its kind ever seen in Newport. Each morning her chauffeur brought the vehicle around to the front door of "The Elms" with the same *cachet* he had produced one of her Cadillacs in happier times. But even Miss Berwind paled before the last of Newport's *grandes dames*, the late Mrs. Hamilton McKown Twombly. The last grandchild of Commodore Cornelius Vanderbilt, Mrs. Twombly died in 1952 at the age of ninety-eight, and this death marked the end of Newport's era of elegance. For more than fifty years Mrs. Twombly had regularly invaded Newport in high style. In her last years she owned fifteen automobiles, ten American, three English and two French, and all of these were painted in her own special shade of maroon; her chauffeurs, butlers, footmen and maids wore livery of the same color. Her famous French chef, M. Josef Donon, received a salary of twenty-five thousand dollars a year and recently built a Newport cottage of his own. Mrs. Twombly herself is perhaps most cherished by Newporters for her determination to attend the wedding in California in 1935 of her grandson and Miss Flobelle Fairbanks, niece of Douglas Fairbanks, Sr. Mrs. Twombly was, even in those days, already in her eighties and a plane trip was out of the question. Nor, since the passing of her private railroad car, would she consider a public train. Driving, too, presented a problem. There was always the chance, during those dark days, of being recognized in the back seat of her Rolls Royce and meeting up, somewhere in the uncharted social wilds, with foul play. But go West the Newport *grande dame* would and she finally decided on the perfect solution. For six thousand miles, going and coming, Mrs. Twombly's maid, dressed as Mrs. Twombly, rode in the back seat of the Rolls, and for six thousand miles, going and coming, Mrs. Twombly, dressed as Mrs. Twombly's maid, rode in the front seat.

Since World War II Newport has seen several candidates for Mrs. Twombly's throne. One of these is Mrs. Sheldon Whitehouse, of "Eastbourne Lodge," the leader of those who have been called Newport's "O.S.S."—the initials standing, of course, not for the Office of Strategic Services but for "Oh So Social." Another of the candidates is Mrs. Robert Young. Raised on a farm at Sun Prairie, Wisconsin, and a sister of the artist, Georgia O'Keeffe, Mrs. Young has entertained lavishly both at "Beechwood," the old Victorian Astor cottage, which she painted a combination of pink and green, and, more recently, at "Fairholm," in which she has not only regularly entertained the Duke and Duchess of Windsor but has also installed a motion picture theater, complete with sound, in a room filled with white plush armchairs and sofas. Even more impressive as a social contender is Mrs. George, or Pearl, Mesta. Oklahoma-oil-rich by birth and the widow of Mesta Machinery by marriage, Mrs. Mesta was in the wintertime—at least up to her diplomatic appointment to Luxembourg—the so-called "Lady Dictator" of Washington Society. At Newport she has been frankly dedicated to making her cottage "Mid-cliffe" a social mecca. A small, dark vivacious woman who neither drinks nor smokes, she had the Vice-president to visit her her very first summer, in 1929, and has ever since been the resort's leading big game hunter. She has no wish to break down Newport *cachet*—"There'll never be any dropping in or that sort of thing here," she says—but she feels the time has come to take the edge off Newport formality. When her male guests, for example, delay in joining the ladies during the after-dinner separation —a custom which, along with that of no one leaving before the guest of honor, is still rigidly enforced at Newport—Mrs. Mesta simply sends in and gets them. "In the old days," says Mrs. Mesta, who does not remember Mrs. Stuyvesant Fish, "having Albert Spaulding would have been Newport's idea of going pretty far. Goodness knows, I have everything from Ike Eisenhower singing 'Drink to Me Only with Thine Eyes' to a roomful of gypsies." Still another Newport hostess, Mrs. Harold Brooks of "Brooks House," has modern entertaining down to a definite system. "I try to take care of every last detail beforehand," she says, "and then I pretend to be one of the guests. A party should be seventy per cent talent and thirty per cent audience."

Unfortunately, neither Newport's *cachet* nor its latter-day hostesses nor such upper-class financial names as the Dukes and the Donahues, the Woolworths and the Hartfords, have been able to stem the tide of the Newport revolution. "Nowadays," says young Mrs. Louis Lorillard, "if I gave a party like Mrs. Fish's and let out a roomful of butterflies, everybody would think they were moths!" Most Newporters have, whether they admit it or not, bowed to the trend. On Coggeshalls' Ledge Frazier Jelke has bought "The Waves," the old John Russell Pope cottage, and has converted it into seven apartments; these apartments, which rent for as little as two thousand dollars a summer, are the first such in Newport history. Out on Ocean Drive John Barry Ryan and his wife, daughter of the late Otto Kahn, have attempted to make their "Moorland Farm" a paying proposition; in the summer of 1952 they counted twenty-three sheep. Two other well-known Newport families, the Grosvenors of "Wyndham" and the Manices of "Edge Hill," have also become sheepherders. But cottage clearance remains Newport's chief revolutionary problem. One of the most curious attempts to solve this was made by the singer Gertrude Niessen who, in 1941, bought the $2,500,000 "Rosecliffe" for $21,000. Miss Niessen, who had spent much of her life in hotel rooms, at first enjoyed the twenty-two bedrooms of the cottage—as well as the twenty-two private baths. Unfortunately she left the cottage one fall without a caretaker and with one of the baths running. By January there was ice several inches thick over the Aubusson carpets and other delicacies of "Rosecliffe" and Miss Niessen was faced with such a large water bill that she decided to sell the cottage to meet it. The current owner of "Rosecliffe," New Orleans' popular J. Edgar Monroe, is unlikely to meet similar difficulties. Monroe's business interests are almost as widespread as his ballroom, which is Newport's largest and measures 82 x 42 feet. "I'm in everything in the South," he says. "With income taxes what they are, a man couldn't live like I live with a million dollars a year."

A striking example of cottage clearance occurred in 1946 when Robert Goelet offered his hundred-room "Ochre Court" to his daughter at Vassar; the latter turned it down with the statement that even the thought of living there "oppressed" her. Finally in 1947 Goelet gave up and delivered the cottage to the Roman Catholic Church for a girls' college. Some idea of the size of this problem at Newport was given by the architect charged with the reconversion of "Ochre Court." Though a specialist in castles, chateaux and manor houses, he was overwhelmed with its grandeur. One stained glass window alone, he declared, was worth $25,000, and the dining room—without one tapestry upon which he felt it was impossible to set a price—he valued at $100,000. "I'm not a temperamental man," he told a visitor, "but I tell you I couldn't sleep or eat for days."

Neither, apparently, could Robert Goelet's father, Ogden Goelet, who built "Ochre Court." In his last years his digestion became so irritable that he was forced to subsist entirely upon hothouse grapes. His son Robert took no such chances. He recently bought a smaller cottage, "Champ Soleil," which takes only five servants to run, in contrast with "Ochre Court's" thirty-five; the change—to remodel "Champ Soleil" to his satisfaction—cost him only $250,000. "This servant thing, you know," says Goelet, "is the biggest thing we have here." Other Newporters agree. The day is gone, they point out, when Mrs. Hermann Oelrichs could keep a card catalogue of her domestics with just three classifications, "Good," "Bad," and "Rotten." The day is also gone when the late Perry Belmont could have a knee-breeched footman holding a candelabra on every sixth step of the staircase of "Belcourt" and could choose these men solely on the basis of the shapeliness of their calves. Further back, old Newporters recall, a footman, on being hired, for fifty dollars a month, would immediately ask, "Do I powder?" If the answer was yes, he expected five dollars a month for the nuisance of brushing the powder out of his hair every time he left the cottage.

At the same time there are also Newporters who feel that the servant problem has been exaggerated. With admirable enterprise they have worked out a smuggling system over the Canadian border, whereby their calls for help can still be satisfactorily answered. In the summer of 1947 one Newport native decided to investigate the servant problem on his own. A discharged veteran and single, he went to an employment agency and procured a position as a pantryman in one of the larger cottages. His working day began at eight o'clock, and except for nights of large dinners, of which he had only eight in three months, he worked just four and a half hours a day, with one complete day off a week. His duties consisted of being in the pantry—never in the kitchen—to prepare trays and wash dishes for three meals a day, from eight to nine-thirty, one to two-thirty and six to seven-thirty, but never for more than three people, which was the normal complement of the front part of the cottage. Mornings from nine-thirty until his lunch, afternoons from two-thirty until his supper, and evenings from eight o'clock on, he was absolutely free. Although he was the only American in the household, he found a certain companionship among his fellow workers and Friday or Saturday evenings regularly attended dances given in a neighboring greenhouse by the leading gardener in Newport's servant hierarchy.

The young man was never responsible for making his own

bed or cleaning his own room—this being done, apparently, by servants' servants. He had no uniform problem since he was never in the front of the cottage and only once all summer did he ever see his real employer. She was sitting on the piazza one day when he went by on his way for his morning swim, and though he waved to her, he was not discouraged by the fact that she didn't wave back—for, as he realized, she had had no opportunity to get to know him. When the butler who first hired him and outlined his duties asked if $250 a month would be acceptable, he almost fell over. At the end of the summer, advised by another servant to ask for a raise, he refused. "I didn't have the gall," he says.

Often overlooked in Newport history, among Newport's eminent hostesses and their quaint counterparts like Ward McAllister and Harry Lehr, have been the rank and file of Newport's male population. From the earliest days these so-called "solid men" played a vital part in the success of the resort. General Cornelius Vanderbilt was never too busy running railroads to give his undivided attention to the carpenters' estimates on reshingling the Casino roof, and Arthur Curtiss James never allowed the directors meetings of his copper companies to interfere with his decision as to the proper rent to be charged for Casino shops. The New York lawyer, Lewis Cass Ledyard, estimated shortly before he died in 1932 that his attention to Newport had cost him a total of two years of his life—that amount of time having been spent on the Fall River Boat. All Newporters took the boat up to New York Sunday night, but Ledyard took it down Friday night also, although this meant docking at 5:00 A.M. Ledyard was on virtually every Newport committee and needed every available minute of Saturday morning at the resort. The New York horseman, Frank K. Sturgis, of Lenox and Bar Harbor as well as Newport, was, at the age of eighty, literally carried to his last meeting in the Casino Governors Rooms; he was supported on one side by his trained nurse and on the other by his valet.

The sturdiest specimen of the hero in Newport history was the late George H. Norman, family-founding forebear of the resort's distinguished Norman dynasty. A dignified gentleman with a long full beard, Norman had no middle name. He thought he ought to have one and so chose the "H," even though the initial never stood for anything. Norman's occupation was that of a hydraulic engineer and, born in Newport, he was a rugged individualist to the end of his days. When a neighbor refused to repaint a barn, which Norman thought was a disagreeable color, Norman, in the owner's absence, had it painted for him. Riding in the train one day in 1900 Norman wrote his will on the back of a paper bag; to this day no one has ever been able to break the trust he thus established.

On another occasion Norman, who never took a parlor car, was reading his paper after the train had started when the conductor, coming through the car, noticed a suitcase in the aisle beside him. The train was crowded and the conductor told Norman sharply that he would have to get the suitcase out of the aisle. "No," said Norman, reading his paper, "I don't." The conductor told Norman that a person who tripped over the suitcase might sue the railroad and it would then be Norman's fault. "I mean it," he said, "move it." Norman paid no attention and the conductor became exasperated. "You may be the largest stockholder of this railroad," he said, "but I'll show you who's the captain of this train. If you don't move that suitcase I'll throw it off." Norman still continued to read. The conductor was furious. "I'll count three," he shouted. "I'll throw it off the train!" As the conductor, red in the face and raging, sounded the counts, Norman still read on. At the third count the conductor seized the suitcase, strode down to the end of the car and hurled it out the door. Coming back he rubbed his hands. "Well," he said, "you Newporters think you own the earth. I guess that will teach you a lesson." For the first time Norman looked up. "Not me, it won't," he said. "It wasn't my suitcase."

Newport's first men's club, the Newport Reading Room, was established in 1854 and antedates all other resort clubs in the country; its proudest boast is that it still operates the oldest flush toilets in existence. Located across Bellevue Avenue from the old Muenchinger King Hotel, it is a small yellow and white frame house with a handsome cupola on top and a wide piazza several steps up off the street which is marked by ancient carriage lamps. In the same way that at Southampton people sit on the porch of the Irving House and stare across at the members on the porch of the Southampton Club, at Newport people sit on the porch of the Muenchinger King and stare across at the Reading Room. "This club," says President Gustave J. S. White, "is a sort of a last stand of old principles." Among these principles are a Spartan diet—canned soup and crackers are the only foods served in the club—and a severe antifeminism. In the old days so severe was this latter principle that a lady who saw one of the Reading Roomers sitting on the porch was not supposed to speak to him, no matter how close he was to her or how well she knew him; the gentleman, for his part, stared solemnly by her as if she was not there at all. If she wished to ask him to dinner, or some such question, she had to go into the Muenchinger King and telephone. Today this tradition has relaxed but the club is still severe. Whereas the porch of the Southampton Club is divided into one side for ladies and gentlemen, and the other side for gentlemen only, the Newport club admits no ladies to the porch or anywhere else except on two days a year. One of these days is for the finals of the annual tournament of *boccie,* an Italian form of English lawn bowling. The other is for what the late Maximilian Agassiz, who died fighting the movement, called "no reason at all."

The club also has an extremely severe set of by-laws. Rule V of these laws reads: "Conversation and drinking are forbidden in the northwest room on the second floor." Actually, conversation is somewhat limited everywhere in the Reading Room. Many of the elderly members are so troubled with deafness that they do not even know whether anyone is talking or not. Often a visitor to the club will have the same experience which he often has after a Newport dinner party when, after the gentlemen are separated from the ladies, two or three gentlemen will start talking at once—each of them not realizing that anyone is talking and thinking their visitor, who cannot possibly parse anything out of the simultaneous deliveries, must be even deafer than they are. At the same time, no visitor to the club can fail to be impressed by its lineal formidability. The club recently boasted no less than ten father-and-son membership combinations, including the Messrs., *père* and *fils,* Bogert, Douglas, Jelke, Manice, Norman, Phelps, Prince, Sheffield and Whitehouse. All these gentlemen take not only the Reading Room but also all Newport with extreme earnestness. Many of them have, in the spirit of Newport's old rank-and-file population, placed with local real estate agents standing offers to meet any cottage property bids of which they disapprove.

Even more recherché than the Reading Room, at least to current Newporters, is the Clambake Club, located out on the end of Easton's Point just beyond an unprepossessing modern development of small houses. Limited to one hundred members, it still features the clambakes and skeet-shooting of yesteryear. This club too can be formidable. It was here that the young golfer T. Suffern Tailer, who had returned to the resort after long absence, admitted to a group of Clambakers, shortly before World War II, that he was going to vote for Roosevelt. One of the gentlemen patted his knee in a fatherly manner. "You've been away a long time, Tommy," he said. "Down here we don't say that even in fun."

Two other once formidable Newport clubs have faded from the scene altogether. One was the Graves Point Fishing Club where the late J. P. Morgan used to fish an average of four hours a year at a cost, Newport statisticians delighted to figure, of five hundred dollars per angling hour. The other was the celebrated Gooseberry Island Club. Located on a small island off Cherry Neck, this club was limited to only fourteen members, was reached only by launch and was never even seen except by members and a few distinguished guests. Membership cards were inherited propositions; for three thousand dollars a year the fortunate holders of them enjoyed Gooseberry's small hunting lodge and enormous bar and devoted themselves to swimming in the nude, then dressing in time to welcome lady guests—via another launch trip—to lunch. The menu for this meal never varied. It consisted of clam chowder, steamed clams, lobster, corn bread and hot waffles, and the amount a man was able to consume was the barometer of his social standing in the club. In the hurricane of 1938 the lodge was utterly destroyed, a colored caretaker drowned and the club never revived.

The whole Newport colossus, and its sturdy social saga, reaches its natural climax in an extremely vital club area of the resort known as Bailey's Beach. That such a name is out of keeping with its grandeur is well known to Newporters; the official name of Bailey's is the Spouting Rock Beach Association. Even its location is significant, for it stands at the end of Cliff Walk and thus brings to an abrupt close the public walk between Newport's cottages and ocean. For generations aspirant millionaires might have been asked to join the Reading Room or the Clambake Club and might even have negotiated one of the "Umbrella Stands" at the Casino; until they were firmly established in a cabana of their own at Bailey's, however, there was still work to be done. Into the American vocabulary they put the phrase, "Bailey's Beach or Bust."

Today the new Bailey's which was rebuilt following the hurricane of 1938 is a gray-brick building with a lemon-colored trim and even an off-tomato-colored bar; it boasts eighty-one outside cabanas. These are known as Bath Houses "A" and consist of two small dressing rooms, a shower and toilet, as well as a porch—upon which, except in case of serious illness, every member of the family owning a cabana must be seen daily from 11:00 A.M. to lunch. There are also two hundred inside cabanas, or Bath Houses "B," as well as an ordinary locker room, in which all Newporters not in the select eighty-one must sit out their turn to get an "A." Like other Newport clubs, Bailey's is run on a double-membership basis; in other words, one must become first a seasonal subscriber, then a stockholder and full-fledged member. Supporting a cabana at Bailey's often runs as high as fifteen hundred dollars a year, because they are owned outright, and the upkeep and all improvements are in the hands of the owner, not the Beach Association. All cabanas have locks, but these locks are not to keep outsiders out; they are to keep the owners out. The superintendent of the beach keeps all keys and every night at seven o'clock locks all cabanas. Then, all night long, every hour a watchman makes the rounds to see that no owners have tried to break in. Bailey's wants no part of after-dark bathing or cabana courtships, and the fact that the younger generation does not like the beach's blue laws does not worry *cachet*-minded Newporters at all. "Young people have a good time at Bailey's," declares Mrs. George Tyson, a sister of Mrs. Mesta and a lady whose cottage overlooks the beach, "but it is a good time in an awfully nice way."

Until 1947 no photographer was ever permitted inside Bailey's. Newspapers and picture magazines were reduced to attempting either airplane shots or telephoto-lens exposure from neighboring rocks. To mark the historic occasion, the first magazine nominated for the honor of picturing the beach was the *National Geographic*. In reality Bailey's, which has no swimming pool of any kind, is not only the best of Newport's many beaches; it is by all odds the worst. Some years ago Mrs. George Henry Warren attended a costume ball dressed as "Miss Bailey's Beach." Her ensemble consisted of a seaweedy-looking dress liberally ornamented with clamshells, bones, banana peels and orange rinds. But Bailey's protocol permits no one to swim anywhere else. A British visitor who, a few summers ago, insisted on going down and taking a dip from off the smooth rocks at the end of the beach was criticized as severely as an American might be for making his own rules at an introduction at the Court of St. James.

Once a person has entered the water from the proper area,

however, Bailey's permits a wide latitude of aquatic enjoyment. The late Evalyn Walsh McLean always swam with two detectives. "Good Lord!" she exclaimed. "I've got to be watched." In more recent times Bailey's outstanding mermaid was Baroness Gourgaud, a lady whose social position at the resort was fortified by the fact that her great-grandfather-in-law had been on St. Helena with Napoleon. The Baroness did not swim a stroke, but she liked to be in the water a full half hour. She solved the difficulty by surrounding herself with a large automobile tube. She also balanced a red parasol over her head—a feat which has been in the tradition of Bailey's great swimmers of the past. Mrs. O. H. P. Belmont also swam with a parasol, although hers was green, while Mrs. James Kernochan, who carried no parasol, successfully avoided the sun, as well as prying eyes, with heavy black bathing shoes, thick black cotton stockings, a pair of large black pantaloons topped off with a full black skirt, a black blouse fastened with pearl buttons, a black jacket with full sleeves tied around her wrists and, finally, an enormous black Mother Hubbard bonnet tied under the chin. Far from a natatory nightmare, Mrs. Kernochan was regarded in her day as a Bailey belle; much more consternation was caused shortly before the First World War when Mrs. Herbert Parsons, the former Miss Clews, became the first lady to appear on the beach without stockings. Even today Bailey's Old Guard ladies may be seen, on unusually hot days, holding their parasols as they gingerly approach the water. Although they no longer actually swim with them, the parasols themselves, stuck in the sand during their swim, are still an important part of beach scenery.

Of Bailey's male swimmers, the late James Van Alen was the most sporty; Van Alen always swam in a white straw hat and puffed a large cigar while he did so. Even more picturesque was the late Hermann Oelrichs. A large round man who felt more at home in the water than he did on dry land, Oelrichs was a veritable water buffalo. For his dip he would equip himself with a dinner pail, a heavy flask and some light reading material, then proceed far out to sea. Unlike Eleanora Sears and other long-distance swimmers of Bailey's history, who at least kept to a charted course, Oelrichs simply drifted about. Saved on some occasions by incoming tides and upon others by the timely arrival of the Coast Guard, he never felt himself in any danger and was particularly indignant about a suggestion, which he traced to the Naval War College, that he was a menace to navigation and should at least mark his position by a buoy. Besides his swimming ability, Oelrichs was also Newport's most fearless raconteur of fishing stories. Once, in describing a catch he had made, he exaggerated the size of his fish to such an extent that a man named Kent challenged him. "Why," he protested indignantly, "that's as large as I am." Oelrichs, a man twice Kent's size, looked him over with some distaste. "With a halfway decent rod and line," he said, "I could land you." Kent wagered he could not and off Bailey's one day the test was made. Kent, fitted out with a cap which was bound to his head and to which a swivel and ring were attached, took to the water. Oelrichs, casting his line from a raft, promptly hooked him. Although Kent was an expert swimmer, Oelrichs had little difficulty reeling him in.

If Bailey's swimmers have deteriorated with the passing years, the Beach's social severity has not. Recently on the bulletin board of Bailey's, just before a junior dance, there appeared the sign: "THIS IS YOUR CLUB. NO INTRODUCTION IS NEEDED." The sign, if not the introduction, was indeed needed. A cabana-owner who some years ago had the temerity to entertain a guest of whom other Newporters disapproved, received a two-week suspension of his privileges—a penalty which had previously been reserved for teen-agers who broke windows or otherwise made nuisances of themselves. At the same time, Bailey's scramble for café royalty had continued almost as vigorously as in the days when Michael Strange noted that, in comparison to it, "football was gentle." Following the wedding of Louise Van Alen to her second Prince Mdivani, one cabana gleamed in the morning sunlight with the sign: "ENGLISH SPOKEN HERE."

Of late years probably the height of Bailey's *cachet* has been the appearance each morning at exactly eleven o'clock of two elderly ladies. Each of them first stands for a while just outside the main door of the cabana area and then takes a seat which affords a commanding view of the Beach. For years they have been coming to Bailey's each morning, they are members of the club and they remain until lunchtime; yet for years hardly anyone has spoken to them. That they would continue to keep coming to the club under such conditions is remarkable enough. What makes their appearance even more remarkable is that they actually seem to be enjoying themselves. "You see," explains Mrs. Hoffman Clinton, "the thing about Bailey's isn't just that we don't speak to them. They don't speak to each other."

In these latter years all Bailey's Beachers awaiting their turn to get a Bath House "A" have spent a good deal of their time inquiring anxiously about the health of Frederick H. Prince. In keeping with his position as master of "Marble House," Prince, a man currently in his middle nineties, is the only Newporter to own three "A's." In the old days when Newport and Bailey's Beach were household words, "Marble House" was the climax of the American social dream. "If every boy can be President," said the late Dixon Wecter, "then surely every girl can sit in 'Marble House' in Newport." Today Prince, who bought the cottage from Mrs. Belmont in 1932 for $100,000, sits in "Marble House" without any girl; his wife died in 1949. Recently when a guest complained of the lack of homeyness, Prince answered the complaint by building inside "Marble House," up on the third floor, a handsome little brick cottage—completely equipped and separately walled and roofed. At Prince's death it is thought possible that this cottage which, out of the way as it is, is one of the few genuine cottages on Bellevue Avenue, will bring a higher price than the eleven-million-dollar castle which surrounds it. Unfortunately, even in this cottage the brick is artificial.

Prince himself, a man of uncertain temper, who usually dresses in riding clothes and carries a whip, admits that his era is gone. Throughout his life he has conducted most of his business on the telephone, and he still talks to people who see him in person as if they were on the receiving end of the wire. "Newport, bah, hello," he says. "Newport is dead, hello. Life is a battle, hello, and those in the front ranks, hello, are always getting shot at, hello. Work is pleasure, hello, and pleasure is work, hello." Prince believes that his own life has been ignored by historians and to remedy this omission recently wrote, in twenty-eight short businesslike paragraphs, a summary of his achievements. Excerpts from this brochure, which he entitled "Mr. Prince's Career," follow:

> Mr. Prince entered into business in 1879 and in 1884 formed an intimate relationship with Governor Smith, the president of the Vermont Central Railroad. He entered into a contract with him to build six steamers to run from Ogdensburg, N. Y., to Chicago. These boats were built in

Cleveland by Mark Hanna's ship yards and through Mr. Hanna and his continual trips to Cleveland he made the acquaintance of John D. Rockefeller and the Standard Oil people.

Mr. Prince became associated with Mr. McLeod, the president of the Reading Road. After the financial difficulties of Mr. McLeod, Mr. Prince was left with the control of the Boston & Maine and other properties.

During all this time Mr. Prince has held large interests in the Union Stock Yard in Chicago, various railroads and carried a large indebtedness with the banks. There never has been a time during the different panics that Mr. Prince has not met all his obligations; in fact his brokers will testify he was one of the few men in Boston who survived the many financial difficulties the country has experienced.

All the thirty-five railroads which Mr. Prince has owned have given him a vast acquaintance and knowledge from operating men.

Around 1900 when Col. Dick had built the Conneaut Road to within three miles of Homestead and was in financial difficulties, Mr. Prince put up the money to save the road from bankruptcy and the control of the road was given to Mr. Prince who undertook on contract with Mr. Carnegie to build it to Homestead. Finally Mr. Carnegie decided to build the road himself. This was the start of the U.S. Steel Co. This brought Mr. Prince into intimate association with Mr. Frick and Mr. Mellon.

Mr. Prince is the oldest member of the New York Stock Exchange and has never been there in his life. He has never been a gambler but has been interested in transportation and the development of industry in this country.

Mr. Prince was associated with Senator William Butler of Massachusetts and worked out a financial plan for his mills, which has been successful. He was intimate with President Calvin Coolidge.

Mr. Prince continually went abroad for recreation for Mrs. Prince.

Last but no means least of the many aspects of the Newport revolution has been the narrowing of the gulf which in Newport's great days always separated the natives from the resorters. Today younger members of Newport's most illustrious resort families, including Van Alens, Lorillards, Phelpses and Auchinclosses, are serving on committees side by side with Newport natives in an effort to promote the new era of good feeling. Even Newport resorters of advanced years are doing their duty on these committees, and though they are not always successful—"I blow in," says Miss Edith Wetmore, "I blow up and I blow out"—the change is a notable one. An enormous indoor tennis and badminton building on Bellevue Avenue, a birthday present to a member of the A & P Hartford family, has been converted into a club for natives, and though the natives still refuse to swim at Bailey's because they have a far better beach of their own, it has now become difficult to distinguish resorters from natives without a blue book. When Newport's own movie star, Van Johnson, son of a local plumber and a young man who started his career as a beach boy at Bailey's, became the first native to move into the same financial league as the resorters, there was even a strong feeling that it would be nice to have the local boy move in on the cottage set and build at least a small camp of his own. Unfortunately Johnson has so far shown little enthusiasm for the movement but his name has given it much impetus. As one of his schoolboy chums expresses it, "It sure would be nice to have just one Van Johnson out there among all those Van Alens, Van Beurens and Van Rensselaers."

Of late years this native-resorter kinship has been kept in the forefront of the Newport picture by a phenomenon which, like the late Coogan ghost house, is unique among resorts. It started back in the 1920's when Timmy and Julia Sullivan, native Newporters and brother and sister, bought at auction for the sum of $6,500 a small gardener's cottage on Bellevue Avenue. Unmindful of the pain it caused their neighbors, who were going in for the social business, the Sullivans went into the junk business. In short order their cottage area became a haven for piles of lumber, bits of furniture, automobile tires, old newspapers and broken-down baby carriages. It still remains so today, a sort of Newport answer to New York's late Collyer brothers, on an outdoor instead of an indoor scale, and Newport's Sullivans are now as sought after by tourists as any of the cottage kings or queens. But Timmy and Julia themselves are no publicity hounds. They shun reporters and forbid even the postman to enter their cottage. In their seventies, they are soft-spoken, kindly people who just like their life, and, having entered their junk business before the days of Newport's now Spartan-strict zoning laws, they know they are safe. In their way they have even developed a certain *cachet* of their own. Each August 31, on the last day of Newport's tax year, they wrap up their tax money in their old newspapers, in dimes, nickels and even in pennies, carry it down to the office of the tax collector and dump it, with some ceremony, on the central desk.

In the past the summer colony made stern efforts to remove the Sullivans. For their half-acre junk heap they were offered as high as $25,000 cash, and three separate efforts were made to declare their cottage, respectively, a fire hazard, a health menace and a public nuisance. Lately, however, with the new era of good feeling between resorter and native, the Sullivans have come to be actually cherished by the summer people and attempts to dislodge them are now looked upon with disfavor. The most curious of these attempts was made by Mrs. Peyton Van Rensselaer, social stormy petrel of Newport and Palm Beach and a lady whose property borders the Sullivans. Mrs. Van Rensselaer knew that the Sullivans had never been away from Newport; if they would allow her to have her gardener clean up the place, she said, then she would make them a gift of a trip to Florida. Timmy and Julia carefully considered the offer, then, with the same *cachet* they pay their taxes, they turned it down cold. Nobody, they informed Mrs. Van Rensselaer indignantly, goes to Florida in the summer.

For many generations a rather more charming demonstration of Newport's native vs. resorter spirit has been carried on by the resort's taxi drivers. These drivers still conduct what were once called "rubbernecking trips" around the estates, and the passing years have merely added to the appeal of their blow-by-blow accounts of life as it used to be lived behind the iron gates. A recent visitor was impressed by a driver's account as he passed "Crossways." "Them was the days," the driver droned philosophically, "when the one was outdoing the other in the parties and Mrs. Stuyvesant Fish up there, she was the greatest of them all. Why, one of her parties—the St. Louis the Seventh, it was . . ." The visitor broke in to inquire what on earth kind of party was that. "It was fancy dress," the driver explained briefly. Once more the visitor was curious. What was fancy dress? The driver looked at him scornfully. "Don't you know?" he asked. "Them was the ones where all the men came in knickerbockers."

Unfortunately the dean of all these Newport drivers is now dead, but his place in Newport history is assured by an event which occurred on one of his last tours. For thirty years he had been taking sight-seers around the cottages without ever once, even by insinuation, breaking the barriers of good taste. He would give names, quote the sizes of the cottages and mention prices, but these were matters of public knowledge. Never would he stoop to editorial comment. Finally one day he had a cabful of visitors and was passing "The Elms," the cottage of E. J. Berwind, Pennsylvania coal baron. This cottage is featured by not one, but three, front doors, thus enabling three carriages, or carloads, of guests to be discharged at once; along its great stone fence are sculptured a large row of heads, all of which bear suspicious resemblance to that of the late Mr. Berwind himself. The driver, of course, was above calling attention to any such details as these. He merely pointed out the cottage, said it was called "The Elms," was the home of E. J. Berwind, the coal baron, had fifty rooms and cost one million dollars; he then went on to add that the cottage was at present being done over and that during the work the baron's sister, Miss Julia Berwind, was living in a stable in the rear. Even this he qualified. The stable was, he said, fitted out for an apartment above and was entirely suitable. On the spur of the moment he went so far as to point it out, down a narrow side road.

A lady in the cab could not let this pass. "What!" she said, leaning forward and looking down the road in great concern, "Miss Berwind! In a stable!"

The driver looked around, saw the lady was past calming, and then he too looked down the road at the stable. All at once thirty years of his good work was forgotten.

"Lady," he said slowly, "if it was good enough for Jesus, I guess it's good enough for Miss Berwind."

IV

Bar Harbor— Walks, Talks and Flirtations

In October, 1947, the front page of a newspaper in Paris, France, *The Figaro,* featured a story about one of America's most famous resorts. The story declared that this resort, which was known as Bar Harbor and located in the State of Maine, had been half destroyed by a fire which had been set by local peasants as a means of protesting the long-continued occupation of their territory by America's landed aristocracy. As it later turned out, this remarkable version of the largest disaster story in the history of American resorts was built up from just one piece of information—one which was nothing more nor less than the name of the fire's place of origin. Unfortunately this place ranks, socially speaking, as the most modest one to be found anywhere in an extremely large and circumspect resort area; it is known as Dolliver's Dump.

If the fire had burned nearby Ellsworth, or Bangor, or even Maine's quiz-question capital, Augusta, it is a reasonable assumption that all the stories about it would have been of far less national interest, and possibly of no international interest. The fire did not, however. It burned a place which has been pronounced, ever since a Bostonian built the first cottage there, as "Baa Habba," which is located on the northeast shore of the island of Mount Desert, pronounced like the final course of a meal, and which is both nationally and internationally accorded a rank second only to Newport in the annals of American resort Society. To a paper like the imaginative *Figaro* the combination of such a place with Dolliver's Dump, pronounced as spelled, was simply too good to be true.

Actually it was too good to be true in more ways than one.

Most Bar Harborites now believe that the fire did not start in Dolliver's at all but forty feet outside, its probable cause being the focusing of the sun's rays through the windshield of an abandoned car. Furthermore, contrary to the general outside impression, which unfortunately still exists, Bar Harbor was not, as a town, half destroyed. There was, of course, severe damage. It could hardly have been otherwise with a blaze which, on top of the worst Indian summer drought in Maine history, was pushed by a wind strong enough, according to one observer, "to split tree trunks apart with cracks like pistol shots." The worst loss was undoubtedly the burning of the Jackson Memorial Laboratory, national center of cancer research, together with its thousands of mice, bred and tested in some cases through 208 consecutive generations.

But even this Laboratory, which received nation-wide publicity and gifts from all over the world, was quickly rebuilt and is now operating on a larger scale than it ever was before the fire. The rest of the town, including Bar Harbor's six churches, four schools and a hospital—as well as all shops, offices and banks—was spared. Two thirds of the famous Acadia National Park, including at least one side of its picture-postcard drive to the top of Mount Cadillac, was also undamaged. In spite of the fact that people had to be evacuated, first to the town athletic field and later down to the very dock itself, where only a last-minute change in wind saved them, only one life was lost as a direct result of the fire—a phenomenon which can be explained only by the heroism and discipline of the fire-fighters themselves. These were led by one of the bravest and most capable firemen in the history of the country, Chief David Sleeper—a man who directed the operation for ninety-six straight hours without any rest and who, when his voice had gone, continued to direct by means of written orders. But, as the Bar Harbor *Times* later editorialized: "Everyone was a hero, even the small puppy with scorched feet who attracted a man's attention to smouldering bushes beside the road to find a larger dog near death from burns."

In respect to the destruction of Bar Harbor as a resort, however, the report of the Paris *Figaro* was more accurate. By cottage count Bar Harbor was not half destroyed but it was almost a third destroyed; it lost some 70 out of a total of 222 cottages. But even here credit to the French paper must be given sparingly. To place so much blame for Bar Harbor's destruction on a fire which occurred in late October and was socially out of season anyway, is as unjust as it is incorrect. Included in the lost column were many cottages which were long unoccupied and whose owners had already planned to have torn down for tax purposes. To more than one owner of a white elephant the fire was actually a blessing in disguise. There were at least three cases in which shrewd owners, receiving prompt reports from their caretakers, were able to increase their insurance after the fire had started. Even those who suffered extreme losses now admit that Bar Harbor cottage life was on the way out long before the fire and that the fire was merely the *coup de grâce*. This cottage life had started in the 1880's and had boomed from the 1890's; then it had begun to collapse. Although it had a brief renaissance in the 1920's and staggered through the depression, it virtually disappeared when World War II gave marching orders to taxes, servants and the Old Way of Life.

How quiet this life had become was illustrated during World War II when a young Navy wife from the Midwest was privileged to be asked to a luncheon at the cottage of the late Frank Skillman of Cincinnati. "Skilly," as he was affectionately known to all Bar Harborites, was a sort of latter-day counterpart of Newport's Harry Lehr, and he really outdid himself on this occasion. The guests were dressed in all their finery, the table was decked out in best china and the cocktails and general accouterments were to the king's taste. The young Navy wife was thrilled with her first taste of the Old Order. Just before she thought they would be going in to sit down she could contain herself no longer. "All my life," she said, waving her hand in the direction of the dining room, "I've been waiting for this." Skilly smiled wanly. "My dear," he said, "so have I."

Mr. Skillman was not joking. His way of life and that of the young Navy wife had met at the crossroads. His last remaining servant had left in an altercation over the hors d'oeuvres, approximately an hour before the guests arrived. Since the young Navy wife soon proved herself, of all the guests, the only capable mistress of the kitchen, her introduction to the Old Order consisted of donning an apron and doing the cooking. Late in the evening Mr. Skillman declared that the party was his last and his life was no longer worth living. "Oh, Skilly," said one of his guests, "be sensible." "I'd rather be insensible," he said.

In the old days it was regarded as dangerous and unhealthy to build right on the water. Ironically, most of the Bar Harbor cottages which were so built escaped damage by the fire. Here in recent summers, dominated by an autocratic widow matriarchy, a vestige of the Good Old Days still goes on. All the major cities of Bar Harbor's social past are represented by at least one *grande dame,* among the most conspicuous of these being Philadelphia's Mrs. Edward Browning of "Pointe d'Acadie," Boston's Mrs. Henry D. Burnham of "Bagatelle," New York's Mrs. Alfred Anson of "The Turrets" and Chicago's Mrs. Potter Palmer, formerly of "Hare Forest" and, since the fire, of an unnamed ex-gardener's cottage. Of these, Mrs. Browning, who first coached up to the resort in a four-in-hand in 1907—a trip that took five weeks—probably describes the Society best. "I am a newcomer," she says.

On many of the doors there are still Indian-made wicker baskets for the benefit of calling cards. These "In" and "Out" signs, however, are no longer manipulated, as they once were, for the benefit of the caller but rather for the benefit of the callee. "What in heaven's name," asks New York's Mrs. William Wickham Hoffman, an exponent of the "Out" sign, "do you *do* with someone at eleven o'clock in the morning?" Butlers are still in evidence in most of the cottages; footmen, on the other hand, have gone with the wind. No longer can one be confident as one approaches a Bar Harbor front door—as one once would have been—that it will be opened by an alert servant before one even presses the bell; indeed on a Thursday afternoon one can be extremely confident that it won't be opened by a servant at all. Bar Harbor dinners are still late, eight or even eight-thirty, and dinner jackets are worn, but tails are as rare as the third-floor maid. At the Bar Harbor Club there are dances, buffet suppers and "Tombola" or prize ticket luncheons, but the only real social rush hour occurs on Sundays between church and lunch, when all Bar Harbor heads for the umbrella tables beside the swimming pool. Old Bar Harborites claim that at this time you can still tell the right people from the wrong people from the fact that, as one comes out of the club toward the swimming pool, the wrong people take the first umbrella to the right and the right people take the first umbrella to the left;

despite this refinement, the fact remains that in the 1920's there were at least six or seven umbrellafuls of both rights and wrongs.

In the face of such destitution, the thinning ranks of Bar Harbor's New Poor are by no means as confident as their Newport comrades of muddling through. While a few of the faithful still have their chins up—"If there are fewer people," says Baltimore's Mrs. William Keyser briskly, "it's so much the better for the rest of us"—the majority are not so sure. This majority viewpoint is briefly expressed by Philadelphia's Mrs. John Dorrance, who summers in "Kenarden," bolstered not only by Campbell's Soup but also by the presence of two married daughters in nearby cottages. "We're all dying," she says. Another Philadelphian, Mrs. John B. Thayer of "Cover Farm," is equally direct. "If you came here to 'come to Bar Harbor,' " she says, "you are going to be disappointed." At the same time Mrs. Thayer is a granddaughter of the late A. J. Cassatt, noted Bar Harborite and president of the Pennsylvania Railroad—in the days when, as Bar Harborites put it, "presidents of railroads were gentlemen." As such, Mrs. Thayer is conscious of the continuation of at least some tradition. "We still eat up and down West Street," she says, "just the way we used to."

Even this is challenged by authoress Mary Roberts Rinehart. A burned-out cottager who summers at the new Hotel Bar Harbor, Mrs. Rinehart has seen a large change in the resort since she first came there twenty years ago. "Then," she says, "you dined out six days a week and on the seventh —a little like God—you rested and gave a dinner for the people who had dined you." Mrs. Rinehart smiles. "Today," she says, "we still know where we're going to eat all right. The trouble is we even know who we're going to sit beside.

There are only five eligible males in Bar Harbor and one of them is pushing ninety." Recently Philadelphia's Tony Stewart, one of the most popular Bar Harbor bachelors, was asked how he was able to undergo the social life at the resort summer after summer with the same few people. He became very thoughtful. "I drink a good deal," he said quietly. "You couldn't do it sober."

It is impossible to dismiss in this fashion, however, an island five hundred miles from New York which through the years has boasted not only generations of Pulitzers and Potter Palmers, Rockefellers and Fords, Stotesburys and Kents, but has also attracted on an individual scale celebrities which have run the gamut from Jane Addams to Evalyn Walsh McLean and from J. P. Morgan to Sumner Welles. With such personal distinction Bar Harbor has also had—and still has, despite the fire—a scenic splendor unequaled by any other American resort. Newport's historical landmarks downtown, as well as its cottage castles along Bellevue Avenue, are unforgettable sights, but Bar Harbor's combination of mountains and ocean dwarfs anything that any other resort offers in natural beauty. When Samuel de Champlain first saw these mountains in September, 1605, they had evidently, even in those days, recently suffered a fire. He called the island "L'isle des Monts Deserts." Today, 350-odd years later, following another fire, they are still in parts deserted, but their rugged beauty still gives Bar Harbor a unique this-is-the-forest-primeval appearance. Inland, among the mountains, there is also a primeval quality to Mount Desert's many lakes. "A land of Canaan look," Mary Cass Canfield described it. "There is a certain Biblical serenity," she wrote, "a wide peace about the views which must broaden your state of mind."

Bar Harbor's cottages are not, like Newport's, awe-inspiring from the road; in fact Bar Harbor's "rubbernecking tours" are conducted by sight-seeing launches. On the other hand, Bar Harbor's Ocean Drive, which has often been compared to the famous Mediterranean Drive from Amalfi to Sorrento, is far more awe-inspiring than Newport's. There is only one beach, but the wild beauty of the Drive is in places breath-taking, and one is not surprised to learn that every landmark on it is a sacred name to all true Bar Harborites—Schooner Head, Spouting Horn, Anemone Cave, Sand Beach, Great Head, Thunder Hole and Otter Cliffs. On the Shore Path which, like Newport's Cliff Walk, affords public access to a view between the cottages and ocean, a phenomenon called Balance Rock is Bar Harbor's version of the Blarney Stone. Shaped like an enormous egg, small end down, this rock perches precariously; but, since it has done so since glacier days, Bar Harborites could wish for nothing more than that their resort Society would continue to balance as well. Bar Harbor's rival resorts on Mount Desert—Northeast Harbor, Seal Harbor and particularly Southwest Harbor, which nestles by the mouth of Somes Sound, which is America's only authentic fiord—are equally cherished scenically, and Robert Haven Schauffler, writing in the *Century* magazine as long ago as August, 1911, warned all future writers against deciding which was the most beautiful. "As for me," he wrote, "I had as lief decide between Chartres Cathedral, the Winged Victory, Leonardo's Last Supper, and the Seventh Symphony."

In order to compare Bar Harbor with Newport, one turns naturally to such a lady as Mrs. Louis Lehr. Though a rather recent addition to the Bar Harbor colony, Mrs. Lehr is a sister-in-law of Newport's late Harry and a lady who had her own coming out at the Rhode Island resort. Mrs. Lehr has little difficulty with such a comparison. "We're just nicer people," she says. While there is a good deal of truth in this statement, it is perhaps necessary to probe even deeper. "The standards of Society here," says Mrs. Robert Codman, who was born a Philadelphian and married a Bostonian, "have always been Philadelphia and Boston, not New York." Referring back to the days when Philadelphia asked who a person was, Boston what he knew and New York how much he was worth, Mrs. Codman feels that Bar Harbor, in contrast to Newport, always looked askance at Manhattan. "If someone was from New York," she says, "you always asked how rich they were." As an example of the Philadelphia tone of the resort she cites the Bar Harbor practice of speeches with dinner parties—first host and then guests as called on by the host—an old Philadelphia custom. For the Boston tone of the resort she has her favorite Bar Harbor story, one which concerns a lady who was in mourning and therefore advised not to go to a certain party. The lady thought little of the idea and in one sentence delivered what may well stand as the keynote of the spirit of Bar Harbor Society. "I shall go," she said, "but I shan't mingle."

Today Bar Harbor's Old Guard remember the resort for good times in their youth. Those who don't, have husbands, or more likely wives, who do. From the days of the late Walter Damrosch to the current Walter Lippmann—both of whom married Bar Harbor girls—an extraordinary number of Bar Harbor ladies have kept their husbands coming back to the resort. Furthermore, in contrast to Newport, the good times they remember were all, apparently, simple ones. Among these were canoeing, sketching and "rocking," or searching for rocks along the shore. There was also, though, the plain and simple matter of walking. In all of Newport's social history only four resorters have ever been remembered as real walkers—Maud Howe Elliott, Mrs. Royal Phelps Carroll, Mrs. Horace Gallatin and James Brett Stokes. Bar Harbor's social history, on the other hand, teems with walkers. For generations Bar Harborites have dutifully trod the hundred miles of tortuous mountain trails which crisscross Mount Desert; at one time a person's social prestige depended on the number of pedestrian miles accomplished up and down hill each summer.

To walking was added, in 1896, another disinction for Bar Harbor. In that year the late Barrett Wendell, Professor of English at Harvard, announced to the waiting world, via the time-honored medium of a letter to the late Boston *Evening Transcript*, that Bar Harbor was the scene of the best conversation to be found anywhere in America. In that same year the writer, F. Marion Crawford, also blessed Bar Harbor conversation on a world-wide scale. "The conversation," he wrote, "does not fall into that jargon of a clique which often makes the talk of the most centralized society, like that of Paris and London, seem narrow and provincial to the unfortunate outsider."

Bar Harbor, then, had its motto—walk and talk. Whether these alone would have been sufficient for the good times remembered by all concerned, however, is extremely doubtful. For hand in hand with walking and talking came a third commodity which was never dignified by being added to the resort's motto but which was always, at least by insiders, known to be included. This commodity was perhaps best expressed by the Harvard *Lampoon* as far back as 1896. Bar Harbor was the place, according to this publication, "where easy-going Philadelphia girls taught slow-going Boston boys how to flirt." Even before the *Lampoon*'s analysis Charles Dudley Warner, fictionally touring American resorts in 1886 for *Harper's Magazine,* was able to report that Bar Harbor was "the finest sanitarium on the continent for flirtations." Warner, author of the line: "Everybody talks about the weather but nobody does anything about it"—one usually credited either to Mark Twain or Will Rogers—wrote that Bar Harbor was unique in one very important matter. "There is no doubt that the American girl is here," he said, "as she is at divers other sea-and-land resorts, but the present peculiarity of this watering-place is that the American young man is here also." The late Ambassador James W. Gerard, speaking of a later era, seconded Warner. "The same mothers and chaperones," he said, "who had been eagle-eyed in town or at Newport, relaxed their vigilance at Bar Harbor." Gerard did not know why. "It was," he said, "for some unexplained reason."

Today Mrs. George McMurtry, wife of the president of the Bar Harbor Club, expresses the resort's flirtation nostalgia as ably as any of the current colony. Born Teresa Fabbri, one of Bar Harbor's geatest belles of the World War I era, she was brought up, in the manner of the day, strictly. "I had three governesses at one time," she says, "one French, one German and one English. Now I ask you—wasn't that hell?" Though this trio was soon reduced by two thirds—the German lady was dismissed for cheating at solitaire and the French lady, who was pretty and read her De Maupassant, met a similar fate when a family uncle took a shine to her—the only time before Miss Fabbri came out, at eighteen, when she was permitted close proximity with a boy was a fifteen-minute period when she was allowed to dance in the ballroom of the old Bar Harbor Club. This was in the morning, and even here she was watched by the last remaining governess. Although she never tasted a cocktail until she was married, she remembers, after her coming out, buckboard parties in which chaperones were left behind, moonlight rides alone with a beau and all kinds of similar iniquities. All these happened at Bar Harbor, and today, looking back on a career which included a period in Reno during 1927 when there were no less than six Bar Harbor girls all getting divorces, she feels that Bar Harbor was the one redeeming feature of an overstrict upbringing which resulted in much unhappiness. "The only good times I had," she says, "were at Bar Harbor."

As Bar Harbor has faded, then, one cannot blame either the fire or, for that matter, merely the lack of money to run the cottages. Rather it appears that Bar Harborites have allowed their three principal social commodities—walking, talking and flirting—to fall into disrepair. Walking, of course, was not aided by the automobile. Some younger stalwarts of the *ancien régime* still sturdily plod the paths, and, maps to the contrary, dutifully call the mountains by their old names—Green instead of Cadillac, Newport instead of Champlain, and Dry instead of Flying Squadron. But by far the majority of Bar Harborites walk only to and from their garages and that only if they can't afford chauffeurs.

The history of Bar Harbor's talking has been an even more lugubrious tale. Philadelphia's Mrs. J. Madison Taylor, distinguished miniature painter and a lady who died in the summer of 1952 as she was preparing to leave for her seventy-fifth consecutive Bar Harbor season, recently admitted that much of the old-time conversation was a matter of what relation who was to whom; at the same time, she felt that the cocktail had done to conversation what the automobile did to walking. "After the second cocktail," she said, "there is no such thing as conversation." A younger authority, New York's Mrs. Shepard Fabbri of "Buonriposo"—she did not come to Bar Harbor until 1885—does not agree that the cocktail is entirely responsible. On the other hand, as a lady whose mother was a granddaughter of Commodore Vanderbilt and whose husband's father was a Morgan partner, she has had wide opportunities for hearing the best of talk all over the world and she feels that general conversation is not understood at all by the present generation. As practiced in the Italy she knew, conversation was, she says, like a centerpiece in the middle of the table with the minds gathered around it "like little searchlights throwing their beams." In Europe, Mrs. Fabbri feels, the women listen to the men; in this country the men listen to the women and the only time the men talk interestingly is when they separate after dinner. Too many women, she declares, have a tendency to turn away entirely and get out of the conversation if they are not themselves being directly addressed.

Still a third authority, Mrs. J. Howland Auchincloss of "Redwood," delivers the final blow. A member of New York's select Fortnightly Discussion Group—a group which has social, if not professional, prestige in the field of talking—Mrs. Auchincloss has been coming to Bar Harbor off and on since 1911. "Frankly," she says, "I haven't heard a good conversation since I got here."

To this sad state of affairs is added, as insult to injury, Bar Harbor's loss of the art of flirtation. Here Miss Alice Van Rensselaer, one of the resort's most distinguished spinsters, takes the stand. "I've lived in two totally different worlds," she says. "There is no illusion anymore. People are too intimate. Flirting isn't even noticed. Why, in the old days, a man noticed everything a girl had on." On this score Miss Van Rensselaer is on firm ground. She remembers playing tennis in a hat pulled down to her eyes, a veil over the rest of her face, a skirt down to her ankles and gloves. Furthermore her opinion, albeit differently expressed, is backed up by most of Bar Harbor's belles of today. One of them, currently regarded as a Bar Harbor–New York "glamour girl," reduces the entire question of modern flirtation to its barest essentials.

"It just isn't any fun any more," she says. "If you even say boo to a man, all he thinks is plop, how soon do we go to bed?"

Abiding strictly by Gresham's Law of artists and intellectuals preceding "solid" people and then first "nice" and finally "naughty" millionaires, Bar Harbor saw the beginning of its summer colony in 1844. In that year, the landscape artist, Thomas Cole, founder of the so-called Hudson River School of Painting, first came to the resort. Cole was armed with a sketchbook to reconnoiter the scenery, the excellence of which he had heard through the artistic grapevine of the day. His sketchbook is today in the Princeton University Art Museum. Following Cole came his pupil, Frederick Edwin Church, as well as such artistic luminaries of the day as Gifford, Hart, Parson, Warren, Bierstadt, Brown and Colman.

This group of easel-wielders, who sound rather like the latter-day batting order of the New York Yankees, soon spread, far and wide, the fame of Mount Desert scenery. Most social resorts have at one time or another been compared to European countries—Lenox, for example, was called the Switzerland of America—but for Bar Harbor one foreign country was not enough. "It is not pure Norway, it is Norway and Italy combined," one of these early-day publicists wrote.

"Days come when the atmosphere has infinite color and softness—has a spongy and velvety feeling to your fingers." While some latter-day realists might believe that such an artist was merely idealizing a typical Bar Harbor fog, the fact remains that these artists started a trend of publicizing the resort's air. In the old days everybody talked about air at resorts and each resort's was always the best. Julia Ward Howe said that Newport's air "made the common breath of life a pleasure." Bar Harbor's air was even more famous; in fact it was regularly compared, albeit by teetotalers, to champagne. Exactly a hundred years after Cole spent his first summer at Mount Desert, the late Mrs. John D. Rockefeller, Jr., whose husband never allowed the serving of cocktails, wrote a friend in 1944 that having grown up at the resort of Narragansett, she was never really happy unless she was near water. "And I am convinced," she added, "that there is no air in the world like the air of Maine."

Soon Bar Harbor's farmhouses had become little boardinghouses, its little boardinghouses bigger boardinghouses, its bigger boardinghouses hotels and finally, in 1867, the Boston merchant named Alpheus Hardy broke away from the hotel field entirely and built a small cottage. Before that, however, the year 1855 is a significant one in Bar Harbor's social history. In that year, on the still-preserved first register of the Agamont House appear the names of painter Church and a friend. Not only were they the first to register at any Bar Harbor hotel but also even the date they signed in, July 5, is significant. Through the years one of the many regular complaints of Bar Harborites is the one that due to the cold the season never really gets going until after the Fourth of July. In the same year, moreover, another friend of Church, the New York lawyer, Charles Tracy, made a pilgrimage to Bar

Harbor. Mr. Tracy's entourage was featured by two items. The first was his daughter Frances Louisa; ten years later she was to become Wife II of J. P. Morgan I. The second item, despite the hardship of Maine travel in those days, was a grand piano. Clearly Bar Harbor was on its way.

All stories of the gaiety of the early days feature Jordan Pond, the place which was usually the mecca of buckboard party pilgrimages and which has always occupied a special nitch in the nostalgia of all true Bar Harborites. Now a part of Acadia National Park, it is located in Seal Harbor on an offshoot of the famous Twenty-two Mile Drive from Bar Harbor to Northeast and almost everything in the area has some sort of romantic association for the Old Guard. The twin mountains at the northern end of Jordan Pond are called "The Bubbles." In hushed voices old-timers happily admit that the name of these mountains was derived from the suggestion of a famous Bar Harbor beau that they be called "The Bubbies"—after the most prominent twin features of the young lady he was courting. In time the name was refined by the change of one letter.

Today at Jordan Pond boats and horses are still for hire as they were in the old days; the feature attraction of Jordan Pond is still, as it has been for half a century, the Jordan Pond House. Boasting two rooms paneled in birch bark, in which many distinguished weddings have taken place, the House is chiefly in demand by Bar Harbor and Northeast Harbor Society for afternoon tea. At this the standard delicacy is the popover, which Bar Harbor is generally credited with making nationally famous. But plaguing Jordan Pond authorities for the recipe is useless. For many years the House has refused any description of its specialty other than that it is "a biscuit gone berserk." In the days when the standard vehicle of the resort was the "cut-under," a Bar Harbor version of the surrey without the fringe on top and with the wheels cut directly under the front seat, the story is told of a European countess who drove over from Bar Harbor to Jordan Pond and left a lasting impression on the place, if not on herself. "I never can remember," she said, "whether I drove over in a 'cut-under' for a 'popover' or in a 'popover' for a 'cut-under.' "

All the great social resorts have been thoroughly exploited as backgrounds for novels, but no resort ever captured the fancy of as many novelists as Bar Harbor. In the early-day novels, there is endless "calling" as well as an almost incessant "tinkle of the tea things." The cottage library is the general trysting place, but the characters also move slowly back and forth, among page-length paragraphs of scenery, between fields and streams, drawing rooms and verandas. In *Love in Idleness, a Tale of Bar Harbor,* Marion Crawford's heroine describes her beau ideal: "It is that he's such a perfect gentleman. You feel that he wouldn't do anything that wasn't quite —quite—don't you know?" All these novels belong to what Carl Brandt has called the "Little-did-she-reck" school of writing; even the late Mount Desert Society journal, the Bar Harbor *Record,* fell into the swing on June 12, 1897, when, harking back to Champlain and his sailors, they reported:

> Little did the storm-tossed sailors, steering from the danger-fraught shores, think their log book would bear the first record of what in future years was to be the scenes of life and pleasure and wealth; and little did the Jesuit monks, chanting their hymns of praise in late years, dream that these quiet valleys and silent mountains would be vocal with the echoes of men and women of fashion—the resting place and summer home of statesmen and leaders in the world of art, science and finance.

Today, of course, the last laugh is on the cottagers rather than on the Jesuit monks; the resort cottages now occupied by the Roman Catholic Church are legion. In the early days the novels all stressed the social motif and particularly the conflict between resorter and native. The island maid of sterling virtue either marries the one true artist among the ne'er-do-well resorters, or the unspoiled island man marries the one truly understanding resort girl among her spoiled contemporaries. Henrietta Rowe, a Maine girl herself, wrote perhaps the most typical of these novels in *A Maid of Bar Harbor*, published in 1902. In this book Comfort, the island maid, is enamored of Robert, the resorting artist, a young man whom she has for years regarded "with reverential awe as of beings too far removed from the dull homeliness of everyday life to be approached with any familiarity by ordinary mortals, but rather as devotees approaching a shrine." Even when Comfort does approach Robert, she does so gingerly, her kisses being described as "a rare expression of affection from this true daughter of New England with whom kisses were too rare and precious a coin for everyday use." But Comfort does want to marry and be a mother. "Happy, thrice happy, the woman who, with conscious pride, wears those love-woven bands as the insignia of a royalty more to be desired than the diadem of princes." Robert, too, is no slouch. He has lost his right arm in the Civil War but he hopes to be able to learn to draw all over again with his left. Unfortunately Robert's mother opposes the match:

> That Robert, fastidious and proud of his name and race, a man of the world, admired and caressed by that world, with high artistic hopes for the future, should stoop to share his name and honors with this little, unknown, untutored rustic, was gall and wormwood to the proud woman whose hopes had all centered in her son from his babyhood—her

> pride in him taking the place of that true unselfish motherly love that it was not in her nature to bestow.
>
> That Comfort was a sweet, modest, gentle-mannered girl she freely admitted. Indeed, she had made no secret of her liking for her or of the pleasure and relief that she found in her tender ministrations. But that Robert, her son, should look upon her with eyes of love, should pass by with cold indifference the wealthy, high-bred girls of his own clique to ally himself with this nameless and dowerless maiden, was something too monstrously absurd to be even thought of as a possibility. But what could she do?

As it turns out, she does plenty. She tells Comfort that she will disinherit Robert if he marries her and that without an income he will be unable to continue his painting. At the same time Comfort also receives another blow. She has inherited a small amount of apparently worthless pasture land; even this her brother tries to take from her: "Comfort's womanly heart shrank with sensitive dread from the thought that her only relative in the wide world—the brother who had lain an innocent baby upon the breast of their sainted mother—could find it in his heart to wrong her." But in the end everything turns out all right. Comfort receives fifty thousand dollars from her land, which a New York millionaire has suddenly coveted, and Robert and Comfort are left to live happily ever after. "You will be," Robert says—a metaphor he has successfully avoided for three hundred pages—"such a comfort to me." Even Robert's mother has a change of heart and "picking at the lace frills of her dressing gown," she sighs resignedly:

> "She is really a very sweet girl, and it is well for her that she won't be left to fall a prey to some designing fortune hunter. I am glad that everything was arranged between her and Robert before this happened, so that nobody can say that he married her for her money."

From 1882 until 1902, in what is now the heart of its business section, Bar Harbor had one hotel which became almost as famous as Bar Harbor itself. Dwarfing such other famous hostelries as the West End, the Malvern, the Newport, the St. Sauveur, the Louisburg, the Hamilton, the Grand Central, it was called, after its builder, Rodick's, and was described by Marion Crawford as the crowning product of the times when the "gnawing tooth of the jig-saw grievously tormented all manner of woodwork." Unlike the Jordan Pond House it no longer still exists; nonetheless it became one of the best known Society hotels in America—as famous for its informality as the hotels of Saratoga and Long Branch were for formality. Run on a sort of go-as-you-please, help-yourself basis, Rodick's was the one hotel, old Bar Harborites agree, where "everyone knew who everyone was"—which must have been some accomplishment. Although Rodick's did not have a single private bathroom and only the old-fashioned "sits" tubs, it was advertised as the largest hotel in New England, had 500 rooms, often served 750 at meals and lured as many as 3,000 people to its twice-a-week dances. Its twenty-foot-wide piazzas, running all along the front and one side—five hundred feet of total piazza length—were the scene of some of the best-mannered walks-and-talks of the day, but even these paled before the main attraction of Rodick's—its main lobby. Here, in contrast to most other resort hotels, in its time and after, the accent was on flirtation; all over the Society grapevine this lobby was known and fearlessly called "The Fish Pond."

In this pond Society girls, talking in fisherman's lingo of nibbles and bites and big ones that got away, unblushingly angled for dates. Not only were chaperones apparently more effectively dodged here than anywhere else but it was also one of the few social meeting grounds of the times in which the male and the female were privileged to introduce themselves to each other without benefit of third party. The competition was keen and Bar Harbor's young men were spoiled. Even at a *thé dansant*, no one was particularly shocked when two young men appeared in striped lawn tennis suits with jockey caps to match. If the young ladies protested there is little evidence of it. Bar Harbor at least had men; the feminine motto was obviously that it was better to be loved in a lawn tennis suit than never to be loved at all. By 1890, in the heyday of Rodick's, Bar Harbor was internationally famous, and a guidebook of resorts was able to go into high gear in reporting those walking down West Street:

> Here comes Peepy Marshmallow and Lina Van Rooster, Chicky Chalmers and Poodle Van Ulster, and the Hon. Hare Hare; and there in the background, in their moire and black lace, are Mrs. Gatling Gown and Mrs. Wellman Heisdeck, and even Mrs. Stylington Ribblehurst herself.

In 1892, ten years after the building of Rodick's, Bar Harbor captured from Newport one of the largest lions of the day in the person of the sixty-three-year-old Philadelphia physician and author, S. Weir Mitchell. His Newport vacations had given him, he declared, "intestinal neuralgia"; the reason he had begun writing novels was that he had been bored in the morning at the Rhode Island resort. From the beginning the good doctor found plenty to do at Bar Harbor. Equally at home, as Anna Robeson Burr noted, in such varying Maine weather as "soft fogs, sparkling northers, crashing nor-easters," the doctor's "knickerbockered shape" was soon a familiar sight on all the mountain trails. Boston's late Bishop

Lawrence was one of the first to sound the newcomer out. The Bishop "covered the mountains" with the doctor, reported back that his companion had "talked most interestingly as he walked." Blessed by the Boston Bishop, the Philadelphia physician, who always bought his neckties in Boston, became the resort's first citizen and its premier walkie-talkie. Elected to every committee formed to keep the beauty of the resort inviolate, Dr. Mitchell particularly liked, among other things, Maine's severe liquor laws. To this day in Maine no one is allowed to drink except at a hotel or private club, to drink on Sundays at all or any other day after midnight, to drink standing up, to carry a drink or to have more than one drink at a time—even just before the midnight deadline. Mitchell approved it all. "There is little heavy drinking here," he once told a guest over two quarts of champagne—the doctor liked a full quart by his own plate—"and less of the Newport ostentation. It is more like the dear old Newport I used to know in the days of Agassiz."

Everyone in Mitchell's circle, which soon extended all the way from "The Field," the most sedate section of Bar Harbor, to "Journey's End," the Northeast Harbor home of Mrs. Casper Wister, was called "dear." First there was, of course, "dear Weir," then there were the Misses Minots and the Misses Irwins, "dear Louisa," "dear Nannie," "dear Sophy" and "dear Agnes," the latter an ex-dean of Radcliffe College. Into this group of dears came professors from Southwest Harbor and all manner of college presidents, including Harvard's Charles William Eliot, Columbia's Seth Low, and Johns Hopkins' Daniel Coit Gilman. Together with such Bar Harborites as Dr. Henry Cadwalader Chapman, another Philadelphia physician, the orator Bourke Cochrane and the author Parke Godwin, these were responsible for Mount

Desert's succeeding Newport as the country's first-ranking intellectual resort. The most rugged of them all was the late Endicott Peabody, headmaster of Groton School. In the days before Northeast Harbor had a swimming pool, the Groton headmaster had to move to Cape Cod one summer so his children could learn to swim in warmer water. "When the children had progressed so far that I could push the boy suddenly off the float and have him come up smiling," Peabody said, "then I moved back to Northeast."

In this period also Mount Desert became a haven for bishops. Bishops Greer and Huntington of New York were inveterate islanders; so, too, was Bishop William Doane of Albany, a gentleman who rivaled Dr. Mitchell himself in social eminence. "Whether you saw Dr. Mitchell in tweeds on a mountain top," one eyewitness wrote, "or Bishop Doane acting coxswain to his grandchildren in a sort of arch-episcopal barge, you knew you were seeing something." Another eyewitness, a German exchange professor on a Mount Desert vacation, put it another way. "I haf nefer," he said, "met so many people of heartfelt reputation in von place gathered."

If Dr. Mitchell was Bar Harbor's Galahad in the fight against the coming of the millionaire cottage-builders, he was as nothing to Bishop Doane at Northeast; indeed, to this day the fact that Northeast is to Bar Harbor what Stockbridge is to Lenox and East Hampton is to Southampton—in other words, the virtuous community alongside the wicked—is generally credited to his late Grace of Albany. Together with Harvard's President Eliot, who kept issuing pamphlets under such titles as "The Proper Development of Mount Desert," the Bishop stood foursquare on the matter of the late dinner. To him this was the entering wedge of Bar Harbor's corruption, and he determined it should not penetrate Northeast

Northeast was to serve "supper," not "dinner," and never after seven. "Of course," said one hostess of the day irritably, "I am perfectly willing to put my soup into cups and call it supper to please the Bishop, but . . ."

Her "but" was never finished. To this day Bishop Doane's influence on Northeast in the matter of suppers at seven still continues—an influence which is all the more remarkable since, like Dr. Mitchell, the Bishop was far from simple in his own tastes. A stanch Anglophile, he even dressed in the fashion of British bishops. Striding back and forth over the mountains in gaiters, aprons and a shovel hat, he was not the slightest disturbed when a native boy once stopped him with the question, "Won't your ma let you put on longs?" As far as Bar Harbor was concerned, Bishop Doane's Anglophilia reached its peak one day when he was signing a hotel register together with a Bishop William David Walker from Buffalo. Accustomed in the British manner to write only his first name and the name of his bishopric, Doane seized the pen with a flourish. "William of Albany," he wrote. Whereupon with an equal flourish Bishop Walker also seized the pen. "Buffalo Bill," he wrote.

In cottage-building, as in the case of Newport and Lenox, Bar Harbor got off to a modest start. Even the first New Yorker to build, Gouverneur Morris Ogden, built simply; the outstanding feature of his cottage was its two front doors. When his first front door, facing the ocean, would not open, on account of the prevailing wind against it, he simply built another, kitty-cornered to the wind, which would. Several years later President Eliot of Harvard, who built at Northeast Harbor, unwittingly gave all of Mount Desert a motto for cottage modesty; this occurred one day when he had a short walk and talk with his guest, Frederick Law Olmsted, the noted landscape architect. "Olmsted," said Eliot in a peremptory Boston manner, "you've been here a week now and you haven't told me what to do with my place." Olmsted stopped short. "Do with it?" he cried. "For heaven's sake, Charles, leave it alone." Unhappily for the long-term future of the resort, not all Bar Harborites remembered the cry. To John S. Kennedy, the New York railroad man, went the honor of "Kennarden Lodge," which was Bar Harbor's first cottage with its own electric power plant. To Cincinnati's J. J. Emery went the honor of "The Turrets," Bar Harbor's first cottage with hanging gardens. The Ledyard Blairs' cottage had a marble elevator and Mrs. Ann Archbold had a motorized dining room table, the center of which traveled between the dining room and the kitchen directly underneath. Mrs. Archbold's apparent purpose was to enable diners to eat without domestics overhearing their conversation, and in her case there was justification for this desire for secrecy. Her social career was such a colorful one that it was made the basis of a novel by her fellow Bar Harborite, the late Arthur Train. The daughter of a Standard Oil man, she had at one time been forced to go to England and kidnap her own children from an estranged English husband; she sailed over and back on a friendly Standard Oil freighter.

From the 1890's to the First World War Bar Harbor's real estate boomed, the most remarkable bonanza being George Vanderbilt's "Pointe d'Acadie." Originally the land was bought by a native for $100. The native, brought up to sell anything when he could receive double what he paid, soon sold it for $200. A few years later the purchaser sold to George —for $200,000. But Vanderbilt also resented the implication that he was Bar Harbor's all-time easy mark. Later in his career, swimming in Bar Harbor's first private swimming pool, he was seized with a cramp and would have drowned but for the timely arrival of a young lady who jumped in with all her clothes on and pulled him out. The next day she confidently awaited a gratuity which she felt would be on a par with the service rendered. Vanderbilt's present, still discussed in Bar Harbor circles, was a bunch of sweet peas.

Bar Harbor's most interesting personality of the era, and indeed one of the most extraordinary success stories in American history, was the elder Joseph Pulitzer. The great newspaper publisher, founder of the awards which bear his name and of the family who pronounce their name, like the Du Ponts, with the accent on the second syllable, Pulitzer was born in Hungary and literally swam to this country. Attempting in France to enlist for the British forces in India, Pulitzer fell in with an agent seeking recruits for the Union Army in America. On the boat he found out that the agent expected to collect a bounty for each recruit. Pulitzer, even at the age of seventeen, was hardly the man for this; dropping over the side just before the boat docked at Boston he swam ashore and hurried over to the recruiting office to collect his own bounty. His first job was as a reporter on a German newspaper in St. Louis; in twenty years he owned two St. Louis newspapers which he combined into the St. Louis *Post-Dispatch*, as well as the New York *World* and was one of the wealthiest men in the country. In 1887, however, he broke down from overwork and became afflicted with a severe nervous disease. This not only resulted in blindness but also made him almost incredibly sensitive to noise. Whenever he slept in a hotel the rooms above, below and on either side of him had to be kept vacant.

Moving to Bar Harbor in 1895 with his beautiful wife, a cousin once removed of Jefferson Davis, Pulitzer built one of the resort's most beautiful cottages—"Chatwold." At a cost of $100,000 he added a huge granite pile which was called the "Tower of Silence." Here he had Bar Harbor's first heated swimming pool—Vanderbilt's was an outside pool fed from the ocean—as well as a bedroom specifically designed to keep out noise. When this proved unsatisfactory he built still another bedroom. In this room, reached through three heavy doors, the floor was on ball bearings, the walls were packed with steel wool and the windows were guarded by triple glass; the only ventilation was through the chimney's fireplace; even this was guarded by silk threads spread to break any sound. "Here, at last," says a biographer, "he found zero. The room was so still as to be uncanny."

Pulitzer's social life at Bar Harbor was also a quiet one. Although he had the entire New York Symphony transported to play for himself and a few guests, he did so only once. Normally he did not even take part in his family's famous horseback paper chases, in which, according to legend, copies of the *World* were used. Instead, fast becoming totally blind, he was limited to quiet rides in which he was led by a groom. He never went out to dinner unless promised by his hostess in advance that he would sit next to two women with soft voices; second only to his own wife, who had an extraordinarily beautiful voice, he preferred the company of Mrs. Walter Damrosch. As for Pulitzer's own dinners, they were an important part of Bar Harbor's conversational history. With his huge red-brown beard quivering in anticipation, Pulitzer would invariably greet his guests with the line, "Tell me a good story." At dinner, when a guest tripped on a fact, or indeed whenever an argument took place, the waiters were forbidden to serve more food; instead they served reference books on the subject under discussion. When the facts were read, then and only then did the dinner proceed.

In 1906 Pulitzer built a yacht well calculated to take its place in Bar Harbor waters alongside Morgan's *Corsair*, Vanderbilt's *Valiant*, Astor's *Nourmahal* and Edgar Scott's *Sagamore*. A vessel three hundred feet over-all, she was called the *Liberty* and boasted both a music room and a gymnasium; Butterfield's, Bar Harbor Society's grocery, still recalls filling one order for $5,600. "I love this boat," wrote Pulitzer. "Here I am at home and comfortable. In a house I am lost in my blindness, always fearful of falling on stairs or obstacles. Here the narrow companionways give me safe guidance and I can find my way about alone. Nothing in my life has given me so much pleasure." In contrast to most of his contemporaries, Pulitzer was forced into his resorting by ill health. With his five secretaries shuttling back and forth from the "Tower of Silence" to the *Liberty*, he ran his newspaper from Bar Harbor just as if he had been in an office. He never visited St. Louis after 1889 and during the last eighteen years of his life he visited his New York office only three times.

Living at Bar Harbor, Pulitzer was naturally intrigued with extravagance. In February of the year of his death, 1911, he wired his editor:

> Somebody should travel in Europe and see how American wives compare with European wives in economy and extravagances. . . . Archbishop Ireland and James J. Hill say that American women are extravagant and that naturally has much to do with the cost of living. It is true. Everybody knows it and yet no paper seems to have the courage to admit it.

The next month found Pulitzer intrigued with the Morgan partners:

> I think it would be a good idea, an interesting feature, to give a full list of all the partners of J. P. Morgan & Co., with a little personal description of each, a little condensed history of their rise to prominence; their education, college, antecedents, how they grew; how the departments are run; the system, the machine, also what young Jack Morgan does, the specific worth of each partner; their age, individual wealth of each. But no exaggeration, for God's sake. There is hardly a statement about any man's wealth that is not exaggerated.

Pulitzer's interest in the Morgans was well-founded. Morgan partners and Standard Oil men were the two bastions of Bar Harbor wealth during the resort's great pre-income tax era. The individual incomes of these men may well have been exaggerated—the Bar Harbor rule of thumb was that a Morgan partner made a million dollars a year—but whatever it was, in a day with virtually no taxes and when a dollar was a dollar, the men were comfortable. Many of these Morgan partners financially emancipated themselves, as well as several generations of their children, so rapidly that they retired early; as a consequence Morgan himself was always out hunting new partners.

But Morgan's trips to Bar Harbor were not business ventures; rather they belonged to the resort's flirtation tradition. As described by old-timers, these trips varied little in essential routine. First the mammoth *Corsair* would enter the harbor and drop anchor. Then, while all manner of sailboats, motorboats, rowboats and even canoes put out from shore and formed an impressively fawning flotilla, chosen representatives from Mount Desert's solid people, such as Dr. Mitchell, Bishop Doane and President Eliot—occasionally mixed with a select few of the better-mannered millionaires—would go on board to deliver the resort's official welcome. Finally, toward evening, his guests ashore, Morgan would give an order and the *Corsair* would weigh anchor and pull out—only to reanchor again a short way down the bay. Here, off a pier which boasted not only a special *Corsair*-size boathouse but also a special lady-in-waiting, Morgan himself, first signaling his move by several vigorous waves of a large handkerchief, would go ashore. His stays varied in length and the *Corsair* always went back to the main harbor anchorage in between times, but one part of the program was especially rigid. On the final day of each of his Bar Harbor visits Morgan would, with some fanfare, drive over to Northeast Harbor and personally deliver a crisp hundred-dollar bill into the hands of Bishop Doane for the church. The following Sunday, at the eleven o'clock service, with even more fanfare, Bishop Doane would announce the donation.

As Morgan extended his Bar Harbor activities, there was, if not criticism, at least comment. High Street, where the financier paid calls on not one, but two ladies, was rechristened "Rotten Row," and at least one discerning eye, that of Bar Harbor's noted abstract painter, A. E. Gallatin, recalled a parallel between the financier's art interest and the advanced age of his lady friends. "Morgan," said Gallatin, "not only collected Old Masters, he also collected old mistresses." So far as Morgan was personally concerned, however, he was only brought to task once—and then he acquitted himself well. At the time his Bar Harbor adventures were at their height a young man in his office became involved in a scandal with a lady in New York. The matter reached the newspapers and the offender was promptly notified that his connection with Morgan & Company was severed. Entering the boss's office the young man protested. "But, Mr. Morgan," he said, "all I did was what you've been doing behind closed doors for years." Morgan was unmoved by the plea. "That, sir," he replied, "is what doors are for."

In an age when Bishop Lawrence reported that Boston thought Bar Harbor "vulgar and rowdy" because the young ladies, walking there, swung their arms—Boston ladies, of course, held their arms properly before them—Morgan's activities were strong evidence of Bar Harbor's double standard of the day. "It isn't that we ever approved of vice," Boston's late Mrs. Augustus Thorndike of "The Crags" used to say. "It's just that if we had to have it we liked it gilded and hung with an orchid." Morgan met the specifications; one of his lady friends received ten thousand dollars a year and another later married a Cabinet member.

At the same time, Bar Harbor's feminine standards were as strict as its male standards, at least as shown by Morgan, were lax. Chicago's Mrs. Joseph T. Bowen, who summered for fifty years at Bar Harbor's famous "Baymeath," tells a story of a double date of her early years. Together with a Boston Peabody girl and two young men, she walked to the top of Green Mountain, intending to descend, before nightfall, via the funicular railroad then in operation. Reaching the top, the party were advised that because of a fire on the way down, the train would not make the trip until the next morning. Although the mountain at that time boasted an excellent thirty-room hotel and although the descent meant literally risking their lives—the blazing branches scorched their faces and the red-hot ashes burnt through the soles of their shoes—they never even considered passing the night. "It would have been," Mrs. Bowen wrote of the event, "as much as any girl's reputation was worth to have done a thing of that kind."

More striking is the story of one of Bar Harbor's most

distinguished citizens, New York's DeForest Grant, of "Reverie Cove." As a young man Grant enjoyed canoeing—an extremely dangerous sport in the open ocean—and he ranked, along with Philadelphia's Llewellyn Barry, as one of the resort's most skillful paddlers. He had a chance to prove this ability one dark evening in 1889 when, out for a paddle with a young lady, he was suddenly overtaken by a storm which made reaching Bar Harbor impossible. Swinging the canoe around, Grant kept it straight with the wind, his only hope being that he might be able to veer just enough to reach the lighthouse station of Egg Rock Light. It was touch and go. Too much of a veer would have meant being tipped over sideways by the force of the wind, not enough would have meant missing Egg Rock entirely and being blown to Africa. Neither Grant nor his date spoke a word as, driven by the full force of the wind, they approached their last hope of safety.

Finally, with a last skillful maneuver, Grant made it. The canoe swept up onto the ledge and they were safe; there was even a lighthouse keeper on hand to help them. Exhausted, Grant sat back. He had saved the young lady from certain death and, turning to her, he expected at the very least a "my hero" look. "Well," snapped the young lady, looking around her in extreme irritation, "you certainly don't expect me to spend the night here, I hope." Thinking she was joking, Grant laughed. But the young lady was not joking. For more than an hour she and Grant argued. Then, before the storm had yet abated and against the protests of the lighthouse keeper, Grant once more risked her life and his to get back to Bar Harbor. Even this, however, was not enough. Feeling that she had been at least partially compromised by so long a trip, the young lady made Grant promise never to reveal her name—a promise which has now been kept for sixty-three years.

Fortunately for Bar Harbor's record, there was at least one young lady who broke with the double standard for once and for all. Mrs. Madison Taylor recalled the story of a family from New York who lived in a large cottage near Duck Brook. The wife's husband, like Morgan, had a way of taking long trips; in his case the trips sometimes lasted as long as three years. Finally, after one of these trips, the wife decided to give her husband a welcome-home party which he would not forget. In the fashion of the day she invited children as well as older people and schooled these children in advance to put on a skit. This skit, watched with pleasure by all the guests, was concerned with the story of a father who was returning after three years to pat his children on the head and tell them of the wonderful places he had seen and the wonderful things he had done. Finally the child playing the part of the father asked, in the time-honored fashion, what their mother had been doing all this time. At this juncture the skit became a reality. The wife suddenly drew back a curtain and exhibited, age one and a half and six months respectively, two new children. "I, too," she said, looking directly at her husband, "have not been idle."

Bar Harbor went into its great days—from the 1890's to World War I—boasting a strong New York front, which was not only securely anchored on its Boston and Philadelphia flanks but was also rapidly mounting a country-wide social offensive. In the mornings Bar Harbor might be swimming to Strauss waltzes by the Boston Symphony, specifically transported to play at the old club during the morning bathing hour; in the afternoons the resort was still walking the mountains to the tune of good conversations. In between times there were Germans, hops, *tableaux vivants, thé dansants,* tally-ho parties, horse shows and canoe tournaments. "Those were the days of gracious living," says Mrs. Robert M. Derby, who remembers one day when she had lunch with Fritz Kreisler and that evening danced the Virginia reel with Paderewski. The most colorful Bar Harbor family was the tribe of New York's William Jay Schieffelin. The entire family, including their Vanderbilt mother, would ride out each morning, eleven strong, on eleven black mounts, each of the nine Masters and Misses Schieffelins going down, like steps, on smaller and smaller ponies, with the last on a tiny black Shetland.

Not the least distinctive feature of the Society of the day was the diplomatic set. Here Bar Harbor outranked even Newport. No Bar Harbor party of the day was complete without the popular Danish Minister, Constantin Brun; on the other hand one had to be without Baron Hengelmuller, the Ambassador from the Austro-Hungarian Empire. A Bar Harbor hostess had inadvertently failed to seat him at her right in a group at which he believed he deserved precedence. Noting his position, the Baron picked up his place card, threw it down, drew himself up and clicked his heels. "My emperor has been insulted," he said and, together with his wife, who invariably smoked cigars, he left the house. The most memorable of all of Bar Harbor's diplomatic visitors, however, was a Vicomte d'Alte, the Minister from Portugal. A man of severe dignity and impeccable ancestry—his grandfather had been Minister to Russia at the court of Catherine the Great—he wore long white gloves and a monocle and spent his daytimes striding along Bar Harbor's Shore Path scanning the horizon with a spyglass. Although no one ever found out what he was looking for, all Bar Harbor faithfully went out to watch his search. But it was as a wine connoisseur that the Vicomte left his lasting mark; at his dinners he invariably served white port instead of the customary red. Finally one Bar Harborite with an imported British accent who fancied himself something of a wine connoisseur himself could stand it no longer. "May I ask," he said one night at dinner, "what you do with your red port?" The Vicomte looked down the table. "What the servants don't require," he said quietly, "I sell to the British nobility."

During both the Spanish-American War and World War I Bar Harbor had some trying times. In the first fray, feeling itself in danger of a possible latter-day Spanish Armada, the resort beseeched Washington for aid, and when pressure commensurate with the prestige of the resort was applied, an aged Civil War cannon was dispatched from the capital. All Bar Harbor rested more easily when the gun was placed in a commanding position at Schooner Head. Close to fifty years later, in World War II, when the gun was donated to the scrap drive, resorters noted for the first time that no ammunition had ever arrived. In World War I the resort was the scene of much excitement as early as August, 1914, when the huge German steamship, the *Kronprinzessin Cecile,* put into port to be interned for the duration. Piloted in by one Bar Harbor passenger, Ledyard Blair, who was on his way abroad, the ship also boasted another distinguished Bar Harborite on its passenger list, Mrs. A. Howard Hinkle of Cincinnati. Waking in the morning, expecting to be far out to sea, Mrs. Hinkle looked out her porthole and saw instead Bar Harbor; later she also witnessed most of her servants out on the lawn engaged in observing the end of what had evidently been an all-night champagne party celebrating her departure. Also during World War I Alessandro Fabbri, who spent his lighter moments racing Edgar Scott in various speedboats, took time out to set up an experimental radio station on a tower at Otter Cliffs; for a brief period his station was the only one in the country with twenty-four-hour contact with European stations.

In between the Spanish War and the First World War Bar Harbor took time out for art. In 1907, in the most ambitious artistic effort ever made at any resort, Bar Harbor erected a rectangular Greek temple with an adjoining amphitheater which was known as the Building of Arts. Designed by Guy Lowell and supported by a galaxy of Bar Harbor's most eminent names, the building was impressively dedicated: "To crystallize the diverse elements that form the summer colony into a real society, having as its objective the highest aesthetic and intellectual stimulation." Whatever the building did, even enthusiastic Bar Harborites admit it did not do this. The Boston Symphony moved over from the swimming pool to play there on occasion, a few flower shows were held, and there were also some of the most curious amateur theatricals ever performed outside of the purlieus of the Junior League of America. Nonetheless, when the fire of 1947 burned the Building of Arts to the ground, as Richard Hale notes, "few tears were shed." Bar Harbor painter A. E. Gallatin recalled that in the entire history of the Building of Arts very few artists or writers were ever even aided, let alone developed, and of the few artists who were, one was particularly unsatisfactory. "Whenever he heard a piece of music he liked," said Gallatin, "he went home and wrote it."

At about the same time as it turned to arts, Bar Harbor turned to something else which was not only distinct from anything at Newport but which has also been a distinct feature of the resort to this day—the building of camps. Usually close to the water, in some cases close to the parent cottage, these camps were, in other cases, far away on another part of the island. If Newport's cottages were not cottages, neither were Bar Harbor's camps correctly named; in fact, during the 1920's, when camp-building reached its peak, they became so elaborate that Bar Harborites often found it necessary to build camps away from camps. But always, to Bar Harborites, camps were sacred, the best illustration of this being given by Philadelphia's Linford Biddle. A pioneer camp-builder, Biddle had built his camp of huge logs specially imported from Canada and made the mistake of lending his camp for lunch one day to a group of Bar Harbor ladies—and then forgetting the fact that he had. When the ladies arrived, Biddle, who had spent the morning in downtown Bar Harbor watching the stock market quotations and had then driven out to his camp, was happily looking forward to cooking his own luncheon. Seeing the ladies, he was distressed by his lapse of memory but also firm in his resolve to ask them to leave. But firm, too, were the ladies. The arguments waxed stronger and stronger. Finally, when the ladies refused all of Biddle's attempts to dislodge them, he suddenly stood up and took his coat off. "What are you going to do?" asked one of the ladies in alarm. "I am going," said Biddle, taking off his coat, "to take all my clothes off." The ladies still hesitated, but only for a moment; when Biddle, as good as his word, began unloosening his belt, the ladies fled the camp in a body.

The combination of the income tax and World War I, together with the deaths of Mount Desert's two great "solid men"—Bishop Doane died in 1913 and Dr. Mitchell a year later—caused a profound change at Bar Harbor. A specific example of this was the fact that when George M. McFadden bought the George Vanderbilt place in 1922, it was the first large piece of Bar Harbor cottage property to change hands in fifteen years. In the next three years no less than forty-seven cottage properties changed hands. Led by such figures as Philadelphia's E. T. Stotesbury and A. Atwater Kent, the resort passed into a white tie era, which if it did not actually mean white tie at least meant that the age-old virtues of Bar Harbor—the walking and talking—were all but forgotten. Ranking as the country's leading symbols of the last gasp of wild resort wealth, Stotesbury and Kent came to Bar Harbor with well-established reputations as men-about-resorts. Both men were self-made and to both of them money was to spend. Both were also determined to have a good time, and at a time in their lives when most men find it impossible to change their habits. "My husband," Mrs. Stotesbury once laughingly declared, "just wants to be a sport." A friend noted that Stotesbury never read a book or a magazine. "He didn't even pride himself on not reading," the friend said. "He just didn't." At the same time, Stotesbury liked to advise young men to live a life of usefulness, cultivate character and practice the virtues of hard work and thrift. "I went into the banking business," he once said, "with the elder Drexel at a salary of $16.60 a month. When I had worked fourteen months I received a Christmas present of $200 from the firm. This I saved. It was my start." A few fortunate Bar Harborites were present at the Bar Harbor Club in August, 1929, when Stotesbury, then at the age of eighty and senior partner of J. P. Morgan & Company, announced in a burst of enthusiasm that he had that day achieved his life's ambition, one which he had possessed ever since, at the age of twelve, living in a walkup over a Philadelphia drugstore, he had first gone to work. "I have today received a letter from my financial adviser," he said, "telling me that I am worth a hundred million dollars."

Stotesbury had waited to surprise his first wife with his success; when she had died, he had been unable to do so. He was therefore determined to deny his second wife nothing. This assignment the second Mrs. Stotesbury was eminently capable of fulfilling. She kept three secretaries, two of them purely social, her own personal fashion designer who was always on hand to sketch new clothes for her, as well as huge scrapbooks of every dinner she had ever given with the table drawn with its seating arrangement and mention of every last item of food served. Upstairs at "Wingwood" Mrs. Stotesbury kept her jewels on a dressing table arranged as in a jewelry store on neck mannikins. Coming downstairs she would often have no idea of who was coming for dinner or how many; a few minutes later, well briefed by her secretary at the foot of the stairs, she was the perfect hostess. "Eva never talked long to anybody," her friend Mrs. McKinlock recalls, "but she made every guest feel as if he or she were the only one asked." Even children's parties sent her into high gear; Mrs. Kent recalls her coming over to "Sonogee" to rearrange the entire Kent cottage for a party of twelve-year-olds.

The career of Atwater Kent was even more notable. Born in Burlington, Vermont, in 1873, the son of a country doctor, he first took apart, at the age of five, the family sewing machine; unlike other children who have performed similar household feats, he put it back together again. At the age of ten he took out the first of his ninety-seven patents—on an electric top he had invented. While still in his teens he made the first outboard motor, and in 1905 he revolutionized automobile ignition systems by his invention of the single-hop spark. In 1923 his Philadelphia plant began turning out radios and by 1929 he was making a million radios a year. Visitors to this thirty-six-acre plant particularly liked peeking through a special window to watch solid gold bars dissolving in acid to supply gold plating for the Atwater Kent trademark. With a fortune which was estimated at fifty million dollars, Kent talked in well-rounded figures. Once asked by Bar Harbor's Mrs. Alfred Anson his advice concerning cutting down a tree which obstructed her vista of the ocean, Kent delivered his opinion unequivocally. "Why?" he asked back, "spoil a million-dollar view with a hundred-dollar tree?"

A far less genial man than Stotesbury, whose nickname was "Little Sunshine," Kent was called "At" and was also a small man, five feet five inches in height. But he outdid even Stotesbury in extravagance. He literally bought everything in sight of "Sonogee," and at one time his empire on Mount Desert included nine cottages. Since he disliked to drive the same car two days in succession, his garages took on the appearance of Manhattan sales rooms. To the Stotesburys, as well as to the Kents, the depression was not vital. "I once asked my grandfather about it," says a Stotesbury granddaughter, "and a sort of vague look of familiarity crossed his face." In the summer of 1932, in the depths of the depression, Kent gave one of his most famous Bar Harbor dances. Three orchestras played until dawn, one in the Kent house, another at the Kent swimming pool, and a third on the Kent yacht. Flower-decked launches carried the guests back and forth. "It was wonderful," says one participant of this latter-day *thé dansant*. "People were falling down all over the place." Kent's best-remembered party was his "Bad Dream Ball" of 1938 in which all Bar Harbor's best went as nightmares. Chicago's elderly Mrs. Charles Pike went as a bride, and Mrs. Kent, who had a strong fear of the water, went in a dress with upturned canoes printed all over it. Prize honors were divided between a Philadelphia *grande dame*, who went as a prostitute wheeling a baby carriage full of dolls, and Mary Roberts Rinehart. Mrs. Rinehart wore a long-sleeve flannel nightgown, a red wig done up in curlers, and carried a hot-water bottle and candles.

When, following the resort's Morgan tradition, Kent began paying attention to a certain red-haired lady and was chided for it, he announced that he had worked all his life and was merely doing what his more fortunate friends at Bar Harbor, Palm Beach and Southampton had been able to do in their sophomore years at Harvard, Yale and Princeton —at a time when he was working in overalls as an electrical repairman. Later Kent took to stifling more severe criticism by giving away Cadillacs to such deserving neighbors as Mrs. Stotesbury and Mrs. Rinehart. Only once was he brought up short, the occasion occurring at a dinner party where he had the poor fortune to be seated next to the sharp-tongued Louise Cromwell, daughter of Mrs. Stotesbury and first wife of General MacArthur. Asked by his dinner partner what he did at Bar Harbor, Kent replied that he had just discovered bicycling, that he bicycled all morning, bicycled all afternoon and even bicycled in the evening. At this his partner looked so surprised that Kent could not resist asking her what was so remarkable about that. "Nothing," she replied archly, "nothing at all—except that I believe that it is the first time that I ever heard of a bicycle with red hair."

Kent apparently learned his lesson. One day long after

he had left the resort, Captain Hayes, who has been running sight-seeing boats around the resort for forty years, saw an officious young man with a brief case get into his launch for the tour. As they went by the cottages, Captain Hayes gave his usual spiel—as always, matter-of-factly and without editorial comment. At the conclusion of the tour, the officious young man shook hands with him. "I am Mr. Kent's secretary," he said. "Mr. Kent wanted to know what you were saying about him."

Actually Captain Hayes had said nothing. There was little to say of Kent's later career. In 1937, after labor troubles at his plant, he completely liquidated his business enterprises, selling two-thirds of his plant to General Motors and the other third to the government. Abandoning his estates in Philadelphia, Bar Harbor, Palm Beach and Southampton, he separated from his wife and settled in Bel Air, California, where he became known as Hollywood's "Mr. Host." Here, among other things, he had four separate lists for his parties. He had two lists which he called "social," which he subdivided into "big" and "little," depending on the prominence of his guests; he also had a "musical and art" group and finally a curious list called "diplomatic service." Once he decided to mix all four lists; that evening he found himself host for 1,738 guests. At one of his last parties he announced to his guests in his halting, half-stammering voice that he was going to perform a balloon trick for them. Holding three balloons in his hand, he waited patiently but was unable to rally his audience. Finally, by the time a few guests had gathered the balloons were deflated.

Kent's death occurred on March 4, 1949. For his funeral he had arranged for a section of bleacher seats to be built outside the Church of the Recessional in Hollywood's Forest Lawn Memorial Park. Since only two hundred mourners appeared, the bleachers remained empty. In his will, by which time his fortune was reduced to less than four million dollars, he mentioned seventy-three friends. Those to whom he left sums of three thousand dollars or more included Edgar Bergen, Billie Burke, Thelma Morgan Furness, Greer Garson, Hedda Hopper, Billie Dove Kenaston, Sir Charles Mendl, Lady Elsie de Wolfe Mendl, Richard Ney, Gloria Morgan Vanderbilt, Cornel Wilde, Claire Windsor and Cobina Wright.

The most significant achievement of the Stotesbury-Kent era was the building of an elaborate new Bar Harbor Club to take the place of the resort's beloved old swimming hole—or "Old Club," as it is still affectionately referred to. The new club, for which Stotesbury and Kent each put up $25,000, not only symbolized the end of the influence of Bar Harbor's "solid men" but it also, when the depression came, symbolized the beginning of the resort's white elephant difficulties. Hard as it is to imagine today, Bar Harbor's most typical early-day club was Spartan in the extreme. Founded in 1887 it was called the Canoe Club and had for its avowed purpose the "developing and perpetuating of birch bark canoeing." In short order a clubhouse was established, first in a cottage in Albert Meadow and later in a boathouse on Bar Island, and, with the assistance of the resort's famed Indian canoeist, Mitchell Loring, as well as various other skilled members of Mount Desert's Penobscot and Passamaquoddy tribes, the club was soon a going concern. Unfortunately, just a year after the club was built, on August 17, 1888, a prominent couple visiting from Newport,

Miss Fannie Milliken of New Orleans and Joel Harmon Reed of Albany, capsized in a canoe and drowned; the canoe was found, floating bottom up, off Egg Rock Light, close to the scene of DeForest Grant's trial a year later. But the bodies of the young couple were never found, and the Canoe Club, although it existed for several years thereafter, suffered a blow from which it never fully recovered.

In August, 1887, the Kebo Valley Club was established by the resort's so-called "Hunt Club" set. With a clubhouse erected on Eagle Lake Road, the club soon boasted a theater, a restaurant, a race track, a golf course and a baseball field, not to mention several tennis courts and a croquet lawn. Primarily famous for golf, Kebo is still operating today; despite the burning of the clubhouse in the fire, it has had only five presidents in its sixty-year history. In the old days Kebo was highly regarded for its parties, one of which was the most memorable in Bar Harbor history. Given in 1899 by Mrs. W. E. D. Stokes, later Mrs. Lydig of Newport fame, it involved a dinner of seventy at which each lady found in front of her place a gilt cage containing a pair of live love birds and each gentleman an Indian basket. The basket was closed but from it there protruded a yellow ribbon attached to a gold safety pin. According to the late Arthur Train, one of the diners, the gentlemen were at first asked not to investigate their favors; then, finally, their hostess was ready:

> Mrs. Stokes, later Mrs. Philip Lydig, arose at an appropriate moment and instructed the gentlemen to attach their ribbons to the tablecloth by means of the pins, and then gave the signal to open the baskets, from each of which instantly leaped a large bullfrog about whose middle was fastened the other end of the ribbon. The bullfrogs, ecstatic

with delight at their release, sprang into the soup plates, the champagne glasses, the laps of the ladies . . . or upon their bare necks and arms. As near to a riot as I have ever seen in high society followed, and when the last half-fainting female guest had been escorted out of the room, only a German count remained stealthily collecting the pins which, by biting, he had ascertained to be genuine 14-carat gold.

Two other well-known Bar Harbor clubs have, unlike Kebo, fallen by the wayside. The first of these, the Bar Harbor Yacht Club, had an unusually trying history, even by resort yacht club standards, and finally passed out of existence during World War II when its officials left for war and forgot where they put the club records. The other, the Bar Harbor Reading Room, went out in more spectacular fashion. Originally named, in honor of the Maine prohibition law, the Oasis Club, it was the first to be founded of all Bar Harbor clubs; in the year 1874 it set itself up in a modest brown cottage as a more or less secret hide-out for liquid refreshment. By 1881, however, it had become powerful enough to defy Maine's law openly and, under the title of the Bar Harbor Reading Room, moved to a handsome new building on the site now occupied by the new Hotel Bar Harbor. Here it stood as a bastion of Bar Harbor's great pre-income tax days and though it suffered some trying times—during the Boer War a member was expelled for flying the Boer flag in the face of a visiting British squadron—it boasted an extremely solvent membership. Abruptly in World War I, membership fell off. By the Stotesbury-Kent era, Bar Harborites were defying the Maine law in their own cottages and no longer felt the need of their Reading Room lockers. All sorts of membership drives were conducted—

and then, inexplicably, these stopped. The club membership, down to three men—Clement Newbold, Llewellyn Barry and A. E. Gallatin—started actually discouraging new members. "When some bird would come along and say this is a nice place you have here and I'd like to join," said Gallatin, "we'd tell him he wouldn't really like it and that it was very dull. If he still insisted, we'd just blackball him." In the last year of the club literally no one escaped being blackballed. It was not until 1921 that the secret of the transformation of the Reading Room from a club desperately in search of new members to one of the most exclusive ones in the history of resorts came out. At that time the three last members of Bar Harbor's Reading Room sold their club to the Maine Central Railroad for a hotel site—a sale which had been arranged for some time and which the Grand Old Men had no wish to share with new members.

A happier story is that of Bar Harbor's famed Pot and Kettle, a club which is still very much of a going concern today. Located up the shore in a simple brown clubhouse at Hull's Cove, it was once legendary in prestige. Although the claim that its fifty-man membership controlled 85 per cent of the wealth of the United States was undeniably exaggerated, the fact remains that in the old days there were often as many as thirty-five yachts anchored off the Pot and Kettle's float, and through the years it has boasted as high a proportion of what John Gunther has called "marmoreally entrenched aristocracy" as has ever been in evidence at any resort club. Even today its reputation is a high one. "If you could find public spirit at Bar Harbor," says Walter Lippmann, "you would find it at the Pot and Kettle."

Founded in 1899 by six members of Philadelphia's famous Rabbit Club, the Pot and Kettle had for its original purpose "to encourage riding, driving and yachting among its members by the maintenance of a country resort for meetings and athletic sports." This was soon simplified into holding dinners at which the idea was, à la Rabbit Club, for the members to do the cooking themselves. Each member was assigned the portion of the meal which he was best fitted to prepare; to be allowed to cook the macaroni, which was the specialty of the house, was the first honor. In short order, however, the members tired of this since it was, according to one past officer, "not conducive to conversation," and today, though the club still insists that each member don a chef's cap and apron before being eligible for a cocktail, the cooking and serving are done by servants. The only duties of the so-called "Caterer" at the regular Thursday luncheon of the club are to give the menu to the cook, provide a guest speaker, and see that the luncheon ends at quarter of three. "Members get restless after that," explains ex-president Eliot Wadsworth of Northeast Harbor. "They want to go play golf." Once, years ago, Philadelphia's Cecil Barret, a rurally inclined member of the club, arrived at the Pot and Kettle with a cow and promptly offered a prize to the member who could get the most milk out of it. The majority failed to get even a drop; the winner, with difficulty, secured a glassful.

The activities of the Pot and Kettle, which on rare occasions permits ladies to afternoon parties, have always been difficult for insiders to explain to outsiders. As one of the club's distinguished directors, the Hon. Hallett Johnson, former Ambassador to Costa Rica, puts it, "It is awfully hard to say what we do in English." High among the traditions for which the club stands, however, is the matter of good conversation. In the old days, when all-day sessions were held in the club, the Pot and Kettle had a ribald reputation. Members would carefully save stories during their winter work and repeat them against a standing prize which was always offered—though, curiously enough, never given—for a story no other member had ever heard before. In more recent years members have felt that their stories, in keeping with the times, should be shorter, although they try to make them just as funny as in the past. "If your story has wit enough to disinfect it," said Charlton Yarnall, who never missed a Pot and Kettle meeting in his fifteen year presidency from 1923 to 1938, "you can get away with it." As an example of a particularly fast and funny effort, several members recall the speaker who got up and said, "There was one fellow who really did see flying saucers—he goosed a waitress, you know."

Particularly impressive are Pot and Kettle's toasts, which are always drunk, with some formality, at every dinner—one to the Pot and Kettle and one to the President of the United States. Despite the fact that Franklin D. Roosevelt was one of the five Presidents who have actually attended a Pot and Kettle dinner, the club made an exception of the toast during what was to members the most unpopular part of his regime in Washington. Instead of a toast to the President of the United States a toast was drunk to the Constitution of the United States. Some idea of the power of the club in attracting guests was given as recently as World War II when Senator Truman, then with the Senate War Investigating Committee, having completed a secret mission to England and being headed back to Washington to report, was persuaded to stop off en route at Bar Harbor and report first to members of the Pot and Kettle assembled for their regular luncheon. At that time, Senator Truman was not judged important enough to sign the guest book. After he became President, the omission was rectified by the simple expedient of sending the book to Washington for his signature—a correction which many Pot and Kettle Constitution-toasters now feel was also a mistake.

The future of the Pot and Kettle, as well as of Bar Harbor, is believed by its members to be a secure one—as witness several stanzas from a poem written by club vice-president Thomas B. Sweeney in 1949 on the occasion of the Pot and Kettle's fiftieth anniversary:

When POT AND KETTLE first was formed
In Eighteen Ninety Nine,
Within its Club House members swarmed
To gamble, talk and dine.

On firm foundations it was laid.
Its flag still flies supreme.
The wit and wisdom here displayed
Re-echo from each beam.

Here confidences have been wrung
From visitors of note—
Because our cocktails free the tongue
For subtle anecdote.

Here lasting friendships have been made.
These rooms contain the ghosts
Of those whose memories never fade.
So here we drink our toasts.

The P. and K. goes flourishing—
We hope a hundred years—
The joy of life for all to bring
Midst laughter's welcome tears.

The problems of the outside world
Are always in a mess,
But POT AND KETTLE's flag unfurled
Brings peace and happiness.

Bar Harbor's chief contrast with Newport is, of course, the fact that, in its great days at least, the Maine resort never allowed the ladies to assume the control which they did at the Rhode Island resort. In 1915, for example, when the Bar Harbor Reading Room gave its first dance up on the second floor of the club, there was such objection to the ladies using the ground floor, even for just their entrance, that a special outside-the-building staircase had to be constructed. This sort of anti-female bias, which was even stronger in the old days, led to more than one attempt on the part of Bar Harbor ladies to band together and form their own clubs. The first of these, founded in 1878 by Mrs. J. Madison Taylor and Mrs. Henry E. Drayton, was the Cooking Club; a second and more successful organization, called the Ladies Club, was founded in 1897 by the same pair together with Mrs. Burton Harrison and Mrs. Cadwalader Jones. Both Mrs. Harrison and Mrs. Jones were authoresses; Mrs. Jones was, in fact, a sister-in-law of Edith Wharton. At a time when feeling ran high in the war between the sexes they might well have sounded off as Newport's Mrs. Belmont was soon to do. Instead, Mrs. Jones spoke out strongly in defense of friendship with men. In *Lantern Slides,* privately printed in 1937, she reviewed her lifelong position on this delicate subject:

> Although I do not agree with Freud's pronouncements, and heartily wish he had never been born, I believe that the most natural friendships are those between men and women. Probably my bringing up has something to do with this conviction, but throughout my life, my intimate friends, with few exceptions, have been men, and I have found that if they are treated fairly, as decent men treat each other, and not tricked or used, as they so often are by women, they "respond to treatment," as the medical jargon has it, admirably.

Unsuccessful as they were as clubwomen, Bar Harbor's ladies produced some remarkable characters in other lines of endeavor. The resort boasted at least four groups of sisters, all of whom were notable walkers and talkers. First of these, in the resort's early days, were Boston's Minot girls, Bessie, Mary and Louisa. All were members of Dr. Mitchell's literary circle and lifelong spinsters; Louisa, with her red wig and loose teeth, which would rattle as she talked, was perhaps the most colorful. Even more endearing were the Hunt sisters, Enid and Bey, both of whom were huge, big-hearted, Brünnehilde-type girls who walked with long man-size strides and, talented musically, talked in rich Massachusetts baritones. As eccentric in actions as they were striking in looks, they shocked Bar Harbor's proper set when they suddenly up and married Boston's wealthy Horatio Slaters—Bey, the younger sister, marrying Horatio Slater *père* and Enid, the older, marrying Horatio Slater *fils*. In the 1920's three other sisters who left their mark on the resort were the three Miss Pattons of Washington; more famed as talkers than walkers, they kept so few secrets that they are still recalled by many Bar Harborites who never knew them. "Telephone or telegraph," the Bar Harborites used to say, "but don't tell a Patton."

Bar Harbor's final pair of famous sisters were two Philadelphians who, though already married when they entered Bar Harbor Society, both made stern social history from that time on. They were Mrs. Edward Coles and Mrs. Edward Markoe. Mrs. Coles, wife of the president of the Philadelphia Club, ranked for many years as the resort's leading conversationalist, while Mrs. Markoe, who fortified her position by regularly entertaining the English banker, Montague Norman, stood, for an even longer period of time, as the resort's leading *grande dame*. Modeled in looks libelously close to the lines of Queen Victoria, Mrs. Markoe started slowly, at first taking interest primarily in young people, to whom she liked to read poetry. Gradually, however, she broadened her field to include control over all culture at the resort. Her *coup de grâce* was administered to the Jessup Memorial Library. Descending on this, through her position as chairman of its book committee, she removed from the shelves all books containing either adultery or split infinitives; in one afternoon, Scott Fitzgerald, Thomas Wolfe and Sinclair Lewis were among those to quickly disappear.

Only once was Mrs. Markoe thwarted. This incident occurred some years ago in Bar Harbor's beloved St. Savior's Episcopal Church. One Saturday night the late Rev. William E. Patterson, on a regular pre-Sunday inspection tour, noted a mouse on the premises. Acting swiftly, he set a trap. The next morning he found his trap with the mouse inside extremely dead; unfortunately the entire church smelled of the decease. Since nothing could be done before the regular eleven o'clock service, Rev. Patterson arranged, after a conference with the senior warden, Dr. Augustus Thorndike, to enter the church following the choir, swinging incense to counteract the odor. All went according to plan until, from her position on the aisle of the second pew, Mrs. Markoe, a vigorous campaigner for Low Episcopalianism, got a sniff. Swinging around, she saw the minister behind the choir. Swinging again, she struck Warden Thorndike, in his position in the pew just in front of her, a smart rap in the back. "Incense," she whispered loudly. "High Church!" Warden Thorndike sang one more line of the hymn, then cupped his hand. "Nonsense," he whispered back. "High Mouse!" The service proceeded.

More famous than Mrs. Markoe on a national scale, of

course, was Chicago's late Jane Addams, the noted settlement worker who used to say that she could raise almost as much money in one summer on Mount Desert as she could all the rest of the year anywhere else. But Bar Harborites remember her less for her money-raising than for the fact that she wore rubbers even on sunny days; also, since she had severe hay fever which came from horses, she was one of the few of the Old Guard to welcome the coming of the motorcar. One Bar Harbor lady, on the other hand, who never welcomed anything new was Miss Edith Boudoin. Daughter of a Morgan partner and a lioness in defense of the S.P.C.A., she even refused to go on Daylight Saving Time. Instead, she preferred to remain, throughout each summer, an hour behind the rest of the summer colony, on what she invariably referred to as "God's time." Two other ladies who showed minds of their own and at the same time furthered the tradition of Bar Harbor's conversation were the mother of George B. Dorr and the wife of John D. Rockefeller, Jr. Mrs. Dorr, author of Bar Harbor's first formal garden, prided herself on her ability to name every point of interest on Mount Desert. Once, questioned at tea by an officious visitor about some particularly remote spot, she was stumped, but only momentarily. "We never answer questions here," she said, "after four o'clock."

The late Abby Aldrich Rockefeller of "The Eyrie" at Seal Harbor, was one of the most loved ladies on the island. As Mary Ellen Chase has recalled, she was asked by her husband if she would keep an expense account. "No," she replied, "I won't." She never did. On another occasion she struck a responsive chord in the hearts of all feminine resorters on the matter of telephoning. On being told by her husband that the Mount Desert phone bills were getting out of hand she faced up to the matter squarely. "John," she said, "has it never occurred to you that you always think *your* telephoning a necessity and *mine* an extravagance?" Despite their mother the Rockefeller children were brought up carefully in the matter of allowances. All the children received as their first weekly wage the sum of fifteen cents; five cents of this was to be saved, five given to charity, and with the rest, David Rockefeller recalls, "we could do pretty much as we pleased." It was such a system, of course, which led to the famous Mount Desert story of young John D. Rockefeller III. On being asked by a young friend why he did not have a certain toy he coveted, John was indignant. "Who do you think we are?" he asked. "Vanderbilts?" A more current Mount Desert story involves the remarriage, in the summer of 1951, of John D. Rockefeller, Jr. Since Mr. Rockefeller married, at the age of seventy-seven, Mrs. Arthur M. Allen, a lady in her fifties, the new Mrs. Rockefeller was jokingly called his child bride. "What did he give her for a wedding present?" a newspaperman asked. "Blocks?" A friend nodded. "Yes," he replied, "he did. Forty-ninth and Fiftieth—on Fifth."

If Bar Harbor outproduced other resorts in walkers and talkers, it also ranked high, at least in its early history, in the matter of belles. Philadelphia took priority in resort beauties, Bella Carter, Helen Sanders and Marie Scott being a trio of Philadelphia girls especially remembered for their charms. One Philadelphia girl who combined walking with her other accomplishments once hiked the entire length of the Twenty-Two Mile Drive in five and a half hours. Other cities, too, had representatives. Baltimore offered Lulu Morris, affectionately remembered among her admirers because of her habit on hot days of sitting under a lawn sprinkler, with all her clothes on, in the middle of Mount Desert Street. Even Boston, back in 1878, appeared on the Bar Harbor scene with a belle of such charm that a future President of the United States attempted to commit suicide one evening in Bar Harbor when she dated someone else. The belle was Alice Hathaway Lee, daughter of Boston merchant George Cabot Lee. The jilted dater, whose attempt was fortunately thwarted, was Theodore Roosevelt. Later Miss Lee, who died in 1884, became the first Mrs. Roosevelt.

In 1878, besides Miss Lee, Boston was also represented on the Bar Harbor scene with a family which was to take its place as the most famous family of belles in the entire history of the resort. Technically Philadelphian, the family was that of Mr. and Mrs. Robert Shaw Sturgis. Nonetheless, both parents had been Boston-born and Sturgis was for a time in Boston's East India trade. There were four daughters in all; at the time of their move to Bar Harbor their mother was a widow who, even without her daughters, would have attracted attention. She was not only beautiful in her own right, but she also had the habit of ruling her daughters with a notably iron hand. Among other things, she made it a practice to go out and look any horse, on which a daughter of hers wished to ride, directly in the eye before allowing the child to mount. For their part the daughters were soon almost as carefully considered by every beau in the entire Mount Desert area. In fact, Susie, the most famous, was so ravishing that an admirer once declared that it was impossible to know what she looked like because you felt, when you saw her, as if you were looking directly at the sun.

After strong competition all three of the older girls settled at relatively early ages for prominent Philadelphians. Rita, like Susie a blonde with bright golden hair and an hourglass figure, became Mrs. Charles E. Ingersoll; Lilly, a darkly handsome girl, became Mrs. James Potter; and Maisie, next to Susie the most beautiful, became Mrs. Edgar Scott. Susie, on the other hand, took her time. She had her first beau in 1882 at the age of twelve and she had other beaux steadily from then until her death in 1941 at the age of seventy-one. An unathletic girl who disliked walking, she had as her sole distinction in Bar Harbor's ambulatory tradition the winning of a cakewalk contest sponsored by the Turkish Ambassador. The award, which was made at a large party on Bar Island, was always under suspicion inasmuch as it was given, like the party by Susie's leading beau of the time. If Susie had certain failings—she liked to boast she had never read a book—she also had definite attributes, not the least of which was her waistline. At the height of her popularity, when she showed signs of increasing this line, a beau offered her a silver belt if she got her waist down to eighteen inches and a gold belt if she got it to seventeen. She failed to win the gold but, measured in on the appointed day at seventeen and a half, received the silver.

In 1897, at the age of twenty-seven, Susie married, her choice falling on the brilliant but erratic Antonio Yznaga Stewart, a Philadelphian and Bar Harborite who claimed descent from Morgan the Pirate. By Stewart she had, in the fashion of the times, six children in eight years. Undeterred by this and living most of the time abroad, she became almost as famous a belle in France and Italy as she had been in Philadelphia and Bar Harbor. Divorcing Stewart in 1914, she married, two years later, the Long Branch-born surgeon, Robert Le Conte.

Following his death, she married for the third and final

time, on this occasion choosing Bar Harbor's famed canoeist, Llewellyn Barry. Though this marriage, like the first, ended in divorce, it was stern evidence of Susie's appeal; Barry, who was fifty-six, had been engaged to Susie first when he was eighteen.

Indeed, to the end of her life Susie remained so charming that only one of all her beaux, her first husband, is generally credited with dropping for once and for all the torch which, once held, Susie's admirers always carried thereafter. Calling at his former home, which was then being occupied by Susie and Dr. Le Conte, the husband who had succeeded him, Stewart met at the door, not his ex-wife whom he expected, but Dr. Le Conte. The latter stood guardedly at the door while Stewart went through a long list of his troubles and told how Susie had taken away his children, his home, and even his new fur coat. When he finished, Le Conte was visibly moved. He said, however, that he was now married to Susie and there was nothing he could do about it; Stewart would just have to get used to life without her. At this he started to close the door, but Stewart, with an effort, pushed it open.

"Sir," he said indignantly, "you are welcome to Susie. I have come to get my coat."

To many old-time Bar Harborites nothing so signified the end of the resort era as the passing of the old "Boston boat." This boat, or rather boats, which traveled under the aegis of the late lamented Eastern Steamship Lines, put several generations of resorters in the "Down East" mood, and, all old-timers agree, today's resort small fry, who travel by automobile or airplane or the Bar Harbor Express, have no idea of the charm of those days—and particularly the 4:00 A.M. arrival of the Boston boat in Rockland, a charm which was always better recognized by male resorters than by female. But the legend did not end at Rockland. The most famous of all the resort ships to have "gone upstream" was the *J. T. Morse*. An old sidewheeler, built in 1903, she succeeded the venerable *Mount Desert* in picking up the passengers at the Rockland dock and taking them across Penobscot Bay to North Haven, to Northeast and finally, to Bar. All true resorters rode the *Morse* and her passenger list, which ranged from Lord Bryce to Hetty Green, reached the social tone pitch of her whistle—which was a piercing E flat above middle C. It was a sad day indeed when the *Morse* made her final Mount Desert run and then disappeared from the resort scene—to end her days, still bravely whistling but far down the social scale, as an excursion boat carrying "trippers" to Coney Island. One Maine paper was moved to an elegiac editorial: "Her stately white hull, with the red paddle wheels churning the green waters into foam and her tall, lean smoke stack trailing a black streamer miles astern as she rolled majestically down Western Way toward Mount Desert, epitomized the leisurely summer life of a comfortable generation."

Old Cap'n Winterbotham was the most famous captain of the *Morse* but the real commander of the ship was Stewardess Maggie Higgins, a lady who for twenty years ruled the realm of saloon, staterooms and pleasure deck. Her cry of "Nawth Haven! Landin' on the lower deck forrard!" still sounds in the ears of the "comfortable generation"—not, however, to all of them pleasantly. To resorters bound for even more hallowed social ports, the stop at the socially minor port of North Haven, where to add to the stigma the *Morse* often grounded itself, could be an extremely irritating delay. Finally one morning, after a three-day rainstorm, a Bar Harbor *grande dame* ignored Maggie Higgins entirely and gave vent to her feelings directly to the master of the ship. "Captain," she said, gazing around her in extreme distaste, "I don't see why the water's always so *low* here—and after all the *rain* we've been having, too."

Such stories are, of course, the delight of the State of Mainers of the area who, of all natives at American resorts, have best managed to maintain their independence from their summer visitors. But not all such stories are nautical; in fact the most cherished Maine story is perhaps the one of the resorter who, on the road from Bangor to Bar Harbor, stops his car and inquires of a State of Mainer by the side of the road if he is on the way to Bar Harbor. "Don't know," replies the native. The resorter then inquires if he is still on the road from Bangor. "Don't know," replies the native. Next the resorter inquires how far it is to the nearest town where he can at least ask the way. "Don't know," the native replies once more. At this the resorter is exasperated. "You don't know a hell of a lot, do you?" he says. The native shakes his head. "Nope," he says. "Ain't lost."

Even the figures of Bar Harbor's native population are notable. Today a town of roughly four thousand year-round people, Bar Harbor has always had, exclusive of its summer visitors, as unchanging a population as any town in the country; by the census of 1940 it had just one less person than it had by the census of 1900. Through the years one of the chief problems of generations of Rodicks, Higginses, Brewers, Hamors and Wasgatts has been the understanding of the term "Old Family" as used by Bar Harbor resort Society. There are more Mayflower descendants among Bar

Harbor natives than there are non-Mayflower descendants, and no less than a score of direct descendants of the signers of the Declaration of Independence. On the letterhead of the Bar Harbor Post Office appear the names of three Tobias Roberts, postmasters; the first took office in 1838, the second, in 1870, and the third, Bar Harbor's current postmaster, in 1936. In contrast with this kind of social stability, these natives have witnessed among their visitors extraordinary ups and downs. Probably the most striking individual case was that of New York's Philip Livingston, the so-called "Commodore" of the Bar Harbor Canoe Club. Commodore Livingston cut a wide social swath not only through Bar Harbor's canoes but also through the resort's horse shows at Robin Hood Park, at which his tandem was always impeccable. Remembered as one of the few resorters in Bar Harbor's social history to wear tails, the Commodore was, in the depression days of the 1930's, a floorwalker at Macy's.

The social stoicism with which the natives have borne their visitors through the years has been exemplary. Only when it came to the matter of the automobile did the natives rise up—and then so effectively that the resorters had to give in. Wishing to keep their resort pure and undefiled, the summer colony had engineered legislation during the summer of 1906 which completely prohibited the importation of cars to Mount Desert. They returned the next year to find that during the winter an enterprising native by the name of Leslie Brewer, using a motorboat engine for power, had built his own automobile. Shortly afterward, the law was changed.

As at other resorts there is a "Village Improvement Society," but it is on an individual scale that the resorters have most severely taxed the natives' patience. Mrs. Markoe's interest in the grammar and morality of the books at the Jessup Library was one of them; another was the millionaire Scotsman, John S. Kennedy, who devoted his Bar Harbor career to attending native card game sessions and routing out what he called "gambling hells." From the natives' point of view the most curious resorter in Bar Harbor's history was the late William Pierson Hamilton, son-in-law of the elder J. P. Morgan. Dissatisfied one season with the lack of publicity his dinner parties were receiving in the Bar Harbor *Times*, Hamilton shipped in a printing press and for the rest of the summer put out his own paper—the Mount Desert *Herald*. During that particular summer Hamilton spent, by a friend's estimate, close to one million dollars; that September he brought a half-empty bottle of ink down to a native in the village and asked him to keep it for him during the winter.

But even Hamilton was, according to the natives, an easier man to work for than Philadelphia's DeGrasse Fox. Having eloped with a Biddle during the Philadelphia Centennial, Fox plunged into Bar Harbor real estate with a bang; among other things he built the Malvern, the resort's largest hostelry since Rodick's. "All I ever got for orders," construction foreman Howard Marshall used to say, "was a few cane marks in the dirt." Another native Bar Harborite recalls that in the same era her grandmother sought employment as a maid in a large cottage estate. At the conclusion of her interview, which had proved a successful one, she was asked what her name was. "Helen," she replied. Her employer looked distressed. "Oh, dear," she said gently, "I'm afraid it would make me self-conscious to call you anything as aristocratic as that. I think we had better call you Hilda."

If there have been unpopular resorters among the natives, there have also been some extremely popular ones. Chief among these by all odds was the late George Bucknam Dorr, father of Acadia National Park—a park which today attracts nearly half a million visitors a year to view its scenic wonders. Described by the famous Bar Harbor barber, Hod Pettingill, as looking "like a forest," Dorr was a scenic wonder himself—a tall, lean man with shaggy eyebrows and a striking down-sweeping mustache. As he walked his beloved mountains, which he wished some day to belong to all, he wore a pith helmet and carried in his pocket a single cold biscuit for his lunch. Scion of an old Boston family and a noted scholar—at the age of ninety he was still reading Homer in the original and inquiring of his younger friends "which text they preferred"—Dorr was a lifelong bachelor who devoted not only his entire career but also his personal fortune to the establishment of the Park. He reached his strategic heights at a vital committee meeting in Washington when a skeptical Congressman asked him if Bar Harbor wasn't too cold for swimming. Dorr, at that time nearing seventy, glared at the man. "Sir," he said, "I swim every day until Christmas." Dorr failed to add, of course, that he was the only Mount Deserter, resorter or native, who ever performed such a feat—and the appropriation was granted.

On their side the Bar Harbor natives have through the years developed notable characters of their own. In the old days the best known of all local characters was Jim Foley, the famous cut-under driver. Foley called all summer people by their first names—a distinction never approached by any other native of the era—and one day took it upon himself to dismiss the resort's summer Society entirely. Driving a cabload of resorters down West Street for a luncheon party, he turned around irritably. "I don't see," he said, "what you folks get out of swapping vittles." But Foley resented criticism himself. One evening, as he was driving his usual snail-slow pace, he had as his passenger DeGrasse Fox, who was in a great hurry. "I say, Foley," said Fox, "is that horse of yours asleep?" Foley swung around. "I don't know," he said, "but if you'll hold the reins I'll get out and see."

Second only to Old Foley was old Bob Sproul of Sproul's Restaurant. Dating from 1870, Sproul's became nationally famous for defying Maine's liquor laws and was so popular socially among resorters that in the old days they made it a practice to announce the engagements of their daughters there. One summer Sproul suffered a poor season; that winter he sent out all his receipted bills. New York's Judge George Ingraham, who always paid Sproul's bill in cash at the end of each season, brought the matter to Sproul's attention at the beginning of the next season. "How about this, Bob?" he said. "You didn't expect me to pay this twice, did you?" Sproul shook his head. "No, Judge," he said, "I didn't. But you'd be surprised how many did."

In the annals of Bar Harbor no native is deserving of a higher place than the late Chet Sprague. The owner of a local paint shop, Sprague was also the owner of a mongrel dog—a male. A Bar Harbor *grande dame* owned a pedigreed *Pekingese*—a bitch. One summer, despite careful supervision, the Pekingese was unfortunately compromised by Sprague's mongrel. Immediately the Bar Harbor lady sent for Sprague. Arriving, he was ushered by the maid into an elaborate marble foyer. He stood there, cap in hand. The lady, in a high state of distress, appeared at the head of the stairs. Without any preliminaries she began an unmerciful tirade against Sprague, the worthlessness of his mongrel, the shame that had fallen to her beloved Pekingese and the general sensual degeneracy of the modern generation. On and on she went—until finally she paused for breath. Sprague, who had not said a word, turned around. At this the lady was completely infuriated. "I'm not through talking to you yet," she screamed. "Where are you going?" Sprague turned back.

"Ma'am," he said quietly, "I was just going home to ask my dog if he'll marry your dog."

V

Palm Beach—
Castles in the Sand

People whose parents came over in steerage
Here entertain only the peerage.
—Old Palm Beach poem, date and author unknown

THE LATE Rev. Endicott Peabody, headmaster of Groton School, made it an annual practice for many years, at the beginning of each Easter vacation, to deliver a farewell address to his troops. While the body of this oration varied slightly from year to year, depending upon which points of outside-Groton deportment he wished to emphasize, the peroration was always the same. "I hope you boys will all have a very good time on your vacation," he would begin this section gently; then in a voice which would have shamed Cotton Mather he would conclude it: *"But do not go to Palm Beach—that den of iniquity."*

That injunction expressed by no means a personal conviction only. To the extreme Right Wing of Old Guard Society, in which the late Rector of Groton occupied the position of commanding general of the Boston area, Palm Beach has long been regarded, at best, as this country's social back door—at worst, as a kind of Buffet Society Babylon which some socially ill-advised soul unfortunately carved out of the wilds of a state which should never have been admitted into the Union, let alone into Society, in the first place. The late resort sport, Alexander Phillips, once admitted that, while in the manner of lifelong resort bachelors, he had experienced a good deal of success in the societies of Newport, Bar Harbor, etc., he had never been as fortunate at Palm Beach. "I did not drink," he explained briefly, "and I had no wife to exchange."

Some such opinions, of course, can be discounted. In comparison with other proper resorts Palm Beach ranks strictly as a Johnny-come-lately; hence there is a jealousy factor involved. Furthermore, since it has held up financially better than any of the others—it is still today the wealthiest township of the ten-thousand class in the country—it is subject to slings and arrows on that score. Nonetheless, even Palm Beachers will admit that Phillips' two specific charges are borne out by even a brief inspection of Palm Beach social history; in fact, from this history it is sternly apparent that, as far back as 1878, the location of the resort was originally chosen under the influence of liquor.

On January 9 of that year—right in season even then—the bark *Providencia,* bound from Havana to Barcelona and bearing a cargo of twenty-thousand coconuts and one hundred cases of Spanish wine, went aground near the site of the resort's present Bath and Tennis Club; the captain, ignoring the coconuts which were in their husks, had nevertheless managed to get at the Spanish wine—which in the fashion of the day was being carried in the hold of the ship to age—and had partaken of it to such extent that he had lost control of his ship. Early Palm Beach pioneers, however, made no such mistake. Seizing the coconuts as they rolled ashore on the waves, they promptly planted them; it was the lush growth of the resulting palms that fifteen years later was chiefly responsible for the fact that the Florida empire-builder, Henry Morrison Flagler, moving down from St. Augustine, chose Palm Beach, seventy miles north of a Miami that had not then been heard of, to build what he determined would be America's most magnificent playground.

Palm Beach social history reads equally sternly on the subject of the resort's matrimonial irresponsibility. "I never design a house," once declared Palm Beach's greatest architect, the late Addison Mizner, "without first imagining some sort of romance in connection with it." Feeling this way, Mizner, whose trade-mark was to forget at least one purely functional item, such as a staircase, on each house he designed, had obviously chosen the right spot in which to work. In company with other circumspect Societies Palm Beachers have always revolved their conversation around what relation who is to whom and who Mrs. So-and-so was; but in the latter case they have rarely meant, as they would have elsewhere, who the lady was before marriage, rather they have meant who she was by her previous marriage. Even before World War I, at a time when American Society elsewhere was still at least reasonably identifiably bedded down, Palm Beach was already setting such a fast marital pace that it hardly stopped to notice the fact that one of its first prominent home-owners, the Tammany Hall leader, Richard Croker, had given up Palm Beach wives entirely; at the age of seventy-three he had set up housekeeping with a full-blooded Indian squaw.

By 1936, when virtually everybody at Palm Beach was an ex-in-law relation of everybody else, *Fortune* magazine made a heroic effort to straighten things out and published a marital anthology of the resort. In this, in four columns, under the heading of "Husbands I, II, III and IV" for the females, and "Wives I, II, III and IV" for the males, the various matrimonial moves of such perennial Palm Beach brides as Marjorie Merriweather Post Close Hutton Davies, Josephine ("Fifi") Widener Leidy Holden Wichfeld and Adeline ("Kim") Stilwell Moran Bamberger Moffett, etc., were faithfully dovetailed with the corresponding altar activity of such ever popular bridegrooms as A. J. Drexel Biddle Jr., James H. R. Cromwell and John M. L. Rutherford. Although some remarkable individual cases were recorded—both the motor fortune's late Delphine Dodge (then Cromwell) and Bromo Seltzer's Margaret Emerson (then Vanderbilt) married, at different times, the same Director of the U.S. Mint—the anthology's only general message seemed to be that, for a Palm Beach marriage, five years was, if anything, a generous par. Today even such a distinguished man of the world as the Duke of Windsor has been known to be brought up short by the resort's attitude. Not long ago, looking at a roomful of Palm Beach ladies, the Duke declared that in all his travels he had never seen such an extraordinarily charming group. His host, railroader Robert R. Young, looked up with a twinkle in his eye. "After all, Sir," he said, "the wealth of the world is concentrated here. Why shouldn't we have the most attractive women?"

A rather different illustration of the resort's reputation also occurred recently when the late Dennis Joseph Cardinal Dougherty, then in his eighties and ranking American dignitary of the Roman Catholic Church, met a Palm Beach lady who was shortly, like himself, to be traveling in Europe. On discovering that they would both be on the same boat, the Cardinal politely expressed his pleasure. The lady too was pleased. "But, Cardinal," she said gently, "won't your wife be along?"

Like Hobe Sounders, their reactionary neighbors to the North, Palm Beachers like to date their social history with Ponce de León and his search for youth. They claim in fact that, in the same manner the *Providencia* chose the Bath and Tennis Club, Señor de León first put ashore on the exact site of "El Mirasol," later home of Palm Beach's great Mrs. Stotesbury. Furthermore, they take some stock in the theory that the good Señor, an elderly man who had just married a young and beautiful Spanish girl, sought out the Fountain of Youth for a very good reason. For all practical purposes, however, Palm Beach history begins in 1867. In that year an explorer named George W. Sears, moving down the Indian River from Titusville toward Miami—at that time a tiny settlement—came upon the area. Bounded on the east by the Atlantic Ocean and on the west by Lake Worth, the area was first viewed by Sears as a long spit of island—one completely uninhabited. Unknown to Sears, however, there was one inhabitant. He was a German named Lang, a Southerner who had run away to avoid Confederate conscription during the Civil War. Later came two other colonists, Captain Albert Geer and a Mr. Charles Moore. Of all Palm Beach's early pioneers, Moore had the most extraordinary tale to tell. This tale, in Moore's own words, was later relayed by E. E. Geer and recorded in the historical edition of the Palm Beach *Daily News*:

> Lang and I were here alone with plenty of game and all the fish we could catch living the life of Reilly when a hurricane hit the island with terrific force one night demolishing our shack and forcing us out into the open. During the next few days we discovered twenty-seven wrecks between Jupiter and Cape Florida. Amid the wreckage of one of the vessels we found a trunk with $8,000 in gold in its battered interior, and a good money belt to carry it in.
>
> After all the years of loneliness in the tropics, $4,000 as my share of the haul proved to be too much for me and after vainly trying to persuade Lang, who was still fearful of

> being caught as a deserter, to accompany me I set out for Jacksonville, traveling most of the way on foot. I arrived in Jacksonville in time to catch a lumber schooner bound for New York. After downing several drinks in a waterfront saloon in New York I hove to around a corner and ran afoul of a lamp post. I woke up in a hospital minus my gold belt. So there was nothing to do but to return to South Florida by devious routes where the news of the cessation of hostilities between the North and South caused Lang to start on a trip of his own.

The man who built Palm Beach was, ironically enough, the son of a Presbyterian minister. Born in 1830, near Canandaigua, New York, Flagler left home and school at the age of fourteen and set out for Republic, Ohio, to work in a store for his half-brother, Daniel Harkness. The first nine miles of the journey, to Medina, Flagler walked; there he shipped on a canal boat, paying for his passage by handling freight; the final part of his journey, from Sandusky to Republic, he again walked. He arrived with a French coin, a nickel and four pennies in his pocket—his entire fortune in 1844. His first salary in his half-brother's store was five dollars per month. Rising in business, he married Mary Harkness, whose uncle, Stephen Harkness, owned the local distillery, and he soon became associated with a young grain merchant who had begun experimenting with oil refining enterprises; the man, nine years younger than Flagler, was John D. Rockefeller.

In 1865, Rockefeller and his friend Samuel Andrews, in need of a loan of seventy thousand dollars, went to Flagler and persuaded him to ask his Uncle Stephen for it. Uncle Stephen, granting the loan, installed Flagler in their office to watch over the money. From that time on, Flagler and Rockefeller were closely associated. "It was," Flagler once said, "a friendship founded on business rather than a business founded on friendship." Whatever it was, out of it came the Standard Oil partnership; originally Flagler's idea rather than Rockefeller's, this partnership made enormously wealthy men of generations of Rockefellers and Andrewses, Harknesses and Flaglers—as well as Archbolds and H. H. Rogerses in later days. No group of American tycoons were ever more forbidding and high and mighty publicly or more gentle and shy and retiring privately. Like Rockefeller, Flagler was a violent teetotaler. He did not swear and "Thunder" was his strongest expression; on becoming provoked with someone he would stamp his cane on the floor and exclaim, "Now wouldn't you think a man would have more sense than that!" Flagler's wife had severe bronchial trouble and for the last seventeen years of her life, from 1864 to 1881, he spent only two evenings away from his home.

In 1874 Flagler had made his first trip to Florida for his wife's health—to Jacksonville—and after their move from Cleveland to New York, each winter he had tried to persuade Mrs. Flagler to go to Florida. They did not go. She was unwilling to go alone without him; and he was unwilling, because of his business, to go with her. The death of Flagler's wife apparently taught him a lesson; from that time on, though he made pleasure a business, never again did he actually put business before pleasure. Two years later, at the age of fifty-three, he married his wife's nurse, a lady of thirty-five, and the next winter the couple began a belated Southern honeymoon—one which soon turned out to be a honeymoon for Florida as well.

At St. Augustine Flagler decided to build the finest hotel in the world. This hotel, the Ponce de Leon, cost $1,250,000, was Spanish Renaissance in design and had 540 rooms. All the rooms had electric lights—which were then some novelty—and the furnishings in each room were advertised as costing $1,000. When these furnishings arrived they were late and Flagler took off his coat and worked with his laborers to transport them to the hotel. With other building problems he had more help. The Ponce was one of the first large structures in the country to be made of poured concrete; since there was no natural building stone in the vicinity, ton after ton of coquina gravel had to be brought over from Anastasia Island to be mixed with it. Flagler engaged twelve hundred Negroes, who literally tramped the mixture as it was poured into the form. Finally completed, on May 30, 1887, the hotel was formally opened on January 10, 1888, its opening being not unlike that of Tuxedo Park far to the north two years earlier. "At a given hour on the appointed day," record Florida historians Alfred and Kathryn Hanna, "a cannon boomed, flags were unfurled, the gates of the Ponce de Leon rose slowly, an orchestra struck up 'The Star-Spangled Banner' and down the street came a great omnibus drawn by six white horses, bringing guests from the station."

For a time fashion flocked to the Ponce. It did not, however, enjoy financial success. Across the street Flagler erected a sister hotel of seventy-five rooms for people of more moderate means and he also bought a third hotel. The fact that the Ponce did not pay worried him not at all. One day the manager wired him in New York asking permission, for the sake of economy, to discharge the expensive French chef and the New York-imported orchestra. Promptly Flagler wired back: HIRE ANOTHER COOK AND TWO MORE ORCHESTRAS. Flagler himself built an expensive house in St. Augustine largely to please his wife. Although he habitually traveled in a private railroad car, the "Alicia"—which had five bedrooms, a dining room and a kitchen—he still continued his habit, when in New York, of carrying his own lunch to work. Coupled with his socially ambitious second wife, Flagler had family troubles left over from his first marriage. His only daughter, by his first wife, died, and though he built her an enormous mausoleum in St. Augustine—which was his manner of expressing his grief—he never got over the loss. He tried hard to interest his son in the business world but, overbearing as he was, he succeeded only in alienating the young man. It was at this time in his life that Flagler expressed to Captain Geer his enigmatical lifetime motto—that "satisfaction and contentment are not synonymous."

Flagler was not interested in other resorts, either in America or abroad; except for one trip to Jamaica and a business journey to the Bahamas, he never went out of the country in his life. He was, however, interested in Florida. Moving down from St. Augustine he became intrigued with the possibilities of Palm Beach. Purchasing some property for what was then the unbelievable sum of $75,000, Flagler announced that he proposed to build not only America's most magnificent resort hotel but also something more. "I shall build upon this spot," he said, "a magnificent playground for the people of the nation." This time even the St. Augustine venture paled in comparison. He built not only Palm Beach but also West Palm Beach—which he described as "the city I am building for my help"—and furthermore he decided, as an additional inducement for his workers, that there would be a race between the building of the hotel and the building of the railroad. On May 1, 1893, the race began. By the next fall the hotel was half completed and the railroad had reached Fort Pierce, fifty-seven miles away. Mercilessly Flagler and his lieutenants spurred the workers on; more than a score were killed because of the haste. Actually the hotel won. It opened on February 11, 1894; at that time the railroad had just reached West Palm Beach.

The largest hotel in the world of its time, the Royal Poinciana, as it was called, was the largest wooden structure ever built anywhere. A six-story building, looking like a skyscraper lying down, it had accommodations for 1,750 guests and had seven miles of hallways; its entire expanse, including its employees' dormitory (a hotel in itself), its gardens, tennis courts, golf courses and famous Coconut Grove, covered thirty-two acres. The dining room seated two thousand people, there were thirty-five assistant headwaiters and the room was, from end to end, said Ring Lardner, "a toll call." One man, in charge of the water bottles, did no other work but to keep them filled. There were fourteen hundred employees in all, a waiter for every four diners, a chambermaid for every four rooms and a bellman in every hall. On a sunny day, as these employees left their dormitory dressed in their uniforms with snowy white shirt bosoms, they looked like a full army advancing on the hotel. Their earnestness not only gave rise to a new name for the Royal Poinciana—the "Royal Pounce-on-'em," it was called—but it also won a new title for the resort itself, that of "Itchy" Palm Beach.

Unlike the Ponce de Leon, the architectural motif of the Royal Poinciana was not Spanish; the exterior of the hotel was painted lemon yellow with white trimmings, and inside the color scheme was green and white. As was the case in St. Augustine, Flagler was not satisfied with merely one hotel. His Poinciana faced the ocean, but a year later he built the Palm Beach Inn, later called the Breakers, directly on the ocean. Burned in 1893, it was rebuilt in 1896, the same year in which Flagler also built a railroad and foot bridge across Lake Worth, connecting the two Palm Beaches. To all Palm Beachers, however, the dearest memory of those days was not the connecting bridge between the two Palm Beaches but rather the famous "mule car" which connected the Royal Poinciana and the Breakers. This car, which resembled a miniature trolley, was on tracks and was drawn by what Palm Beach youngsters described as the "little horse"; it was not only the accepted mode of transportation back and forth to the Breakers Beach, but it was also, to the children at least, an entertainment which rivaled the swimming itself.

The year 1896 also saw, on March 14, the first train to cross Flagler Bridge. The passengers on this train ride, which young Miss Gladys Vanderbilt (Countess Széchényi) recalls as being "like a house party," numbered just seventeen. All were among the leaders of the "Four Hundred" of the day and were the kind of social avant-garde which had already made Newport, Bar Harbor, Tuxedo and other resorts. They were equally effective at Palm Beach. Life at the Royal Poinciana and the Breakers was in those days the closest to an era of simplicity as Palm Beach ever had; actually the life was a strange combination of simplicity and elegance. Mornings were spent on the old Breakers Beach where the famous "Connie" Lewis, ex-minor league baseball player, was beach censor. The resort rules declared that every lady should wear stockings with her bathing suit, that the stockings should be black in color and that they should reach the suit with no flesh visible. Lewis' famous cry, on seeing bare skin, is still remembered: "Ladies, rules is rules!"

At one o'clock the beach was deserted and everyone gathered for an eight-course lunch and a dance or two afterward. The rest of the afternoon usually involved, first of all, a trip down to see "Alligator Joe" Frazier. Frazier's domain, to the south of the island, comprised what is now the Everglades Club; with his sea-lions and his turtles, his side shows were always a favorite diversion. The feature attraction was his wrestling match with one of his tame 'gators. There were also pleasant afternoon drives in "afromobiles." Flagler allowed no horses on the island and these wheeled hybrids, half chair and half cycle, were the only mode of transportation. Originally they had the Negro pedaler in front; since the pedaler spoiled the view, the design of the chair was changed to have the driver in the rear. By five o'clock everyone hustled over for tea in the Poinciana's Coconut Grove and to eat Mrs. Roche's famous coconut cakes. At seven-forty-five Dabney's orchestra played its last tango and everyone went in to dress again—at least their fifth change for the day—for dinner. In the evening there was more Coconut Grove dancing and, every Saturday night, a cakewalk. In this performance, the forerunner of the tap dance, the contestants, colored servants who worked in the hotel, competed for a cake by dressing in extraordinary costumes and shuffling, strutting and striking extravagant postures in time to the music; the winner, judged by audience applause, "took the cake." Songs like "Georgia Camp Meeting," "Too Much Mustard" and "Waiting for the Robert E. Lee" were played to accompany the darktown strutters; the most famous song was "De Cake Walk Queen," a tune which is still wreathed in sentiment for Palm Beach old-timers:

Dar's a meeting of all de high society,
To decide what dancers has most variety,
And a prize they offer with all propriety,
And de winner shall be de cake walk queen!
Come you children, dar's a priety.
Der gal dat wins it shall be de cake walk queen!

Flagler's success at Palm Beach was such that Henry Bradley Plant, engaged in developing Florida's West Coast, could not avoid an expression of jealousy. One day he met Flagler in New York. "Friend Flagler," he asked, "where is that place you call Palm Beach?" Flagler smiled. "Friend Plant," he replied, "just follow the crowd." At the same time Flagler's personal life left much to be desired. His second wife, who had been leading him a difficult social chase, finally went insane and was committed to a sanitarium in 1897. A curious Society legend surrounds Flagler's meeting with the lady who was to be his third wife. Miss Mary Lily Kenan by name, she was a so-called poor relation of the high and mighty Pembroke Joneses and lived at their "Sherwood" cottage in Newport, according to the legend, "somewhere at the top of that enormous house, in a tiny room among the servants." Miss Kenan, who did the Jones' family sewing, was not beautiful and, at thirty-four, was described as "rather like a little mouse." At the same time, still according to the legend, she always dreamed that a Prince Charming would come into her life someday and take her away from the tiny room and the sewing machine. One day the seventy-one-year-old Flagler arrived in Newport to visit the Joneses. "He saw her," the legend concludes, "asked her to sew a button on his coat, proposed to and married her."

Actually Flagler's third courtship was equally colorful but hardly as dramatic. Flagler had first met Miss Kenan in 1891 when she was visiting the Pembroke Joneses in St. Augustine; at the time she was twenty-four and not thirty-four and he was sixty-one and not seventy-one. For ten years Palm Beach gossiped of their intimacy and Flagler had lavished expensive gifts on her. In 1899, having tried and failed to get a divorce in New York, he changed his residence to Florida, giving as his reason his desire to avoid excessive New York inheritance taxes. The whole state was shocked to learn, on April 9, 1901, that Flagler had been responsible for the introduction of a bill into the Florida Senate—one which enabled a divorce to be granted on grounds of insanity. Furthermore, the bill was rushed through, Standard Oil style; two weeks from the day the bill was introduced, it was signed by the Governor and became law. Called the "Flagler Divorce Law," the bill was specifically tailored to meet Flagler's personal requirements; four years later it was repealed. In the meantime Flagler, in the manner of the empire-builders of the day, had what he wanted, and on August 24, 1901, in the presence of a few friends, the seventy-one-year-old was married to his thirty-four-year-old bride in "Liberty Hall," Kenansville, North Carolina. "His advancing years," recorded the local paper, "were hidden behind a beaming countenance."

"Poor relation" as she may have been to the upstart Joneses, Miss Kenan of Kenansville soon put even the Joneses of Newport to shame. First and foremost she wanted a Palm Beach cottage and told her husband so. Flagler promptly went to the architectural firm of Messrs. Carrere and Hastings in New York. "Build me," he said, "the finest residence you can think of." The firm did as they were told. "Whitehall" today, run by Bostonian A. M. Sonnabend, is Palm Beach's most impressive hotel. As a resort cottage, the most remarkable thing about "Whitehall" was its time of building. Like other Flagler projects it was a record—eight months. Rugs that could have taken five years were woven in five months; one cost $35,000 alone. The total cost of "Whitehall" was three million dollars. Stately bronze doors, curtained with hand-made Arabian lace, led to its so-called "Marble Hall," 110 feet long and 40 feet wide, which was decorated in no less than seven shades of marble, including off-white, pink, dove-gray, cream-yellow, baby blue, light violet and pea-green. Supported by sixteen bronze-capped pillars of solid marble, a domed ceiling depicted "The Crowning of Knowledge," "Prosperity" and "Happiness." All over the first floor were—and indeed are still—tapestries of all kinds, which cover even the windows, as well as a host of gold and crystal chandeliers, jeweled mirrors, antique Florentine chests, Boucher panels, Carrara marble settees, satinwood love seats and wine-red velvet portieres, not to neglect a clock, nine feet high, representing "Time Riding the World in a Cloud"—an interesting feature in view of the disparity of ages between "Whitehall's" master and mistress. Along with the Marble Hall also went a French salon of Louis XVI period, an ivory and gold-décored ballroom of Louis XIV period, a Chinese billiard room, a Renaissance library paneled with lion's heads, a dining room including some fifty dining room chairs each one covered with its own individual Aubusson tapestry, and finally a gold-satin and antique-white music room of Louis XV period. In this room was the largest pipe organ ever placed in a private home in this country.

Upstairs, in its Flagler days, "Whitehall" boasted sixteen suites of guest rooms, each with a different design, representing different epochs in the world's history and each with its own private hallway leading to the main hall. Italy, France, Spain, England and the Orient were all represented; significantly the only suite which was "modern" American in motif boasted Florida's first twin beds—an American Society innovation in the early 1900's. Mrs. Flagler's own suite was ornate even by "Whitehall" standards. The walls and window draperies were silk damask, the bed was draped with a canopy of gold damask—which was embellished with a panel of supposedly the finest lace Cluny ever made—and all four corners of this bed were decorated with female bronze busts. Mrs. Flagler's bathroom, which was seventeen feet long and eleven feet wide, contained the country's first sunken tub and opened on a so-called "closet." This, a small house in itself, was surrounded by armoires of glass doors, each affording enormous compartments for Mrs. Flagler's several hundred dresses and hats—none of which, she liked to boast, she ever wore twice. Later, when "Whitehall" entertaining was in full swing, she also boasted that she could have fifty guests for dinner each night in the week and still use a different dinner service every time. Once a friend commented to Flagler on the beauty of his palace. "I wish I could swap it for a little shack," Flagler replied. At another time his financial adviser came up and informed him that the Standard Oil Company had just been fined $29,000,000. Flagler nodded absently. "Do you happen to have those 'Whitehall' plumbing bills handy?" he asked.

In his last years Flagler had just two ambitions—to build up Miami as he had Palm Beach and to see his railroad reach Key West. Although he did not live to see Miami follow Palm Beach, and then far surpass it in size, he did live to see the completion of his so-called "railroad that went to sea" —at the cost of scores of lives of his workers. In 1912 his first train moved slowly into Key West. A year later, on January 15, 1913, moving precariously down the last three steps of "Whitehall's" grand marble staircase, he himself suffered a fall from which he never recovered. His son, who had refused to see him since his third marriage, came to "Whitehall" for the first time the day before his father died; Flagler was by this time so ill he did not recognize him. The "Father of Palm Beach" as well as the "Father of Miami" left an estate of close to $100,000,000. Since he had spent some $50,000,-

000 in Florida and had already given his second wife some $15,000,000 more, this $100,000,000 fortune was evidence that it was almost impossible, in those days at least, to dispense with a Standard Oil fortune. At his own wish he was buried in his mausoleum at St. Augustine in preference to Palm Beach, a community which had never taken as kindly to him since his "Divorce Law" as he felt it should. Shortly before his death, as Sidney Martin records, he himself expressed his feelings on this subject to his friend, T. T. Reese, president of the Palm Beach Farmers Bank and Trust Company:

> I have lived too long and have been a target too often to allow myself to be disturbed by the jealousy of others who have been less fortunate. I don't know of anyone who has been successful, but that he has been compelled to pay some price for success. Some get it at the loss of their health; others forego the pleasures of home and spend their years in the forests or mines; some acquire success at the loss of their reputation; others at loss of character, and so it goes; many prices paid, but there is one universal price that I have never known any successful man to escape, and that is the jealousy of many of the community in which he moves.

It was Flagler's custom to build, along with his hotels, two other subsidiary edifices—one a church and the other a gambling house. At St. Augustine he had his Memorial Presbyterian Church and his Bacchus Club; at Palm Beach he had his Royal Poinciana Chapel and his Beach Club. For the operation of the latter he selected one of the two brothers who operated the Bacchus Club, and this man, Colonel Edward Riley Bradley, soon ranked, second only to Flagler himself, as the most important man in Palm Beach social history. Born December 12, 1859, in Johnstown, Pennsylvania, the son of a steel worker, Bradley, like Flagler, left home at fourteen; in Bradley's case it was a matter of actually running away. The year before, at the age of thirteen, he had been put to work in the steel mills. The young man preferred to go West. Working his way as a dishwasher he got as far as Arizona and was variously a cowboy, a miner and an Indian scout; in after years he was fond of saying he had participated in the capture of the famous Apache chief, Geronimo. Later he was a bookmaker in Little Rock and Hot Springs, Arkansas; when bookmaking failed, he was often again reduced to dishwashing. His first successful gambling enterprise was located in Silver City, New Mexico. From 1870 to 1890 he owned the Del Prado Hotel on Chicago's South Side. In 1890, having suffered a heart attack, he moved to Lexington, Kentucky, where he established his famous racing stable, the Idle Hour Farm, a farm which later became a four-time winner of the Kentucky Derby. Moving to Florida with his brother, he ran the Bacchus Club along with other casinos located in as widely separated areas as Rockaway, Long Island, and Long Branch, New Jersey.

Small and kind-faced, a devout Catholic and a man who wore a stiff collar even on the hottest days, Bradley looked anything but a gambler. To the stern Presbyterian Flagler, as indeed to several generations of Palm Beachers, he was eminently respectable. Above all, he was honest. The only people he feared were those who did not tell the truth. "You can protect yourself against a thief," he once said. "There is no protection against a liar." Once on the witness stand he disconcerted a United States Senate Investigation by his reply to the question as to what was his profession. "I am," he stated with some pride, "a gambler." Late in life, at the age of eighty-three, he was asked if after long years of betting at tracks, he had been able, with all of his connections among other owners, jockeys, trainers, etc., to beat the races. "I have not," he said. "I have kept a record. I am just ten per cent behind—the amount the tracks keep for themselves."

In sharp contrast to Canfield's ornate Temples of Chance in New York, Saratoga and Newport, Bradley's Beach Club, which opened in 1898, was a modest white frame house which cost only $3,500 and was located on the corner of Lake Worth and what was then Main Street. The charter was just eighteen words: "To run such games of amusement as the management and members may from time to time agree upon." In its first year the club, which was operated "for gentlemen only," lost money. It was then suggested that Bradley relax his rules. These rules were also brief. No native of Florida, no man who did not *look* twenty-five, no man who was under the influence of liquor, and no man not in evening clothes was permitted to gamble.

Bradley particularly held out against a suggestion that he give, in the manner of other gambling institutions before his time and after, free liquor; drinks must be paid for and the farthest the Colonel would go in the direction of stimulus was to put yeast tablets in the Beach Club's special cocktail. But finally he did give in to another suggestion—one to which Flagler was particularly strongly opposed. This was the question of admitting ladies. The lady must be escorted, the rules said, but from 1899 on, she was admitted; from 1899 on, the Beach Club prospered. In 1912 it moved to new quarters. Here its octagonal gambling room, decorated in the emerald green and white colors of Bradley's racing stable, was a replica of the Poinciana's ballroom. The Beach Club was still, however, simply marked "B.C." and was a plain white clapboard house standing back of a trim expanse of lawn. The signs inside were still models of decorum. One read: "GENTLEMEN ARE REQUESTED NOT TO SMOKE IN THE BALLROOM." Another, in the gambling room, read: "LADIES AND GENTLEMEN ARE RESPECTFULLY REQUESTED TO REFRAIN FROM LOUD TALK AND LAUGHTER." The only rule Bradley ever relaxed was the matter of evening clothes; if you were taking the old three-thirty train back North you were, for that evening only, permitted without dinner jacket.

Early in its career, Bradley's established a high reputation for its food; in the days before George Lamaze's famous Colony Restaurant, it was the only socially approved mealtime rendezvous in Palm Beach. Its famous Swiss chef, Conrad Schmitt, first introduced green turtle soup early in the 1900's —at what was the unbelievable price of one dollar per portion. Later, with his French chef, Jean Broca, Bradley's introduced the custom of a fixed-price luncheon and dinner, and these were reduced to such a point that Bradley used to say he lost two dollars on every lunch and four dollars on every dinner. Palm Beachers claim that in the course of an average year Bradley gave away ninety per cent of his net profits. Whether this was true or not, two of his favorite sayings were, "There are no pockets in shrouds," and "I don't want to be the richest man in the cemetery."

Notably strict with his croupiers, cashiers and dealers, Bradley hired only those who were single and the few exceptions he permitted were not allowed to bring their wives to Florida during the season. Bradley's own wife died in 1926 and he had no family. His horses, he used to say, were "his children." He also used to say he only "tolerated" women; he never believed they mixed with gambling. He housed his employees in a special building called "The Barracks." Here they were guarded at all times and were never permitted, even in their leisure time, to mingle with the patrons of the club. Bradley paid his employees well—up to fifty dollars a day, with room and board—and he held their salaries in trust until the end of each season, at which time he would add a 10 per cent bonus. Many of his employees served him for more than forty years.

The Beach Club itself served Palm Beach continuously from 1898 until Bradley's own death in 1941. From 1905 on, neither taxes, reform waves, gambling investigations nor any other outside influence ever disturbed its operation. Aided by its own platoon of eighteen Pinkerton men, by control of two Palm Beach newspapers, and partial control of a third, as well as by contributions made to both political parties and to churches of all denominations, it was virtually a law unto itself. Around the walls, high above the heads of the players in the octagonal gambling room, there was a white trellis, behind which there were guards armed with machine guns; in the entire history of the club it never suffered a holdup. At Bradley's death, by the terms of the Colonel's will, the club was torn down, the land given to Palm Beach as a public park and the gambling equipment towed out to sea and sunk. Palm Beachers themselves have been, by their own admission, sunk ever since. Chicago's Mrs. John C. King, a niece of Marshall Field and a lady who claims to be the resort's oldest continuously operating colonist—she first arrived in 1904—is perhaps the most nostalgic. "Bradley's," she says, "was everything." Mrs. King feels that no restaurant in Paris was ever better than Bradley's and that the gambling was better than the Riviera's. "It made Palm Beach cozy," she adds.

Disregarding Herbert Bayard Swope's famous resort dictum—never to bet on anything that "walks, talks or squawks"

—Palm Beachers have always loved to gamble. In the old days, gathering in their curiously named private railroad cars—Harry Payne Whitney's "Adios," Harry F. Sinclair's "Sinco," Joshua Cosden's "Roamer" and J. Leonard Replogle's "Westmount"—they would bet on anything from, as Swope puts it, "which lump of sugar a fly will light on to which man a woman would marry next." They would also conduct poker games, some idea of the size of which may be gathered from the fact that when the late George Loft, of Loft's candy, entered one game with a flourish and produced a crisp roll of ten thousand dollars, he was given one white chip. The late John Studebaker, president of the motor car company, lost $200,000 in one evening at roulette, while Albert Lasker, pioneer advertising executive, once declared himself out after a $175,000 reverse. Bradley's met even these figures. In 1923, the year that *chemin de fer* was added to roulette and hazard—which were, up to that time, Bradley's only two games—over three million dollars changed hands at the so-called "chimmy" table. From that time on Bradley's limits were higher than Monte Carlo's. On many occasions not only the men but even Palm Beach's famous lady gamblers wagered as much as fifty thousand dollars on the turn of one card. At the same time, Bradley knew exactly how far each of his customers was able to go, and they were never permitted an extension of credit beyond this sum. If you lost heavily one evening, the Colonel invariably offered you at the door one throw of the dice—doubles or quits. If you expressed doubt that your losses might be due to something besides bad luck, he would give you every cent of your money back and then ask you, in his presence, to tear up your membership card.

Bradley's judgment of people was almost infallible. Palm

Beachers still cherish the story of the young lady who came into his private office at the club one night, tears in her eyes, and told him that she and her husband were on their honeymoon in Palm Beach and that her husband had just lost their entire savings of five thousand dollars. Bradley looked at her closely, then reached in his drawer and took out five thousand-dollar bills. "I shall give you these," he said, "on condition you promise me that neither you nor your husband will ever enter this club again." Still tearful, the girl agreed, then at the door asked the Colonel for his promise that, if she pointed out her husband, he would not speak to him; her husband didn't know she had been going to see the Colonel and she didn't wish him to make a scene. To this condition, as she had to his, Bradley agreed. At the door the girl pointed out her husband, a man who was already going out the door. Bradley took one look, then went back to his office.

The next night the Colonel, touring his tables, was brought up short; there was the young man the girl had pointed out gambling away as if nothing had happened. Bradley stalked into his office and immediately sent for the man. "You were told never to come here again," he stormed. "You cannot afford that kind of money. Your wife agreed." The young man looked surprised. "My what?" he said. "Your wife," repeated Bradley. The young man smiled. "Colonel Bradley," he said, "I am not married." Bradley looked amazed. "As far as not affording it, Colonel Bradley, I think I can. My name is Russell Firestone."

Up to the time of his death Bradley was regularly asked by any person who had heard the story what he did about it. "Do about it?" the Colonel would roar. "I didn't do a damn thing. Any girl who can get the best of a tough old goat like me is welcome to five thousand dollars."

As Palm Beach never had an era of genuine simplicity, so too its eras of "nice millionaires" and "naughty millionaires" are somewhat confused. In early 1917, however, two men began at the resort a completely new era; their names were Paris Singer and Addison Mizner. As Society types they were unusual, even for Palm Beach. Singer was one of twenty-five children of the sewing machine tycoon, Isaac Merritt Singer. Eight of these children were legitimate but Paris was not one of them. He received his name because he was born in the French capital. Nonetheless, he inherited a large share of the sewing machine fortune and tall, blond and full-bearded, was the answer to a maiden's prayer—the maiden, at least in his later life, being the dancer, Isadora Duncan. In 1908 Miss Duncan was penniless. "I must find a millionaire," she prayed. "I must find a millionaire." Singer, whom she met at the funeral of her previous patron, Prince de Polignac, was her man. From that time on he was her so-called "Lohengrin." Previous to Singer's first appearance in Palm Beach, the couple already had enjoyed a tempestuous eight-year love affair at five Singer residences—at his estate in Paignton, England, at his villa at Cap Ferrat, at a country home in Paris and at two town houses in London. Although Singer brought Miss Duncan to Palm Beach several times in later years, he first arrived alone, exhausted and ill; he was literally carried off the train on a stretcher. Gradually, he started to recover. His first cottage at Palm Beach, a small frame house on Peruvian Avenue, he called "Chinese Villa." Painted orange, green, yellow and blue, it was decorated with a stuffed alligator which perched precariously on the ridgepole. Singer's own dressing was equally exotic. He wore voluminous Côte d'Azur trousers, gaily striped Riviera shirts, a

Basque beret and purple Basque espadrilles. Soon Palm Beach stores were stocked with similar items—although the resort did not also follow Singer's formal side. Suffering from weak eyes, he spent his time listening to a hired reader who daily read him biographies of the French court—Marie Antoinette, Madame de Maintenon, Madame Recamier, etc. Little did Palm Beach realize it then, but their distinguished visitor was already dreaming of bringing to the resort something of European life and culture.

Mizner was also cosmopolitan and world-wanderer. A jolly round man, with infectious gaiety, he was by profession an architect but he worked hardest at being an international resort sport. Born in San Francisco, he had prospected for Gold in Alaska, had lived in Guatemala, Hawaii, China and Australia and had been entertained at Court abroad and by Mrs. Stuyvesant Fish at Newport. He had, however, become bored with it all. Once dining with Mrs. Fish and having embarked upon a story, he noticed that no one was listening to him. Catching the eye of a footman, he took out his billfold. "Here," he said, "if you will be good enough to listen to the end of this story I will give you five dollars." Like all Mizners, Addison was noted for his maxims. "Everything troublesome in Florida," he used to say, "becomes trivial." Even Paris Singer he tolerated, though Isadora Duncan became troublesome; he called her "Is-a-bore when drunken." His brother Wilson, whom he later induced to come to the resort, was the most famous of all Palm Beach wits. Although Wilson Mizner is not even accorded mention in several anthologies of quotations, he was responsible for such abiding aphorisms as: "Life's a tough proposition but the first hundred years are the hardest," "Be nice to people on your way up because you'll meet them on your way down," "Treat a whore like a lady and a lady like a whore," and "if you copy from one author it's plagiarism, if you copy from two it's research."

One morning in January of the year 1917 Paris Singer and Addison Mizner sat rocking on the porch of the old Royal Poinciana. Both were bored. "Mizner," said Singer abruptly, "you know I came here expecting to die, but I'm damned if I feel like it." Mizner shrugged. "What are you going to do about it?" he asked. It was Singer's turn to shrug. "What would you do about it," he said, "if you could do anything you wanted?" Mizner suddenly became earnest. With a sweeping gesture he took in Palm Beach's Poinciana, its Breakers, its station and its half a hundred shingled cottages. "I'll tell you what I'd do," he said. "I'd build something that wasn't made of wood, and I wouldn't paint it yellow."

This conversation sparked a Palm Beach renaissance. Singer had already given some hospitals to England and France and he promptly commissioned Mizner to design a convalescent home for servicemen—the resort's renowned Everglades Club. Mizner was given carte blanche as far as design was concerned and to start off Singer first bargained for eighty acres of land. He received them literally for nothing, and when the deeds were delivered to him, he found that he had been given 160 acres. Protesting, he said he did not want so much and that he did not wish the responsibility of clearing it and paying the taxes, not to mention the difficulty of killing the rattlesnakes. The man who had given him the land, however, refused to take it back. Ten years later Singer's land lay in the very heart of Palm Beach's Gold Coast; at that time he refused to accept an offer of ten thousand dollars a foot.

A year from the time Singer and Mizner had started, the Everglades Club was completed. Paths were cut through the jungle for wheelchairs and houseboats were tethered at the docks on the lake and in the coves of near-by streams. The idea was that the mentally disturbed patients would be aided by such peaceful splendor. Finally Singer and Mizner were ready to send out their invitations. No less than 300,000 men were invited to come to Palm Beach, at Singer's expense, and enjoy, free of charge, their new facilities. Just thirty-three replies were received.

To this day Palm Beachers cannot explain the lack of popular enthusiasm for the club. Mizner felt that it was because the resort was too far away geographically, Singer because it was too far away socially. In any case, Palm Beachers did not spend long grieving. Moving with their customary dispatch, they promptly made their service club into a real club. At a grand opening party held on February 4, 1919, the guest list was studded with such distinguished resort names as Dr. and Mrs. Maitland Alexander, Mr. and Mrs. Pierre Barbey, Mr. and Mrs. Theodore Frelinghuysen, Mr. and Mrs. John C. King, Mr. and Mrs. Frederick H. Prince, Mr. and Mrs. E. T. Stotesbury, Dr. and Mrs. Herbert Endicott Warren and half a dozen Phippses. Just before the opening a Palm Beach newspaper lady rushed into a corner of the dining room to get the guest list from the maître d'hôtel. Singer, on an inspection tour, spotted her. "Don't you ever come in here again after sundown," he said, "unless you are dressed in evening clothes." This, from a man who had started Palm Beach's most eccentric dress styles, was hard to take, but the lady joined other Palm Beach papers in waxing ecstatic over the opening of what was, in those days at least, the country's premier resort club:

> A little bit of Seville and the Alhambra, a dash of Madeira and Algiers, an Italian lagoon and Terraced Garden and the incomparable Florida sunshine and climate combine to make of the club and its surroundings a wondrous combination of the Old World and the New.

For Mizner the Everglades Club was just the beginning. Palm Beach's building boom had begun and he was ready to branch out toward the ocean. Sunset Avenue, he felt, was too crowded. "You can hear people making up their minds in the next house," he said. He was besieged with commissions for private cottages; his first was "El Mirasol" for the Stotesburys. Extending all the way from Lake Worth to the Atlantic Ocean, the cottage started out along the lines of a Spanish convent and ended up as a Spanish castle. There were half a dozen patios, a swimming pool lighted from underneath and even a private zoo. There were also thirty-seven rooms, including an enormous sunroom auditorium. Exclusive of its forty-car garage, "El Mirasol" cost well over one million dollars, and Mizner characteristically forgot to send a bill. He also, in the beginning at least, forgot to include a kitchen. To this day all Palm Beach owners of Mizner cottages will tell you as a mark of special pride that Mizner forgot something or other for them, too. This forgetfulness was his trade-mark. It was even more notable than his curious manner of personally "antiquing" figurines—by taking a hammer and knocking off a nose or an arm—or his equally ingenious method of "aging" furniture—by burning it with a hot paper fire. Mizner's most famous example of forgetfulness was his omission of any staircase in the old Rasmussen house. At the last moment he designed a turret for the house and put an outside spiral staircase around it; the cottage promptly became a Palm Beach showplace.

After "El Mirador" Mizner had to be begged to design a cottage. Lying on the beach or lolling in the Everglades Club, he would first demand the story of the life of the prospective architect-hunter and then if he found the story romantic enough to interest him, he would sketch something on the back of an envelope. Then if properly encouraged he would proceed even further. If ever discouraged he would immediately lose all interest in his plan. In this manner he designed some fifty million dollars worth of Palm Beach real estate, not to mention the Gulf Stream Club at Delray and his ill-fated Boca Raton project even farther south. In short order he designed "Amado" and "Louwana" for Charles and Gurnee Munn, "Sin Cuidado" and "Collado Hueco" for Edward S. and Paul Moore, "Casa Bendita" for John S. Phipps, "Lagomar" for Mrs. Henry Rea, "El Solano" for Harold Vanderbilt, "Playa Reinte" for Joshua Cosden—as well as a host of other equally quaintly named cottages for such Mizner favorites as A. J. Drexel Biddle, Jr., Arthur B. Claflin, John F. Harris, George Luke Mesker, Rodman Wanamaker, Major Barclay Warburton and Dr. Preston Pope Satterwhite. In the end, after the Florida boom, Mizner died, like Paris Singer, not only without money but actually in debt—and it remained for his brother Wilson to provide the finale for the great Mizner boom-and-bust. Wilson was forced to appear on the witness stand and testify as to some real estate shenanigans in which he and his brother had participated. "Did you or did you not," shouted the opposing lawyer, "tell my client he could *grow nuts* on this land?" "I did not," Wilson shouted back. "I told him he could *go nuts* on it."

Nothing so symbolized Palm Beach's great 1920's as the individual features of its houses. The Mesker cottage took first honors. It featured Lord Nelson's own bar, which Mrs.

Mesker had bought in London, stained glass windows, which had also been bought abroad, and, finally, oriental rugs which led right out the front door and down over the lawn to the edge of the swimming pool. "Playa Reinte," the resort's largest private cottage and in many ways Mizner's most remarkable, also has a rug story; its living room rug, with raised flowers on it, is today valued at $500,000. The cottage itself was built in 1923 at a cost of $1,800,000 by the late oilman, Joshua Cosden, a man who Palm Beachers say was worth $75,000,000 when he was thirty-eight and, at the age of fifty-eight, died "broke," or what to Palm Beachers was apparently the same thing—worth under one million dollars. The outstanding feature of this cottage is its ballroom which hangs right out over the ocean and is decorated with nine enormous paintings by the famous Waldorf and Radio City muralist, José Sert. When two years after the cottage was built, Mrs. Cosden sold it to Mrs. Horace Dodge, then Mrs. Hugh Dillman, for $2,800,000—Mrs. Dodge having in the meantime sold the Dodge Motor Company for $150,000,000, or, as she puts it, "perhaps a few million more"—the story was printed that the sale was concluded because the thirty Cosden servants, who had thirty rooms of their own, were nonetheless frightened by the elephants in the largest Sert painting and had left in a body. Today Mrs. Cosden indignantly denies this story. "I sold because I made a million dollars in two years," she says. "Wouldn't you?"

Looking back on the Palm Beach 1920's, Mrs. Cosden feels that people often think of them in the same way people look back on the 1890's—as being populated only by the elderly. "Don't write about us," she says. "Write about the Stotesburys, the Phippses and the Munns. If you have to say something about us, say how *young* we were. Why, my husband was in his thirties and I was in my twenties, and we had the largest independent oil refinery in the world!" Asked if she misses those days now, Mrs. Cosden shakes her head. "I never miss anything I've had," she says, "as long as I've had it."

Unfortunately the philosophy of the 1920's no longer pervades the resort today. "The trouble with Palm Beach," says forty-year-old Robert Kintner, president of the A.B.C. Network, "is that by the time you can afford it, you're too old to enjoy it." In the summer of 1952, Charles Merrill, senior partner of New York's largest brokerage firm, Merrill Lynch, Pierce, Fenner & Beane, declared in court that though he estimated his worth at $5,000,000 he could no longer afford his third Palm Beach wife. She spent, he said in his suit for divorce, $360,000 a year. Even Mr. Stotesbury, who weighed into Palm Beach Society in his prime at $75,000,000, found the resort expensive. Finally he made a valiant attempt to budget his wife on household expenses—at $12,500 per Palm Beach week. One day not long after the midnight-to-morning redoing of one of the patios of "El Mirasol," Stotesbury visited a lady neighbor who started to tell him of some work she proposed to have done as a surprise for her husband. Stotesbury stopped her. "Don't," he said quickly. "Don't do it. Husbands don't like surprises." Frazier Jelke recalls that his parents paid three thousand dollars a month for four rooms at the Everglades Club. Later, after the new Breakers Hotel had been built following the fire of March, 1925, his parents moved there and paid six thousand dollars a month—but this time meals were included. Again considering the value of the 1920's dollar, these prices were no bargains, but they were a definite part of the appeal of the resort. "Nobody," declared the late Arthur Keller, first secretary of the Bath and Tennis Club, "should come to Palm Beach who doesn't have money."

The Bath and Tennis Club, a reaction against Paris Singer's highhanded behavior in running the Everglades Club, was far from a financial reaction; in fact, it was perhaps the outstanding example of the extravagances of the era. Formed by many of the same Palm Beachers who, led by the popular "Tony" Biddle, had, in the old Breakers Beach days, roped off a clubable-size portion of the beach for themselves, the Bath and Tennis was built in 1926 and its semi-Moorish splendor outdid all the other great resort clubs of those days. Still today Palm Beach's most desirable club, the Bath and Tennis charged ten thousand dollars for founder memberships; so great was their demand that Secretary Keller had to send back over a quarter of a million dollars in checks after the quota had been filled.

Ziegfeld designer Joseph Urban, who conceived the Bath and Tennis, was also responsible for the cottage which of all Palm Beach estates best exemplified what Palm Beacher Mrs. Axel Jonsson has called the resort's "early Bastardian Spanish period." Called "Mar-a-lago," the home of Mrs. Davies—who was at the time of its building married to Edward F. Hutton—it is located next to the Bath and Tennis Club and promptly outranked all the Postum heiress' other hideaways. This was no mean accomplishment, since Mrs. Hutton's hideaways included a seventy-room triplex penthouse apartment in New York, her famous "Hillwood" estate in Roslyn, Long Island, her sixteen-thousand-acre shooting rendezvous up the Combahee River in South Carolina and her incredible "Camp Topridge" at Upper St. Regis in the Adirondacks; the latter boasted, among other conveniences, an escalator from the lake to the camp. Urban did his best, however, and what he failed to provide in the way of an Arabian Nights setting was ably seconded by a Venetian artist named Ju-Ju de Blas. Ju-Ju visited the Huttons for two winters and ad-libbed a remarkable series of water colors. Outside the cottage had its own golf course and inside there was almost enough room for one. A million-dollar inlaid marble dining room table was the cottage's individual feature, but Mrs. Davies' boudoir was not far behind; a visitor compared it to Versailles. Another visitor declared pointedly, after his first tour of inspection of the cottage, that there was gold everywhere but on the front door. Returning some time later he declared there was then gold everywhere; he had evidently been overheard and, in the interim, the door had been hung with several gold cupids. But it remained for the late Harry K. Thaw, slayer of Stanford White, to provide the most awe-inspiring comment. Thaw first gazed at the cottage silently for several seconds, then turned to a friend. "My God," he said quietly, "I shot the wrong architect."

It is hardly surprising that, with "Mar-a-lago," the Huttons were enabled to rival even the Stotesburys in Palm Beach partying. On more than one occasion, for an audience of perhaps two hundred guests, the Huttons provided a full-length play by a full Broadway cast; once, after the performance in 1930 of *Stepping Out,* the cast had a full week's vacation as Mrs. Hutton's guests before returning to Broadway. Other Palm Beachers were also doing their level party best. The author Kenneth Roberts, journeying down from Kennebunk, Maine, reported in his *Florida,* published in 1926, a typical Palm Beach day:

> The conscientious seeker after diversion at Palm Beach arises at a fairly early hour, indulges in eighteen holes of golf, hastens to the beach to mingle amiably with the K.

Lespindrawl Bunns, the W. Shiver Triplechins and other members of the seven upper circles of Palm Beach society, and to procure an earful of the scandalous developments of the preceding evening.

At 12:30 he rushes away to join a cocktail party at a private residence; moves directly from the cocktail party to luncheon; hastens to the tennis courts for a light work-out; repairs to the home of a friend at 4:30 for a game of bridge; and dashes away at six to attend any one of a large series of before-dinner cocktail parties, where he gets himself pleasantly mulled.

At eight he tears himself away and races home to dress; hurries to dinner at 8:30 and engages in brilliant social conversation at the dinner-table as to who such-and-such a person is and who Mrs. Thus-and-So has been seen with lately; makes a neat get-away at ten o'clock and visits the first of a series of after-dinner parties, where he sops up enough highballs to enable him to get his bearings.

At eleven he eases out and visits a second one; breaks away from the second one at 11:30 and looks in on a third; decides the second party was the best, so ducks the third party at midnight, returns to the second party, and remains there until three or four o'clock in the morning—or even five or six o'clock, provided that sufficient amusement is provided.

On the following day he gets up and goes through the entire program again; and if, by any mischance, there happens to be a single hour in his day that is not filled with some kind of *divertissement* or distraction, he almost goes mad with boredom and distress.

In the old days—an expression which Palm Beachers use much to the irritation of the more venerable Newporters and Bar Harborites—Palm Beachers left the resort following the gala Washington's Birthday Ball at the Royal Poinciana.

Nowadays Palm Beachers make a far longer season; at least one up-and-coming club, the Coral Beach, stays open all year round. This does not mean, however, that Palm Beach seasons are that much more attractive. Members of the hotel contingent stay primarily because the hotel rates go down steadily from March 15 on, the cottage colonists, at least in a great many cases, because they have to. In order to make Florida their permanent residence and thus avoid state income taxes elsewhere, they must remain at the resort long enough to show "intent of domicile." While this time limit varies and Florida addresses have been rather freely interpreted, the fact remains that resorters are often forced to resort longer than they might wish. Actually Palm Beach's weather, which for the past twenty years or so, has been described to visitors as unusual, has steadily been getting, to put it gently, more unusual. Palm Beachers deny this, of course. Comparing their sunsets with those of Egypt, a place where a great many of them have apparently spent a good deal of time, they ignore the stark fact that, as New York's winters have become warmer, Florida's have become colder. The resort's Januarys and Februarys are by no means the dine-out-of-doors months they once were, and even in March the famous artificially lighted patios, once standard equipment for all Palm Beach dinner parties, are now little used. A final straw has been the emergence of late years of a peculiar form of stinging jellyfish known as Portuguese men-of-war. These fish, whose sting can be fatal and who seem to prefer the waters around Palm Beach and Hobe Sound to less fashionable piscatorial areas, are now in the process of transferring the resort—at least for periods of varying duration each season—from an ocean-swimming to a swimming-pool community.

In view of such disadvantages it may be wondered why

Palm Beach is not in an even worse position than the other great social resorts, and, in fact, why it is still inhabited at all. There are a number of reasons. The resort, which may still be visualized as the explorer Sears first saw it—as a narrow stretch of land between the Atlantic Ocean on one side and Lake Worth on the other—is scenically rewarding. The ocean drive, along Ocean Boulevard and County Road, affords perhaps the most immediately arresting view of the area, but to Palm Beachers their favorite sight is the Lake Trail, or the Jungle Trail as it used to be called, where no automobiles are allowed and the old "afromobiles," though fast disappearing, are still in evidence. Worth Avenue, Palm Beach's main street, is undoubtedly the most exciting resort thoroughfare in the country. Beginning a block down from the new Colony Hotel, it offers chic white Fifth Avenue stores which first mingle with fascinating Old World vias, such as Via Mizner and Via Parigia, and then later end, on a high ancient note, with the Everglades Club. Almost equally exciting are Palm Beach's great hotels, the mammoth Whitehall, the blockbusting Breakers and the Palm Beach Biltmore. Lit up at night, these hotels are spectacles in themselves and the night entertainment they provide leaves little to be desired; the Whitehall, for example, has for many years featured, in its handsome outdoor ballroom, Ruby Newman's famous Boston Society Orchestra.

Besides these sights the resort has at least one Miami-type nightspot which advertises itself as Palm Beach's place "to see and be seen"—the Patio. The owners of the Patio, Dan Shalek and Val Ernie, are long-time students of Palm Beach Society and in their frank opinion a strong reason for the success of the resort is that it is no place for happily married couples. "A man married to a beautiful girl," says Shalek with some pride, "has more chance of losing her in Palm Beach than anywhere else in the country." For his part, Ernie is equally proud of the resort's social severity and points to the fact that Adelaide Moffat, premier debutante singer, was not nervous singing in New York, Hollywood or Miami; at Palm Beach, he says, she invariably broke out in a cold sweat. As an example of the kind of thing which evidently turns impressionable heads, both owners point back to the night of St. Valentine's Day, 1938. At that time Chicago's late Kenneth Smith, president of Pepsodent, celebrated his forty-sixth birthday by having the Patio orchestra play for him until early the next morning; he then presented the leader with a Packard car and all nine orchestra members with Pontiacs.

The outstanding scenic feature of the Patio is its sliding roof which may be, at a moment's notice, like a convertible car, changed from completely closed to wide-open or, in medium temperatures, halfway in between. On top of this roof, on special occasions, the entire orchestra renders, by violin, the song, "Florida, the Moon and You." This song, from Florenz Ziegfeld's *No Foolin'*, is a memorable one to all Palm Beachers since Ziegfeld gave the first performance of his show in Palm Beach in the winter of 1926 and allowed the resort belles of the day to take parts in the chorus. But even to outsiders, the song, played by a full orchestra of violins from the edge of an open roof, becomes unforgettable —and it is not surprising that it was used in both *Palm Beach Girl* and Ziegfeld's *American Review* and has since become recognized as the Palm Beach theme song:

Here beneath the stars,
While soft guitars,
We hear a strumming,

I want you to know
I love you so
And that's why I'm humming.

It's heaven to be here with you,
Underneath the moon in Florida.
I love everything that you do,
It's paradise here in Florida.
Your smile, your sighs, your wonderful charms,
Your lips, your eyes, your two loving arms.
I love you, my darling, I do,
Florida, the moon and you!

Even more important than the resort's scenic qualifications for success is the fact that what might be drawbacks to the average person are not drawbacks to Palm Beachers. In particular they take severe pride in the proximity of the Everglades Jungle, in which may still be found genuine Seminole Indians, bobcats and man-eating alligators, and the Everglades Club, in which there are all manner of suspect social pilgrims, playboys and marriage-minded heiresses. "This is the last frontier" is a phrase Palm Beachers use a good deal and while it is not always clear whether they are speaking geographically or socially, the difference is at any rate not a large one. When John S. Phipps recently trapped, right on the manicured lawn of his "Casa Bendita," a huge bobcat, the event was celebrated in much the same manner as the landing of a new husband on the part of the resort's ever-popular social charmer, Countess Dolly Hylan Heminway Fleischmann O'Brien Dorelis. Together with this spirit of roughing it, there is also a remarkable obliviousness, at least on the part of many Palm Beachers, to the expense of the resort; this spirit is particularly notable in the matter of Palm Beach charities. Mrs. Wiley Reynolds has been running Palm Beach's Crippled Children's

Society for ten years. "We do have a little trouble getting publicity," she says. "We don't have dukes and duchesses on our board. But just the same, we've never had to ask anybody for a nickel." The reaction of Palm Beachers to their current climate difficulties is equally exemplary. When they notice the bad weather at all, they blame it either on the experimentation with the atomic bomb—which they claim has disturbed the Gulf Stream—or else on taxes, the younger generation or the late Franklin D. Roosevelt. In any case, these climatic difficulties have not yet affected the modest amount of golf, tennis, polo, fishing, etc., in which they indulge; as for the chain reaction of the luncheons, teas, cocktails and dinners, these would proceed equally well if the climate became as cold as New York. "Frankly," says Mrs. Latham Reed, who has been called the "Voice" of Palm Beach Society, "I hate people in the daytime."

Even if it has deteriorated geographically, Palm Beach is still psychologically an almost ideal climate for its patrons. From the moment you cross the drawbridges over Lake Worth from West Palm Beach—a place which, though now eleven times the size of Palm Beach, still suffers socially from Flagler's description of it as his "help" city—you enter what amounts to an island of privilege, in many ways the most remarkable one left in this country. The two main gateways, appropriately enough, are called Royal Poinciana and Royal Palm Way, and the regal impression continues all the way from the resort's morning newspaper, the Palm Beach *Daily News*, which is printed on shiny paper and advertises itself as "for 55 years devoted to the cottage, club and hotel life of Palm Beach," to the resort's traditional, though unwritten, curfew law which forbids any colored person, not employed in a Palm Beach home, to be on the streets after dark. In a distance of more than six miles there are only four blocks of public beach; the entire area is either privately or club-owned, strictly zoned and controlled by all manner of deed restrictions. The contrast with the nine-mile stretch of Miami Beach, seventy miles to the south, at the southern end of the Florida Gold Coast, is inevitable. Miami Beach is also an island resort; it is a city, separate from Miami, with no manufacturing, no railroad, no airport, no cemetery and no Negro residential area. But here the comparison ends and the contrast begins. The honky-tonk Broadway-Bagdad atmosphere of Miami Beach is entirely lacking at Palm Beach, and Palm Beachers who journey down to bet on the races at Hialeah—a track rebuilt in 1931, complete with 550 pink flamingos, by the late Palm Beacher, Joseph E. Widener—could wish for no worse fate than to have to spend even one night in their sister resort.

This is, of course, a difficult attitude to understand since to the average vacationist the night life at Miami is as attractive as that offered by any American resort; it varies from the "world's fastest sport"—the pari-mutuel Jai-Alai offered at the Biscayne Fronton—to the "world's most beautiful girls" offered at the Norman Bel Geddes-designed Copa City. In its early days Miami Beach had an even more remarkable growth than Palm Beach. Developed by Indiana's late Carl Fisher, called by Will Rogers "the midwife of Florida," Miami Beach had 60 hotels by 1930, 250 by Fisher's death in 1939, and today—still in a nine-mile area—close to 400.

This "Four Hundred" of hotel Society is in its way, and despite Palm Beach's attitude toward it, as regal as Palm Beach's cottage Society. A newcomer, proudly stating the name of the hotel where he is staying, is likely to be stopped short by, "Oh, last year's hotel!" Miami's hotels offer, besides their own individual bathing clubs and all manner of cocktail lounges, patios and pavilions, such services as that of printing their guests' names on stationery and having it delivered to their rooms a few minutes after arrival. Along Lincoln Road, which is called "The Most Beautiful Shopping Lane in the World"—it was formerly called "The Fifth Avenue of the South"—it is possible to spend fifteen hundred dollars on a necktie, a difficult task in Palm Beach. At the same time, while there are some Miamians, notably Baruchs and Briggses, Fishers and Firestones, Ketterings, Knudsens, Sorensons and Kresges, who still winter relatively quietly, Palm Beach style, in private estates, Miami Beach in general is as blatantly publicity-conscious as Palm Beach at least pretends to be publicity-shy. Cartoonist Gluyas Williams, traveling to both Palm Beach and Miami Beach in pursuit of his "America's Favorite Playgrounds" series, recalls the sharp contrast which greeted him at the two resorts. At Palm Beach he was reduced to drawing the backs of a crowd of people outside the fast-closed gates of "Mar-a-lago." At Miami, taking a sight-seeing tour around the resort's famous artificial islands, he listened while the announcer intoned that Such-and-such estate was owned by So-and-so of the Something Company who paid for it X dollars and cents—when, all of a sudden, the owner himself appeared on his patio, beamed at the spectators and then proudly shook his hands over his head in the traditional prize-fight victory gesture.

Between Palm Beach and Miami are located several intermediate resorts, among them Fort Lauderdale, Florida's canal-streeted Venice, Hollywood-by-the-Sea and Boca Raton, once known as the "world's most luxurious private club." Salvaged after the bursting of its Mizner bubble by the late

Clarence Geist, a public utilities magnate who, like Carl Fisher, was an Indianian, Boca Raton has had, despite its Latin-Gothic lavishness, many ups and downs. Still called a club, it no longer has the anti-Semitic reputation of, for example, Fort Lauderdale. Nonetheless, all along the Gold Coast this question cannot be ignored. Several Miami clubs have extraordinary long-standing anti-Semitic reputations; so too do several of the hotels on upper Miami Beach. The Kenilworth, in particular, goes so far as to add postscripts to its letters drumming up trade from previous patrons. The letters themselves are long, including several paragraphs about "sun-siestas" and "fun-fiestas"; the postscripts, on the other hand, are brief: "As always, restricted clientele."

Back at Palm Beach, this question is also in evidence. One does not have to stay at the resort long to understand why it was at Palm Beach that the late Otto Kahn made his telling definition of the word "kike." "A Jewish gentleman," said Kahn, "who has just left the room." At the same time there are all varieties of hotels in Palm Beach—there is even one especially for chauffeurs—and these hotels have given rise to at least one humorous story on the subject. As the story is generally told, a man attempted to register at the Breakers Hotel and said that he was Jewish; he was informed by the desk clerk that the hotel, while not actually restricted, nonetheless catered primarily to a Christian clientele. Going over to another hotel the man said he was Christian; by the desk clerk there he was told that the hotel's clientele was primarily Jewish. "Well," said the man, by this time extremely irritated with Palm Beach social protocol, "I'll be a son of a bitch." To this, according to the story, the desk clerk had an immediate answer. "If you can prove that, sir," he said, "I can get you in anywhere."

Although some Palm Beachers like to boast that, in contrast to Newport, they have no Old Guard, the fact remains that they not only have one but also have something which Newport has not, an Old Guard Society. An organization of golfers who used to gather on the wide west veranda of the old Poinciana, the Society started—in the same way the Bath and Tennis started by roping off the Breakers Beach—by reserving the chairs on the veranda. Today the society, whose membership is limited to one hundred and whose members have ranged from the late Sir Harry Oakes to John Charles Thomas, still operates, although in reduced circumstances, on the second floor of a golf caddyhouse.

Palm Beach's real Old Guard, however, is made up, as at other social resorts, of a far more powerful group—an autocratic widow matriarchy. This group consists of at least one representative from a variety of societies, including New York's Mrs. Edward Shearson, Long Island's Mrs. Dodge Sloane, Tuxedo's Mrs. Theodore Frelinghuysen, Philadelphia's Mrs. Atwater Kent, Detroit's Mrs. Horace Dodge and Chicago's Mrs. G. Alexander McKinlock. It is Palm Beach in spirit—no Bostonian is represented and even New York's Mrs. Shearson once proudly rode a large elephant in a Palm Beach parade—but at the same time it is a powerful force for tradition. In a purely social way this group takes upon itself the "sponsoring," as it is still called, of properly qualified new visitors into Palm Beach Society—there is a saying at the resort that no single man with a dinner coat ever needs to buy himself a dinner—and has also been responsible for maintaining what is left of the original Philadelphia tone of the resort. Dating back to the days when Biddles, Wanamakers, Warburtons, Wideners, etc., frequented the old Breakers cottages, they still use such anti-New Jersey expressions as "going Jersey" for a Dutch treat party. But in a political way, too, this Old Guard has been known to bare its teeth. In 1950, when a plan was on foot to have the Everglades Club sell some of its property to interests which the Old Guard felt undesirable, the entire group gathered, over a hundred strong, from all sections of the country, in the middle of the summer, at New York's Metropolitan Club, and sternly vetoed the proposal.

Today Chicago's Mrs. McKinlock, first president of the Garden Club of Palm Beach, perhaps best expresses the feeling of the resort's old-timers. "Palm Beach is sanctuary," she said, "for those of us who are left." The widow of the organizer of Chicago's Central Electric Company and herself the donor of Harvard's McKinlock Hall—given in memory of her only son, George Alexander, Jr., who was killed in action in the First World War—Mrs. McKinlock lives in the Vita Serena area in a cathedral-like villa named "Casa Alejandro." With an efficient staff and with a beautiful garden patio shaded by palm and banana trees and separated from the rest of Vita Serena by a high wall trellised with ivy and Bougainvillaea, Mrs. McKinlock has lived alone in her cathedral-cottage since the death of her husband in 1936; she came to Palm Beach, however, many years before. "In those days," she says, "it was just as unendurable to come to Palm Beach from Chicago as it was to go to Boston. I know, I was in Boston." But Mrs. McKinlock found the tone of Palm Beach not Bostonian but Philadelphian. "I used to call the Philadelphia people 'the Mercuries,' " she recalls. "They stuck together so—you just couldn't separate them at parties."

Mrs. McKinlock also recalls the great Long Island invasion in the 1920's; one lady called her and told her she wanted to have her for dinner but she said she couldn't. "I'm just having Long Island people," she said. In time, Mrs. McKinlock learned from this sort of Society a severe dignity of her own. In the winter of 1951, returning from a party at an hour which she felt was too late to disturb her servants, she suddenly found herself in immediate need of assistance in extricating herself from a stubborn ball dress. Promptly she called the Palm Beach police. The latter, in short order, landed and took the situation in hand. No small part of Palm Beach's quaint atmosphere, these police make a habit of questioning any stranger in the Palm Beach area who acts even remotely out of line, yet are tolerant of all sorts of vagaries on the part of their regular customers; for many years two handsome brothers on the force faithfully mingled with the resorters at even the most *intime* social functions.

Ex-Ambassador Joseph P. Kennedy, who has cottaged at Palm Beach for more years than he cares to remember, recalls being told by newspaper publishers that, as a dateline on a news story, the name Palm Beach has never been equaled in reader-draw. Kennedy attributes this to a combination of personality and place—in other words, that the combination of Old Guard personalities disporting themselves against a backdrop of Florida sunshine was at least once, from the point of view of glamour, an unbeatable one. Although the Palm Beach Suit was not a Florida product—it was developed by the Goodall Sanford Company of Maine—the examples of Palm Beach's name appeal are legion. Perhaps the most graphic illustration of this appeal followed the finding, on the morning of June 11, 1920, of Joseph Elwell, New York and Palm Beach bridge expert and roué, seated downstairs in his New York home, with his pajamas on and his toupee off, and a bullet through his head. In the subsequent investigation of what turned out to be one of New York's most famous unsolved cases, it was clearly established, by Elwell's chauffeur, that his employer, riding in the back seat of his car, was able to pick up, on the streets of New York, virtually any girl he wished by merely opening the door and saying, with extreme conviction, "Why, I haven't seen you since Palm Beach!" When the outsider attempts to introduce himself to the Palm Beacher, however, the shoe is likely to be on the other foot. Not long ago oilman C. B. Wrightsman was stopped on Worth Avenue by a lady acquaintance who took the liberty of introducing another lady to him. That evening the first lady received a call from Wrightsman. "I wish you wouldn't introduce me to people on the street," he said. "I know too many people as it is and I have too many responsibilities and obligations."

"Palm Beach," says Mrs. Axel Jonsson, "can be a very demoralizing place for people who don't realize that life isn't like this." Mrs. Atwater Kent agrees with Mrs. Jonsson. Still wintering at the famous "Nautilus Cottage" on Breakers Row and asked which, Palm Beach or Bar Harbor, she likes better, Mrs. Kent replies quickly, "Oh, there's no comparison. Palm Beach is much worse." While it takes a moment or two to understand the meaning of such remarks, they can be clarified. Newell Tilton, a Palm Beacher of such eminence that he had a bar named for him, explains the resort with his characteristic wryness. "In case you don't want to know," he says, "Palm Beach has always been about as cheeky as they come." As an example of this cheekiness, another Palm Beach old-timer points to the fact that when Mrs. Dodge Sloane, owner of the Brookmeade Stables, went to the hospital for a few days during a recent winter, the regular hangers-on around her swimming pool and cottage continued to use all her facilities and servants—even her dinner table and manicurist—just as if she were still there. What annoyed Mrs. Sloane most was the fact that, upon her return, the same hangers-on gave no indication that they even knew she had been away.

Palm Beach undeniably has a flavor boasted by no other resort. Not even Newport, for example, can outdo the story of the Palm Beach lady who, failing to be invited to a party to which she felt entitled to an invitation, started legal proceedings against her prospective hostess and was barely dissuaded from pursuing the matter right into court. Nor did Newport ever suffer the spectacle of having one of its most remarkable fancy dress balls attended by the late Arthur Somers Roche. An inveterate Palm Beacher, Roche appeared at an Everglades Club costume affair dressed as a social climber with a ladder on his back; on the ladder were four rungs, painted from bottom to top, with the words "Common People," "People," "Nice People" and "Right People."

In this kind of social jungle gym, it is not surprising that there have been some notable individual careers, and all Palm Beachers today still enjoy, in retrospect, looking back at them. "Take E. Clarence Jones," says Messmore Kendall of "Kendall's Corner." "Why, he caused a terrific fuss down here. They called him the arbiter of Palm Beach Society and you weren't anybody if you weren't in with Clarence. In New York he was just a name in the telephone book." Actually Jones, who also had a colorful career at Saratoga, was one of the first New Yorkers to take root at the resort; his cottage was located on the present site of the Patio Restaurant. A good-looking gray-mustached Wall Street bachelor, he was Palm Beach's leading resort sport—even after his marriage to the beautiful widow of playwright Henry Blossom. Jones was also one of the first to see the possibilities of combining business with pleasure at the resort. A heavy speculator both in stocks and real estate, he gave and received tips at every party and ended, among other things, with control of the entire Vita Serena area. But all Palm Beachers agree that whatever Jones' shortcomings he died, as they put it, "a gentleman." "You see," they say, "he left his wife everything." Jones was succeeded as Palm Beach's male arbiter by a very different kind of leader and the resort's all-time popular sport, Tony Biddle—a man who has since graduated to a higher calling. With his Oasis Club, his Bath and Tennis Club as well as his "Coconuts"—a group of Palm Beach bachelors who gave spectacular balls once a year to return their invitations—Biddle cut a social swath at Palm Beach that no other man ever equaled. His long suit was his ability to remember names. "When you shook hands with him for the first time," says one admirer, "he made you think that you were going to be his best friend." Another admirer recalls testing Biddle's name-remembering ability one day in New York's Racquet Club. "Tony gave me a greeting downstairs I'll never forget," he says. "He said he hadn't seen me for years and he had been desolate about it. A few minutes later I saw him upstairs and he gave me the same greeting all over again. That time I was desolate."

To Palm Beach's credit, at least some of its leading citizens have developed considerable aplomb in dealing with difficult social situations. High among these is Charles A. Munn of "Amado," whose mother was a Breakers Row cottager. As the patent-holder of the totalizator, he is one of Palm Beach's most publicized figures—his name appears on the back of all pari-mutuel race-track tickets—and some years ago, in an effort to escape from his publicity, he bought a large and elaborate trailer and took it to Paris. Unfortunately, the trailer proved too large to drive on the streets downtown. Munn was forced to park it on the outskirts of the city in an extremely radical district. One evening he returned late to find a large crowd stoning his vehicle. Munn hesitated only a second. Seeing that to claim his vehicle under such circumstances would be foolhardy, he nonetheless refused to desert the scene entirely. With a display of spirit that still brings a tingle to the spine of all true Palm Beachers, he promptly leaned over, selected a large rock and joined in the stoning. Back in Palm Beach Munn added to his distinction by making what is perhaps the resort's most memorable definition of a gentleman. "A man," he said, "who for three generations has pronounced 'to-may-to' 'to-mah-to.' "

Many a Palm Beach hostess has demonstrated, in a more quiet way, equally telling examples of poise. One is Mrs. Alexander Dallas Bache Pratt, the former Mrs. Louis Kaufman, a lady who has been coming to Palm Beach for sixty-three years and who, in happier days, was widely publicized as receiving a million dollars from her father, the late Chicago merchant, Otto Young, every time she had a baby. Mrs. Pratt, or rather Mrs. Kaufman, had eight children, a Moorish houseboat designed by Mizner specifically for parties, as well as a large interest in horses. Mr. Kaufman, president of two banks and a director of the Empire State Building, approved the children and the houseboat but objected to his wife's other interests. "I don't like your being a horsewoman," he said. His wife was firm. "I don't like your being a banker," she replied. Although the Kaufman children are credited with having had more marriages and divorces than any other

Palm Beach family—their average is close to three per child or some twenty in all—Mrs. Pratt no longer overly concerns herself with each subsequent wedding. "I've only been to three of them that I can remember," she says.

Equally self-possessed was Palm Beach's beautiful Mona Strader Schlesinger Bush Williams, the Mrs. Harrison Williams of perennial "best-dressed" acclaim. Mrs. Williams came to Palm Beach in 1930 at the peak of her social career with a necklace and bracelet which, a mathematically minded Palm Beacher declares, consisted of 129 square-cut sapphires, 144 square-cut emeralds, 762 small round diamonds and 79 pearls. Born the daughter of a Lexington, Kentucky, horse-trainer, she first married, at the age of eighteen, the thirty-seven-year-old Milwaukee bachelor, Harry Schlesinger, in whose racing stables her father served as overseer; her honeymoon, in the manner of Southern belles, had been spent at White Sulphur Springs. Divorced in 1920, she received a sum of $200,000; her husband kept the child. After another five-year marriage, to another Milwaukean, James Irving Bush, she was divorced again and this time married utilities man Williams. Some twenty-five years his wife's senior, Williams had once been a barefoot boy himself—in Avon, Ohio—and had been a guest at her second wedding. He had been married once—and almost twice; three days after his second engagement had been announced, his bride-to-be had eloped with her ex-husband. In any case, Palm Beach regarded the Williamses as eminently qualified on all counts, and the couple's entry into the resort's Society, with some 700,000,000 of "newspaper dollars," was an anchor to windward in the dark days of the depression. Mrs. Williams' charm, her Persian cat eyes, her taste for modern white-and-black décor, her clothes imported from France and her accent imported from England, all formed an irresistible combination. Together with them went her tact; at one time, during the depression, she stated that she never spent more than twenty thousand dollars a year on her wardrobe. Once at a dinner party the author Joseph Hergesheimer attempted to pull her leg. "Mrs. Williams," he asked, gazing around at the lavish appointments of one of Palm Beach's most memorable dinner parties, "are you satisfied with your life?" Mrs. Williams gazed back. "Mr. Hergesheimer," she replied, "is anyone ever satisfied?"

Such an answer is in the Palm Beach poise tradition. Back in the days when Louise Cromwell was honeymooning at the resort with one of her husbands, General Douglas MacArthur, and Palm Beach couples were going in heavily for the sport of joint cycling, Mrs. MacArthur was queried as to why she, who was after all a bride on her honeymoon, indulged in the sport all by herself. The answer also took the form of a question. "Can you imagine Douglas," she asked, "on a bicycle?"

Even Louise Cromwell's mother, the resort's greatest hostess, the late Mrs. Stotesbury, was no exception to the Palm Beach rule of aplomb. Once at a warbond rally she was asked, as the wife of the senior partner of J. P. Morgan & Company, if she would say a few words. Mrs. Stotesbury arose. "The only successful financial transaction I ever made in my life," she said, "was when I married Mr. Stotesbury." What Mrs. Stuyvesant Fish was to Newport, Mrs. Stotesbury was, in her way, to Palm Beach—although she always maintained she liked Bar Harbor better. Together, she and her husband were a curious couple, Mrs. Stotesbury always fifteen minutes early to everything, Mr. Stotesbury always fifteen minutes late. Mrs. Stotesbury never went out for lunch or cocktails—just to dinner—while Mr. Stotesbury would go anywhere, at least if it did not interfere with sittings for his portraits. A rival of his wife in the matter of clothes, he had no less than 150 fancy dress costumes and was invariably, no matter what he wore, awarded first prize at the Everglades Club's annual costume ball. In "El Mirasol's" zoo the Stotesburys had twenty-five monkeys, an equal number of parrots, as well as a baker's dozen of parakeets and love birds; house guests at "El Mirasol" were equally numerous and equally catholic. To each of them each morning went a schedule for the day as well as a blank menu for food and and drink orders. "Mrs. Stotesbury," Bulgarian Prince Cyril once complained, "you never have what I order." Mrs. Stotesbury smiled. "Prince," she replied, "you never order what I have."

Actually, with seventy-five servants and three secretaries, not to mention forty cars, "El Mirasol" could supply most normal desires. But Mrs. Stotesbury's most exemplary aplomb was reserved for her parties. Whether it was to be a small birthday ball for her son, Jimmy Cromwell, at the Bath and Tennis Club—at one of these the men wore bathing trunks, full dress shirts and opera hats—or a large affair at "El Mirasol"—often there were so many people that it was a physical impossibility for them all to get in the house—Mrs. Stotesbury stuck to one abiding motto: "A nervous hostess makes an unhappy guest." This composure was put to its test once a season on February 26, at Mr. Stotesbury's own annual birthday parties. The most cherished affairs on the Palm Beach social calendar, these parties were often attended by so many people that it was impossible to tell where, outside of "El Mirasol," the party ended and Palm Beach began. Invariably, just at midnight, Mr. Stotesbury, who claimed he had seen service as a Civil War drummer boy, went over and did a drum solo of Civil War marching songs; on his death in May, 1938, a small trap drum, with appropriate ceremony, was hung in a corner of his coffin.

As memorable as Mr. Stotesbury's drum-beating was, immediately following, his solo rendition of his favorite song —one which today still ranks with "Florida, the Moon and You" in the affection of Palm Beach old-timers. Entitled "The Old Family Toothbrush That Hangs on the Sink," Mr. Stotesbury sang the song, as nearly as it was possible to ascertain, to the tune of "The Old Oaken Bucket." In any case, the picture of the dapper "Little Sunshine," the country's outstanding banker, who was still doing his act on his eighty-seventh birthday in 1936, singing in his high, quaking voice to five hundred champagne-soaked Palm Beachers, is an unforgettable resort vignette:

The old family toothbrush,
The old family toothbrush,
The old family toothbrush
That hangs on the sink.
First it was father's,
Then it was mother's,
Then it was sister's,
Now it is mine.

Only once did Palm Beach's poise ever suffer a real blow. This occurred many years ago and was delivered by the late James P. Donahue, husband of Jessie Woolworth. At Southampton Donahue had once urged a fellow resorter to look at his dining room. "Come on in and see it," he said. "All the silver's gold." At Palm Beach Donahue's difficulties occurred in the field of art. A man who knew little about music, he nonetheless had a ballroom in his "Cielito Lindo" which was acoustically excellent, and he had agreed, as a generous gesture, to act as host for a Palm Beach performance of Mrs. Seward Webb's famous New York string quartet. No one could have shown greater enthusiasm. Preceding the concert Donahue decked not only his ballroom but also all of "Cielito Lindo" with white orchids; an hour before the event he was personally making a last-minute inspection tour when he was informed the musicians, specially transported from New York, had already arrived and were assembling at the piano. Rushing through the ballroom door, arms outstretched to greet the men of whom he expected so much, Donahue stopped in his tracks. "What!" he exclaimed, in a voice no member of the quartet would ever forget, "are there only *four* of you?"

Today this story is to some extent perpetuated at the resort since Palm Beach's most famous artistic center, on Royal Palm Way, is now known as the Society of the Four Arts; there is, however, no connection. Established largely through the efforts of Palm Beach's Newport contingent, with the late Maud Howe Elliott leading the way—Mrs. Elliott's cry, during dark days, of "Stick by the flag!" is still recalled by Mrs. Lorenzo Woodhouse—the Society has been ably accompanied artistically by other successful ventures. Among these are the famous Norton Gallery and School of Art—which Chicagoan Ralph Hubbard Norton significantly established in West Palm Beach in preference to Palm—as well as a theater, first started by Muriel McCormick Hubbard, whose mother had studied with Freud in Vienna, and also Maude Miner Hadden's so-called "Round Table" and Grace Thompson Seton's "Quills," or penwomen.

If the resort has refused to be a period piece artistically, it has been less successful in the political sphere. "Do you not find," asks Sumner Welles with a wry smile, "that this little resort of ours is the most enlightened, progressive, forward-looking community you have ever encountered?" The answer, of course, is obvious. Charles Francis Coe, editor and publisher of two Palm Beach newspapers, has written, by his own count, close to a million words a year of editorials against the past Democratic administration. As a man who once wrote a *Saturday Evening Post* serial in one rainy week end, "Socker," as he is affectionately called by Palm Beachers, is an old hand at speed and his editorials are, if nothing else, a vacation solace for Chicago's Colonel Robert R. McCormick, a man who, symbolically enough, owns a solid mile of Palm Beach beach. But even such a political-minded citizen as Coe can, if the occasion arises, move into the social sphere. "I don't talk family," he says, "but if anybody wants to, do you know who the daughter of John and Priscilla Alden married?—a Coe!"

Equally symbolic of the resort are the opinions of Palm Beach's evangelist of free enterprise, stock-exchanger Edward F. Hutton of "Four Winds." For many years Hutton's advertisements blanketed Palm Beach papers simultaneously with their appearance in such other mass media as the *New York Times;* in Hutton's view, often expressed at the resort, being a Democrat is a disease. In the days when he was married to the present Mrs. Davies, Hutton commissioned, in 1931, from the Krupps works at Kiel, the largest sailing yacht in the world—*The Hussar.* Costing $900,000, *The Hussar,* now owned by Mrs. Davies and registered under the name of *Sea Cloud,* is a four-masted square-rigged bark, has two Diesel engines and is 316 feet long. Furnished in the Louis XIV manner below deck, this yacht has inspired a number of legends, one of them being that even the "lifeboats carry lifeboats." No legend, however, is the expense of *Sea Cloud*; its crew of seventy-two has a monthly payroll of twenty thousand dollars and Mrs. Davies, who likes their uniforms changed twice a year, pays twenty thousand dollars twice yearly for this item alone. Hutton, who operated the yacht all during the dark days of the 1930's, urged his fellow yachtsmen to do likewise. "He seemed to feel," said Ferdinand Lundberg, "that if all the big boat-owners would follow his suggestion, the nation might yacht its way out of the depression."

Perhaps fortunately, not all Palm Beachers take their politics as earnestly. In the winter of 1951, at a time when President Truman was vacationing at Key West, Palm Beacher James Cameron Clark gave a dinner in honor of another distinguished Florida visitor, Warren Austin, Ambassador to the United Nations. Among the guests was Mrs. William Hayward, of Newport and Palm Beach, a lady who promptly seized the opportunity to question Austin. "Ambassador," she began gently, "you know this fellow Truman pretty well, don't you?" Since world affairs were at that moment in a severe crisis, all conversation ceased and everyone listened intently. Austin admitted that he was seeing the President frequently. "Well then," said Mrs. Hayward vigorously, "can't *you* do something about those shirts he wears?"

All this does not, unhappily or otherwise, add up to an unchanged social picture. The swimming pool of the late Vincent Bendix is no longer filled, as it was in the 1920's, with Poland water, and even the Bendix cottage's cottage, connected by an underground tunnel to the cottage proper, is now a curio. Among its features is an arrangement for nude drinking. Between the two dressing rooms, one for ladies and one for men, stands a bar with a set of double-door windows on each side. In happier times the bather, nude, would call his order and the bartender would open one door and set the drink out and then close the door again; then the bather would open the other door and take the drink. The famous million-dollar hole of the Gulf Stream Club—its members, just prior to the 1929 crash, refused an offer of that sum to sell their eighteenth hole for ocean-front property—is today merely the loss leader of Palm Beach price tags; it is closely seconded by the million-dollar Paramount movie theater. This theater, which used to cost Palm Beachers one thousand dollars a box per season, was designed on a table-cloth by Joseph Urban as an underwater scene—complete with a fish-and-fungi *décor*. To Palm Beachers today the scene is no longer as funny as it once was. Equally desperate is the situation among the resort's most fabulous cottages of the past. The two outstanding white elephants, the Stotesbury's "El Mirasol," which ran to twenty-five acres, and the Donahue-Woolworth "Cielito Lindo," in which the master bed alone was described as large enough for a political party, have been chopped up and subdivided. "El Mirasol" is now thirty small homes, and a large road, bordering five twelve-room homes, now goes directly through what was once the living room of "Cielito Lindo." The estate of the late Otto Kahn—once described by its colored caretaker in a burst of enthusiasm as "equal to few and surpassed by many"—is now Palm Beach's Graham Eckes School, and even the resort's largest currently operating menage, the Cosden-Dillman-Dodge "Playa Reinte," is now down to a skeleton staff of twenty servants.

The situation in the Stotesbury family, whose seventy-five

or one hundred million went with the wind and Mrs. Stotesbury, is perhaps the more acute. A Stotesbury granddaughter has recently been operating a small inn, which she calls "Madhouse Manor," while her young son, affording Palm Beach's best illustration of shirtsleeves to shirtsleeves in three generations, is currently working in a filling station. Taxes are, Palm Beachers claim, the main reason for the woe. Coupled with taxes, however, is a general social disintegration which is perhaps best symbolized by the fact that no contender for Palm Beach's social heavyweight throne, vacant since the death of Mrs. Stotesbury in 1946, has even taken the trouble to compete for the honor. One possible contender, Mrs. Harrison Williams, deserted the resort in favor of the island of Capri and a fortress built by Tiberius in the first century. Another, Mrs. Joseph Davies, declares that since she cannot afford the operation of both "Mar-a-lago" and *Sea Cloud*, she had to choose between them. She chose *Sea Cloud*.

"The tide's turning all over the country," says Ruby Edna Pierce, for forty years editor of the Palm Beach *Daily News*. "Palm Beach isn't what it was ten years ago and ten years ago it wasn't what it was ten years before that. Why, I'm featuring people in my paper today I wouldn't have mentioned in my guest list fifteen years ago." Miss Pierce's motion is seconded by virtually every cottage colonist at the resort. "Our little country town is gone," sighs Mrs. Leray Berdeau, whose modern "Villa Aujourd'hui" is the center of the resort's arty set. "Why Palm Beach is a *city*!" Equally firm is Mrs. McKinlock. "Palm Beach has lost its personality," she says. "Today it is like Miami. It used to be *poetic*!" Charles A. Munn speaks for another group. "I used to know everybody," he says. "Now I don't know anybody." Speaking for the Old Guard, Philadelphian Charlton Yarnall, a Palm Beacher since 1900, shakes his head. "It's not one thing or the other," he declares. "It's an *omnium gatherum.*" Tuxedo's Worthington Hine sums up the case with a brief story. Absent from Palm Beach for some time he returned with a new wife to ask his friend, the artist Murray Hoffman, who the nice people were. Hoffman was incredulous. "Why, haven't you heard?" he said. "There aren't any."

In the same way that Palm Beachers boil down their pleasures of the Good Old Days to the time when, as they say, "There was just the Poinciana and the old Breakers, the rest was *all jungle*"—this latter invariably accompanied by a sweeping wave of the hand—they boil down their grievances of today to the specific question of the increased membership of the Everglades Club. Originally the maximum membership was three hundred; today there are close to fourteen hundred, and old-time Palm Beachers, who have seen the same social inflation duplicated at the Bath and Tennis Club, the Seminole Club, and even, to a lesser extent, at the Gulf Stream, have never taken kindly to the change. "When you used to go there," says Mrs. Horace Dodge, "you knew everybody. Now if you know three people you're doing well and you don't want to know them." Harvey Ladew expresses this majority opinion even more strongly. A former Maryland Master of Fox Hounds and a nephew of Saratoga's E. Berry Wall, King of the Dudes, Ladew has now deserted Palm Beach entirely and has moved down to Delray Beach. "Belonging to the Everglades Club today," he says, "is like belonging to Grand Central Station." With these views the man who for many years has personified Palm Beach Society, Hugh Dillman, is in hearty assent. Born in Chesterville, Ohio, ex-juvenile actor, ex-secretary of Joseph Riter, ex-husband of Mrs. Dodge, and, as of 1952, ex-president of the Everglades Club, Dillman has made a lifetime career of Palm Beach and is even able to refine the resort with such divisions as Old New Guard and New Old Guard; nonetheless, at the height of the 1951 season, he not only resigned his presidency of the Everglades but he also abandoned the resort altogether to take a brief rest back in Ohio. "I just don't know these people," he says. "I don't know who they are."

Alone of the cottage colony set, Princess Laura Rospigliosi refuses to subscribe to the voices of social doom around her. One of the legendary Stallo sisters of Cincinnati—her sister married Prince Murat—she came to the resort when she was prenatal and now lives in it year round. "It's not true at all," she says. "Palm Beach and Rome have held up socially better than any other places in the world. They're the last places left where you can still feel like a lady and a gentleman. Why, everybody comes to Palm Beach!" Even this minority view, however, was sharply answered, and by no less a Palm Beacher than H. T. Webster. As the Caspar Milquetoast-"Life's Darkest Moment" cartoonist, Webster was, until his death this fall, reputed to be the only person at the resort who actually worked in the winter. He was philosophical. "Yes," he said quietly. "Everybody comes to Palm Beach, all right. That's why I have an unlisted phone number."

It is not surprising, in view of such feeling, that many Palm Beachers have retreated—either northward to Hobe Sound or southward toward Delray Beach. Even Palm Beach's Phippses, who not only own their own real estate company, the Bessemer Properties, but also a large per cent of the total resort, feel under constant obligation to explain themselves. Representing the third Palm Beach generation of a family which has been called the "beefsteak" of the Palm Beach social menu, the athletic Ogden Phipps makes a brave effort to state the case. "We never came here for business purposes," he says. "We just kept trying to get away. The trouble was that Palm Beach kept catching up with us."

One family who have made, of all Palm Beachers, the most interesting getaway are the Gerard B. Lamberts; indeed the Lambert home, built as recently as 1946, is undoubtedly the most spectacular present-day resort cottage anywhere in the country. Mrs. Lambert wanted to be right on the ocean, Mr. Lambert wanted to be on the lake; no compromise was apparently possible, and the only solution was to build down towards Delray, at Boynton Beach, where the distance between ocean and lake is narrow enough so that the cottage can overlook both. At the same time, of course, there still remained the problem of the road. Fortunately this road—Florida's Route A-1-A to Miami—was relatively high at this point so that the Lamberts' cottage, which is built literally under the road, can still overlook both the ocean and the lake.

The cottage itself, a breath-taking blend of modern and Pompeian, was designed by Marion Sims Wyeth; fifteen feet of insulation between the road and the room of the cottage which is directly under it make this room so quiet that, despite the passing cars overhead, the Lamberts decided, at the suggestion of their friend Noel Coward, to call this room their music room; they now have an organ in it. They resisted another friend's suggestion that they call the whole cottage "Burrow Hall"; the cottage is nameless.

Nameless or not, the cottage provides Palm Beach's most elegant standards of living—for Mrs. Lambert lives completely in her ocean half of the cottage and Mr. Lambert completely in his lake half. Along with one of Palm Beach's most extraordinary art collections—the Lamberts are amateur artists themselves as well as generous art patrons—they have two complete sets of bedrooms, dressing rooms, living rooms, dining rooms, kitchens and servants' rooms. They also have two complete sets of servants, colored on the lake side and white on the ocean side. On Christmas, 1950, the servants all got together for the first time for their holiday dinner on the lake side, and Mrs. Lambert, who also goes over to her husband's side of the cottage from time to time, applauded the move. "I thought it was nice," she says. Though one of the resort's most charming hostesses, she has never allowed her cottage to be photographed or written up in Society magazines, and she has a good deal of trouble with tourists who drive out from Palm Beach prospecting for it. Only once has she permitted the cottage even to be seen by any large number of people; the occasion was for the benefit of the Delray Garden Club and so great was the appeal that the traffic jam on the roof lasted for several hours. Actually the cottage, complete with swimming pool on lake side and private beach on ocean side, is perhaps the most tasteful of all Palm Beach showplaces. The interior decoration picks up the greens from the ocean and the blues from the lake and these are carried, in decreasing intensity, to the middle of the cottage. The furnishings throughout are almost incredibly handsome, but even more incredible than the cottage's interior is its exterior landscaping. The driveway, which comes up to the road some distance from the cottage itself, is well disguised and the cottage itself is completely hidden as one drives over the road.

This feature pleases the Lamberts most. In contrast to such aboveground castles as "Mar-a-lago" and "Playa Reinte," the

Lambert cottage foxhole, which is worth as much in dollars and cents as both of the others put together, represents the most militant example of present-day defensive wealth. Indeed, the Lamberts themselves, having burrowed underground, obviously represent the country's most militant example of the hidden rich. Nor is their divided manner of living without its significance for these modern times; both Mr. and Mrs. Lambert have been married before but their present marriage has already outdistanced the average Palm Beach blend by at least a decade.

Mr. Lambert was not always so publicity-shy. A former America's Cup Defender Yachtsman, he is the inheritor of the fabulous Listerine fortune. At first he had little to do with the company but in 1921 he shocked his brother inheritors by stepping in and suggesting that the then quietly operating mouthwash should be dramatized by a direct appeal to the public. As a new vice-president of the company in 1921 he summoned two men from the Chicago advertising agency which handled the account. He closed his office door. "We are not leaving here," he announced, "until we've got an idea, a hot idea, for popularizing Listerine."

The conference took several hours. Finally a brother of Lambert called in the company's chief chemist, a gentleman known as "Old Man Deacon." Lambert demanded that he enumerate all possible uses of the mouthwash. Deacon went through them and finally said something about "halitosis." Immediately Lambert swung around. "What's that?" he asked. Deacon looked over his glasses. "Latin for unpleasant breath," he replied. "Say it again," barked Lambert. "Halitosis," barked Deacon. Lambert made for the door. "That's something we can hang our hat on," he said. Within an hour he had purchased a portrait of a model whom he named

Ernestine and, concludes Jack Alexander, reporting the event, "the great Halitosis campaign was on":

> Ernestine was supplanted by girls who were neglected by the stagline or were bridesmaids but never brides; by salesmen who wondered why purchasing agents avoided them; by businessmen whose secretaries turned away during dictation; by husbands whose wives averted their heads; by barbers who could never understand why their patrons left only nickel tips.

That a man who was personally responsible for what was perhaps the country's most successful publicity campaign should today own the country's most publicity-shy resort cottage may seem an anomaly, but Lambert is no ordinary resorter. Not long after his success he began to have periodic spells of soul-searching in which he wondered whether, if he had started off without inherited money or social background, he would have amounted to anything. On one occasion he even went so far as to plan a completely new life—one which would involve disappearing from his regular career entirely and starting out, with a new name and in a new town, all over again. He chose the town—Canton, Ohio—but at this stage in his plans he took up J-boat yacht-racing instead. On another occasion he became so intrigued with resort social-climbing that he wrote a book entitled *Murder at Newport*. In this book the son of a "nice millionaire" who has committed suicide after being ruined financially by a "naughty millionaire," murders the "naughty millionaire"; the latter, in turn, has been betrayed by what the author calls his "social complex" which led him to ruin the "nice millionaire" who had once snubbed him. Today Lambert himself has no such shortcoming. As a Palm Beach friend puts it, "A fellow who lives below road level can hardly be accused of social-climbing."

The death of gambling all over the country has, of course, affected all the resorts, but Palm Beach and Saratoga have suffered most. "When Bradley's went," says ex-Ambassador Kennedy, "this place lost its zipperoo." The Kennedy children, all of whom would, in earlier days, have perhaps been happy there, now vastly prefer Cape Cod. "It's nice," says Miss Patricia Kennedy, "to go to a resort where you can walk down the street without a clean white blouse and a clean white pressed pair of shorts." At the same time, it would not be in the spirit of Palm Beach if the more elderly resorters permitted the public greyhound racing provided by the local kennel club to be their only gambling outlet. In recent years there have been outstanding instances of gambling for charity. A few seasons ago the high-water mark of such activity was reached at one of Palm Beach's so-called "Chinese auctions"—one which was held at the Everglades Club for the benefit of St. Mary's Catholic Hospital. In such auctions, the bidder pays only the difference between the previous bid and his bid, but all previous bidders have already contributed to the pot and, unless they bid again, have no chance of winning. Thus a man who makes a thousand dollar bid over a nine hundred dollar bid pays just one hundred dollars but all the other bidders have contributed to the pot all the way up. In the case of the Everglades Club auction, with such ardent bidders as Kennedy, ex-Ambassador Davies, Brigadier General Ralph Robertson and Thomas J. Watson, the bidding on a Cadillac car, originally given by Kennedy, soon reached such a frenzy that when a large Texas oilman put in a bid after Ambassador Davies he was, in the confusion, immediately hailed as an ambassador himself. Pleased, he put in several more bids and when Florida's Attorney General, who had journeyed from Tallahassee to regulate matters, attempted to knock the car down, Palm Beachers in turn rose in a body and knocked him down. Finally the car was won for a sum of over $100,000. "It was," says Harry Bull of Delray, "a grievous money jag."

Almost equally exhausting is the seriousness with which Palm Beachers take their betting at backgammon and other games. Card-playing, an intrinsic feature of resort life at Newport, Bar Harbor, Southampton, etc., is nowhere taken more earnestly than at Palm Beach. Afternoon luncheons, evening dinners and sometimes even late breakfasts are hardly pushed aside before all rush to their places at the table. For cards, and cards alone, Palm Beachers are even inclined to forget their social distinctions; in the words of Mrs. Henry Carnegie Phipps, "If they play good bridge, who cares about their souls?" Not long ago some ladies new to the resort ambled leisurely to a table where they found an elderly Palm Beach lady had beaten them to the draw; already seated, she had even picked up her hand. The ladies, surprised, nonetheless attempted to introduce themselves. "I'm Mrs. So-and-so," said the first, while the other two also gave their names. For the first time the Palm Beach lady looked up. "I'm the dealer," she said, "and I bid four spades."

Harold S. Vanderbilt, a Palm Beacher himself, recalls that the first game of contract bridge was played in the autumn of 1926 on board the *S.S. Finland* enroute from San Pedro, California, to the Canal Zone. "The scoring and other features of the game which I invented at that time," he says, "and which were used by myself and three other friends on board, are almost identical with those used today." The word "vulnerable," Vanderbilt declares, was originally suggested by "a young lady passenger on board" whose name Vanderbilt cannot remember. "She had played," he concludes, "some other game in which the term 'vulnerable' was used."

Not content with ordinary bridge, or for that matter, with gin rummy or canasta—in the words of Philo Calhoun, the former is "a bore," the latter, "a complicated bore"—Palm Beachers have even refined Vanderbilt's contract game into their own variant called "towie" (rhymes with "zowie"). Invented by the late Pittsburgh steeler, J. Leonard Replogle, whom Palm Beachers remember as such a poor bridge-player that nobody wanted him for a partner, towie requires no partners and is played by only three players at a time. For many years Palm Beachers played it when it had no name; then one memorable evening Pauline Wanamaker, who had one of the resort's most notable Philadelphia baby-talk accents, went down one thousand points. "Oh deawie," she exclaimed, "I'm down a towie!" From that day forward, towie became the game's name and, ably promoted by Replogle, with an assist from the Palm Beach architect, Maurice Fatio, it is still played at Newport, Bar Harbor, Southampton, Santa Barbara, Hot Springs, as well as in New York's Racquet Club and a few other select locations. Ely Culbertson has called towie the best three-handed bridge game in existence, and Palm Beach missionaries specifically credited with carrying towie to other resorts are the Crawford Hills to Newport, the Hugh Nesbitt Kirklands to Santa Barbara, the William Greves to Southampton, Mrs. Frederic Owsley to the hunting set in Virginia and Mrs. O'Malley-Keyes to Biarritz.

Towie's rules are relatively simple. With six cards of the hand opposite the dealer turned up after the deal, all players bid on the basis of their hands plus what they believe to be the total strength of the partly turned-up hand; this then becomes the dummy of the player who has made the highest bid. If there is no game bid, the hand is not played, as it is in bridge, at all. Instead a goulash is dealt with six cards in the dummy hand again being turned up. Four or even five players can play towie as well as three; in these cases one or two players sit out and then cut in, in turn, after a player has made a game. Since a score of five hundred is given for the first game and one thousand for the rubber game and since a player who goes down pays all opponents separately, the scoring in towie varies considerably from bridge and also, with its many goulashes and resulting slams, runs considerably higher. Palm Beachers especially enjoy this feature of the game. They find that their two-cents-a-point towie, not unusual at the resort, is roughly comparable to five-cents-a-point bridge; outsiders to the resort, who generally take one full season to learn the game, find it roughly comparable to owning a yacht.

The enjoyment which Palm Beachers, regardless of their wealth, take in winning at towie must be seen to be believed. Many of them maintain special checking accounts for their gambling and they watch over their ups and downs with the same eagerness with which they used to watch the turn of the wheel at Bradley's. Mrs. Horace Dodge, coming out of the Everglades Club one night after an extraordinarily close towie session, was asked how she made out. Mrs. Dodge beamed. "I won *five* dollars," she said. This sum represented approximately one thirty-millionth of her total assets. It was, however, money which she had made herself, which she had seen pass from an opponent directly to her and which was, at that time, far more enjoyable than any amount of good news brought from her seemingly far-removed Detroit bankers concerning stocks, bonds or even tax-exempt securities. Old-time Newporters recall similar instances of this idiosyncrasy at their resort. Washington's Dr. Walter Wells remembers that in the days when Arthur Curtiss James was losing a million dollars a day in the stock market the fact "didn't seem to bother him at all"; at the same time, James was desperately downcast over losing five or six dollars at mah-jongg. "I felt quite ashamed," recalls Dr. Wells, "to take it."

Actually, in these difficult times, towie has bolstered many an otherwise deflated Palm Beach ego to the point where certain Palm Beachers can at least attempt to put on their old-time dog. Some years ago Paulding Fosdick, regarded as the resort's leading towie-player, even went so far as to boast inordinately, in the old-time manner, of the sterling virtues of his butler. Other Palm Beachers, inclined to doubt that such virtues still existed, badgered Fosdick to such an extent that, as they tell the story, Fosdick was placed in such a position that he was obliged to prove his case. Down late in the season and alone in his cottage, he heard his butler coming and suddenly threw himself on his living room floor, held his breath and feigned sudden death; he was confident that his butler, on discovering him, would provide the kind of touching scene which would prove his point for once and for all. The butler entered the room and took one look. "My God," he said, "I've lost my job."

At least one vital tradition of Palm Beach Society still continues intact through all the changes which have taken place. This is the attention to titles. On this subject, since she herself married one of Palm Beach's titular personalities, the American-born Countess Dolly Dorelis ranks as at least one authority. "Foreigners are irresistibly drawn here," she says. "I never could figure out why." Princess Rospigliosi agrees. "They just come down here," she says, "select the house they like, meet the hostess and move in." In fairness to the titles, however, one thing is certain. Even more than Newport, a resort which has always held open house for royalty, or than Tuxedo, notably regal for its size, Palm Beach has had the reputation for having more than met its visitors halfway. One monocled Marquis, for example, just off the boat, was introduced to a Palm Beach lady. In a direct American manner she immediately asked if she might inquire as to the purpose of his trip. The Marquis, taken rather aback, replied that he had not expected to come to Palm Beach at all, that he was actually on his way to visit a lady in Pittsburgh. Then, making a joke of the whole thing, he admitted that he had no money and had been advised to come over to this country and look for a rich American widow. "Look no further, Marquis," said the lady sharply. The Marquis did not; shortly thereafter, in the best Palm Beach tradition, the lady, in between husbands at the time, became a Marchioness.

But if forthright in the actual title search, Palm Beachers have been notably softhearted once the title is trapped. Mrs. Stotesbury, on one memorable occasion, refused to curtsy to the Earl and Countess of Athlone, but, at other times, all the leaders of the resort Society have not only bowed the head and bent the knee but have also cheerfully accepted whatever treatment they have received at the hands of their distinguished visitors. One English Countess, visiting Mrs. Davies, refused to leave at the appointed conclusion of her visit and then remained a full week longer to register her distaste at being reminded of it. This Achilles' heel in an otherwise well-armored Society was perhaps best expressed by the mother of Palm Beach's popular Joseph Leiter, who was once asked why she was so fond of the wife of the British Ambassador, a lady who did not appear to be too fond of her.

Mrs. Leiter thought a moment, then brightened. "She always speaks to me," she said with some pride, "no matter whom she's with."

Assurance of this kind of appealing hospitality have apparently traveled the international grapevine; in any case, waves of visiting titles have regularly washed ashore at Palm Beach ever since the original coconuts. In the Singer-Mizner regime at the Everglades Club their guests included the Prince of Monaco, Prince Philip of Bulgaria, Princess Alexandria, the Grand Duke Nicholas and the Duke du Richelieu, and even as recently as 1951 the associate editor of the *Palm Beach Social Directory* was no less a personage than the Archduke Franz-Josef. The mid-1920's were especially good vintage years for titles, and in 1925, when the present Palm Beach Biltmore was being constructed, so great was the titular enthusiasm that it was decided to name the hotel in honor of the Spanish nobleman, the Duke of Alba, who graciously agreed to come over for the opening celebration. Unfortunately, in spite of elaborate preparations, the Duke did not appear and Palm Beachers were forced to put on the show just as if he had, with Jimmy Cromwell playing the title role. Even Indian princes have been known to cause some consternation at the resort, an example being the recent arrival of India's popular Maharaja of Baroda. The Maharaja, who receives each year a tax-free salary of some 2,000,000 rupees, or $400,000, had the idea, apparently after his first season at Palm Beach, that the princes of India should form themselves into a trade union. While Palm Beachers approved of the plan, Indian authorities did not, and the Indian Government back home took away his title and gave it to his son. Palm Beachers now call him "Major General."

Of late years one of the most familiar figures on the Palm

Beach scene is the arresting Count José Rex Holstein Dorelis, who first came to the resort in 1939. Rumanian-born, the Count is a Count from a country which has no counts. His title was granted him by the King of Bulgaria, and is so often challenged that he usually carries his title papers with him wherever he goes. A perfumer by trade, he carries, besides these papers, not one but two monocles and is also distinguished by a handsome gold tassel which protrudes from an antique flint box in his right rear pocket. Formerly married to Palm Beach's Dolly Dorelis, the Count, born in 1898, married in 1952 a young Hollywood starlet named Margaret Deegan; thus, despite the lack of counts in Rumania, Palm Beach is now able to boast two Rumanian countesses. In a Patio competition, the new Countess Dorelis, who was wearing a pale pink dress with black stripes and old-fashioned hoops, won the prize as Palm Beach's best-dressed lady of the season of 1952. Daughter of a Philadelphia insurance man, she feels that her husband is wasting his time being a perfumer and hopes that he will write plays. "He writes wonderful," she says, "and in nine languages, too." Conscious of the fact that her husband's title is often challenged by cynics, the Countess had no doubts about this herself. "His mother's side," she says, "is all royal." As for her own family, the Countess is equally secure about that. "My grandfather was very wealthy," she says. "Him and Henry Ford were pioneers together."

Among all of Palm Beach's titles, by all odds the most interesting to the Palm Beach man in the street have been, for the past several winters, the Duke and Duchess of Windsor. They began by staying at the Everglades Club on their first trip to this country together, and they have since visited the resort almost every season. To Palm Beachers the Windsors have been, ever since the abdication, the leading figures in a kind of world-wide Viennese opera.

The Duke and Duchess were originally shepherded into the Palm Beach fold by another Englishman, Captain Alistair Mackintosh, popular proprietor of the famous "Alibi" bar—one which was named after him. Son of a Scottish wine merchant, Captain Mackintosh was in turn introduced into the resort by Palm Beach's pioneer title, the Hon. Charles Winn, whose first American wife was a niece of Harry Payne Whitney. Neither Captain Mackintosh nor the Hon. Winn goes to Palm Beach any longer. "I wouldn't take a house there now," says Winn, today a confirmed Southamptonite, "if you gave it to me." Today the Duke and Duchess, although they miss Mackintosh and Winn, have an ever widening circle of friends to make up for their loss. Among these are the Robert R. Youngs, the C. B. Wrightsmans, Mrs. George F. Baker, the first Countess Dorelis, the Rt. Hon. and Mrs. Winston Frederick Churchill Guest, Charles Cushing, Woolworth Donahue, Herbert Pulitzer, Christopher Dunphy and Milton Holden. Mrs. Baker is the daughter-in-law of Tuxedo's great banker, but many of the others who surround the ex-king and his wife are also ex's in their own right. Countess Dorelis is, in her own way, an ex-Countess, Mrs. Guest is both an ex-Boston debutante and an ex-Ziegfeld Follies girl, Mr. Dunphy is an ex-caddy and Mr. Holden is an ex-husband of the popular bride, "Fifi" Widener; altogether the group has been called a "study in perpetual social motion."

Besides this group, the regular Windsor entourage, which precedes their Palm Beach visits, caravan-style, includes two secretaries and two chauffeurs, two personal maids of the Duchess and the Duke's valet, as well as an upstairs maid, a maître d'hôtel and two dogs. The cottage into which they regularly move at the resort is known as "The Towers." Built by the late Leonard Wood of the American Woolen Company, it was next occupied by the late Atwater Kent and is now the property of Robert R. Young. Railroader Young first met the Duke at a small luncheon of businessmen given by Winthrop Aldrich at the Chase Bank in May, 1943, and has been entertaining him both at Newport and Palm Beach, as well as at White Sulphur Springs, ever since. But Young does not come under the old Palm Beach poem about people whose parents came over in steerage entertaining only the peerage; his father, in fact, was an American cowboy. Furthermore, he makes clear that he has often visited the Windsors, not only in France, which is their favored residence, but also elsewhere, and that he is as socially obligated to them as they are to him. At the same time, a keen student of protocol, he grants his visitors all the various prerogatives which, though they evidently irritated the Duke at the time he was King, have become increasingly important, at least to those around him, now that he is not.

Among these prerogatives, invariably fascinating to outsiders, is the fact that all guests must be assembled at any function, down to a breakfast, at which the Duke and Duchess are to appear, and all must be briefed as to the correct form of address and in the matter of the curtsy. The Duke, who is addressed simply as "Sir," is entitled to the curtsy at all times, while the Duchess, who is not entitled to the curtsy, is addressed as "Your Grace." These matters, which have proved ticklish to American Society in other parts of the country, are faithfully observed at Palm Beach, at least in the Windsor circle, a group which includes such excellent curtsyers as Mrs. Young, Mrs. Wrightsman, Mrs. Boettcher, and Countess Dorelis. Even more important is the matter of table-seating. At the Youngs, for example, the Duchess is not placed at Mr. Young's right at dinner, Mr. Young instead is at the Duchess' right, and the Duke and Duchess, not Mr. and Mrs. Young, are at the heads of the table. In this matter Palm Beach follows the ancient English custom. Since every house, down to the meanest cottage, technically at least, belonged to the King, he has always sat at the head of the table wherever he was. Recently, according to the Lord Chamberlain, England has changed this custom. Palm Beach, however, still abides by it.

If the Duke and Duchess have been to recent Palm Beachers the most interesting of the resort's titled visitors, to old-timers they are clearly outranked in lasting fame by the Hon. Hugo Cecil Levinge Rumbold. A short, dapper gentleman, the half-brother of a British Ambassador to Germany, Rumbold spoke with a pronounced stammer and was, in his pre-Palm Beach days, a stage artist and theatrical designer, a Lieutenant in the British Grenadier Guards and a Chevalier of the Order of Leopold of Belgium. At Palm Beach he was known primarily as an accomplished mimic, one who could impersonate anyone from a Japanese statesman giving a speech to a Palm Beach hostess giving a party. At various times he took every male title in the Palm Beach book, as well as several female ones. At such times, during his female impersonations, his stammering, which he claimed had been the result of spending a night in a haunted house as a child, deserted him almost completely.

On one occasion creating the role of an English Countess at a Stotesbury fancy dress ball, Hugo went through the entire evening undetected even by his closest friends. Palm Beach's only irritation with his performance occurred some time later when it was discovered that he had used the ladies' dressing room in preference to the men's. At another time Rumbold's career extended to Sarasota. Having fallen in love with a Palm Beach interior decorator, who was opening a branch of her business at the famous Florida West Coast resort, Rumbold followed faithfully along in the capacity of her personal maid. Visiting the Honore Palmers and other Sarasota families, he spent several weeks at the resort and even emerged unscathed from a beach party where the Sarasotians, hearing the refined maid of their Palm Beach visitor begin stuttering in a peculiar male voice, merely thought that the maid was doing an impersonating act of a man. Rumbold's final escapade was his most brilliant. Having fallen in love again, this time with a Palm Beach married lady, he persuaded her to take him, along with her husband, on a trip to Europe; again the disguise was as the personal maid and, according to Palm Beachers at least, on the entire trip, through six countries and back, Rumbold was never discovered by the lady's husband.

Unfortunately for Palm Beach, the Hon. Hugo, in many ways a throwback to the great days of the resort, turned respectable in time. Marrying the distinguished playwright Zoë Akins, he spent the last years of his life, at his own wish, in relative social obscurity. Even his friends were sternly forbidden to recall memories of his illustrious past. As for his death, this occurred, ironically enough, at what might be considered, at least in comparison to Palm Beach, at the bottom of the social scale. Suffering a heart attack, he succumbed in a dentist chair in Hollywood, California.

Illustrations

"Shadowbrook," a Berkshire "cottage." (*Berkshire Eagle.*) *Inset:* A flower-bedecked coach—part of one of the Berkshires' famous "Tub Parades." "Shadowbrook," built by Anson Phelps Stokes at Lenox, contains 100 rooms. In 1916 it was bought by Andrew Carnegie and following his death there in 1922 it was sold, like so many resort cottages since, to the Roman Catholic Church. To this cottage Canon Anson Phelps Stokes, son of the builder and a young man attending Yale in the class of 1896, wired his mother, ARRIVING THIS EVENING WITH CROWD OF NINETY-SIX MEN—only to receive from Mrs. Stokes the return wire, MANY GUESTS ALREADY HERE. HAVE ONLY ROOM FOR FIFTY.

Bailey's Beach at Newport. *Inset:* Swimming in the old days. (*Underwood & Underwood.*) Until 1947 no photographer was ever permitted inside Bailey's and newspapers and picture magazines were reduced to attempting either airplane shots or telephoto-lens exposure from neighboring rocks. To mark the historic occasion the first magazine permitted was the *National Geographic,* and here, by courtesy of that magazine, is the resulting picture.

Reception Day at the old Bar Harbor Reading Room. *Inset:* Lawn party, "Mistletoe Cottage," Jekyll Island. Bar Harbor's Reading Room rarely admitted ladies and was at one time the most exclusive of all resort clubs. Now site of new Hotel Bar Harbor.

Left: A present-day New York model, Argentina-born Gloria Case, outside the Springs House at White Sulphur in an old-time Southern Belle costume designed by Dorothy Draper and Helene Pons. "Florence," Greenbrier Mammy, arranges the gown. *Right:* Saratoga's Grand Union Hotel, last of the great nineteenth-century caravansaries, soon to be torn down. The amount of marble in the hotel would cover a solid acre; the amount of carpeting, twelve acres. (*H. B. Settle.*)

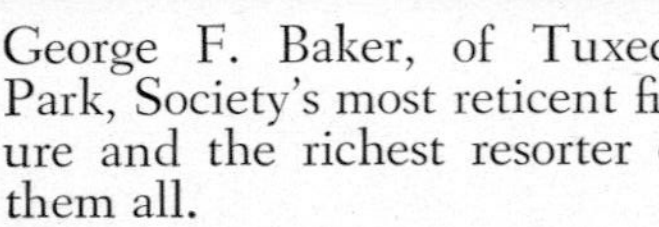

George F. Baker, of Tuxedo Park, Society's most reticent figure and the richest resorter of them all.

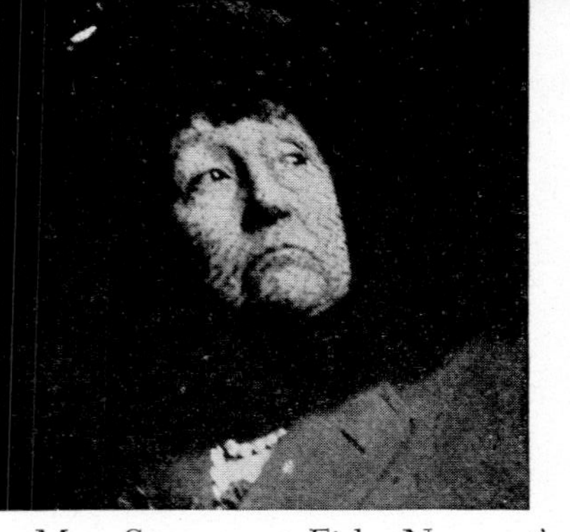

Above: Mrs. Stuyvesant Fish, Newport's *enfant terrible*. *Below:* Jewel queens. Mrs. E. T. Stotesbury vs. Mrs. Evalyn Walsh McLean and the Hope Diamond.

Joseph H. Choate, of the Berkshires, Society's greatest wit and the most popular resorter of his day.

The three great eras of resort life. *Left:* The Gay Nineties. Tuxedo's Mrs. Grenville Kane at Narragansett Pier. *Center:* The Boom Twenties. Mr. and Mrs. E. T. Stotesbury at Palm Beach. (*Underwood & Underwood.*) *Right:* Today. The Duke and Duchess of Windsor and "Mr. Thomas," outside the Robert Youngs' cottage at Newport.

Southampton. Looking across Lake Agawam from swimming pool of the Southampton Beach Club. *Left to right*, the cottages visible are those of Chester Dale, Mrs. Dwight Davis, Sr., and Mrs. Goodhue Livingston. In pool is John Funk, grandson of Southampton's Wilfred Funk. *Below:* Facing the other way, the Beach Club with reflection from pool during the annual August Full Moon Ball. (*Irving Cantor*.)

Palm Springs, California. The Racquet Club pool. (*Bernard of Hollywood.*) From the springboard of this pool the dive of Charles Farrell, in white tie, top hat and tails, during the annual fashion show officially opens each Palm Springs social season. *Below:* The way Palm Springs was promoted in its early days. Underwater picture at El Mirado pool of embrace between swimmer Marjorie Gestring and diver Harold "Dutch" Smith. (*Acme Photo.*)

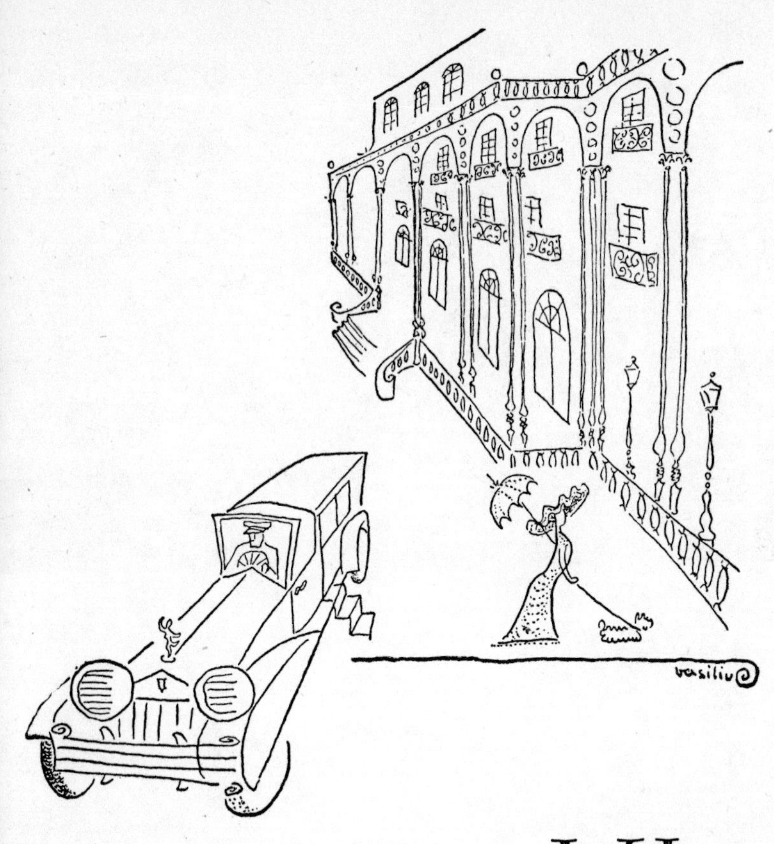

VI

Saratoga and the Social Springs —White, Hot, Sweet and Palm

Of all the gay places the world can afford,
By gentle and simple for pastime adored,
Fine balls and fine singing, fine buildings and springs
Fine rides and fine views, and a thousand fine things
(Not to mention the sweet situation and air),
What place with these springs can ever compare?
First in manners, in dress, and in fashions to shine,
Saratoga, the glory must ever be thine!

As THE story of this country's great social resorts begins with a spring, the little village of Stafford Springs, Connecticut, so it is proper that it should end with one, *le dernier cri* itself, Palm Springs, California. In between, however, it is also proper to consider the rise and fall of this country's two greatest social springs—Saratoga, the king of the Northern Springs, and, considered together, Saratoga's Southern counterparts, the famous Virginia Springs, the old White, the old Warm, the old Hot, the old Sweet, and the old Salt. All of these are, of course, spas rather than resorts, and it should be made clear at the outset that the word "spa," known to moderns only as a drugstore, is not only far more venerable than any drugstore but also implies, in contrast to the word "resort," the presence of mineral springs, either for drinking, for bathing or for both.

The poem quoted above was originally penned in honor of the venerable spa of Bath, England; it was adapted for the use of Saratoga by an anonymous Saratoga poet as far back as 1830. Saratoga itself goes much further back than that. Second in age only to the Virginia Springs, it goes back, like

Stafford Springs, to the Indians, its pioneer non-Indian springsgoer being the Hon. Sir William Johnson, British Superintendent of Indian Affairs. Sir William visited the Mohawks' "Medicine Waters of the Great Spirit," later called the High Rock Spring, in August, 1767, but the springs were then secret and Sir William was permitted to visit them only because he was popular among the Indians and was, in fact, called the "Great White Father"—a title which he did his best to maintain since he sired, through a succession of Indian mistresses, no less than one hundred children. Saratoga's own name is also of Indian origin. It is derived from a contraction of the Iroquois word "*Se-rach-to-que*." Unhappily, this word was, up until ten years ago, translated by an official publication of New York State as "Floating Scum upon the Water." To Saratogians—they are never called just "Saratogans"—who have had a good deal to put up with in these modern times, the translation was the last straw, and they finally prevailed upon the authorities to make a new one. Today "*Se-rach-to-que*" is translated, far more satisfactorily, "Hillside Country of a Great River."

However good this current translation is as Indian scholarship, it is not so good as a description of the resort today. Saratoga is not on a hill and it is not by a river; in fact, it can honestly lay no claim to being a beauty spot at all. Saratoga has its famous Saratoga Lake which was in the old days a center of intercollegiate rowing, but this is the only body of water anywhere around, and while the mountains may be seen from certain vantage points the land is generally flat and there is no such scenic splendor as at Bar Harbor. The contrasting charms of Newport, with its Colonial downtown and its cottage-castle uptown, or of Palm Beach, with its Mizner *palazzi* mixed with modern Fifth Avenue stores, are missing.

Saratoga has contrasts, all right, but they are not necessarily charming ones. The railroad tracks still cross Saratoga's main street, its famous Broadway, and, although the train passengers no longer hang out the windows to see the Society, as they did in the old days, Broadway itself is still in places a handsome tree-lined sight.

At the same time, Broadway, and indeed Saratoga in general, is, in many other places, a crowded jumble of honky-tonk hotels and motels, roadhouses and boardinghouses. A town which has, in fact, no industry except health and recreation, Saratoga also offers its Skidmore College, where over one thousand girls come from all parts of the country, and its Yaddo, where, as at the MacDowell Colony in Peterboro, New Hampshire, real live authors and artists may be seen in what their patrons apparently believe are their natural habitats. The name "Yaddo," incidentally, is not of Indian origin. As Yaddo's struggling poets tire of explaining to Yaddo sight-seers, the four-year-old daughter of Saratoga's late Spencer Trask made up the word in a not entirely successful attempt to pronounce the word "shadow."

Saratoga's chief contrast is, of course, the fact that it has, on the one hand, the country's oldest continuously operating race track—at least except during World War II—and on the other, the country's most modern spa development—the ten-million-dollar Saratoga Springs Authority. Here there are three bathhouses, the Lincoln, Washington and Roosevelt (F. D.), a "Hall of Springs" offering the three famous Saratoga waters, the Geyser, Hathorn and Coesa, the Gideon Putnam Hotel, which is named for Saratoga's first hotel-builder, as well as a Research Institute and all manner of recreational facilities, including a therapeutic golf course where no grade runs steeper than 5 per cent. In 1951 the per cent of ailments of Spa Association patients ran as follows: heart trouble, 31 per cent; rheumatic conditions, 24 per cent; stomach and intestinal disorders, 18 per cent; nervous conditions, 8 per cent; glandular disturbances, 4 per cent; skin diseases, 2 per cent; miscellaneous, 3 per cent; and no disease but generally "run-down," 10 per cent. Although many old-time resorters who stop at Saratoga for post-Newport or post-Palm Beach recuperative periods still persist in the old regimen of twenty-one baths—because of the old belief in the magic value in a multiple of the number seven—the doctors at the Spa Association take little stock in the old mystic traditions and their modern regimen contrasts sharply with a guidebook's description of the benefit of Saratoga waters, as of the year 1821:

> The most prominent and perceptible effects of these waters when taken into the stomach are Cathartick, Diuretick and Tonick. They are much used in a great variety of complaints; but the diseases in which they are most efficacious are, Jaundice and billious affections generally, Dyspepsia, Habitual Costiveness, Hypochondrical Complaints, Depraved appetite, Calculous and nephritic complaints, Phagedenic or ill conditioned species or states of gout, some species of dropsy, Scrofula, paralysis, Scorbutic affections and old Scorbutic ulcers, Amenorrhea, Dysmenorrhea and Chlorosis.

Most social resorts are not around the corner, and Saratoga is no exception. Located in northern New York State at the gateway to the Adirondacks, Saratoga is, if it is around the corner from anywhere, around from Albany, from which it is thirty-five miles north and which is a difficult city to avoid if one drives to the Springs from New York. A hazard of going to Saratoga even in the height of its August racing season—when the year-round population of fifteen thousand swells to over forty thousand—is the possibility of going to Saratoga itself. Saratoga is where the Battle of Saratoga was fought and it is fourteen miles away from Saratoga *Springs,* which is where the resort is, and which is always called, confusingly enough, Saratoga. As for the hazard of going to Saratoga in any off-season period, the sad possibilities of this were illustrated shortly before World War II when the novelist, Edna Ferber, persuaded the playwright, George Kaufman, to accompany her on a tour of inspection of the resort in a winter season. Miss Ferber intended, with Mr. Kaufman's collaboration, to write a play about Saratoga, but Mr. Kaufman, who had a cold anyway, was almost overcome by his first encounter with a draught whistling down a hotel corridor. Promptly he turned around and went back to New York, refusing to have anything more to do with the project. Equally promptly Miss Ferber decided to write a novel instead of a play and shortly thereafter gave birth to *Saratoga Trunk.*

Miss Ferber's "trunk" was a railroad trunk line over which millionaires were squabbling for control, but her title was also, of course, a play on the words of the real Saratoga trunk. Iron-bound and, to the despair of porters, curved on top, this wondrous piece of luggage spread Saratoga's fame far and wide a century ago. It took two strong men to lift and was capable of holding a month's changes even for the clotheshorse belles of those bygone years.

Almost equally renowned was the Saratoga chip, a specialty which was to the Saratoga potato even more than the popover was to the Bar Harbor biscuit. First served almost exactly one hundred years ago, at Moon's Lake House in 1853, the development of the chip was the result of a cook's outburst of temper. The cook of the old Moon's was an irascible half-breed named George Crum, the son of a mulatto jockey and an Indian woman. No man to trifle with, he had no less than five wives, all of whom he apparently kept happy at once and all of whom served as waitresses in his establishment. When a fastidious diner sent back Crum's French fried potatoes with the comment that he wished them sliced thinner, Crum, in the time-honored manner of cooks, hit the ceiling. He shaved off some potato slices paper-thin, wrapped them in a napkin and plunged them into a tub of ice water. Then, after he had kept the diner waiting for a full half hour, he first dropped the chilled slices into a kettle of boiling grease, then ladled them out and salted them, and, finally, more or less as a practical joke, sent them in to the diner by one of his wife-waitresses. Instead of the commotion and indignation Crum expected, the diner promptly called for more. Then and there the Saratoga chip was born. Moon's immediately saw in the discovery an excellent thirst-producer, one well calculated to increase liquor consumption, and that very day distributed the chips free to patrons in paper cornucopias; by the next day chips were placed in a huge bowl on the bar with a sign reading, Saratoga style, "HELP YOURSELF."

As it took more than the Tuxedo coat and the Palm Beach suit to make those resorts, so it took more than a trunk and a potato chip to make Saratoga. Two other items sufficed. One was the growth of gambling; the other was the growth of the grand hotel. The "elegant hells" were what Saratoga's gambling casinos were called in their great days—and, poetically enough, the grand hotels were primarily famous for their "elegant belles." Today, of course, the sad state of both the hells and the belles, Saratoga's two great recreational commodities, is responsible for the sad fact that no great resort is more a shadow of its former social self than Saratoga. Except for the one month of pari-mutuel day flat racing and three months of excellent pari-mutuel night harness racing, gambling at Saratoga is today as dead as it is anywhere east of Nevada. A guard at Canfield's famous old red Club House, which has ever since 1911 been a part of Canfield Park, expresses it briefly. "We've all got Kefauver Fever," he says. Furthermore, despite the fact that Canfield's has downstairs an excellent new Museum of Racing, the Club House's old museum upstairs boasts not a single memento of Saratoga's greatest gambler, and instead stocks only a quaint collection of armor, old costumes and Indian relics. Elsewhere in the Club House a recent visitor to what was once the most elegant of all Saratoga's "elegant hells" was amazed to find a thriving convention of—of all people—Jehovah's Witnesses.

No less extraordinary is Saratoga's hotel situation. Of Saratoga's great nineteenth-century hostelries, the first of which was built in 1802, only one remains. This building, the Grand Union, which was not built but *rebuilt* in 1864—parts of it go back to 1836—still gives Saratoga's Broadway what nineteenth-century atmosphere remains at the resort, but the Union's esteemed contemporary, the United States Hotel, was a World War II casualty. Furthermore, following the razing of the "States," a bulldozer was brought in and the old elms which shaded the court of the hotel were uprooted. Of all the unkind blows which modern times have dealt Saratoga, nothing today rankles old Saratogians as much as the matter of these trees. In the old days a village bylaw provided for a highway tax rebate of sixty-two and a half cents for each tree planted by a taxpayer, and Saratogians, with such inducement, planted with a will. One old-timer in the 1850's planted with his own hands a row of 360 maples. But the elms were always particularly sacred at Saratoga and it was almost unbearable that one wanton bulldozer should destroy, almost in one afternoon, elms which had stood for three-quarters of a century.

Whether death, as it must to all grand hotels, will come with equal outrage to the Grand Union, no one knows. But one thing is certain; the handwriting is on the wall. In fact, the handwriting may be said to be literally on the wall because, for the past two summers, a sign over the Union's basement advertises the fact that the last of Saratoga's caravansaries has now gone into its own antique business. "ORIGINAL ANTIQUES FOR SALE," the sign reads. "PERIOD FURNITURE USED AT THE TIME OF LILLIAN RUSSELL, DIAMOND JIM BRADY, OTIS SKINNER, VICTOR HERBERT, JOHN DREW, A. T. STEWART." One of the last chances to save the Union appears to have disappeared with the recent attempt of Cornelius Vanderbilt Whitney to buy the hotel and make it some kind of permanent Saratoga memorial. Nebulous as some parts of the plan were, the idea was highly applauded, and when Whitney's offer was met by such a staggering increase in the asking price that even he could not meet it, old Saratogians, bitterly discouraged, all but gave up the ghost. Today they have some hope that the state will take over the Union and use it as a base for the State University which is about to be ousted from Plattsburg—but this, too, remains nebulous. Currently only in the month of August is the Grand Union open at all, and, even at that time, it is only partly open. The 306-foot long main dining hall, where the gourmets of yesterday did battle, thrice daily, is now for the first time closed even in August, and it is a safe prediction that the day is coming, in another August or two, when Saratoga will be without any grand hotels at all.

This is a pity. In the same way Newport's "Breakers" and Palm Beach's "Playa Reinte" are the end of their eras, Saratoga's Grand Union is the end of its era; indeed, in many ways, it is perhaps the most nostalgic sight of the Good Old Days of resorts which is still visible. Outside, its white-elephantine splendor is actually enhanced by its grotesque gingerbread architecture and it still boasts, from ballroom to bandstand, the longest single porch in the world—just over a quarter of a mile. Inside, many of its features date to Civil War days, including black walnut staircases, mahogany bedroom suites, massive imported French mirrors, Irish hand-pointed needlework draperies and Waterford cut crystal chandeliers adorning hand-frescoed ceilings. The barroom, with its original solid mahogany bar, remains today just as it did when General Grant bent an elbow there, and the hotel elevators, among the first ever installed by the brothers Otis, are still operated by the same steam engine which first operated them in 1875. The amount of marble in the hotel would cover a solid acre; the amount of carpeting would cover more than twelve acres.

Among the sights still to be seen in this last stand of the nineteenth century, none is more awe-inspiring than the so-called "Grand Centennial Painting." This work, which is actually entitled "The Genius of America," hangs in the main ballroom. One of the largest paintings in the world, it was commissioned in 1870 from the French artist, Yvon, by A. T. Stewart, the dry-goods merchant. Reputed to be one of the three wealthiest men in the country of his time—Commodore Vanderbilt and John Jacob Astor were the other two—Stewart had originally commissioned the painting for his New York home but when Yvon had finished—he took two years and charged Stewart $100,000—Stewart found that he could not even get the painting into his house, let alone hang it there. Promptly he shipped it up to the Grand Union—a hotel which he had bought in 1872 in an attempt to realize his ambition to "own the largest hotel in the world." Today this "Grand Centennial Painting," which ever since 1876 has covered, from floor to ceiling, the entire west wall of the Union ballroom, is valued at a sum considerably in excess of the crumbling hotel around it, and no visit to Saratoga is complete without a careful scrutiny not only of the painting itself but also of the description of its allegory. According to a recent brochure of the hotel, the painting "depicts America, represented by a beautiful woman of Amazonian stature and proportions, dispensing from a huge Horn of Plenty, learning, culture, healing and largesse generally, to the assembled nations of the world."

James Gordon Bennett once called Saratoga the "seraglio of the prurient aristocracy." Translating "seraglio" as harem, and "prurient" as lewd, the description was not a flattering one. Nor can it be denied that in Saratoga's great days its houses of ill fame were a vital part of its total resort picture. Madame Grace Sinclair and Madame Landry, and later Hattie Adams, were by no means backward about exhibiting their wares, and no coaching parade to the lake, race track, or Club House was complete without the sight of their girls sitting, complete with picture hats and parasols, like a carefully thought-out flower arrangement, on top of handsomely appointed coaches.

Despite Mr. Bennett and the Mesdames, Saratoga's grand hotels were, in the days of the 1880's and 1890's, extremely circumspect about the registration of the male and the female without benefit of marital vows. There were, of course, exceptions. At the United States Hotel one day, the resort sport, Evander Berry Wall, King of the Dudes, signed in with his manservant. "Wall and Valet," he wrote. Wall was followed by the millionaire horse-breeder, "White Hat" McCarty and a young lady friend. McCarty first looked at the Wall signature and then at his lady friend, then seized the pen. "McCarty," he wrote, "and Valise."

Mr. McCarty, whose son still lives in Saratoga as a handicapper, was admitted, but the case was a rare one. Beyond this refinement, the hotels maintained a strict feminine curfew. When the old-time Saratogian staggered up to the steps of the so-called "Millionaires' Piazza" of the old States, or to the Grand Union, he was by no means a free man. After eleven o'clock every entrance of the States and the Union, except the main one, was locked, and even this was guarded by a husky attendant. The latter not only refused to chaperon any unregistered ladies but also maintained a corps of assistants who all night long patrolled the lengthy piazzas against any attempt at female bootlegging. Such severity, which is contrary to the general view of the Saratoga of those days, was, of course, responsible for the immediate social popularity of the adjoining hotel cottages. Here, no such conventions were applied. "In accordance," said Saratoga's late Hugh Bradley, "with the still-prevalent American belief that sin becomes somehow sanctified if a sitting room is attached to the bedchamber, the cottages solved the problems of numerous lonesome Wall Street tycoons and Western copper kings."

In certain instances Saratoga's love-in-a-cottage motif reached extraordinary heights. One oil millionaire is still remembered as being so occupied with business that he was forced to share his cottage with no less than five secretaries. The number of beautiful but obscure nieces who also took up cottage-keeping for their uncles was also extraordinary. Just how many proper Saratogians were fooled by the fiction, and how many overlooked the fact, it is difficult to say, but a story of President Chester A. Arthur is perhaps typical of the majority spirit. The President, snubbed by Mrs. DeWitt Clinton, was nonetheless given a dinner by another Saratoga hostess and was asked for his views on alcohol. "Madam," he said, "I may be President of the United States, but my private life is nobody's damn business."

The importance of the hotel cottages—which, as has been noted, started the use of the word "cottage" to begin with—cannot be overestimated in its future effect on Saratoga Society. The cottage colonies of Newport and Bar Harbor and the other great resorts were soon entirely free of their hotel beginnings—at Newport the hotels all but disappeared entirely—but at Saratoga, where the grand hotels still flourished, the cottage colony still retained the gay, early-day spirit. One manifestation of this gaiety was in the mixing of Society with stage celebrities. Up until the First World War there was at other resorts a great gulf between Society and the stage; even Newport's Mrs. Fish failed to break it down completely. "You must remember," said Berry Wall, who spoke for the Newport-Tuxedo circuit, "that Broadway only cuts across Fifth Avenue; it never parallels it." Saratoga's Broadway did parallel it. What Harry Lehr and Mrs. Fish were to Newport, Diamond Jim Brady and Lillian Russell were, in their way, to Saratoga, and while neither that well-traveled salesman nor "that woman," as old-time Saratogians still recall her, would have attempted setting up cottage-keeping at Newport, they were, at Saratoga, the uncrowned rulers of the spa.

Nor did Saratoga's gaiety end with Diamond Jim and Miss Russell. Palm Beach's Mrs. George A. McKinlock, a relatively recent convert to Saratoga, finds the spa far gayer, at least in one respect, than the Beach. "Liaisons are accepted in Saratoga," she says. "They haven't yet been in Palm Beach." Mrs. Dodge Sloane, also of both Palm Beach and Saratoga, finds the latter so gay that she often makes it a point to take the Saratoga baths for two weeks before the August season even starts. Mrs. Sloane feels that Palm Beach has been, as she puts it, in "a social slump" but she feels that, at Saratoga, Society, apparently something like hope, springs eternal. "It's a fascinating place," she says. "Everybody in the world comes to Saratoga in August."

Equally sure of the gaiety is such a relatively new Saratogian as Mrs. John A. Morris, the former Edna Brokaw, whose husband is the vice-president of the Saratoga Association for the Improvement of the Breed of Horses. "It's a fun gay wonderful four-week job," she says. Mrs. Morris feels that raising horses is very expensive but that this is all the better from the point of view of Society. "You see," she explains, "it's so expensive that it takes more than one generation of money." Mrs. Morris also feels that, for Saratoga Society, one should be, as she puts it, "internationally geared." "Otherwise," she says, "you're a character and then the party has to be just for you or for people who can get along with you." Certainly Mrs. Morris' own August life at the spa is a highly geared one. "We only have two guest rooms full of guests," she says, "two couples, that is, because we feel that six in the total group with my husband and myself is enough. We have breakfast seven-thirty to eleven, trays going up, guests coming down, then tennis or nine holes of golf or perhaps even a drink of the waters, then back before lunch to kiss or spank the children depending on their behavior, then off to the track for lunch and the races, then back either to go to a cocktail party or give one, then either go to a dinner or give one, then bridge or Canasta till I don't know when—well, one, maybe—then bed. The next day we get up and do it all over again—for four weeks."

Gay as this resort regimen sounds, it is not, in the opinion of older Saratogians, anything to what the resort was in the old days. "Saratoga today," says Mrs. Edward Hamilton Hough, "is no more like the old days than anything in the world." Mrs. Hough, one of the distinguished Vassar sisters of Ballston Spa, ranks as a *grande dame* of a resort which goes back to the eighteenth century and looks on Saratoga as a nineteenth-century upstart. As of 1952 Mrs. Hough feels that the chief difference between the Saratoga Society of yesterday and the Saratoga Society of today is that, today, there is no such thing as Saratoga Society. In the old days, she remembers, people came for all summer long. Nowadays they either come for a short while, as at Virginia Hot Springs, to take the waters and baths following the Newport or Palm Beach seasons, or else they are the horse Society which comes just for August for the races. In the latter case, Mrs. Hough is not at all sure she is glad they come at all. "Horse Society," she says, "is a hodgepodge. It's anybody who owns a horse."

Evelyn Barrett Britten of *The Saratogian*, a lady who has been writing up Saratoga Society ever since 1910, agrees with Mrs. Hough's view: "You can get into Saratoga Society today," she says, "if you want to." Mrs. Britten feels that there has not been an acknowledged leader of Saratoga Society for so long that even she, Saratoga's official historian, cannot recall one. "I guess you have to go back to the Civil War," she says.

Saratoga's summer cottage directory would seem a point in

proof of these changes. It is now reduced to the point where it is nothing more than a typewritten list put out by the local real estate agent. While this directory still boasts such eminent racing names as Iselins and Igleharts, Whitneys and Wideners, Vanderbilts and Von Stades, it cannot, even though it separately lists all clubs and hotels, muster even a "One Hundred," let alone a "Four Hundred." Compared with today's cottage rentals, which often run well under $1,000, Saratogians can recall rentals in the summer of 1929 which ranged as high as $10,500; this sum Mrs. R. Amcotts Wilson received for "Broadview," a none too elaborate cottage on North Broadway, and for just the month of August. In those days August rentals of $6,000 or better were by no means unusual and were cheerfully paid by such upper-case Saratogians as Virginia "Birdie" Vanderbilt, "Sally" Hitt. Harry Sinclair and William Ziegler.

Saratoga never went in for marble palaces and baroque villas in the manner of Newport. In fact, old Saratogians regard as typical of old-fashioned Saratoga summer living a cottage known as "Inniscarra," the home of the late Irish songster, Chauncey Olcott. One of Saratoga's best-remembered hostesses, Mrs. Olcott, who died in 1949, chose the cottage, which was always called "The Candy House," for just one reason—its apple trees—but the place was especially beloved by her song-writing and singing husband, a man who was born in Buffalo and never saw Ireland until he was famous and went over to brush up on his brogue. Mrs. Edmund Johnstone, the former Janet Olcott Cavanagh and the present owner of "The Candy House," rented the cottage for the summer of 1952 to Mrs. Widener Wichfeld; she herself feels that Saratoga is nothing like it was. Mrs. Johnstone remembers as a young girl getting out of bed on nights of dinner parties and rushing first to stick her head through the banisters and see the grownups inside and then rushing to the windows to watch them outside. She liked the garden sights best. "It was all lit up," she recalls, "and it seemed to me like fairyland. It was very romantic, too. I even saw Sam Riddle and Elizabeth Arden spooning." Today Mrs. Johnstone feels so strongly about what has happened to the resort that she would very much like to move "The Candy House" out of Saratoga altogether. "I'd like to move it to Long Island or Connecticut or somewhere," she says, "but they gave me an estimate on it and they said it would cost $100,000."

John Hay Whitney and his sister, Mrs. Charles Shipman Payson, joint owners of the famous Greentree Stables of their late mother, Mrs. Payne Whitney, also recall their childhood life at Saratoga with relish. "We used to feel sorry for our Newport cousins," says Mrs. Payson. "We had a wonderful time. We dressed in overalls all the time. We were the other side of snobs." Although Mrs. Payson is now a Hobe Sounder and her brother is a Fishers Islander, and they spend only the August racing season at the spa, they make clear that their love of Saratoga has never been financially motivated. They recall that their mother made money out of Greentree only one year out of all the years she ran it, and despite the fact that they have already had two winning years out of the eight they have run the stables, they do not feel that horse-racing is a money-making proposition.

Other Saratoga Society stable-owners support this view. In their opinion the only owners who regularly make money are the so-called "gyp," or gypsy, stables; these have only one or two horses and just enter them in races when they know they have an excellent chance to win. Saratogian Alfred Gwynne Vanderbilt, who was running his own stable at the age of twenty-one, won $300,000 in purses one of his first years. He was asked how the stable had made out for the whole year. "They haven't figured it out yet," said Vanderbilt. "I'm either ten dollars ahead or ten dollars behind."

Saratoga's beloved "Three Musketeers," actor Monty Woolley, humorist Frank Sullivan and ex-Mayor Clarence Knapp, all of whom live in the resort the year round, are particularly amazed at the changes. Today Knapp, a distinguished Saratoga historian, has formed with Sullivan a two-man Society for the Restoration and Preservation of Nineteenth-Century Saratoga. "We are keeping Woolley out," says Sullivan. "That's what clubs are for, aren't they? Anyway, he didn't get here until he was almost three years old. He's a carpetbagger."

For his part Woolley, the Third Musketeer, yields to no one in his love of the old days. The son of the Grand Union's great proprietor, W. Edgar Woolley, Monty recalls that his father had no worries about the fact that W. B. Gage, proprietor of the United States Hotel, had a higher proportion of the *haut monde* than the Grand Union. "Gage can have the Vanderbilts," the elder Woolley once declared. "I'll take the money." As a young boy Monty remembers morning and evening symphony concerts, band music and floral *fêtes*, as well as balls which would open at either the Grand Union or the United States, move on to Congress Hall and then back to whichever hotel, the Union or the States, they had not begun. When he was four years old Woolley got his thespian start by dancing a sailor's hornpipe on a grass stage; on his seventh birthday he was allowed to conduct Victor Herbert's fifty-four-piece symphony orchestra in the "Little Edgar Polka." "There was in those days," he says, "a wonderful slow tempo to life. Even the weather was warmer. God, what a lovely time it was to live!" Today Woolley believes the times have passed Saratoga by. A Yale man, he is particularly unimpressed with the kind of present-day greeting offered by F. S. Von Stade, a Harvard man and president of the Saratoga Association for the Improvement of the Breed of Horses. "Every year," says Woolley, "Skiddy gives me two languid Harvard fingers for a handshake."

Even the younger members of Saratoga's horse Society seem to have quieted down in the opinion of old-timers. It was only yesterday, they feel, when such youngsters were really horsing around in style. Although they do not like to dwell on the more difficult case histories, such as those of Cornelius Vanderbilt Whitney, "Fifi" Widener or Mrs. Dodge Sloane, they enjoy recalling the gayer episodes—how, for example, "Liz" Whitney used to wear an emerald necklace with riding clothes one day and the next would arrive at the track, direct from a night club, wearing an evening dress and accompanied by a small herd of dogs. They also recall the time when "Ella" Widener threw an egg at a judge in night court, and when young Alfred Gwynne Vanderbilt sent a hopeless horse out to race in the Saratoga Cup, and, knowing his jockey would be out a long time, gave him, in lieu of riding orders, a sandwich, a container of milk and a wrist compass.

Today, old-timers feel, all these comparative youngsters have completely deserted their character roles. C. V. or "Sonny" Whitney has married an ex-choir-singer and happily raises Black Angus cattle, "Liz" Whitney has married a doctor named Perssons and lives relatively quietly, albeit still with her dogs, in Virginia, and even the still incredibly young-looking Alfred Vanderbilt has given up his wild-oats days and settled down with one of Southampton's Murray girls. Further back, the old-timers look back to the even wilder days when old Sam Riddle, owner of Man o' War, was in his prime and was serving mint juleps at all hours of the night; conversely, Colonel Edward Riley Bradley was—in all hours of the morning—serving his famous stable breakfasts which began with the dawntime "breezes," or workouts of the horses, and often lasted until racetime.

The late George H. Bull, who was president of the Saratoga Racing Association until his recent death, was perhaps the resort's most noted personality. A brother of Aiken's Henry Bull, who lives at what is undoubtedly the country's most correct resort address—the corner of Whiskey Road and Easy Street—George used to rent three adjoining houses at Saratoga each summer, and, a baldish, paunchy bachelor variously called "Judge" and "Ferdinand," Bull would dispense lavish hospitality which began with his own habit of drinking a dozen cocktails before dinner. Bull maintained that horse Society was difficult at best. "Horses are like children," he used to say. "Everybody wants to talk about their own horses but nobody wants to hear about other people's." By the end of his life Bull was also convinced that the pari-mutuel would be the finishing blow to Saratoga socially—an opinion which, since he died in 1942 three years after the pari-mutuels appeared, he lived to see well substantiated.

Old Saratogians agree that the best place to see what is left of Saratoga horse Society is in the annual yearling sales which occur during the second and third weeks of August. Held at nine o'clock in the evening, the show opens with the arrival, one by one, of the elders of Saratoga Society in their chauffeur-driven limousines. Moving past the bright lights of the boxing-ring enclosures, they take their box seats with their time-honored assurance. Then, one by one, the horses themselves are brought in to stand, in the bright lights, usually with considerably less assurance. A groom holds the horse in front, a stableboy sweeps up behind, and an auctioneer sounds off: "Ladies and gentlemen, that's mighty little money and a whole lot of horse." The bids are not delivered to the auctioneer at all but are relayed by delicate signals forwarded by ushers in the aisles. Indeed, so delicate are these signals that, for a nonbidding spectator, it is dangerous to make any motion at all; turf-writer Joe Palmer recalls accepting a $15,000 bid by a gentleman who was trying to brush a fly off his neck.

Like the Saratoga race track, which is known as the graveyard of favorites, the yearling sales have over the years provided some startling results. The most famous yearling ever sold, of course, was Man o' War, who went to Sam Riddle in 1917 for $5,000; in purses and stud fees "Big Red," as he was called, brought in over $3,000,000. In contrast, Man o' War's son, Broadway Limited, cost W. T. Waggoner $65,000 in 1928. Broadway Limited never won a race and finally, attempting to win a $900 purse in 1930, he rounded the stretch turn in front and, finding himself for the first time in his life ahead, suddenly dropped dead.

Even the yearling sales, however, do not seem to old Saratogians to have held up as well as they should have. "Years ago," says Mrs. John F. C. Bryce, a former Newporter, "you used to know everybody, and everybody came in evening clothes. Now everybody comes in anything, and you're lucky if you know the first five rows." The characters, too, at the sales seem to have deteriorated. Mrs. Payne Whitney had the reputation of buying any horse which looked at her sadly; at one sale she bought seventeen horses. Curiously enough, this deterioration in horse Society has been accompanied, in the view of old-timers, by a deterioration in the actual races themselves. The old-timers will tell you that they don't have races any more the way they did, the way, for example, they did on August 13, 1919, when, at Saratoga, of course, Man o' War was beaten for the first and only time in his career—and by a horse, of course, named Upset.

But the most famous race in Saratoga's history was reserved for a rainy afternoon of August 16, 1930, and the running of the Travers Stakes. Named for the great resort wit, Saratoga's beloved "Old Billy" Travers, the oldest of America's stake races at the oldest of America's tracks, the Travers at Saratoga is always a special race, but this particular Travers, run in the rain and the gloom of that stormy day twenty years ago, will never be forgotten. Today when old Saratogians gather at the Grand Union or the Worden Bar and talk of the old days, the story of that Travers is still told.

There were just four horses in the race that day, but two of them were the greatest race horses in America. One was William Woodward's Gallant Fox, a big white-eyed horse who had already won the Derby, the Preakness and the Belmont; he was ridden by the country's greatest jockey, the fabulous Earl Sande, and the odds were one to two. The other was Harry Payne Whitney's brown colt, Whichone. King of the two-year-olds of 1929 and ready for this race of 1930. Whichone was a fast horse in the break and the horse who was rated to hold the Fox if such a feat could be done. His price was six to five. With Sonny Workman up, it was a race not only between the country's two best horses but also between the country's two best jockeys.

The other two horses were both outsiders. One was Sun Falcon, and the other a particularly rank outsider named Jim

Dandy. A chestnut horse which had been out of the money in sixteen of his twenty starts, he had earned only $125 all season. His trainer, a red-faced man named Johnny McKee, had faith in Jim Dandy and had persuaded his owner to buy him. The owner, however, had lost faith. He was not even at the track that day and, as the horses paraded to the post, Jim Dandy was one hundred to one. Hugh Bradley best tells the story of Saratoga's race of races:

> A flash of tape, a confused roar, two smoothly gliding machines move to the front. The duel is even as they dart past the clubhouse turn. There Sonny Workman bends closer to Whichone's ears.
>
> Whichone goes to the front, but Gallant Fox is not to be run off his feet as the Whitney stable hopes. Earl Sande croons songs of the Western plains to his mounts, and music has its charms today. At the furlong pole the Fox draws even again; at the quarter he gets his neck ahead.
>
> It is the high point of the race, or so they think. Now that the Fox has taken command, he never will be headed, they scream from the stands.
>
> Yes? Then you have forgotten Sonny Workman and the brown colt which was king of the two-year-olds. Clods of mud catapult under frantic hooves as they fly to the far turn. Whichone moves up, is a scant head in the lead.
>
> OOoooOOH!
>
> You have forgotten something else. There has been a silence, then a strange babbling undertone, now this high pierced shriek of the crowd surprised.
>
> Inside, next to the rail where the mud has not yet been churned into glue, a horse is slipping through, sailing past the leaders.
>
> His chestnut coat is spattered, for a moment you do not know him even though only four started. But old Johnny McKee has known all along. Yet the white creeps under the florid mask of his face, and thick fingers clinch.
>
> On they come. Sande croons to his mount. Workman's

shoulders heave as he tries to hurl the brown colt home. Baker, obscure jockey in mud-spattered silks, sits quietly. He does not have to move; matters are out of his hands. Destiny is riding the chestnut today.

Surely, though, he is only a false alarm, breathe the thirty thousand. Surely he cannot outrun the greatest colts of the year. Wait a second, he will shoot his bolt and then drop back to where he belongs.

It is a long second, and then even the doubters know. Daylight lengthens between the upstart and those supposed to humble him. Sande still sings to Gallant Fox and pleads, but it is no use. Whichone slows, seems to be in distress. Jim Dandy is six lengths in front, merely galloping.

He still is there at the wire while his jockey looks back and grins over Destiny's shoulder, wonders what has become of the champions.

In the sport and on the track which know the name so well, a dark horse has triumphed. It has been the greatest upset in American turf history, greater than the day when Upset outdistanced Man o' War, when Sysonsby, at 1 to 40, finished in a dead heat in the Metropolitan, when Fashion beat Boston, sire of the mighty Lexington.

Johnny McKee's gray hair bristles in triumph; the red is back in his face when he comes to the judges' stand. He pats Jim Dandy behind the ears, whispers to him as they listen to the roar of the crowd.

Perhaps Whichone did pull a tendon and break down at the head of the stretch. Perhaps Sande and Workman will meet in the jockeys' room to settle their end of the abortive duel with fists. No matter.

Old Johnny, whose friends said he was stubborn, and Jim Dandy, son of a mare who won her first race at a fair for colored folks, are happy. 100 to 1 in the books, 30,000 to 1 in the crowd. The memory will sustain them far longer than the fifteen months which must end before they win another race.

Such also was Saratoga.

As in the case of Newport, Saratoga had been deserted by its social Southerners following the Civil War. The resort made up for this loss by attracting not only Westerners but also a steady procession of political bigwigs; in this sphere the spa even outranked the Atlantic City of Boies Penrose and the French Lick of the elder Tom Taggert. By the Gay Nineties Saratoga was, more than any other resort, the tintype of the Flash Age, and the names of Saratogians were as flashy as their personalities. There was "Diamond Jim" Brady, of course, and "White Hat" McCarty, "Coal Oil Johnny" Steele and "Lucky" Baldwin, "Bet-a-Million" Gates and "Pittsburgh Phil" Smith. Even the bookies who followed them wore their nicknames with pride—"Irish John" Cavanaugh, Joe Yaeger "The Boy Plunger," Joe "Big Store" Ullman and Joe "The Orator" Gleason, Orlando "Fashion Plate" Jones and "Tiffany" Wolfgang—the latter so named because he guaranteed his prices to be as good as anything in the Grand Union branch store of the famous New York jeweler.

"Diamond Jim" was the flashiest of all. He had thirty complete sets of jewels, one for each day in the month, and each set included a watch, watch chain, ring, scarf pin, necktie pin, necktie clasp, pen, pencil, cufflinks, belt buckle, eyeglass case, pocketbook clasp and J.B.B. monogram, not to mention shirt studs, collar buttons and even underwear buttons. The most ornate of all his sets was his so-called "Transportation Set." One shirt stud had a bicycle made of 119 diamonds; the eyeglass case was a locomotive of 210 diamonds. No less than 2,548 diamonds were included in the whole set. Even on the rare occasions when Brady arrived in Saratoga without Lillian Russell, he made up for the lack in style. In the summer of 1896 he arrived with a silver-plated railroad undertruck, Miss Russell's gold-plated bicycle and twenty-seven Japanese houseboys. One of these boys acquired so many fifty-cent Havana cigars that, after Brady returned to New York, he opened a cigar store.

For her part the great Miss Russell was equally conspicuous. If Brady had his Japanese houseboys, Miss Russell had a famous Japanese spaniel, complete with an eighteen hundred dollar collar, and when her gold-plated bicycle bored her, she had a carriage with solid-silver trimmings and dazzling white doeskin reins. Each summer Miss Russell rented a cottage and brought with her a coterie of her girl friends—her "Farm Flirts" she called them—to entertain the menfolk. Fighting a constantly losing battle with her waistline, she insisted on all her guests' exercising severely each day. Then each night she would seize the bedpost while the maid, who often neglected to pull down the shades, would seize the corset strings and endeavor to get her mistress in shape for dinner. Among eyewitnesses to the resort's most celebrated tug-of-war was Saratoga's young Charles Brackett, now of Hollywood. Despite the fact that he loves telling the story, his friend Frank Sullivan refuses to believe it. "I presume Mr. Brackett," says Sullivan, "then as now an honorable gentleman, spoke from hearsay."

Married three times before she had ever appeared on the Saratoga scene, Miss Russell was never, according to Saratogians, the mistress of Brady. To the well-known resort sport, Jesse Lewisohn, went that honor. Nonetheless, when Lewisohn was advised by his doctor that he would have to choose between Miss Russell and his health, Lewisohn chose his health. Thereafter the Brady-Russell-Lewisohn relationship was further complicated by the fact that, during Lewisohn's recuperation at Brady's farm, he fell in love with Edna McCauley, a lady who for ten years had been Brady's mistress. When Lewisohn married Miss McCauley, Saratoga's most beautiful triangle was dissolved. But even this failed to irritate Brady for long. Lewisohn was soon back on the so-called "active list" of the Brady Beneficent Society. Through this organization Brady gave three hundred people presents each week—the first week, a five-pound box of Page and Shaw candy; the second, a huge basket of fruit; the third, another box of candy; and the fourth, flowers. The fifth week the routine started all over again. Finally one of Brady's friends complained. "Goddamn it," said Brady, "if it gives me pleasure to send you presents, I'm gonna go right on sending 'em whether you like it or not."

Brady in all his magnificence was by no means alone in what Lucius Beebe has called the "Augustan Age of American Clownery" at Saratoga. A companion period piece was the celebrated English sportsman, Squire Abington Baird. The Squire assured reporters that his Saratoga supply of walking sticks, of which he had a separate one for each of his dress ensembles, cost ten thousand dollars. He was equally proud of his position as patron and inseparable companion of the famous boxer, Charley Mitchell, a man who had once fought a three-hour draw with John L. Sullivan. One evening in the bar the Squire and Mitchell had an argument. Suddenly the Squire slapped Mitchell in the face. To the amazement of the onlookers the quick-tempered Mitchell did nothing. The same scene was repeated in various other Saratoga bars until finally one day a friend asked Mitchell how he could stand such treatment. Mitchell smiled. "The truth is," he said, "I enjoy it. The Squire pays me one hundred dollars for every blow he lands."

Dapperest of all Saratoga's Dapper Dans was Berry Wall. One evening in August, 1888, he announced that the next day he would appear in forty complete changes of costume. The next morning before breakfast the crowd began gathering in front of the United States Hotel, where Wall had a first-floor room. Out on the street no less a figure than John L. Sullivan started making book on the outcome of Saratoga's greatest sartorial steeplechase.

Just before breakfast Wall appeared. He was dressed in a handsome black and white costume. He stood on the piazza, waved and talked a moment or two with his friends, took a quick stroll up and down, then disappeared inside. A few moments later he was out again, this time garbed in white linen and this time he took a quick walk around the block. All through the day he continued the parade. Sometimes he strolled across to the bar for a drink, sometimes he strolled down to the springs, sometimes over to the Grand Union, but always he was back for another change—to his room where his unseen valet was methodically assisting him, hanging out each new outfit in fireman's fashion. Finally, just at dinnertime, John L. Sullivan led the crowd in three long cheers, the band out under the trees struck up "Hail, the Conquering Hero Comes" and Wall, for the fortieth time, appeared. As his final outfit he wore a Prince Albert, white tie, boiled shirt and poke collar. The title of "The King of the Dudes" was his forever.

The charm of Saratoga in those days lay, of course, in its utter lack of self-consciousness and in its lack of any defensive feeling toward wealth—a feeling which has been the bane of all social resorts in these latter days. This spirit was perhaps best exemplified by the peerless prince of the Erie Railroad, "Colonel" Jim Fisk, Jr. Fisk's colonelcy was of New

York's Ninth National Guard Regiment which he financed and which, in full uniform with its own band, usually accompanied him to Saratoga. A true Saratogian at heart, "Prince Jim" was later to lose his life at the hands of Edward T. Stokes in a quarrel over their joint mistress, Josie Mansfield. But whatever Fisk's shortcomings, he never, in the words of the song written about him, "turned his back on the poor." In fact, journeying down from Saratoga in the summer of 1870, he delivered a speech to six hundred mechanics in the machine shops of Susquehanna, Pennsylvania, which faced up to the matter of poverty in no uncertain manner. This speech not only illustrates the sentiment of the haves for the have-nots of those days but also, more important, the sentiment which the haves wished the have-nots to return:

> It may seem to you a fine thing to be able to wear a diamond and a velvet coat, and to be stared at and run after by a hungry, curious crowd, whichever way you may turn; but I can assure you it is not half so big a thing as it seems. I hope none of you will hanker after big diamonds and velvet coats, for I know you will be far happier without them.
>
> I see before me men who, I will venture to say, are rising sixty years old, but who can't show as many gray hairs on their heads as can be found under the velvet cap that I wear. Sleepless nights and work that never ends are not your portion. Your homes may be humble, but your toil is over when you straddle the legs of your supper table. Don't think that all the work on this road is done at the vise and the lathe, for it ain't. The man who thinks that all Jim Fisk and Jay Gould have to do is to sit in a gilded office at one end of the road, and pass the time away by writing free passes and reading telegraph dispatches, has got a false impression.
>
> You enjoy your evenings in the presence of your little families, while Jim Fisk and the heads of the road fre-

quently spend the greater part of the night studying how to meet a debt of a hundred thousand dollars by noon the next day, when they don't know where to turn for twenty dollars; and all this, it may be, to feed you and your fellow workers. We have to study and work—work hard for your interests as well as our own, for our interests are combined! (*Cheers.*)

The mechanic and the laborer in the United States command respect from all. You are the foundation stone of society. You are the honest sons of honest toil, and you reap the rewards of honest toil. Again I tell you those rewards are far greater than the rewards of those who work with the brain alone, and not with hardened hands.

And again I say, don't hanker after kid gloves and high stovepipe hats, and velvet coats, and diamond pins, and gorgeous neckties, for they will afford you no real comfort. I know I should be far happier running one of those lathes, with no other care on my mind.

I have been connected with the management of this road for some years, and this is the first time that I have enjoyed the privilege of meeting you. I am glad to see you and glad to be seen by you. (*Cheers.*) You have my best wishes and shall have my best efforts for your welfare. If any of you ever come to New York, and I can assist you, I shall be most happy to see you. Good-bye! (*Loud cheers.*)

In the same year in which Jim Fisk gave that speech the young son of an improvident New Bedford printer went to work, at the age of fifteen, in the shipping department of a company in which "Prince Jim" had a partnership—the firm of Jordan, Marsh & Company, in Boston. His name was Richard Albert Canfield and his salary was two dollars a week. Two years before, at the graduation exercises of the Brimmer Grammar School in Providence, Master Canfield had been one of the five children chosen to deliver class declamations. Canfield had chosen Josiah Quincy's "Our

Obligations to the Fathers of New England," an oration he learned so well that forty years later, in an upstairs room at Delmonico's in New York, he repeated it verbatim for the edification of a champagne supper which he had given for members of the Four Hundred.

Unhappily, one sight of the peerless "Prince Jim" on one of his trips to Boston apparently made the impressionable young shipping clerk forget all about his obligations to his Fathers. He did not even wait to hear the Prince's theories of the superior happiness of the working man; instead the young Canfield promptly quarreled with his Jordan, Marsh superior, quit his job and took up gambling.

Although he never in his life played the game of solitaire to which he gave his name, Canfield early learned everything there was to know about his trade—in Pawtucket, Providence, Boston and New York. At the age of twenty he was worth, by his own estimate, twenty thousand dollars. The next year he toured the casinos of Europe and, studying them carefully, returned penniless. Always popular with the ladies—he later married a Pawtucket girl—he was far from backward in preparing himself for Saratoga's Flash Age. Even when he was between jobs his suits, jewelry and cigars were the best money could borrow, if not buy, and his suave manners, studied courtesy and remarkable ability to remember names won him not only respect but also jobs.

Then, at the age of thirty, Canfield saw his faro house in Providence raided and he was sentenced to six months in jail. Furthermore, the sentence, unusually severe for the times, stuck; friends of Canfield always believed its severity was caused by the jealousy of a prominent Rhode Island businessman with whose wife Canfield had, before his own marriage, been intimate. Instead of breaking the rising young gambler, however, the jail sentence made him. "Jail," he used to say in after years, "was my Harvard." From the prison library he procured all kinds of books, on history, literature and particularly art. Once a free man, he was able to mingle with those whom he regarded as his betters without the fear of being humiliated by his lack of education. He took his self-improvement with extreme seriousness. Later in his life returning incognito from an art-buying trip abroad, he was faced with filling in, on his customs declarations, the space after the word "business." He found it no problem. "Gentleman," he wrote.

The only portrait of Canfield in existence was painted by his friend Whistler. In this, Canfield, dressed in dark robes, has his chunky hands clasped piously over his chest, a sanctimonious smile on his round, clean-shaven face, and one of his eyes half shut. Whistler called the portrait "His Reverence"—a title which Canfield, who never went to church, cherished. Since he was the living symbol of their great days, old-time Saratogians remember him equally reverently. "If there is such a thing as an honest gambler," says Monty Woolley, whose father was one of Canfield's closest friends, "Canfield was that man."

In Saratoga's pre-Canfield days a few men had been allowed credit. John Morrissey, for example, allowed Cornelius Vanderbilt, son of the old Commodore, to write out a blank check before starting to play. But Canfield was the first American gambler to extend credit on a large scale. "Canfield expected his patrons to wear evening clothes," says Alexander Gardiner, "and it was his theory that a man clad in a dress suit or a tuxedo did not care to carry a large amount of currency with him." Although Canfield took some severe losses on this theory—one man who gave him an I.O.U. for

$137,000 and never paid is still alive today—the result was remarkably in his favor. His Club House became the most successful gambling house in resort history, and it changed the character of Saratoga from a fading resort of politicians and show-offs to one which was, for a brief last gasp at least, a social rival of Newport and Bar Harbor. This record was the more extraordinary since the Club House was in operation only from 1894 to 1907.

Like Bradley's at Palm Beach, Canfield permitted no native to gamble. Unlike Bradley, however, he never permitted ladies in the gambling rooms. But ladies as well as gentlemen enjoyed Canfield's cuisine. He paid his French chef, Jean Columbin, five thousand dollars for a two-month season and the rest of the year gave him an expense account to travel to Europe to look for new ideas for dishes. Although Canfield's prices were higher than Sherry's or Delmonico's and many of the "American Plan" hotel guests ate even their breakfasts there, the restaurant invariably lost money. Canfield did not mind in the slightest. For him the restaurant was only the come-on, and indeed its outstanding feature—its fish pool—was actually a come-on. In this fish pool near the Club House were trout and bass and all manner of piscatorial delicacies gaily swimming. Patrons ordering fish courses were invited to go out to this pool and pick out their choice. Then the fish was, before the diner's very eyes, scooped out with a net, placed in a basket and taken to the kitchen. What the diner's eye did not see, of course, was the fact that there was a pipe connecting the kitchen with the pool, and when the fish was safely in the kitchen, it was substituted by another and slid back into the pool.

In the gaming rooms Canfield needed no such chicanery. Once asked point-blank if he had ever permitted crooked paraphernalia, he said he had not. "All any gambler wants is to have play for a long enough time and he'll get all the money any player has. In business if you or I can lend money enough at 5 per cent we think we are doing pretty well. Every time a roulette wheel is spun, the percentage on a thirty-six-inch wheel is $5\frac{5}{19}$ per cent against the player. Therefore, you will say that I get an interest on my money of $5\frac{5}{19}$ per cent every time a roulette wheel is spun."

Saratogians still measure time by how many years have passed since the great goings-on at Canfield's Club House. All of Saratoga's other fabled gambling establishments, Riley's, Newman's, the Arrowhead and Piping Rock—not to neglect Arnold Rothstein's Brook and "Lucky" Luciano's Chicago Club—had their fabulous gambling periods, but Canfield's was in a class by itself. Here each evening chef Columbin personally prepared Lillian Russell's sweet corn and crépes suzette and here the playboy, Freddie Gebhard, who had won ten thousand dollars, joshed Canfield late one night. "Don't worry, Dick," he said, "I'll come over for breakfast in the morning and you can get even."

Canfield's was not all actresses and playboys, or, for that matter, all Vanderbilts and Whitneys. Here also the famous bookmaker, Fred Burton, took his meals. One day after he had laid too good a price on a winning favorite, Burton was disgusted. He entered Canfield's and ordered a massive porterhouse and all the trimmings, together with potatoes, vegetables and side dishes. When the waiter brought the food, Burton just sat there looking at it but not touching it for a full hour. Then he got up, paid the check and left. Later his amazed waiter recalled that over and over again Burton had kept repeating, in a quiet but clear whisper, the same words: "Starve, you sucker, starve."

In Canfield's gaming room the play was on a scale commensurate with the size of the rug—one which was reportedly the largest ever woven in one piece. In Canfield's safe, which had five combinations and three heavy steel doors, there was a million dollars in cash, half of it in thousand-dollar bills, the rest in five hundreds, one hundreds and fifties. Ordinarily, white chips were worth $1; red, $5; blue, $10; yellow, $100; and special large-size brown chips, $1,000. The private roulette wheel upstairs, however, sometimes saw the white chip raised to $100 and the brown to $100,000. The biggest game ever played in Canfield's, or in fact at any gambling house in resort history, was played in one of these upstairs rooms on an August evening in 1902. The player was John W. "Bet-a-Million" Gates. A former barbed-wire salesman from Chicago and a millionaire by the time he was thirty, Gates was a large, gross man whose vulgarity so offended J. P. Morgan that the latter excluded him from the billion-dollar United States Steel Corporation, even though the project had been Gates' original idea. Vulgar or not, Gates had no equal as a gambler. "There's no fun in it," he used to say, "unless I risk getting hurt or can hurt the other fellow."

That afternoon fifty years ago Gates had a most unsuccessful day at the track. His system of pyramiding his bets had backfired since having lost race after race, he could no longer place bets large enough to get back even. To one bookmaker alone he had lost $30,000. That evening he had dinner at Canfield's and made his way to the downstairs gaming room. Here, at the faro table, he took the regular limit, $500 on case cards and $1,000 on doubles. He lost steadily and, in order to change his luck, went to a private room upstairs. Here the limit was raised to $2,500 and $5,000. Still Gates lost.

At ten o'clock, out some $150,000 Gates asked for higher

limits. "Billy" Coe, Canfield's manager, told him only Canfield himself could give a higher limit. "I'll see him," said Gates, and went downstairs.

He found Canfield and asked that the limits be raised to $5,000 and $10,000. "You may have it," said Canfield quietly. Then as Gates turned back, Canfield added, "If that isn't enough, come back and see me." Between ten o'clock and midnight Gates had won back the $150,000 he had lost. By the time the game ended at eight o'clock the next morning, Gates was $150,000 ahead.

Even Canfield's famous establishment at 5 East Forty-fourth Street in New York—one which is today occupied by the Keep Shirt Company—never saw anything like that Gates all-night stand fifty years ago. Besides these two establishments, however, Canfield had still a third casino, the Nautilus Club at Newport which he had bought in 1897 for $65,000 and operated for seven years. Canfield rarely appeared in Newport himself and the discreet little house on Bath Road, under his managers, Bucklin and Coe, was never a great success. At the end of the 1904 season he took a trip down to the Rhode Island resort and, superintending the closing of the house, found that the profits were just eleven hundred dollars for the season. The day after he closed, Reggie Vanderbilt and a party of friends walked in and begged for one chance to play. Canfield agreed to one spin of the wheel. Vanderbilt put a thousand-dollar bill on the red. The wheel spun, and red it was. The season had then netted Canfield but one hundred dollars and that winter, disgusted, Canfield sold the property to Bucklin and Coe for a song.

If Canfield was no success at Newport, however, he remains today at Saratoga a living legend. Pontifical and humorless, he stood only five foot eight in height, yet he weighed, by the 1900's, close to 250 pounds. He wore corsets and, as he grew older, inclined to severe blacks and grays in his suits. Although he drank severely, Saratogians recall that he never had to be helped to bed and was always able to pull his old-fashioned nightgown over his head—which was, in the words of one intimate, "no small feat on occasion." After such a night he would eat enormous portions of corned beef hash for breakfast but otherwise show no sign of wear. "Nothing," his manager Jack Northrop recalled, "ever ruffled him."

After the raid on his New York casino in December, 1902, he was offered a salary of thirty thousand dollars a year to manage a casino in Monte Carlo. "I was sorely tempted to take it," he told a reporter. "The casino would have on its board of directors men whose names were prominent in society, finance, and even in royal court circles."

"Why," asked the reporter, "didn't you?"

"Because a little twelve-year-old girl asked me not to. She thought that I already had reputation enough in that direction."

"Do you mind telling me who the little girl was?"

"Certainly not. My daughter."

Actually, while Canfield was known as a "good family man," Saratogians used the phrase in typical resort Society fashion. He visited his wife and son and daughter once a month in Providence, but none of them ever came to Saratoga, or even near-by Newport, and even in the winter months Canfield always lived in New York alone. "I do not know that I have any code of ethics," he once said. "I do not care a rap what other people think about me. I never did. As morals are considered by most people, I have no more than a cat. The only person whose respect and good opinion I want is that of Richard A. Canfield. . . . I have made it a rule to look at myself in the mirror every morning and I feel that if I can look in my own eyes and be satisfied with the examination, then I have no reason to regret anything I have done. That is my personal standard and has been for years."

Because of the publicity surrounding the raids on his houses, and his subsequent suits with his lawyers—he quarreled, before he was through, with even those on his side—resorters generally have the impression that Canfield came to no good end. In fact, due to the confusion with his earlier jail sentence, there is a widespread impression that he ended his days penniless and in jail. This is false. Worth some $12,000,000 in 1907 at the time he closed the Saratoga Club House, he lost in the panic of that year at least half his fortune in the stock market. In one day he lost $1,500,000. But at his own death his estate was appraised at $841,485, and he was by no means a broken man. In 1910 his assiduously cultivated friendship with art connoisseurs and literary men had resulted in his membership in the Walpole Society; in 1914 he was still nursing the hope that he would be included in the next edition of *Who's Who in America.*

Seven years earlier he had, at the time of the Saratoga Club House closing, made a prediction about the future of gambling. "There will come a day," he said, "perhaps not in our lifetime, when gambling will be licensed. The reason why I am convinced that there will eventually be a license is that gambling cannot be stopped. As has been done with liquor, it will be found that the best public policy is to regulate it and to obtain a revenue for the state."

Canfield never lived to see either his gambling legal or his name in *Who's Who.* On the morning of December 11, 1914, at the age of fifty-nine, the Prince of Gamblers at the King of Spas took a subway trip to Brooklyn. Becoming confused, like many lesser people before his time and after, he got off his train at Fourteenth Street thinking it was Grand Central. Halfway up the stairs, he realized his mistake and, in an attempt to get down the stairs before the car doors closed, he slipped and fell. The next morning he was dead.

In 1830, at the same time as the anonymous poet told the world that Saratoga was "first in manners, in dress, and in fashions to shine," another poet, a young Maryland lawyer, discussed Saratoga's Southern counterpart, the Virginia Springs. In the War of 1812, in a cavalier attempt to rescue a British-imprisoned client, the young man had been a chance spectator of the bombardment of Fort McHenry and had written, on the spot, a poem in honor of the occasion; his name was Francis Scott Key and his poem was "The Star-Spangled Banner." Key's poem in honor of the Virginia Springs was also written on the spot, jotted down, in a whimsical moment, in the diary of a Virginia belle, Miss Cornelia Lomax. Not heretofore published in its entirety, this poem was some years ago presented to the Old White Museum by a granddaughter of Key's belle:

A word of advice about matters and things
May be useful to those who visit the Springs;
So list' to the muse as she kindly sings
All for your good, ye folks at the Springs.

I purpose to tell you of all the fine things
That are here to be seen at these Sulphur Springs:
First there's a bell in the morning that rings
To awaken the other belles at the Springs;
And the belles fix their ribbands and tie up their strings
And look very beautiful here at the Springs;

And then they all fly as if they had wings
  To eat the hot cakes that abound at the Springs.

There's an insect or two called a flea, that here stings
  The skins of the people who stay at the Springs;
There's a broom and a half here for nobody brings
  Such articles here to sweep out the Springs;
There's a maid and a half, too, for one of them swings
  Rather much to one side, for she's lame at the Springs;
There's mint in great plenty for juleps and slings,
  When the water's too cold or too weak at the Springs.

There's a bawling all day—but the ball at night clings
  The most to my fancy of all at the Springs—
To conclude, though some things here might e'en do for kings,
  If you wish to fare well, say farewell to the Springs.

In the museum's version of the poem four lines are omitted —the two lines at the head of the second stanza which deal with the insects and also the concluding lines which deal with the farewells. Such editing of the past is still characteristic at the Virginia Springs today. Nestling in the bosom of the Allegheny Mountains—the Hot Springs in the far western part of Virginia and the White Sulphur in the far eastern part of West Virginia—the springs region of Virginia might be said to be in the middle of nowhere and is today, in fact, known only for two last resort hotels, the Homestead at Hot Springs and the Greenbrier, sixty miles away, at White Sulphur. Both of these hotels are confident that they have all the modern conveniences and yet at the same time have preserved the best of all the old traditions. At the Homestead, despite a "Palm Beach Corridor," a "Homestead Theater" and other modern trimmings, guests may have, if they wish, their own "personal boy," and thus live under the illusion that they are old-time Southerners with a body servant. Another tradition of the hotel is that the waiters carry trays on their heads; for this purpose they wear small circular crowns between head and tray.

At the Greenbrier there is also a heroic effort in the direction of the old traditions. The hotel may advertise itself as "America's smartest—and gayest—resort," but at night the signs in the corridor read, "QUIET PLEASE—IT'S SLEEPY TIME DOWN SOUTH." In the same way, despite its "Celebrity Corridor," its "Little Fifth Avenue" and an ultramodern *décor* which allows no two of the six hundred rooms to be identical, the hotel operates an ancient tallyho for horse-minded patrons and also boasts an apparently genuine Southern Mammy to serve tea and coffee. For many years the Greenbrier has also held such events as "Old White Week," "Lee Week" and even a "Spring Festival Week." The Old White Week was in honor of the Greenbrier's famous predecessor, the Old White Hotel, and Lee Week was, of course, in honor of the great Confederate General, but the Spring Festival has frankly baffled many outsiders. Finally a former manager of the Greenbrier was asked, after a long and particularly harassing day, just what the Spring Festival was a symbol of. For a moment the manager appeared to be in deep thought, then suddenly something seemed to snap. "It's the symbol," he said firmly, "of making money."

Actually, comparison between the Homestead and the Greenbrier is ticklish at best because the hotels are earnest rivals and are even reached by the same Chesapeake and Ohio train from New York—the so-called "F.F.V."—the Homestead and the Hot being reached by a spur line from Covington, Virginia, and the Greenbrier and the White being reached direct. Nonetheless, old-time resorters agree that generally speaking the Hot has more of what is left of old-time resort Society. "You can see it right on the train," says Worthington Hine. "The people you would want to be with are all going to the Hot." Since Hine is an ex-White Sulphurite, not to mention a Tuxedoite, Southamptonite and Palm Beacher, this is high praise indeed. Furthermore, it is strongly seconded by Fay Ingalls, for many years owner and manager of the Homestead. Ingalls maintains that the Homestead has fewer conventions than the Greenbrier and also believes that his colored help, which he describes as "Old School" Southern, are less tip-conscious than the Greenbrier's. He is particularly proud of the fact that he has a sterner policy toward supporting celebrities. "Once in a while we may give somebody 25 per cent off," he says, "but we don't take people free the way the Greenbrier does."

Robert R. Young, chairman of the board of the Chesapeake and Ohio Railway which owns the Greenbrier, answers such charges not by words but by actions. For the Grand Reopening of his new Greenbrier in April, 1948, Young took four hundred people free—all for a four-day house party from Thursday through Sunday. Not even incidentals were charged and the affair was the outstanding resort Society function in modern social history. Alphabetically, on the invitation list, Mr. and Mrs. John Jacob Astor found themselves beside Mr. and Mrs. Fred Astaire, Mr. and Mrs. Robert Goelet beside Mr. and Mrs. Samuel Goldwyn, Mr. and Mrs. Herbert Hoover beside Mr. and Mrs. Bob Hope, Miss Elsa Maxwell beside Mr. Louis B. Mayer, Mr. and Mrs. Arthur H. Sulzberger beside the Duke and Duchess of Sutherland, Mr. and Mrs. Juan Trippe beside President and Mrs. Harry S. Truman, and Mr. and Mrs. Harrison Williams beside the Duke and Duchess of Windsor.

Possibly fearing more uncomfortable juxtapositions, all of

these invited dignitaries did not, of course, appear. Nonetheless, the turnout was ample evidence that Society at the Greenbrier is gayer, if less august, than that at the Homestead. "Ex-wives of ex-husbands, and ex-husbands of ex-wives," says Mrs. William Randolph Hearst, Jr., the former Mrs. Igor Cassini, "rubbed elbows like olives in the same bottle." Cassini himself, the present Cholly Knickerbocker, called the assembled group the "*crème de la crème* of American capitalism," and John Jacob Astor declared that in his opinion the nearest thing to the Greenbrier house party in history was the entertainments of the kings of France at Versailles. Bing Crosby was particularly awed. "I had to wash and iron my shirt," he says, "before sending it to the laundry." Crosby was also frightened by his maid. "She used a lorgnette," he declares, "to look under the bed." At the Grand Ball Saturday night an anonymous and rather sinister figure approached orchestra leader Meyer Davis. "This is the last of the great social events of a changing age," he said darkly. "Civilization may be dancing at the brink of a precipice." Davis too looked gloomy, then suddenly brightened. "Whenever civilization dances at the brink of a precipice," he said, "it's always to the music of Meyer Davis."

Ex-Tuxedoite Dorothy Draper, who decorated the new Greenbrier, is adamant in its defense. Although her decoration of the new hotel is often accused of being less of "romance and rhododendrons"—its supposed theme—than it is of dollars and cents, she herself welcomes criticism. "If everybody liked it," she says, "then it wouldn't be thought-provoking and it wouldn't have the publicity value. Frankly, I think too many people like it as it is." Mrs. Draper particularly enjoys the occasions when Old Greenbrierites, or even

Old Whiters, point to the chandelier in the ballroom and say, "Well, at least that woman couldn't ruin this room. How I remember dancing under that chandelier!" Mrs. Draper smiles. "That chandelier didn't exist before we did the job," she says. "We copied it out of an old Russian book."

Whatever the outcome of the war between the pro-Homesteaders and the pro-Greenbrierites, the fact remains that at both resorts the old cottage colonies are currently living in equal states of social ghostdom. As at Saratoga, the chief complaint is that, while a few social people still come for a short time during the spring and fall seasons, they no longer come for all summer as they did in the old days, or even, for that matter, for regular fall or spring visits. Washington's Mrs. Francis Whitten, who was optimistic enough to build, just before World War II, "Three Valleys," the large hillside showplace at White Sulphur, is now sorry she did and has put her place up for sale. "Goodness gracious," she said, "I was all alone." A friend of Mrs. Whitten also moved away. She now understands her place is being turned into a gambling house. "I was suspicious," she says, "the minute I heard they were putting red lights on the gates." Down at Hot Springs, the situation is equally sad. For many years, because of the prevalence of rich widows, the area was known as "The Valley of the Kept Men." Today Washington's Colonel McKee Dunn, whose "Gramercy Farm" covers a whole mountain and includes an old stone house which dates back to 1790, speaks for a dwindling cottage contingent of perhaps twenty-five families. "In the old days," he says, "we had everybody. We had Vanderbilts and Whitneys and we had Mrs. Stuyvesant Fish and Governor Livingston Beeckman from Newport and we even had a Miss Postlethwaite from Boston—oodles of people like that. Now we don't have anybody. Everything has gone to hell in the last twenty years. Roosevelt and Truman and all those people have given everybody the idea they're just as good as everybody else."

Mrs. Jackson Boyd, who has cottaged at Hot Springs since 1909, is more philosophical on the subject of the deterioration of Springs Society. "I have given it up completely," she says. "I've taken up baseball. I spend most of my time listening to the games. They're very hard to hear, too, there's so much static on account of the mountains. The only other person who listens is the man who carves the roasts at the Casino luncheons. He's a Brooklyn Dodgers fan." Asked what team she prefers, Mrs. Boyd, whose winter home is in Florida, says she used to be for the New York Yankees but she now prefers the Philadelphia Phillies. "You see," she says, "I'm so intimate with them in the training season in Clearwater."

One difficulty of Springs Society in modern times has, of course, been the matter of the springs themselves. For many years the owners of both the Greenbrier and the Homestead have not wanted to attract too many invalids and yet have, at the same time, not wanted to admit that the baths and mineral waters were just a period fad. Their attitude was perhaps best expressed by the late Dr. John Freeland, Richmond bachelor who cut a large social swath in the cottage colony at White Sulphur in the 1920's. "The baths and waters are good for you if you're all right," he used to say, "but they're bad for you if you're not." Today probably the best place to see the last remnants of bath Society as it once was is at the Warm Springs pool. This pool, though run by the Homestead, contrasts sharply with the main spas run by the Greenbrier and Homestead which are now advertised primarily for businessmen's checkups. An old-fashioned circular building which looks rather like a large wooden well, the Warm Springs pool boasts a startling sign which reads, "MAN'S POOL OPENED 1761, LADIES' POOL OPENED 1836." Here George Washington, Thomas Jefferson and Alexander Hamilton all bathed and here the die-hards of Virginia Springs Society still take their last bathing stands.

Actually this last stand is made on stones, which come out from the sides of the pool. Rubber or elastic bathing suits cannot be worn because the minerals eat them up, and, with the ninety-eight-degree water up to their necks, the resorters hang on to ropes, the men in the nude and the women—in a different pool—in Mother Hubbard romper suits. Every so often, in the women's pool, a mixed party is held and at this the men, as well as the women, dress in romper suits, and the food and drinks are floated out on trays. Unhappily, even these parties can no longer be what they were in the old days, as state liquor laws forbid the serving of alcoholic beverages in public. At both the Greenbrier and the Homestead the law is circumvented by so-called "clubs," which claim to be operated independently of the hotels, but since the little Warm Springs pool is no club—baths cost fifty cents and are open to *anyone*—the old days of mint juleps being floated out on the trays have gone with the wind. Atmospherically, the chief charm is provided by Horace Tonsler, the colored caretaker whose father held the same position before him and whose grandmother was one of the Springs' most beloved characters. "Aunt Fanny," as she was always called, handled all bathers, regardless of their social eminence, in the great Mammy tradition, and one day when a lady asked her to turn her back while she put on her romper suit, Aunt Fanny laughed out loud. "Lawsy, Ma'am," she said, "don't pay that no mind. Nekedness ain't no treat to me."

In the very old days this same Warm Springs was both the

beginning and the end of the Grand Tour of the Springs—one which became as famous a hundred years ago to the Southerners as the recognized Grand Tours of the Northerners in the early 1900's. The road originally dictated the order in which the Old South took the waters. The first turnpike which entered the springs region was laid over the top of Warm Springs Mountain and then down to skirt the Warm's bubbling baths. The total tour by this turnpike, and feeder roads, was about 170 miles. Beginning at the Warm, the Springs-goer of the day attacked in order the Healing, the Hot, the White, the Red Sweet, the Sweet, the Salt Sulphur, the Red Sulphur, and then, in later years, either went on up to the Blue Sulphur and back via the Rockridge Alum and the Bath Alum or down to the Gray Sulphur and back via the Yellow Sulphur and the Montgomery White.

Where the turnpike led, health, generally speaking, followed—although the usual practice was to skip the Hot and the Healing on the way to the White and take them coming back. At the Warm, the landlord, Colonel John Fry, welcomed his coming, sped his parting, guests, all with the same line. "Go," he used to say, "get well charged at the White, well salted at the Salt, well sweetened at the Sweet, well boiled at the Hot, and then return to me and I will Fry you." Doctors, too, applauded the turnpike prescription for Springs fever. In those days, in a high spirit of "Physician, heal thyself," they themselves took the waters before advising their patients to do so. One doctor, however, advised doubling back for a second dose of the Salt before the Sweet; he thus routed his patients Warm, White, Salt, Red, Sweet, Healing, Hot and Warm. Another doctor was bold enough to try a different tour altogether. He started at the Red Sulphur, but, as he later reported in a pamphlet, he found that, though he had started at the right end for phthisis, he had started at the wrong end for dyspepsia.

In the early days the facilities of the Springs were simple in the extreme, either log cabins, frame boardinghouses, or small, vastly overcrowded hotels. But gradually, as fashion supplanted health in the Springs Tour, larger hotels with cottage rows began to make their appearance. The most famous of all of these was, of course, the White Sulphur Springs Hotel, or the "Old White," as it was called. Today, on the lawn in back of the new Greenbrier, there is a small and dignified monument before whose touching inscription all true resorters, Northern and Southern, make obeisance:

1858–1922
HERE STOOD A FAMOUS HOSTELRY
AFFECTIONATELY KNOWN AS
THE OLD WHITE
ONCE THE PRIDE OF THE OLD DOMINION
WHOSE GRACIOUS HOSPITALITY, BEAUTIFUL
SURROUNDINGS AND HEALING WATERS GAINED
NATIONAL RENOWN AND MADE IT THE OBJECT
OF MANY A PILGRIMAGE
HERE GATHERED FROM THE NORTH AND SOUTH
GREAT GENERALS, FAMOUS STATESMEN AND
PHILANTHROPISTS, LOVELY LADIES AND
REIGNING BELLES WHO LEFT UPON THE SILENT
SHORE OF MEMORY IMAGES AND PRECIOUS
THOUGHTS THAT SHALL NOT DIE, AND
CANNOT BE DESTROYED

ERECTED BY ITS SUCCESSOR
THE GREENBRIER
1940

Here, at the Old White in a dark cool barroom at the bottom of a beautiful spiral staircase, the mint julep was born in 1858—created of pure French brandy, old-fashioned cut-loaf sugar, limestone water, crushed ice, and young, home-grown mountain mint. Here also, in 1878, Governor Zebulon B. Vance of North Carolina made his famous remark to Governor Wade Hampton of South Carolina. "It's a long time between drinks." In that same year *Harper's Magazine* reported that White Sulphur was free of the presence of both the *nouveau riche* and what the magazine called the "Messrs. Tag, Rag, and Bobtail" who were apparently, in the age-old complaint of resorts, plaguing the other Springs. "In the midst of the fast and somewhat pretentious and shoddy existence of the present time," *Harper's* reported—as of August, 1878—"you find here the same air of high-breeding and rational relaxation which characterized the White Sulphur during the *ancien régime* before the modern spirit of democracy had levelled everything to so distressing a uniformity."

One story of the White Sulphur of not many years after this is still told at the resort today. Richmond's young Mrs. Beverly Dandridge Tucker, the former Anna Maria Washington and the mother of Virginia's fabulous Tucker brothers, was visiting at White Sulphur and was called up to a porch on which were sitting a group of what constituted White Sulphur's newer element of the times. One of the ladies introduced the young Virginia girl. During the meeting the talk turned to the occupations of the girls' fathers. One of the new group's father was the president of a Pittsburgh steel company, one was president of a Western copper company, and another president of a Chicago meat-packing concern. Finally Mrs. Tucker was asked what her father did. "He's a farmer," she replied. Later, after Mrs. Tucker had left, the newer element raised their collective eyebrows. "A farmer's daughter!" said one. "What on earth is the White coming to?" The lady who had introduced Mrs. Tucker interrupted. "I do not think," she said, "my friend told you the name of her farm." The other lady shook her head. "No," she said, trying to be interested, "she did not. What is it?" The first lady smiled. "Mount Vernon," she said.

The greatest contribution of the Virginia Springs to resort life was by all odds its belles. No other resort compared to the Virginia Springs in this regard. Furthermore, the belles were unmarried. At Saratoga the belle could have her wedding cake and eat it too. It was the same at Newport and the other watering places. There a belle was a matron, a hostess, even, in some cases, almost a *grande dame*. But down South the brief and merry chase from Warm to Healing to Hot to White to Salt to Sweet—which ended at the altar—also ended the belle. In the days before the First World War newspapers did not use the names of the belles in print; they appeared only as Miss M—— or Miss R——. One of these papers, however, could not resist comment on the awful change from Miss to Mrs.:

> Oh! piteous to behold, that sad class of beings, young married ladies; like dethroned Princesses they witness triumphs that once were theirs; there they waste their sweetness on the indolent beaux that are too lazy to dance, or some antiquated hero of the old school who compassionates their lonely and deserted state.

"The South," says Perceval Reniers, "in its contemplation and adoration of its belles got as much satisfaction as the North got from counting the cost of Cornelius Vanderbilt's horses or Jay Gould's yacht." Actually the age of Southern belles may be said to have begun at White Sulphur as far back as the 1830's. In that decade the famous Colonel William Pope—all landlords of the day became colonels automatically—conceived the idea of his so-called Billing, Wooing and Cooing Society. The articles of the constitution of this Society, which prescribed well-defined rules for the pursuit of belles by beaux, as well as its membership list, which soon counted seventeen hundred names, was written on a long roll of pink paper and hung in a ballroom. When the Old White appeared on the scene, it was admirably equipped to handle all these ex-Billers, Wooers and Cooers. Besides its famous Baltimore Row, Carolina Row, Virginia Row, Colonnade Row and Paradise Row—in the old days there was even, for bachelors, a Wolf Row—there was also a variety of surrounding paths. These, too, were circumspectly named. One was Lovers' Walk; another, Lovers' Rest; a third, Courtship Maze; and a fourth, Hesitance, the latter leading, of course, either to Acceptance Way, to Paradise or to Rejection, and then, finally, to Lovers' Leap. Each path has its own legends. Along Lovers' Walk, for example, all newcomers would be told the story of the famous belle who had the entire Springs at her feet. One suitor, unable to make any impression, determined to win her by strategy. One late afternoon he took her along the walk, and when she was, as usual, as cool as a julep to his intentions, he stopped and started talking with her. Another couple approached, and just as they came in sight, he suddenly stopped talking and kissed her. Although the witnesses immediately turned back, in half an hour the whole Springs knew of the compromise. No explanations were possible. Fortunately, the belle was as game as they come. "That evening," records Charles Dudley Warner, "the engagement was announced in the drawing room."

Along with the walks and the talks on the paths there was also the famous "Treadmill" at the Old White. This Treadmill was the stately promenade taken each night directly after dinner, or supper as it was called. Legend has it that the Treadmill began on the spur of the moment one evening when Henry Clay offered his arm to Mrs. John Preston and began to march around the great uncarpeted space of the parlor. Clay's action was seconded by John Caldwell Calhoun, who walked with a Mrs. Rhett. Thereafter the Treadmill, which carried on out to the piazza, became an important daily event and one which was, for the belles, almost as important as the morning or evening cotillion. Whether she was a Queen of the Blue Grass from Kentucky or a Queen of the Mardi Gras from New Orleans, the Treadmill was her chance to pass in review with all her art of coquetry. The beaux, too, kept the code. "The discarded suitor who had been given his *congé* that afternoon at Lovers' Leap," Alexander MacCorkle recalls, "gallantly faced his rival as they met in the Treadmill's tortuous wind."

MacCorkle also remembers "the awful night" at Treadmill when it became known that a beautiful young lady from the West had been divorced. A dowager from South Carolina sounded the voice of doom. "She should have gone to the Warm," she said. Even more severe was the penalty for the great belle of St. Louis, Nellie Hazeltine. Forced into engagement by an ambitious mother with Samuel Tilden, Democratic nominee for president and a man old enough to be her father, Miss Hazeltine returned to St. Louis after a gay summer at the White and one evening, accompanied by a throng of fashionables, attended the opera. The tenor, a handsome blond youth, cast an eye of admiration in the direction of "the most beautiful girl born west of the

Mississippi," and, according to several people present, Miss Hazeltine returned the glance. The next morning the newspapers gave vivid accounts of the flirtation, Tilden canceled the engagement, and Miss Hazeltine was never again a belle of the White.

One day after the war, in July, 1867, there arrived at the White, to stay at the famous Baltimore Cottage "G," the greatest personality in the history of the springs, General Lee. To the new generation of belles the presence of the great Southern leader, whose wife was ill with arthritis, more than made up for the postwar lack of eligible beaux; Lee's coming may be said to have launched the Golden Age of Springs belledom. At last, however, there came the evening when a group of Northerners were left alone across the ballroom. Lee approached a group of Southern belles who believed that the Northerners were present only to gloat over their defeat and smile at their makeshift dresses. "I have tried in vain," said Lee, indicating the strangers, "to find any lady who is able to present me. I shall now introduce myself, and shall be glad to present any of you who will accompany me." Baltimore's Christiana Bond alone arose. "I will go, General Lee," she said, "under your orders." Lee gave his arm. "Not under my orders," he corrected, "but it will gratify me deeply to have your assistance."

Halfway across the room, directly under the brilliant crystal chandelier, Miss Bond herself asked the General the fateful question. "Did you never," she asked, "feel resentment toward the North?" ("Yankees," Miss Bond recalled, was a name one might not say in his presence.) Lee stopped. "I believe I may say," he said, "looking into my own heart, and speaking as in the presence of God, that I have never known one moment of bitterness or resentment."

From the late 1860's to the late 1890's belledom at the Springs was the ambition of every Southern girl. As often as not, her parents could not afford the trip. In such cases, the girl joined other girls and came anyway; sometimes as many as half a dozen girls grouped themselves under a chaperone. One belle wrote the well-known W. W. Corcoran, Washington banker and inheritor of Colonel Singleton's Colonnade. "Please, Mr. Corcoran," she wrote, "send me one hundred dollars so that I can go to the Springs and be a belle." Corcoran sent the one hundred dollars. The whole routine of the day was, if not a beau ideal, at least a belle ideal. In the morning there was first springs-drinking and then breakfast, a morning German at eleven, a lawn party complete with iced champagne and frozen watermelon at noon and a midday dinner at one. In the afternoon the older people took siestas but the belles had their date books filled for coaching parties, horseback rides and walks. In the late afternoon there was another lawn party, a pink tea or a band concert and then an early supper. In the evening there was first Treadmill, of course, and finally, every single night in the week, a ball. No other Springs could equal the balls at the White in the heyday of belledom. Led by the famous "General" Jo Lane Stern—even the title of colonel was not enough for him—these balls included the greatest cotillions ever seen at any resort. The two most famous figures were the Butterfly, in which the belles fluttered about the ballroom waving large wings of chiffon and pursued by beaux with long-handled butterfly nets, and the Coach-and-Four, in which the beaux literally drove the belles around the ballroom—harnessed four abreast and covered with jingling ornaments.

Perhaps the most appealing of all the Springs' belles was the celebrated Mattie Ould—pronounced "old"—daughter of

Richmond's Judge Ould. Beguilingly round-faced and curly-haired, she had an extraordinary wide-eyed expression, the latter the perfect background for her greatest appeal—her quick-wittedness. Plays on words were the accepted form of wit of the day, and at this Miss Ould had no peer, particularly with names. As a young girl she had laid her head on the shoulders of General Young. "It was a case," she said, "of Ould head on Young shoulders." On another occasion she was asked by a young girl whether she would marry a Mr. Wise or a Mr. Morrison. "Oh, hasten, sinner, to be wise," she replied, "stay not for tomorrow's sun." One day she dropped a glove and an elderly but not acceptable admirer named Mr. Page retrieved it. He bowed and presented her the glove with a couplet:

> If from your glove you take the letter *g*,
> Your glove is love and that I bear for thee.

Miss Ould flashed:

> If from your name you take the letter *P*,
> Your Page is age, that will not do for me.

That couplet expressed Miss Ould's contempt for the general practice of the "reigning belles"—which was to make a "brilliant match" with an elderly and wealthy beau. One summer Miss Ould in mid-August went down to the Montgomery White. There she scandalized Society by eloping to nearby Salem with a young Richmond editor named Oliver Schoolcraft. Miss Ould was twenty-three, her husband twenty-four. Although on her return to Richmond her father ordered the ceremony performed again, he never forgave his daughter and would not go to her when, the very next spring, she lay on her deathbed, dying in childbirth. All the South, however, mourned its wittiest belle.

Outranking even Mattie Ould was Richmond's Mary Triplett, a belle who was the cause of the last duel fought in Virginia. In face and figure no belle of the Springs was the equal of this beautiful blue-eyed golden-blonde beauty. Mattie Ould herself, a rival, had toasted her. "Here's to beauty, grace, and wit, which united make a Triplett." Miss Triplett, like Miss Ould, was loved by a journalist; in her case, however, there were two journalists, McCarthy, a brilliant young Irishman, and Mordecai, a young man to whom she was apparently betrothed. Unfortunately, in the columns of a Richmond paper there appeared some verses, written in pain and anger at being rejected, by McCarthy:

When Mary's queenly form I press
In Strauss' latest waltz
I would I could those lips caress,
Although those lips be false.

Immediately on reading the verses, Mordecai challenged McCarthy; in the subsequent duel Mordecai was mortally wounded. But Miss Triplett, as it turned out, never had any plan of marrying either Mordecai or McCarthy. Instead she chose Philip Haxall, a textile man and one of the few Southerners of the day who had managed to amass a sizeable fortune. With her marriage, Miss Triplett's crown fell to Mattie Ould's sister Sallie. But Miss Sallie preferred the parlor's whist to the ballroom's cotillion and finally the crown settled firmly on the head of the Oulds' stepsister, the great May Handy.

Miss Handy was schooled for belledom as a race horse is schooled for the track. No one ever saw a hair of her beautiful coiffure, which she wore coiled on her head, out of place. Her "daily constitutional" was a community event. Wearing her Palmer violets—standard equipment for all belles—she always "smelled delicious," in the words of one young admirer. In Richmond when the unsuspecting traveler alighted from the train and asked the colored driver the fare to the hotel, he would always receive the same answer. "One dollar," the driver would say, "but two dollars to go by Franklin Street. You just might see Miss May Handy." Miss Handy, in the manner of belles of the day, starred not only all along the circuit at the Springs, but she also made the Northern tour of Newport, Bar Harbor, Lenox and Saratoga. In the end, too, she married not only a Yankee but a divorced Yankee as well, Tuxedo's James Brown Potter. Southern Society was shocked, of course, but less than they were by Miss Handy's leading rival, Mrs. Willie Allen.

Born Minnie Anderson, in Savannah, Mrs. Allen was the first Southern *femme fatale* who refused to give up belledom just because she was married. Her husband, a Virginia gentleman, was always in the background, but Mrs. Willie was always front and center. Reporters of the day bracketed her with the unmarried belles; she herself made no secret of snaring Henry Grafton Dulany, the so-called "Catch of the Springs" away from all other rivals. A Virginia gentleman with an English fortune, Dulany was virtually the owner of the Old White when he died in 1890, but he was by no means Mrs. Allen's only extramarital attachment. Furthermore, when one of these attachments, a dignified Virginia lawyer, suddenly gave her up and decided to marry somebody else, Mrs. Allen dared to publish, out of spite, a brief volume called *The Love Letters of a Liar*. Dedicating her book to "the men who couldn't wouldn't and didn't write these letters," Mrs. Allen signed the amorous epistles with a pseudonym, "Lawrence Goddard," but the letters were obviously real. "Do you remember what I told you was my dream last night," one letter ran, "how mad and bad and glad it was, but then *how it was sweet?*" Later the irritated lover, a man well known in his day, answered in a poem of his own. "Thank God," his last line ran, "that I lost you, Bonny Lorraine."

The greatest single *cause célèbre* in the era of belledom was also caused by a married belle, Mrs. Bettina Ordway Padelford. Daughter of a Richmond provost marshal, Mrs. Padelford was, as an eighteen-year-old bride, on her way upstairs to bed with her husband one night when Hal Dulany begged her to come down and chaperon a midnight supper. During this supper the talk turned to the ancient Polish custom of drinking wine from the bride's slipper at weddings. Hal Dulany declared he would not drink from any girl's slipper, but another member of the party, the young Charlottesville lawyer, George Morris, said, with a glance at Mrs. Padelford, that it depended on the lady. Whereupon Mrs. Padelford promptly took off her slipper. "There," she said, "is your challenge." Bravely Morris caught up the slipper from the floor, poured champagne in it and quaffed.

By the next morning, of course, the entire social world had heard the story, generally in a vastly exaggerated version, and the custom of slipper-drinking was already on its way to becoming a national fad. At Saratoga or Long Branch, the affair might have been forgiven, but not at White Sulphur. "The moral and social structure of the famous resort," says Major Hale, "was almost demolished." For the culprit, Morris, banishment and lifelong exile were immediately prescribed. Although he later became a state senator, he was, to the end of his life, a marked man. As for Mrs. Padelford, her part in the event launched a stage career. Within a year she had left her husband and, for twenty years, with six succeeding husbands, she starred from coast to coast in stage plays and vaudeville.

Most Springs old-timers today believe that the belledom was killed by two forces. First, of course, was the emancipation of women and the removing of the pedestal on which they stood—a factor which was also influenced by girls' going into athletics. Second was the same social disintegration which affected the Northern "Four Hundred." Nonetheless, faint echoes of belledom reverberated at the Springs well into the 1920's, and in this latter era there were at least two events which came close to rivaling Mrs. Padelford's slipper. One was the near elopement of a beautiful belle appropriately named Miss Katherine Bonnie. Miss Bonnie had a beau who was a jockey, and her mother, who did not approve the young man, locked her in a cottage at the Hot and took away her clothes. The jockey, however, was not so easily forestalled. Having finished riding in a race in the vicinity, he appeared on the scene one early evening and, lending the belle his silks and white breeches, he rode romantically away with her to White Sulphur. To this day no one is quite sure what the jockey wore, but in any case, Miss Bonnie's angry parents retrieved the couple before bedtime.

The second great *cause célèbre* of latter-day Springs belledom occurred earlier, in the autumn of 1911. This affair began innocently enough when, in the little round card room at the Homestead, a group of belles, including Clarice French, Elinor Bright, Margaret Luce, Prudence Sterry, Lillian Palmer, and Harriet McCook, were playing hearts with two schoolboys named William Chappell and Gaines Gwathmey. Suddenly the door burst open and admitted the late Seth Barton French, Jr., a brother of one of the belles.

French had obviously been drinking and he was wearing a cowboy hat and waving a pistol. In an effort to stage a Western version of Southern belledom, he declared, in a thick voice, that the belles would have to get up on the table and dance; otherwise he would shoot. The belles, in the game tradition, promptly refused and went on with their hearts. No one knows whether French would have made good his threat or not. For, equally gamely, Gaines Gwathmey, today a distinguished Long Islander, immediately slipped down under the table and dove at French's knees. In a moment French was disarmed and the flower of Hot womanhood was thus saved from what might have been lasting disgrace.

For many old-timers the most memorable evening in the history of Springs belledom occurred as far back as 1889. One evening in July of that year, a group of young people were sitting, dangle-legged and starry-eyed, on a window sill of the Old White ballroom. They were watching the first hour of the ball before the parents sent them to bed. Suddenly the Philadelphian beau, William Wright, spotted one of them—a beautiful girl with golden hair, an hourglass figure, and bright blue eyes which he later described as "glowing with liquid fire." He strode over and asked her how old she was. "Sixteen," she replied. "Well, then," said Wright, "it's time you were out." With that he took her twenty-inch waist in his two hands and swooped her in a high, wide arc up from the window sill and down to the ballroom floor—and thus, in one fell swoop, the greatest of the Springs' belles made her informal debut.

There were many other belles of this era—Ellie Bosher, Anne Carter, Martha Bagby, Judith Carrington, and the beautiful Petersburg sisters, Anne and Eugenia Tennant—

but the belle who was launched from the window sill that night was the most famous of them all. Curiously enough, today the belle herself remembers everything about that fateful night except who else was on the sill. "I can't remember who I was sitting with," she says, "but I remember who I was in love with. I was in love with Nicholas Longworth." Four years later, at a horse show, the belle met a Yankee, and that meeting proved even more memorable than her debut. She never forgot his first words. "Why," he asked her, "did you wear such a funny hat?" A year later the engagement of Miss Irene Langhorne to Mr. Charles Dana Gibson was announced—and, with the ex-Miss Langhorne as the model for the artist's Gibson Girl, a new era began.

Today Mrs. Gibson remembers her sub-belle days at the Old White with almost as much affection as her belle days. The Langhorne family were all crowded together in "Bruce Cottage" on Virginia Row, including, besides Irene and her father and mother, Nannie (now Lady Astor), Lizzie, Phyllis, Nora, Buck, Harry and Keene as well as several colored nursemaids. They also had a pair of goats and a goat-cart. In those days, Mrs. Gibson remembers, the beaux used to pay her boxes of candy to go out and spy on the paths and come back and tell them which belle was with which beau. Later, after her leap from the window sill, her happiness knew no bounds—although she never used the word "belle." "I loved it, loved it, loved it," she says. "I never wore a speck of make-up of any kind—not even powder—and I ate everything. Big breakfasts, big dinners, and big suppers. Hot breads and beaten biscuits too." Despite only mild exercising in the form of "gentle" tennis and side-saddle horseback-riding, Miss Langhorne kept her twenty-inch waist. "The beaux were supposed to be able to put their hands around it," she says, "but my father never let them."

Mrs. Gibson's youngest sister Nora, who won the White Sulphur baby prize at the age of two, recalls that her father had no use either for etiquette or for fashion as they are now thought of. "Etiquette is for people who have no breeding," Mr. Langhorne used to say. "Fashion is for people who have no taste." Once his oldest daughter had the audacity to take an artificial rose from her hat and rub a little red on her cheeks. Her father promptly branded her a "brazen hussy" and there was such a to-do about the matter that Miss Langhorne went to bed for a week. Other old-time Springs belles recall similar instances of parental severity. Chaperonage was in many instances actually militant. The Memphis belle Ada Thompson Norfleet was breakfasting one morning at the Homestead with a young man from Pau. Her eagle-eyed chaperone soon spotted them and promptly broke up the meal. At the door, in her slow Southern drawl, she delivered her memorable ultimatum. "You all may have any meal you wish with any man you wish," she said, "but you may never have *breakfast* with a *Frenchman.*"

Vigilant chaperonage was particularly in evidence in the evening. "Young people of this generation," says Mrs. Lavalette Keiley, greatest of the belles of the Old Sweet Springs, "have no idea of the fear of the dark in those days. The idea was that the dark changed even the mildest male into a raging lion. Even being engaged to a man didn't entitle you to go anywhere with him in the dark."

Mrs. Keiley's great-great-grandfather, John Lewis, originally settled the Old Sweet Springs; she herself, now in her seventies, still lives there. Looking back on the age of belledom, she recalls daytimes which consisted of a German with one beau, a Lovers' Walk with another beau, a tallyho ride with a third, and a Treadmill with a fourth. But after the ball at night there were no such *à deux* iniquities. "The last oil lamp on the porch was by the water cooler," she says. "You could walk with your beau that far but no farther. It was considered breathlessly fast even to go a few steps beyond. It was almost like going away for the weekend, although of course we hadn't heard of that." Mrs. Keiley's Old Sweet Springs is today an Old People's Home. In its heyday, however, it was as socially select as the White and, in some respects, more so. For one thing, there were fewer Yankees. "I still don't know," Mrs. Keiley sighs, "why Northern men always feel that before they give a compliment they must take it away in the corner and brood over it."

No picture of the great belles of White Sulphur's past would be complete without the Duchess of Windsor, a lady who is not only the greatest of White Sulphur's annually returning belles of today but who is also, in season, an admitted social star of both Newport and Palm Beach. The legal residence of the Duke and Duchess of Windsor is in France; their off-season residence in this country is in New York's Waldorf Towers. In between times, with their perennial hosts, the Robert R. Youngs, they have been resorting for a full decade. Nor have they any definite future plans. "We just don't make any plans at all," says the Duchess. "We just read the plans the newspapermen make for us and then we pick the one which pleases us the most."

Born in a resort to begin with—Blue Ridge Summit, Pennsylvania, a summer rendezvous then heavily patronized by Baltimoreans—the Duchess first came to the Old White as a little girl and stayed in a cottage on Baltimore Row. "I cannot remember when it was," she says. "I have no memory for dates." Her chaperone was her grandmother, Mrs. Henry Mactier Warfield, a lady who was largely responsible for bringing her up in her Baltimore days and who was herself a White Sulphurite of an earlier era. Today the Duchess remembers that her grandmother laid down two immutable laws to her grandchild. "She told me never to marry a Yankee," she says, "and never to marry a man who kissed my hand. She said they weren't the marrying kind anyway." The Duchess smiles. "What my grandmother would have thought of this new jive generation—or, I guess, of me—I'm afraid just isn't worth thinking." In the course of three marriages, two Yankee and one English, the Duchess has lost all trace of her Southern accent; at the same time she still retains a strong love for the South. "One evening we were all sitting around at dinner," she recalls, "and someone said something ugly about the South. I jumped right up. So did Nora Flynn —she is Mrs. Gibson's sister, you know—and just as we got going we caught ourselves and laughed out loud. 'Here we are,' we said, 'fighting the War Between the States all over again.' And we were, too."

The Duke, who describes himself as "a Southerner by marriage," was also at White Sulphur in an earlier day. At the time of his first American tour as Prince of Wales he went to the old Greenbrier in 1919. "Your State Department arranged the trip for six of us," he says modestly, "and they were awfully good to us. They even arranged for six awfully pretty girls to be there at the same time we were." Part of the Prince's White Sulphur entertainment included, besides the girls, a Sunday morning church service in which an old prayerbook was used. From this prayerbook the congregation was treated to a prayer which included the lines, "God bless the Prince and Princess of Wales." "I took a bit of ribbing on that," the Duke recalls, "but it's rather more amusing to look back on now, don't you think?"

Ever since the opening of the new Greenbrier the Duke

and Duchess, ably promoted by Robert Young, have been the feature attraction. Young frankly describes his prized guests as "the world's most interesting personalities." Even in Mexico, he points out, where he accompanied the Duke and Duchess on an extended trip in 1951, there were flowers and bands and dancing girls, even at the smallest whistle-stops. "There was admiration written in every face," he declares, "down to the lowest peon." At the Greenbrier's annual Spring Festival there are no peons, but every move of the Duke and Duchess is watched with an all-consuming interest, and even the daily walk of "Mr. Thomas," the Duke's Scotch Cairn terrier, who is escorted by the Duke's valet, is a well-attended event. Like the Duchess, Mr. Thomas travels everywhere the Duke goes except to England. "I can't take him there," says the Duke. "It's because of the six-month quarantine."

The regular Windsor entourage which accompanies them to the Greenbrier consists, roughly, of the same group which surrounds them at Palm Beach. Besides Mr. Thomas, this group includes the Youngs, Wrightsmans, Guests, Cushings, Donahues, etc., as well as various other individuals who have either inherited or, at one time or another, married fortunes. "I like small Society," says the Duchess. "Big things scare me. Outside of the official things we had to do at Nassau we've never had more than twenty-nine to dinner." Both the Windsors maintain that of all the entertaining that has been done for them they enjoyed most a simple dinner of four in a young couple's apartment. "I did the cooking," says the Duchess, "and the Duke wanted to do the dishes but they had a dishwasher."

At the Greenbrier the "world's most interesting personalities" do no cooking or dishwashing. Furthermore, the Duchess nowadays lives in a style which contrasts sharply with the days of Mrs. Gibson's crowded cottage. With her husband and the Youngs, she occupies what is known as the Presidential Suite, which is not to be confused with the President's Cottage; the latter, known as "America's First Summer White House," is a relatively simple affair, left over from Old White days, outside the hotel. The Presidential Suite, on the other hand, is not simple. A two-story house built inside the hotel, it has, downstairs, a formal entrance foyer, a drawing room, den and powder room, as well as a dining room, kitchen and pantry; upstairs, which is reached by a handsome fifty thousand dollar circular staircase, there are five attractively furnished master bedrooms as well as separate servants' rooms each with an individual telephone. The Duchess' bathroom is perhaps Dorothy Draper's chef d'œuvre. It boasts various splashes of wild colors which on distant examination—at close range they are blinding—prove to be a giant version of a bleeding heart fuchsia pattern. The cost of the entire suite is $225 per day plus an extra charge for meals of $10 per day per person.

The Duchess, in the great tradition of Southern belles, indulges in no resort athletics except swimming. Nonetheless, with her husband, she invariably wins the annual Spring Festival waltz contest at the Pink Champagne Ball and during the Amateur-Professional Golf Tournament, as the country's most distinguished golf widow, she sits on the porch of the Casino to watch her husband going and coming. In common with other amateurs in this tournament, the Duke is always teamed with a professional golfer for a thirty-six-hole best-ball contest which is also featured by a secret "Calcutta" pool. Bidding on the teams often goes over $100,000 and the winning team stands to win some $50,000. In

1952 the Duke, playing with a handicap of eighteen, largest in the tournament, shot an eighty-two on his own ball on the final day. In the words of his fellow competitor, Sam Snead, "The Duke takes his golf more serious than any man I ever saw." Teeing off in a driving rainstorm, the event was watched not only by the Duchess and her circle but also by the entire paying clientele of the Greenbrier as well as a large group of the working help. Over the loudspeaker the contestants were methodically announced: "Ed 'Porky' Oliver from Lemont, Illinois; Vic Ghezzi from Inwood, New York; Jim Ferrier from San Francisco, California," etc.

Then there was a pause. Up to the tee stepped a small pipe-smoking bronze-tanned man. He was nearing sixty but with his quick-moving manner and boyish smile he looked like a young man in his twenties. Out on the tee, facing the driving rain and holding an umbrella, he looked to his admiring audience like a lost little man all alone against the elements. As he leaned over to tee up his ball, there was a thunderclap followed by an even stronger downpour. Suddenly over the loudspeaker the announcer began again—only this time in a far different voice: "It is an honor and a privilege to introduce the next contestant. His endeavors to play the game of golf have endeared him to all of us. Ladies and gentlemen, His Royal Highness, the Duke of Windsor."

The crowd was silent. The Duke put down his pipe and his umbrella, took a quick nervous practice swing and then stepped up to his ball. To his admirers the suspense was breath-taking—but the drive was a good one, long and high down the middle of the fairway. The crowd, tense to the breaking point, broke into loud cheers and handclaps. The Duke first watched the ball, then turned to the crowd, smiled quickly and half waved his hand. Then he turned, reached down, picked up his pipe and umbrella and followed his ball down from the tee and off into the rain.

As the first of this country's resorts, Stafford Springs, Connecticut, found its social consciousness in the Podunk-Nipmuck Indian feud of about 1650, so it is a matter of final justice that a large part of what may be considered the country's last social resort, Palm Springs, California, should be given, as of 1950, back to the Indians. By a Supreme Court decision, 3,337 acres of Palm Springs were awarded to seventy-one surviving members of the Agua Caliente Band of the Cahuilla tribe.

These Indians were the original settlers of the resort and each one received two acres in downtown Palm Springs, five acres in uptown Palm Springs, and forty acres in suburban Palm Springs. Since the Indians, even before the decision, already owned a large portion of the area, including the four hot-sand springs which originally gave Palm Springs its name, they may now be said to be in a commanding position at the resort. They are, however, reluctant to assume the honor. One Indian, in the fall of 1951, sold back to the Whites over sixty thousand dollars' worth of his property. "I would have sold the rest," he said, "but I didn't like the class of people who were interested."

On first sight there is perhaps no social resort area which is more disappointing. A wind-swept oasis, located one hundred miles southeast of Los Angeles, on the edge of a desert which backs up against the eleven thousand-foot Mount San Jacinto, Palm Springs resembles an abandoned Cecil B. DeMille movie set—full of glorified bungalow courts, honky-tonk motels, traffic jams and the strangest inhabitants to be found anywhere west of the Bronx Zoo. These inhabitants are generally kindly and apparently harmless. They grow grapefruit so sweet you do not need any sugar on it and they grow lawns, without topsoil, from seeding to cutting, in seven days. They speak a weird dialect composed chiefly of the words "but," "yet," and "so," all of them often in the same sentence. ("He's loaded—but loaded, but you're so right, I should live so long yet.") Outside of the Indians, who dress conservatively, the gentlemen of Palm Springs wear the most extraordinary colored shirts and shorts to be found at any resort, and the ladies wear bejeweled dark glasses and as little else as the law allows. "Even I gave up dressing here," says Adolphe Menjou, a pioneer cottage-builder. "I would call Palm Springs," he adds, "the home of the varicose vein."

Not the least of the resort's curiosities are the springs themselves. In these baths, if the visitor is a confirmed health-through-misery seeker, he can dunk himself chest-deep in slimy sulphurous quicksand, and, held up by the pressure of the bubbling, may stay for a period of twenty minutes for a charge of seventy-five cents. Although the Indians now make a ten-cent cover charge for the use of a towel, this is still the longest period anyone can remain in Palm Springs for such a small expenditure.

Just how such a place became America's most fashionable desert resort—it is not only the Palm Beach of the West but also the mecca of the Hollywood mink shift—has baffled many observers. It would seem to have taken miracles, and, roughly speaking, it did. Among other things it took such widely different personalities as the late Marilyn Miller and Albert Einstein, such widely different events as a New York City political scandal and the suicide of an Australian tobacco millionaire, and, finally, such widely different influences as the sun-tan craze and the emergence of a "400" reduced to $3.98. But these miracles were more than enough. From May to October the area had, not so many years ago, a population of less than three thousand. Today, from November to April, it has more than thirty thousand; it also has the highest per capita swimming pool rate in the country—over six hundred pools. Altogether, no area is a better example of the fact that while the East's social resorts are withering on the vine, the West's are blooming. For years the favorite running gag of "The Springs," as the resort is affectionately called, has been told of someone looking at some obviously underprivileged Palm Springsians and saying, "Well, *they're* certainly not millionaires." To which the obvious answer is, "No, but they were when they got here."

Compared to Newport or Palm Beach, or even with its fellow springs in Saratoga or Virginia, Palm Springs seems, to put it mildly, artificial. It is, however, as good an example of the new in resort Society as exists anywhere. It is also honestly artificial. The motto of the Springs might well be the favorite line of Earl Coffman, owner of the Desert Inn, the most conservative in town. "Early to bed and early to rise," says Earl, "and you meet few prominent people."

From its airport, which is larger than La Guardia and is run by an attractive divorced grandmother named Zaddie Bunker, to its jail, which has good Western sun exposure and takes its prisoners out to all meals, Palm Springs sells glamour. It has no business except resort business and few people who, whether Hollywoodians or otherwise, are not show people at heart. "Palm Springs is really a very unfunny place," says Cary Grant, who recalls circus parties where real lions have gotten loose. "Nobody ever thinks anything about it," he says. "People just think they're from Metro and treat them like important guests. The lions love it and it all seems to be part of the show."

Bob Hope has for many years been the honorary mayor of Palm Springs; the real mayor has for several terms been Charlie Farrell. At a recent meeting on a particularly hotly debated subject—whether or not to allow horse-racing—Farrell banged down hard with his gavel. "Now listen here, you," he said, "there isn't going to be no hissing and there isn't going to be no applause. This meeting's going to be orderly and if nobody can't be orderly and not speak in an orderly manner, everybody's going to be put the hell out."

For many years, outside of the horse-racing, which was voted down, and gambling, which has been closed down, Palm Springs has had just about everything. Even the resort's newest financial institution, the Desert Bank, puts "Where Living Is Better" right on its checks, and in the lobby of the bank there is a silver dish filled with dates. Fifteen miles outside of the resort there is even a dude ranch for dogs. Furthermore, the resort's dollar sign is not delicately hidden but blatantly out in the open. "DON'T BAWL OUT OUR WAITERS," reads the sign in Rogers' Ranch, one of the best-patronized restaurants. "IN THEIR BRACKET THEY DON'T HAVE TO TAKE IT." When business at the bar slackens late in the evening, Trav Rogers, the popular proprietor, bellows, "Everybody buy a drink!"—and everybody does. Rogers' so-called "Mink and Manure Club" is a social feature of the resort. Started by actor William Gargan, the club donates all membership fees to the local hospital and boasts branch charters as far as New York's Twenty-One Club. Anyone who donates ten dollars has his name painted on a panel over the bar; for fifty dollars his name is given a whole lamp shade to itself.

One thing, however, Palm Springs did not have—a public rest room. Throughout the early course of its history the only rest rooms were in the gas stations. Finally in 1950, after years of agitation, the resort built two truly gorgeous rest rooms right in the front of the firehouse, one for ladies and one for gentlemen. So great was the enthusiasm for these "Firehouse Facilities," as they were called, that not until the venture was almost completed did the Fire Chief notice that the Facilities made it necessary for the engines to back out of the station and make two extra turns to get started for a fire. But by this time he did not care; all over town he was known as the "Chief of the Head."

One of the rest room's first explorers was an old-time Eastern lady who ventured, rather timorously, into the ladies' wing of the Firehouse Facilities. Gingerly she experimented with the gaudy new plumbing and, on the spur of the moment, decided to make a trial flush. Instantly there was a deafening shriek above her and the full blast of the fire sirens pierced the siesta-time quiet of a desert afternoon. Running outside, the lady, by now in a high state of social shock, was promptly greeted by every able-bodied male Palm Springsian over the age of fourteen—all members of the resort's volunteer fire department and all hurrying to answer a call of duty which, because of the continued screams of the sirens, they felt must be either a four-alarm fire or perhaps even an atomic bomb explosion. As it turned out, of course, the sirens heralded no bomb scare, nor, for that matter, even a false alarm. Unknown to the volunteer firemen, whom the Chief of the Head had neglected to inform, the sirens had sounded off solely for the purpose of signaling the arrival, out at the airport, of Honorary Mayor Bob Hope. Of all participants the Eastern lady who believed she had started the trouble was, after being revived, the most relieved. "I knew it couldn't have been me," she said, "I just went in to look around."

"The early history of Palm Springs," say the booklets advertising the resort, "is lost in antiquity." The father of the town was Judge John Guthrie McCallum, who was a San Francisco attorney but not a judge and who in 1884 first sought out the mineral baths in Palm Springs for the health of a son who had contracted tuberculosis. Hard on the heels of the Judge who was not a judge arrived a doctor who was not a doctor but who always prefixed his name with "Dr." His name was Welwood Murray, and in 1886, in a building which he characteristically borrowed instead of bought from McCallum, he established the town's first hotel. Mrs. Pearl McManus, McCallum's daughter and today dean of Palm Springs historians, recalls the advice given her father at the time he made the deal. As nearly as she remembers it, this ran: "You'll rue the day, Judge, you brought Murray in."

It was good advice, but Judge McCallum did not take it. A lanky, colorful Scot, "Pop" Murray, as he was affectionately called, set a fast pace at his hotel during the Gay Nineties, which was the forerunner of The Springs' illustrious future. Attracting such guests as Robert Louis Stevenson, explorer George Wharton James, geologist John Muir, and Vice-president Fairbanks, Murray not only attempted to doctor them with remarkable medical theories but also firmly established the area's tradition of immodesty. In the evenings he entertained with tales of his world-wide travels. "No matter what town you would mention," says a guest of those days, "Murray had always been there and had founded the most famous business."

In 1908 Murray had as one of his last guests the late

Mrs. Nellie Coffman, the daughter of a Santa Monica hotel-keeper. Mrs. Coffman had an earache when she arrived, and though she was, throughout her eighty-odd years, a firm believer in a sort of desert Christian Science for all types of illness, she had a hard time at first. "That first night at Murray's," she said, "I prayed I might leave the desert." But a year after she arrived, on $2,000 down, and $2,500 mortgage and a ninety-day grocery credit, she founded the Desert Inn, which today sprawls over thirty-two acres on land which would sell in the neighborhood of $2,000 per front foot. "I had a conviction," Mrs. Coffman stated, "that Los Angeles would some day be a big, crowded, noisy city. I wanted a sand pile for them to play in."

Curiously enough, the first time the Desert Inn was filled to capacity was in 1916 when a movie company, thus establishing a precedent for later days, came to town on location. "That was in the days," says Hollywood director Leo McCarey, "when they'd load up a truck with a camera and a girl and a boy and a villain, go out on the desert and come back with a movie." Rudolph Valentino, Charlie Chaplin, Lawrence Tibbett and Alla Nazimova were the resort's first large-name personalities; Valentino is the best remembered since there was some girl trouble in connection with his stay and Mrs. Coffman ordered him to leave the hotel. When Valentino refused, Mrs. Coffman promptly had the couple packed, bag and baggage, out on the driveway. "I can still see," says one Springs old-timer, "Valentino and his girl sitting on their luggage outside the Inn waiting for a ride back to Hollywood."

In 1926 Mrs. Coffman and her Desert Inn were treated to the advent of two distinguished authors, England's John Galsworthy and America's Louella Parsons. Mr. Galsworthy stayed for a short time only, but Miss Parsons stayed throughout the season, fortifying her prestige by completely monopolizing the lobby telephone, at that time the only one in Palm Springs. Miss Parsons clearly states her connection with the growth of the resort. "The movie people started coming down from Hollywood to see me," she says, "and before either of us knew it, Nellie had more business than she could handle."

Actually, the rise of Palm Springs as a fashionable resort did not become noticeable to the uninitiated until some five years after Miss Parsons had left. Even Mrs. Coffman was none too responsible, for the rise took place, not at the Desert Inn at all, but at a far wilder and woolier establishment known as the El Mirador. This hotel, complete with the resort's largest swimming pool, was built in 1928 at a cost of close to a million dollars; following the 1929 crash it looked like a hotel version of the kind of club and cottage albatross which was weighing down the Eastern resorts. In contrast to their fellow resorters in the East, however, Palm Springsians moved fast. A group of the leading American Plan hotel men in town, more or less reluctantly joined by the conservative Coffmans, banded together into an organization known as the Palm Springs Associates. With the aid of $100,000 and the services of two able promotion men, Tony Burke and Frank Bogert, the former a British newspaperman and ex-Hollywood extra and the latter an ex-stableboy from the Deep Well Ranch who had a borrowed Leica camera, they made Palm Springs a household word in America, or at least came as close to this as possible in view of the material with which they had to work.

Particularly useful to the Associates in their early days was the late Samuel Untermyer. Widely publicized as the first lawyer in the country to charge a million-dollar fee, Untermyer built a concrete Mediterranean-style house terraced in three tiers into Mount San Jacinto. Untermyer liked publicity himself and he liked guests with large news names. In 1934, topping his list, he invited Mr. and Mrs. Albert Einstein, then fleeing the Nazis, to visit him. Einstein did not like publicity as well as his host, but he was easy prey for the resort's promoters because he spoke practically no English. On one trip to the desert on which he was shadowed he commented, "*Gut,*" to some bit of scenery, and this was freely translated into a nation-wide interview in which the scientist credited Palm Springs with virtually everything unobtainable elsewhere in the world.

In the same manner the late Mayor Jimmy Walker, fleeing investigation proceedings in New York and stopping first at the Untermyer home and later at the Mirador, was nationally quoted as having found his Shangri-La in Palm Springs. At that particular moment, of course, Shangri-La for the Mayor was as far from New York as possible. Then as now, Palm Springs was reached by no direct air service from the East—only by shuttle line from Los Angeles—but then as now, the railroad station was ten miles from town. Furthermore, Walker made the statement to a none too reliable source—Little Bear, a Cherokee Indian who headed the welcoming committee who staged a mock holdup of Walker's train.

The Associates were not averse to random scenic shots but they concentrated on the Mirador. "The Mirador was the kind of a place," says one old-timer, "where John J. Raskob could have cocktails with the I. Magnin salesgirl and neither of them would feel uncomfortable." Since Mr. Raskob was at that time a man approaching sixty with twelve children, there could, in the opinion of Palm Springsians, be no higher praise for a resort hotel. No representative of the press was ever charged a nickel at the Mirador and those attracted ran the gamut from the late George Horace Lorimer and H. G. Wells to Lord Beaverbrook and Cornelius Vanderbilt, Jr. When the father of Barbara Hutton pulled into town with two Rolls-Royces—the second drawing a trailerful of servants—and ignored the Mirador in favor of camping on the desert, irate Palm Springsians promptly declared open season on him. In short order he reported to the police the loss of all his dress clothes, including a complete set of black pearl studs and cuff links.

The Mirador pool was the first swimming pool in the country to have a trough dug underneath and a plate glass window installed for taking underwater pictures. Besides this photography, which always concentrated on the sex motif, the Palm Springs promoters also made a heroic effort to popularize the rickshaw in the manner of Palm Beach's "afromobile." "But we weren't going to make it appear we were abusing colored people," says one of the Associates, "so we used college boys with pith helmets." Unfortunately, the rickshaw dated itself by the success of the rest of the promotions. As Palm Springs streets became crowded by automobiles, the rickshaws were abandoned. The promotion of bicycling also became difficult, although several stars and starlets were photographed on them. Finally Palm Springs attempted, for a brief period, a bicycle with an egg-shaped rear wheel. Nothing like it had ever been seen in the country before—and it was not long visible in Palm Springs.

The resort's two crowning achievements of the era were the bare midriff dress, which originated beside the Mirador pool, and ladies' shorts. Tony Burke, the Britisher, was responsible for this latter innovation, which he remembers occurred in the 1929-30 season. Burke got his idea from soldiering in Egypt with the British Army in World War I; the only shorts available were a pair of seventy-five cent men's underwear which he bought in a local department store. Burke also recalls that they had to photograph the girl carefully in order not to show the buttons in front, but he maintains that his first subject, Martha Worden, daughter of a Beverly Hills financier, was eminently respectable. "She had nothing to do with the movies," he says firmly, "at all."

The first picture of Miss Worden in shorts appeared in the *Police Gazette*, but by the next year I. Magnin had started making shorts for ladies and the craze was on. Ordinarily the Palm Springs promoters had no idea where their pictures would appear. One member of the Associates recalls that foreign newspapers invariably confused Palm Springs with Palm Beach, and even in this country there was enough postal confusion to alienate Palm Beachers to such an extent that the feud has never been healed. One thing is certain; the work of the Associates paid off. Palm Springs doubled in size even in the depression years, 1929 to 1933, doubled again from 1934 to 1939, and has lately, from World War II to the present, doubled still a third time. In the fall of 1952, even the El Mirador, closed since its World War II days as an Army Hospital, was again reopened. Redesigned by the noted Negro architect, Paul Williams, the new Mirador saw a second rebuilding job which cost another million dollars and also saw the hanging of murals which, in keeping with the hotel's past, are advertised as "unequaled in glamour and daring anywhere in the West."

After the Associates had convinced Hollywood, if not the

rest of the world, that Palm Springs was the place where, as the slogan ran, "The Sun Shines on the Stars," the motion picture colony began to take root. Among the pioneers was Paul Lukas who in 1935, on one acre for which he paid $500, built a conservative two-bedroom cottage which cost $4,750. Although his cottage has no swimming pool and thus is socially suspect, Lukas declares he was recently offered $42,000 for it and also maintains that the land on which it is located now runs over $4,000 an acre. Along with Lukas came Harold Lloyd, George Brent, Joseph Schenck, Glenda Farrell and many others. Of late years the outstanding Hollywood cottages have been those owned by the late Al Jolson, in which the interior was conceived by the art director of Columbia Pictures, by Darryl Zanuck, whose lawn is lighted for night croquet and hence is called "The Ball Park," and by Frank Sinatra. The latter's cottage was built in sixty days in the winter of 1948 and cost $110,000 exclusive of a swimming pool built in the shape of a grand piano. Sinatra is proud of his pool but declares that he is even prouder of the fact that his cottage is the only one he knows of which has a master shower bath with sunken faucets. A thin man, he is easily disturbed by knocks, and to visitors he likes to go right into his shower and demonstrate that it is completely bump-proof.

In recent years Palm Springs' front-running showplace has been "Tierra Caliente," the cottage of industrial designer Raymond Loewy. The author of the Studebaker car and well known in the streamlining field, Loewy designed his cottage in one evening on Racquet Club stationery and, equally abruptly, carried Palm Springs' swimming pool architecture to its logical conclusion. Loewy's pool, which is kidney-shaped, occupies more than one-half of the total floor area of his cottage and even penetrates well inside of the living room, where a white carpet reaches its edge. In the entire cottage the transition between indoors and outdoors is as nearly imperceptible as possible, and at night Loewy illuminates not only his pool but also, by virtue of a three-thousand-watt projector on a fifty-foot mast, a large part of the surrounding Indian Reservation. In spite of this illumination the swimming pool is so difficult to avoid that at a recent "Tierra Caliente" party two of Loewy's guests, actor William Powell and singer Tony Martin, took a step backward from the front door in the course of saying good-by and fell in. Promptly Loewy also took a full-clothes dip, a practice which he believes makes his guests in such a situation feel more comfortable. In between parties Loewy, a New Yorker, found his desert retreat so quiet that he finally installed an elaborate mechanism which constantly sends loud drops of water into his pool. This was not an expensive operation, however, and Loewy maintains that the cost of "Tierra Caliente," which has only two bedrooms, quarters for only one servant and no dining room at all, was, as he puts it, "well under" $100,000. "The philosophy of this place," he says, "is that the day is over for expensive houses."

More important to Palm Springs social life than any private cottage is Charlie Farrell's Racquet Club; in fact, its fashion show, which takes place on or about October 15 each year, regularly opens the resort's social season and Farrell himself, at least up to the time he became mayor, officially christened each season by dressing in white tie, top hat and tails and somersaulting into the swimming pool. A good-natured, nervous, absent-minded man, Farrell has actually starred in more talking pictures than he has silent ones. To his rare irritation, however, he is best remembered for the silent pictures and in particular for *Seventh Heaven* which his friends now describe as a "nineteenth-Century-Fox release." In 1934, with his friend Ralph Bellamy, he founded his club—"as a hangout for the gang," he puts it—and is now sole owner. He can put up seventy-five guests at a time and the club does half a million dollars worth of business a year. The club has some two hundred yearly members as well as fifty-odd season members, all of whom use the club fairly regularly, together with a host of rather nebulous members-in-waiting who are always talking about joining but never do, and meanwhile continue to use the facilities of the club on guest cards or through "knowing Charlie." The club is built around a large bar, which has glass walls on two sides, one facing the tennis courts and the other the swimming pool, and thus gives even nonparticipants in athletics the impression of activity. The lawn is decorated by a remarkable set of two-foot-high chessman. There is also an elaborate buzz system at the gate, and officers of the club are proud of its reputation for exclusiveness. "We've stopped a lot of important people," one declares. "We stopped Mickey Rooney three times."

In 1934, before the club even had a bar, it attracted in one week-end a foursome which consisted of Mary Pickford, Douglas Fairbanks, Marlene Dietrich and Leslie Howard, and it has been doing just as well ever since. Spencer Tracy and several other stars have at one time or another had their own permanent cottages and Hollywoodians like Samuel Goldwyn and the Marx brothers still regularly vie for rooms with Manhattanites like Jack Dempsey and the brothers Kriendler. Although actual swimming is looked upon with some disfavor, tennis is of a high order, and movie stars play side by side with such Racquet Club notables as Pauline

Betz, Donald Budge and Frank Shields. Some idea of the informal tone of the club was indicated by a letter Farrell sent out to all members in the heat of a recent season:

> When calling for reservations, please call reservations and not C. Farrell unless you want to drive me ca-razy. And, No. 1, if you want to make friends and influence people, please don't make a reservation and then send someone else. No. 2, please don't send people to the club that you wouldn't bring with you or have at your house. No. 3, please have a little consideration for the reservation department as we have 35 rooms and over 200 members. If everyone wants to send their friends and relatives our 35 rooms won't last very long. We want to add a few more bungalows so that people that want a couple of rooms rather than just one can have them. But, at fifteen or sixteen thousand a crack we can only build a few hundred a year.
>
> Just keep your sense of humor and don't give me a hard time because you can't always get the reservation you want.
>
> And I love you too,
>
> CHARLIE

The Racquet Club is by no means Palm Springs' only club; indeed, its clubs have steadily increased in recent years. The new Thunderbird Country Club, backed by Bing Crosby and Randolph Scott, as well as the Governor of Colorado and the founder of Consolidated Aircraft, is perhaps the most impressive venture, but it is being hard pushed by the even newer Tamarisk Country Club, backed by Seattle's auto magnate, M. O. Anderson, as well as the Marx brothers and Ben Hogan. Also still operating is the old Tennis Club, which is old, in the Palm Springs sense, since it was built as far back as 1939. This breath-taking establishment was designed by Paul Williams and was built right into the San Jacinto mountainside. The Club was originally conceived by the stricter element of Palm Springs Society which, with the exception of Walter Pidgeon, who is acceptable even in Pasadena, has little to do with the movie set. "We had just the quieter ones," ex-President Lee Bering declared, "like Rudy Vallee and Bob Hope."

In contrast to the Racquet Club, which allows children on the premises only two weeks a year, at Thanksgiving and Easter, the Tennis Club prides itself on being a family club. It also has as impressively aristocratic a fishing custom as exists anywhere in the West—one which undoubtedly had its genesis from Canfield's old casino at Saratoga. Every evening at cocktail time, Tennis Club members who wish trout for dinner are privileged to catch their own. The fish, brought into the club in aerated tanks or iced milk cans, are locked in a small brook, and as each member steps up to his position, he is handed a ready-baited line by a white-coated waiter. After he has caught his fish, he hands his line back to the waiter, who unhooks it and carries it to the chef carefully marked so that each member can get the fish he himself caught. Unfortunately, during the past few seasons there has been no fishing at the Tennis Club. There have been plenty of fish but there has been no water to put them in. There has been a drought.

Altogether, the new American Society, of which Palm Springs is perhaps the most prominent resort example, consists of the Maharajas of moviedom blended as conspicuously as possible with an assortment of industrial moguls. This assortment, at the Racquet Club at least, has included everything from the country's largest banker to a bona fide yo-yo king. Shunned by most fashionable Easterners, with the exception of New York's Stork and Twenty One set and a few New York pioneers such as Howard Cullman and

Stewart Hopps, the resort is also traditionally avoided by San Franciscans. The latter regard Palm Springs as one of Southern California's major evils and have their own Carmel for lengthy stays and Lake Tahoe for briefer periods. Resorts like Arrowhead Springs and Aspen have also made some inroads on Palm Springs' popularity, and The Springs is, of course, ignored entirely by august Santa Barbarans. Nonetheless, Palm Springs draws heavily from the Midwest—Chicago, Detroit, Cleveland, St. Louis, Cincinnati, and Minneapolis are always represented—and also does surprisingly well in the Northwest. "I'll take Seattle people," says Frank Bogert, manager of the new Thunderbird Club, who is well aware that Los Angeles guests sometimes depart for home during bad weather. "When the wind blows, they're here." The appeal of the resort among such stalwart Palm Springsians as Townsend and Irving Netcher goes far beyond the matter of climate. Two Chicago brothers who inherited their money from The Boston Store, they are internationally known resort sports who invariably stay the full Palm Springs season. In a recent March, Mrs. Irving Netcher, formerly Roszika Dolly of the Dolly sisters, suggested to her husband that just for a change they should leave Palm Springs a month before the end of the season. Her husband's reply was clearly audible throughout the Racquet Club bar. "There's nowhere else to go," he said. "It's too early for the Riviera."

Wherever its members come from, Palm Springs Society is Hollywood-dominated. "It's a potpourri, I suppose," says Ginger Rogers philosophically, "but when you come right down to it, there's everybody here—producers, directors, actors and everybody." The new field of television has as yet offered no competition to this domination, since, with a two-mile mountain on top of the resort, Palm Springs is still free of this disturbing element. Around the Racquet Club bar and other social rendezvous the talk is almost invariably of *the* industry, and there is no mistaking which industry this is. Even such an accomplished name-man as Walter Winchell has been brought up short. Learning from a long-distance telephone conversation at the Racquet Club bar that George Marshall wanted copies of a recent column, Winchell was delighted. "George Marshall wants them!" he said happily to Farrell. The owner of the Racquet Club feigned a puzzled look, then asked quietly, "Which George Marshall, Walter?"

Farrell then explained to Winchell that as far as he was concerned there were three George Marshalls—first, the director who gave him his first lead in a picture; second, the owner of the Washington Redskins; and third, and finally, the General and Secretary of State. "Hell," he says affably, "the first two are both good customers. The General hasn't ever even been to the club."

Farrell was joking, of course, but there is no question that just as Newporters get excited over the appearance of Mrs. Vanderbilt at Bailey's Beach, or Palm Beachers welcome the Duke and Duchess of Windsor, the Racquet Club is brought to life by the advent of its most distinguished members. When news is passed around that Joan Crawford has phoned from Beverly Hills and is on her way, everyone wonders whether the waiters will have her milk and crackers—she likes them ready in her room when she arrives—prepared to her satisfaction, and also who will be with her. This latter is always an important question. Everyone wants to know who will be with Clark Gable, in between his marriages, and, by way of contrast, the arrival of Errol Flynn, with Mrs. Flynn, can prove almost equally interesting.

"The climate here," says Priscilla Chaffey, for many years editor of the *Limelight News*, "is sexy." As a young reporter she recalls jokingly asking the late Alvah Hicks, head of the Palm Springs waterworks, what was the latest scandal in town. "There isn't any," replied Hicks briefly. "We're too broad-minded for scandal." Although no one individual has ever matched the standing record of the Southwest in drinking—it was set by the late Herbert Uihlein, of Milwaukee, at the Arizona Biltmore Hotel in Phoenix, at seventy-five highballs in one day—the liquor consumption at the resort is also extremely heavy. This is in keeping with a social life whose pace is so demanding that at a resort Big Top Ball, the season's outstanding fancy dress affair, the prize-winning costume was that of a man who came in bathrobe and slippers with painted circles under his eyes and announced himself as a Palm Springs house guest. If the pace and laxity of Palm Springs is celebrated, however, Palm Springs culture is not. The Palm Springs Book Shop has the dubious distinction, among people in the book business, of having what they call "the cleanest stock in the West." By this they mean that there is a better turnover of old books than at any other store of comparable size. The shop accomplishes this, it readily admits, by catering to the wishes of many actors and actresses and other Palm Springs cottagers who wish books for their libraries but are not particular about content. "We have a flat rate per shelf," says one bookseller, "and we can get rid of anything if the color on the jacket's all right with the interior decorator."

Nonmovie talk around Palm Springs pools often concerns itself with the ever pressing problem of the turn-in prices on Cadillacs and the perennial complaint of all resorters, particularly charming in the case of The Springs, that the place isn't what it used to be and that it is too bad the visitor didn't see it in the old days before all the riffraff came. Apparently one of the chief charms of these old days was the gambling. One patron declared that after several sessions at the celebrated Dunes Club he would not go to the place again without rubber gloves because he did not like to get close to so many electric wires without them, and a lady once registered formal notice to the management that the magnets on the roulette wheel had enticed the hairpins out of her coiffure. Even as recently as the days of the "139" and the "Cove" there were some memorable games, a particular favorite being the time Jack Benny saw a friend of his lose ten thousand dollars in one evening. Benny, one of Palm Springs' most popular cottage-owners, worked at the time on an average of three days a week on his radio program—a meeting with his writers to discuss the script on Friday, a rehearsal on Saturday, and the show itself on Sunday. At the same time, through radio and motion picture work, he was drawing a salary in the neighborhood of fifteen thousand dollars a week. The evening after seeing his friend lose the ten thousand dollars Benny returned to his Palm Springs cottage in a philosophical mood. He paced up and down while one of his writers, George Balzer, sprawled lazily on a sofa. Finally Benny stopped. "You know, George," he said, "if I lost ten thousand dollars in one evening, I'd feel like slitting my throat the next morning." Balzer nodded. "Yeah, Jack," he said quietly, "just think—two whole days' work."

Of late years there has been a disturbing trend on the part of more conservative groups at the resort to beat a path out to the desert away from Palm Springs. Off to a good start in this race, since they left years ago, are the resort's oldest ranches, Smoke Tree and Deep Well. Besides these, ten miles outside of the Springs, there is an even sharper illustration of the trend in the form of a sixteen-hundred-acre, twelve-hundred-membership venture known as the Shadow Mountain Club. With a board of directors which includes Edgar Bergen and Harold Lloyd, the Shadow Mountain Club has from the beginning advertised that it is not only a new kind of resort but a complete dream community. Apparently beyond the stage of calling attention only to such features as a 130-foot figure-8 swimming pool, one roadside sign declared firmly, "WE ARE GOING TO HAVE A LIBRARY AND AN ART MUSEUM."

Farther out, some twenty miles from Palm Springs lies La Quinta. The so-called "Ritz of the Desert," La Quinta has a loyal clientele which includes the heads of Neiman-Marcus, Climax Molybdenum and Superior Oil, as well as celebrities who range from Greta Garbo to Bennett Cerf, all of whom feel that they have culturally or socially outgrown Palm Springs. "We have a few writers," says Cerf, "but it's a pretty expensive place for them." Five miles beyond La Quinta lies the thousand-acre ranch of industrial merger-maker Floyd Odlum and his wife, the speed aviatrix, Jacqueline Cochran. Perhaps the most famous private ranch in the West, it has entertained as many as three full generals in one week-end and has not only the best golf course anywhere in the vicinity but also guest cottages, each of which has its own individual sand dune. Odlum opens his golf course to the public and, despite the fact that he is the president of the $75,000,000 Atlas Corporation, charges greens fees which enable him to operate it at a profit; golfers are also privileged to buy Jacqueline Cochran cosmetics direct at the caddy-house.

Palm Springs' answer to this disturbing trend to get away is entirely in character with the resort's past history. It is undoubtedly the most ambitious project ever attempted at any resort anywhere in the world—a ten million dollar undertaking which will eventually enable resorters to be carried by aerial tramway from tropical Palm Springs to the snow-capped crest of the eleven thousand-foot Mount San Jacinto all in a matter of twelve minutes. Although steel and other strategic materials have not yet been allocated for the purpose, the remarkable project is expected to make Palm Springs not only a desert resort and a ski resort at the same time, but also a permanent resort where people will live all year round.

Whether or not such a project will ever be entirely successful, time alone, of course, will tell. But at the very least it is possible to look forward to a bright new day when both old-time Eastern resorters and new-time Western resorters may meet together in the lordly lobby of an aerial Desert Inn and sing with cowboy minstrel, Johnny Boyle, his famous Palm Springs theme song—one which may well serve as both the swan song of the old, and the herald of the new, in resort history:

Oh, give me a home
Where the millionaires roam,
And the dear little glamor girls play—
Where seldom is heard
An intelligent word,
And we round up the dollars all day.

Index

Set in Linotype Fairfield
Format by Robert Cheney
Manufactured by The Haddon Craftsmen, Inc.
Published by HARPER & BROTHERS, *New York*

SOUTHAMPTON
PALM
PALM
PRINGS
TUXEDO
PARK
NO TRESPASSING
BAR
HARBOR
Vasilíu